Also Available from ASQ Quality Press

Implementing ISO 14001
Marilyn R. Block

The ISO 14000 Handbook
Joseph Cascio, editor

Integrating ISO 14001 into a Quality Management System
Marilyn R. Block and I. Robert Marash

ANSI/ISO 14010-1996
Guidelines for Environmental Auditing—General Principles on
Environmental Auditing

ANSI/ISO 14011-1996
Guidelines for Environmental Auditing—Audit Procedures—Auditing
of Environmental Management Systems

ANSI/ISO 14012-1996
Guidelines for Environmental Auditing—Qualification Criteria for
Environmental Auditors

To request a complimentary catalog of ASQ Quality Press
publications, call 800-248-1946.

Identifying Environmental Aspects and Impacts

Identifying Environmental Aspects and Impacts
Marilyn R. Block

Library of Congress Cataloging-in-Publication Data

Block, Marilyn R.
    Identifying environmental aspects and impacts / Marilyn R. Block.
        p.   cm.
    Includes index.
    ISBN 0-87389-446-4 (alk. paper)
        1. —Production management—Environmental aspects.   2. ISO 14000
    Series Standards Case studies.   I. Title.
    TS155.7.B558   1999
    658.4'08—dc21   99-35572
                                                                      CIP

© 1999 by ASQ

10 9 8 7 6 5 4 3 2

ISBN

Acquisitions Editor: Ken Zielske
Project Editor: Annemieke Koudstaal
Production Coordinator: Shawn Dohogne

ASQ Mission: The American Society for Quality advances individual and organizational performance excellence worldwide by providing opportunities for learning, quality improvement, and knowledge exchange.

Attention: Bookstores, Wholesalers, Schools and Corporations:
ASQ Quality Press books, videotapes, audiotapes, and software are available at quantity discounts with bulk purchases for business, educational, or instructional use. For information, please contact ASQ Quality Press at 800-248-1946, or write to ASQ Quality Press, P.O. Box 3005, Milwaukee, WI 53201-3005.

To place orders or to request a free copy of the ASQ Quality Press Publications Catalog, including ASQ membership information, call 800-248-1946. Visit our web site at http://www.asq.org.

Printed in the United States of America

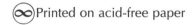 Printed on acid-free paper

American Society for Quality

Quality Press
611 East Wisconsin Avenue
Milwaukee, Wisconsin 53202
Call toll free 800-248-1946
http://www.asq.org
http://standardsgroup.asq.org

Identifying Environmental Aspects and Impacts

Marilyn R. Block

ASQ Quality Presss
Milwaukee, Wisconsin

CONTENTS

LIST OF FIGURES

ACKNOWLEDGMENTS

I am indebted to a number of organizations and individuals for their contributions to this workbook.

My thanks to the many companies with which I have been privileged to work. The results of your efforts to fully understand your environmental aspects and impacts are woven into the discussion and examples presented here.

My sincere appreciation to those who graciously shared their procedures for identifying environmental aspects and impacts:

Robert P. Blair, Purolator

Caryn E. Coyne, Panasonic

B. Tod Delaney, First Environment

Michele DeWeese, MKA

James D. Heeren, First Environment

Alma MacCallum, Panasonic

Jim Merriam, BOC Gases

Steve Ross, Purolator

Deb Weimer, MKA

Tom Whipple, Con Ed

Your generosity is greatly appreciated.

INTRODUCTION

Implementation of an environmental management system (EMS) is intended to result in improved environmental performance. Because a company's environmental performance is directly related to the effect that its activities have on the surroundings in which it operates, the efficacy of an EMS hinges on a thorough understanding of those elements of their activities that can significantly effect the environment. Although the terminology of "aspects and impacts" was coined by ISO 14001, *Environmental management systems—Specification with guidance for use*, the underlying concept has appeared in numerous EMS standards and industry codes of practice.

The single most important element of any EMS involves the identification of environmental aspects and impacts. In ISO 14001, for example, the information resulting from the procedures and activities mandated by clause 4.3.1, Environmental aspects, provides the foundation for seven other activities required by the standard.

- Ensuring that the environmental policy is appropriate to the nature, scale, and environmental impacts of an organization's activities, products, and services

- Establishing objectives and targets that are consistent with the commitment to prevention of pollution

- Identifying the training needs of all personnel whose work may have a significant impact on the environment

- Communicating internally between the various levels and functions of the organization

- Identifying operations and activities, including maintenance, that are associated with identified significant environmental aspects and developing appropriate work instructions

- Identifying the potential for accidents and emergency situations

- Monitoring and measuring the key characteristics of operations and activities that can have a significant impact on the environment

Despite its importance, this activity is poorly understood. Most organizations going through the ISO 14001 implementation process indicate that they need help with this requirement.

Whether an organization needs to identify aspects and impacts in order to conform to the requirements imposed by an EMS standard or industry code of practice, or whether it simply wants to gain a better understanding of the effect that its activities have on the environment, this workbook provides that help. *Identifying Environmental Aspects and Impacts* defines environmental aspects and impacts (chapter 1) and provides a step-by-step approach for identifying aspects (chapter 2), determining their impacts (chapter 3), and defining significance (chapter 4). Each section is accompanied by work sheets that can be adapted for use within a particular setting.

Where specific examples are presented, ISO 14001 is used throughout the workbook. Examples that reflect the requirements imposed by a single standard enhance the reader's ability to move easily through the sequence of steps required by the identification and evaluation process. ISO 14001 was selected because of its worldwide acceptance and use. The methods and work sheets presented, however, are applicable for use with any EMS.

The transition from theory to practice is assisted by examples of how companies have elected to identify and evaluate their own aspects and impacts. Six ISO 14001–registered companies share their procedures for environmental aspects and impacts (chapter 6). These examples are not intended as templates. Companies must develop their own procedures to reflect their management systems and business activities.

The companies presented in chapter 6 were selected because they reflect varied industry sectors with different kinds of environmental impacts. BOC Gases manufactures and supplies industrial gases. Consolidated Edison, a utility, manages an extensive transportation function. First Environment, an environmental consulting company, represents the services sector. MKA, Panasonic, and Purolator are manufacturing companies in the electronics, communications, and automotive sectors, respectively.

CHAPTER 1

EXPLANATION OF ASPECTS AND IMPACTS

ISO 14001, 4.3.1 Environmental aspects

The organization shall establish and maintain (a) procedure(s) to identify the environmental aspects of its activities, products, or services that it can control and over which it can be expected to have an influence, in order to determine those which have or can have significant impacts on the environment. The organization shall ensure that the aspects related to these significant impacts are considered in setting its environmental objectives.

The organization shall keep this information up-to-date.

Definition of Aspects and Impacts

So, what *is* an environmental aspect? According to ISO 14001, an environmental aspect is defined as an *element of an organization's activities, products, or services that can interact with the environment*. In other words, an aspect (or element) is a constituent part of the business in which an organization is engaged. In a manufacturing environment, constituent parts often are thought of as inputs to the manufacturing process—that is, use of raw materials, chemicals, and natural resources.

It is important to remember that the procedure mandated by ISO 14001 is intended to identify aspects associated with *activities, products, and services*. This means that inputs to the manufacturing process alone do not comprise *all* aspects. It is possible to have aspects that are not inputs. For example, fuel storage on site constitutes an aspect. The packaging that accompanies raw materials is also an aspect, as are office supplies, paper, toner cartridges, and other items associated with the front office. More about aspects can be found in chapter 2.

ISO 14001 defines an environmental impact as *any change to the environment, whether adverse or beneficial, wholly or partially resulting from an organization's activities, products, or services*. Impacts often are viewed as outputs; however, it is more accurate to view impacts as the result of outputs. Examples of outputs are air emissions and wastewater discharges. An adverse change to the environment resulting from a wastewater discharge might be increased concentrations of heavy metals in a receiving stream. A beneficial change to the environment might be reforestation. (Impacts are discussed in chapter 3.)

Examples of aspects and impacts related to a process, product, and service are illustrated in Figure 1.1.

Figure 1.1. Examples of aspects and impacts.

	Aspect	Impact
Process: Manufacture of acrylonitrile monomer	Injection of ammonium sulfate into deep wells	Groundwater contamination
Product: Aerosol hair spray	propellant; solvent	Chlorinated solvent released to air
Service: Lawn maintenance	Application of herbicides	Nonpoint source pollution

The progression from identifying aspects to determining impacts to evaluating significance creates a funnel effect. A company may identify 50 aspects of which only 35 have an environmental impact. In some cases, an environmental aspect may have more than one impact. Therefore, in this example, the 35 aspects may create 35 impacts or there may be 40 or 60 impacts. Of the identified impacts, only 10 may be significant. The 10 significant aspects (that is, those aspects that create a significant environmental impact) must be considered in establishing objectives and targets.

ISO 14001 does not require objectives and targets for every significant aspect. Companies are free to prioritize and select significant aspects based on regulatory requirements, technological options, financial and business considerations, and the views of interested parties. Therefore, a list of 50 environmental aspects, where 10 aspects are deemed significant, may ultimately result in prevention of pollution objectives and targets for only three or four significant aspects.

Categories of Environmental Aspects

Aspects fall into three distinct categories.

- Aspects related to a company's operations: Operational aspects typically receive the greatest emphasis, largely because they are more familiar than aspects in the other two categories. Typically, these aspects are directly associated with a company's core business, such as the manufacture of product, the extraction of a natural resource, or the assembly of component parts.

- Aspects related to services offered or used by a company: Service aspects are indirectly associated with a company's core business. Service aspects typically encompass shipping/transportation, maintenance of equipment and facilities, and support functions such as groundskeeping.

- Aspects related to a company's products: Typically, these aspects are associated with packaging and use of a finished product (as opposed to aspects associated with the manufacture of a product). Ultimately, some potential environmental impacts are outside a company's control. For example, a manufacturer may attempt to minimize landfill waste by providing its product in a recyclable container, but it is up to the consumer to determine whether the container will be recycled or disposed of in another manner.

Figure 1.2 provides examples of categories of aspects associated with operations, services, and products and aspects within those categories. These lists are neither exhaustive nor inviolate; rather, they are intended to illustrate the kinds of aspects that often are identified. Some aspects appear on more than one list. For example, packaging is associated with operations and product. The former focuses on the manner in which incoming supplies and materials are packaged, while the latter focuses on the kind of packaging used for the manufactured product.

Readers of this workbook may discover additional categories of aspects that are unique to their particular business. They should feel free to add those categories if warranted by the nature of the organization in which the EMS is being implemented.

Keeping Information Current

ISO 14001 states that information about environmental aspects and impacts must be kept up-to-date. Some companies interpret this to mean that they must go through the entire identification and evaluation procedure at specified intervals (this usually is done annually). If absolutely nothing in a process changes—that is, the same materials are used in the same amounts within the same process—then aspects

Figure 1.2. Categories of environmental aspects.

Operational Aspect Categories	Service Aspect Categories	Product Aspect Categories
Energy	Janitorial/Cleaning	Power Source
• Natural gas	• Detergents	• Battery
• Electricity	• Aerosol cleaners	• Electricity
• Fossil fuel	• Water	• Fossil fuel
Materials	• Paper	• Solar
• Raw materials	• Rags	Packaging
• Processed materials	Groundskeeping	• Paper
• Recycled materials	• Fertilizer	• Cardboard
• Reused materials	• Herbicides	• Plastic
Natural Resources	• Grass/yard clippings	• Aluminum
• Water	• Power equipment	• Steel
• Land use	Maintenance	• Wood
Chemicals	• Solvents	Transport and Delivery
Packaging	• Oil	• Fuel
• Paper	• Grease	• Oil
• Cardboard	Transport and Delivery	• Grease
• Plastic	• Fuel	• Fluids (e.g., coolant)
• Aluminum	• Oil	Communication
• Steel	• Grease	• Paper
• Wood	• Fluids (e.g., coolant)	• Inks
Facilities and Equipment	Food/Catering	Use and Disposal
• Design	• Paper/plastic dishes, utensils	
• Operation	• Packaging	
• Maintenance	• Bottles, cans	
Office Administration	• Food	
• Paper	• Ranges, ovens	
• Toner cartridges	• Microwave ovens	
	• Dishwashers	
	Pest Control	
	Fire Prevention Systems	
	Facility	
	• Building	
	• Parking lots	
	• Drainage	

and associated impacts remain unchanged. Reevaluation of the identical process, simply because a year has elapsed, may be a waste of resources.

It is far more effective to rely on a change to any internal process as the trigger for reevaluation. When a company modifies any component of its business by changing the amounts of materials used, substituting one material for another, introducing new technology, or otherwise changing a process, then aspects have changed and must be evaluated to see whether associated impacts are significant. Reevaluation also can be triggered by externally imposed changes. For example, a company's supplier may change the kind of packaging in which it delivers goods. Because incoming packaging is an aspect, the company must evaluate the environmental impact associated with that change in packaging.

Any procedure for identifying environmental aspects must indicate how the information will be kept current. Therefore, a company must be able to demonstrate that, at any given time, it is familiar with its aspects and their associated impacts. Reevaluating changes within a specified time period after the changes have occurred is more likely to keep information up-to-date than an annual review.

Some companies hedge their bets by combining both activities into the procedure. They reevaluate whenever a change occurs. However, in the absence of any changes during a specified period (for example, 12 months), they reevaluate to make sure nothing has been overlooked.

Any of these three approaches to reevaluation—after a specified period of time, after a change, or a combination—will fulfill the ISO 14001 requirement.

CHAPTER 2

IDENTIFYING ENVIRONMENTAL ASPECTS

> **From ISO 14001:**
>
> Identify the environmental aspects of activities, products, or services that can be controlled or influenced (section 4.3.1)
>
> Environmental aspect—element of an organization's activities, products, or services that can interact with the environment (section 3.3)

Different methods for identifying aspects provide different kinds of information, thereby creating different gaps. The following methods have been used with varying degrees of success.

Value Chain Method: This method focuses on the environmental aspects present throughout the entire value chain of a company, from suppliers, through manufacture and distribution, up to and including product disposition. This approach typically involves life cycle analysis, which creates an emphasis on mass and energy balance.

Materials Identification Method: This method focuses on all of the materials (and their constituent parts) used in production. This approach tends to capture information about chemical and hazardous substances, but often overlooks aspects such as water and energy.

Regulatory Compliance Method: This method focuses on the substances that are regulated by federal, state, and local environmental agencies. Obviously, aspects that are not regulated—for example, many forms of packaging waste—will not be addressed.

Process Flow Method

The easiest and most comprehensive way to identify environmental aspects is the *process flow* approach. This method breaks the organization into manageable chunks by delineating every process and support activity on a process flow diagram, then each process and activity is individually examined to identify associated aspects. This approach expedites the identification of aspects in relation to those processes and activities. It has the added benefit of fulfilling the ISO 14001 requirement contained in clause 4.4.6, Operational control, to "identify those operations and activities that are associated with identified significant environmental aspects."

Specific activities that facilitate successful completion of the process flow diagram are as follows:

Establish a cross-functional team. This workbook espouses a team approach. The author's experience has demonstrated time and time again that many heads are better than one. Depending on the nature of a particular business, team participants will come from the sales, purchasing, production, shipping, distribution, and environmental functions. For those companies with a quality system, the quality function also should participate.

The cross-functional team has overall authority for aspect identification. This does not mean that the cross-functional team does all the work. In many organizations, it is beneficial for the cross-functional team to establish a number of smaller teams composed of people who are responsible for a process or activity under review— that is, those whose actions initiate an activity, those who perform that activity, and those who receive the result of that activity.

Remember that those involved with an activity may be physically located in an area of the facility other than where that activity is performed. For example, aspect identification of activities associated with the receiving department would include individuals from the purchasing department (because they determine what will be delivered to the company) and the warehouse/storage facility (because they are the *customers* in this particular activity) in addition to those from the receiving department.

Similarly, aspects identification associated with the warehouse would include individuals from the receiving department (because their actions initiate the warehouse function), warehouse employees, and those individuals who obtain materials from the warehouse (customers).

Diagram the process flow. Once the cross-functional team is assembled, its first task is to ascertain what processes and activities occur within the organization and their interrelationships. This can be accomplished at a meeting at which participants sequentially *walk through* their own component of the operation.

The process is greatly enhanced by a facilitator, whose role is to ensure that all processes and activities, including hand-offs between departments and functions, are identified. Typically, the facilitator initiates the process by asking two questions.

First, participants are asked to describe the event that initiates activity within the organization. The response (for example, customer order) becomes the starting point.

Second, participants are asked what event concludes activity within the organization. This response (for example, receipt of payment) becomes the end point. The facilitator's job is to ensure that participants delineate every step between these two points.

Realistically, participants are unlikely to identify key steps in sequence. There is a great deal of going back and forth as information about one portion of the organization's activities triggers information about others. The most effective way to capture such information is by creating a process flow diagram that depicts all organizational processes and hand-offs.

Most companies focus on their core business. A printing company, for example, will address the processes and activities involved in setting up a press and printing an order. Once all activities related to the operational facet are identified, the facilitator must ensure that support and ancillary services are considered. Typical services are

- Transportation and distribution

- Construction

- Equipment maintenance

- Janitorial/cleaning services

- Grounds maintenance

- Food service

- Waste disposal services

- Administrative activities

After the cross-functional team develops the general process flow diagram, the smaller working teams should review the diagram to ensure that all steps have been included. Each working team reviews those components of the diagram with which its members are associated. If a particular process involves more than one department, representatives from all relevant departments should participate in enhancing that portion of the process flow diagram.

For example, the cross-functional team at a printing company might identify the following eight key steps on the process flow diagram:

1. Job award

2. Production process

3. Art flow

4. Pre press process

5. Platemaking process

6. Press process

7. Finishing process

8. Job completion

A small working team involved with the platemaking process adds to the diagram by detailing the specific tasks involved.

5. Platemaking process

   a. Obtain flats from stripping department
   b. Compare flats to layout, job ticket, and proofs for accuracy
   c. Burn image into plates
   d. Process plates through the developer
   e. Check plates against proofs for broken type, holes, and color break
   f. Send plates to the press

The cross-functional team should review the completed process flow diagram when all operational and supporting activities (for example, sales, maintenance) have been described in detail and inserted into the original overview diagram.

Based on the process flow diagram, the inputs and outputs associated with each step can be identified. These inputs and outputs provide the basis for identifying aspects.

The concept of a process flow diagram can be intimidating, especially to those with limited access to sophisticated computer graphics software. In fact, the ability to create flow charts or other similar graphics is unnecessary. Figure 2.1 depicts a process flow diagram that presents information about the manufacture of street signs in tabular form. Because this figure is intended to illustrate how a process flow diagram is formatted, key support activities are missing. A comprehensive process flow diagram must include all nonmanufacturing activities, such as sales, receiving, storage, shipping, accounting, and so on.

Figure 2.1. Process flow diagram.

Process Inputs	Process Flow	Process Outputs
Steel sheets	The sign blank is cut from a sheet of steel by a metal shear machine. Corners are rounded on a punch machine. Holes for mounting the sign are punched by a punch machine.	Scrap steel
Liquid zinc	The sign is coated with zinc to prevent rusting.	Liquid zinc
Cellophane tape Water	The blank is checked for cleanliness. A tape snap test checks for dirt by applying cellophane tape to the blank and pulling it away. The presence of color or particles on the tape indicates dirt. Water is poured over the surface. Beading action indicates the presence of oil or grease.	Used cellophane tape Water/oil mixture
Mineral spirits/naphtha Clean cotton cloths Trichloroethylene (TCE) or Perchloroethylene (PCE)	The blank surface is wiped with mineral spirits (or naphtha) to remove grease and dried with a lint-free cloth. The blank is then immersed in a bath of TCE or PCE vapor.	Cloths saturated with mineral spirits (or naphtha)
Wallboard Nails Band saw Indelible marking pens Retroreflective sheets	The shape of the sign is transferred to thin wallboard. The wallboard is placed on multiple retroreflective sheets and secured to a hardboard cutting base. The sheets are cut with a bandsaw.	Scrap wallboard Used nails Used pens Scrap steel Used hardboard Scrap retroreflective material

Figure 2.1. Process flow diagram (continued).

Process Inputs	Process Flow	Process Outputs
Retroreflective sheets Cutting dies	Retroreflective sheets are placed in a clicker press. Cutting dies are used to produce letters and symbols.	Scrap retroeflective material
Steel blanks Cut retroreflective sheets	The adhesive liner on the back of the background sheeting is removed and the sheeting is applied to the dry steel blank. The sign is pressed between rollers to ensure a smooth, even application. The edges are trimmed.	Adhesive liner Scrap steel and retroreflective sheeting
Die-cut letters Plastic slipsheets	The sign is set in a heat lamp vacuum applicator and cooled. Letters, symbols, and other copy are placed on the sign. The sign is pressed between rollers to ensure a smooth, even application. The sign is covered with a plastic slipsheet and heated and cooled.	Scrap retroreflective sheeting Adhesive backing Scrap plastic slipsheets
Cardboard cartons Packing tape Wooden pallets Plastic strapping	Signs are boxed according to type and sent to warehouse for shipping	Scrap cardboard Scrap packing tape Scrap plastic strapping Damaged pallets

Identification of environmental aspects. Once the process flow diagram is complete, the small working teams are in a position to examine every step in every identified process and activity in order to delineate any associated environmental aspects. This approach serves two purposes. First, it enables the organization to identify aspects in small, manageable chunks, thereby decreasing the likelihood that significant aspects will be overlooked. Second, it enables the organization to link its aspects to specific operations and activities as required by ISO 14001, clause 4.4.6, Operational control. A comprehensive process flow diagram will delineate

- Where every process or activity begins, in terms of the receipt of materials or intermediate products

- The nature of any transformations that occur as part of the process or activity

- Where every process or activity ends, in terms of intermediate or final products

Depending on the nature of the specific process or activity under review, consideration usually is given to

- Use of processed materials

- Use of recycled materials

- Use of reused materials

- Use of raw materials

- Use of chemicals

- Use of natural resources

- Use of energy

- Packaging on incoming items

Teams focused on aspects related to products tend to focus on

- Design

- Fabrication

- Storage

- Distribution

- Packaging

- Use

- Disposal

The impacts of these (or other) aspects typically are viewed as emissions to air, releases to water, contamination of land, and depletion of natural resources. (Impacts are discussed in chapter 3.)

Many companies erroneously evaluate their environmental aspects only within the context of normal operating conditions. This overlooks aspects that may be associated with shut-down and start-up conditions or emergency situations. For example, a fire (emergency) may trigger a halon system (aspect) that is not a consideration under normal operating conditions. Consideration of emergency situations has the added benefit of fulfilling the requirement in ISO 14001, clause 4.4.7, Emergency preparedness and response, to identify the potential for accidents and emergency situations.

The easiest way to identify aspects is to create a questionnaire that guides a working team through the process. Obviously, such a tool should be customized to reflect the nature of a company's activities. Figure 2.2 provides an example of how such a tool might be constructed.

The questionnaire can be customized to better reflect the nature of a company's activities and to make it easier to use. For example, the kinds of packaging associated with a company's materials and supplies could be listed, thereby requiring recognition by the individual completing this form rather than recall. The ability to check off the kind of packaging rather than having to write it out could save time. If this approach is employed, be sure to include *other* as an item. This allows the user to add information in case the list of choices is not complete.

Similar questionnaires can be constructed for services and other nonoperational activities and products. Figure 2.3 is designed to accommodate service activities performed on a company's premises, either by its own employees or by subcontractors. The form also is applicable for situations in which a company's employees provide service to a customer.

Figure 2.4 focuses on aspects associated with a finished product. Therefore, the emphasis here is limited to product packaging, use, and disposal. Aspects related to product manufacture should be captured when operational aspects are identified (refer to Figure 2.2).

Figure 2.2. Identification of operational environmental aspects.

Operational Area:			
Activity/Task:			
Form Completed by:			Date:

Yes	No	Questions	Aspects (Complete this section for any "yes" response.)
		1. Is energy used?	List the kinds and amount for normal operations. List the kinds and amount, if different, for: Shut-down: Start-up: Potential emergency situations:
		2. Are natural resources used?	List the kinds and amount for normal operations. List the kinds and amount, if different, for: Shut-down: Start-up. Potential emergency situations:
		3. Are chemicals used?	List the kinds and amount for normal operations. List the kinds and amount, if different, for: Shut-down: Start-up: Potential emergency situations:
		4. Are other materials used?	List the kinds and amount for normal operations. List the kinds and amount, if different, for: Shut-down: Start-up: Potential emergency situations:
		5. Is any packaging associated with items 1–4?	List the kinds and amount for normal operations. List the kinds and amount, if different, for: Shut-down: Start-up: Potential emergency situations:

Figure 2.3. Identification of service environmental aspects.

Nature of service:			
Activity/Task:			
Task Performed by: ☐ Employee ☐ Subcontractor			
Form Completed by:			Date:
Yes	No	Questions	Aspects (Complete this selection for any "yes" response.)
		1. Is service provided on company premises?	Identify the location(s).
		2. Is service provided on customer premises?	Indicate the nature of transportation used to get there.
		3. Is energy used?	List the kinds and amount.
		4. Are natural resources used?	List the kinds and amount.
		5. Are chemicals used?	List the kinds and amount.
		6. Are other materials used?	List the kinds and amount.
		7. Is any packaging associated with items 3–6?	List the kinds and amount.

Figure 2.4. Identification of product environmental aspects.

Product:			
End User:	❏ Original Equipment Manufacturer (OEM) ❏ Consumer ❏ Other (specify)		
Form Completed by:			Date:
Yes	No	Questions	Aspect (Complete this section for any "yes" response.)
		1. Does the product require enclosure in a container?	Describe the nature of the container.
		2. Is the product (or its container) enclosed in any packaging?	List the kinds and amount.
		3. Does the company have a take-back program for the product, container, or packaging?	List the materials that are taken back and amount.
		4. Is any portion of the product, container, or packaging reusable or recyclable?	List the materials that are reusable and explain how they are reused. List the materials that are recyclable.
		5. Does proper use of the product rely on an energy source?	Describe the kind of energy and the amount.
		6. Is the packaging disposed of by the end user?	Describe typical manner of disposition and amount.
		7. Is the container disposed of by the end user?	Describe typical manner of disposition and amount.
		8. Is the product disposed of by the end user?	Describe typical manner of disposition and amount.

Identification of Positive Aspects

Environmental aspects typically are viewed as having an adverse impact on the environment. The focus of environmental objectives and targets, therefore, is to eliminate or reduce the aspect, thereby preventing or reducing pollution. The emphasis in ISO 14001 on prevention of pollution fosters this perception.

It is important to understand that an environmental aspect can have a beneficial impact on the environment. Examples are few—because most aspects *do* have an adverse impact—but include planting trees, creating wetlands, donating or selling land to conservancy organizations, and other similar activities.

CHAPTER 3

ASSESSING ENVIRONMENTAL IMPACTS

From ISO 14001:

Determine those [aspects] which have or can have significant impacts upon the environment (section 4.3.1)

Environmental impact—any change to the environment, whether adverse or beneficial, wholly or partially resulting from an organization's activities, products, or services.

Identification of Environmental Impacts

Just as aspects can be categorized in terms of processes, products, and services, the impacts resulting from those aspects can be similarly classified. ISO 14001, Annex A, states explicitly that organizations do not have to evaluate each product, component, or raw material input. They may select categories of activities, products, or services to identify those aspects most likely to have a significant impact.

It is not necessary for an aspect to have an *actual* impact; the *potential* for a significant impact is sufficient to designate an aspect as significant. Thus, organizations that are successfully managing aspects to avoid a significant impact should identify and evaluate their potential impacts to avoid an adverse environmental impact in the future. Figure 3.1 lists common categories of environmental impacts.

Figure 3.1. Common environmental impact categories.

Operational Impact Categories	Service Impact Categories	Product Impact Categories
Consumption/depletion of energy	Wastewater discharges	Toxic substances
Consumption/depletion of natural resources	Disposal of chemicals	Chemical substances
Air contaminants	Disposal of solvents	Packaging disposal
Wastewater discharges	Disposal of used parts	Product disposal
Storm water runoff		Noise
Land contamination		
Hazardous waste disposal		
Solid waste disposal		
Noise		
Odor		

Environmental impacts can be identified in much the same manner as environmental aspects. The most effective method is to build on existing information. If a template (such as the example offered in Figure 2.2) was used to identify environmental aspects, that information becomes the foundation upon which the list of environmental impacts is built.

Figure 3.2 provides an example of an impact identification form that guides this effort. Note that a separate form is used for each environmental aspect. This allows a company to organize the forms in whatever manner is most useful by using information in selected boxes. For example, aspects can be organized by

- Operational area: This assists in identifying environmental aspects and impacts that are associated with specific tasks, work stations, or other activities. Such categorization will be helpful in fulfilling other requirements imposed by ISO 14001, such as providing training to employees whose jobs may create a significant environmental impact (clause 4.4.2), and identifying those operations and activities that are associated with identified significant environmental aspects (clause 4.4.6). Information in the Activity/Task box of Figure 3.2 provides the means for organization.

- Media: This approach clusters all water-related impacts as one grouping, all air-related impacts as another grouping, and so forth, regardless of the functional area in which the impact is generated. It assists in identifying the legal

Figure 3.2. Identification of environmental impacts.

Operational Area:			
Activity/Task:			
Aspect (from Figure 2.2):			
Form Completed by:			Date:
Yes	No	Questions	Impacts (Complete this section for any "yes" response.)
		1. Does any component of this aspect reenter the process from which it was generated?	List the component(s) and amount.
		2. Does any component of this aspect enter another internal process?	List the component(s) and amount.
		3. Is any component of this aspect sent off-site for recycling?	List the component(s) and amount.
		4. Is any component of this aspect sent off-site for reprocessing?	List the component(s) and amount.
		5. Is any component of this aspect sent off-site for reuse?	List the component(s) and amount.
		6. Is any component of this aspect emitted to the air (either directly or as fugitive emissions)?	List the component(s) and amount.
		7. Is any component of this aspect discharged to water?	List the component(s) and amount.
		8. Is any component of this aspect handled as solid waste?	List the component(s) and amount.
		9. Is any component of this aspect handled as hazardous waste?	List the component(s) and amount.
		10. Could this aspect contribute to an accident?	Identify the type of accident, the conditions under which it could occur, and the result.
		11. Could this aspect create an emergency situation?	Identify the type of emergency, the conditions under which it could occur, and the result.

requirements that are applicable to a company's environmental aspects (clause 4.3.2). Information in boxes 6 through 9 of Figure 3.2 serves as the basis for organization.

- Potential for accidents and emergency situations: This categorization assists in fulfilling the requirement imposed by clause 4.4.7, Emergency preparedness and response. Impacts in this category are organized on the basis of information in boxes 10 and 11 of Figure 3.2.

- Actual impacts: This consolidates the total array of impacts by treating multiple examples of the same impact (for example, air emissions from a web press on the east end of a building and air emissions from a sheet-fed press on the west end of the same building) as one impact (emission of VOCs from ink). It also can elevate an impact from minor to significant. Consider a complex process in which each of 10 workstations generates a small amount of solid waste (200 pounds/week). Individual evaluations might conclude that solid waste is not significant. However, when the 10 small amounts are considered as one total amount (one ton/week), the solid waste evaluation can result in a score that defines it as a significant impact. Information in boxes 1 through 9 on Figure 3.2 is used for organization.

Selecting Evaluation Criteria

Once environmental impacts are identified, each must be evaluated to establish the magnitude of the impact. This evaluation becomes the basis for determining significance (see chapter 4).

A common error is evaluating impacts only under normal operating conditions. A comprehensive evaluation effort will also consider abnormal operating conditions, shut-down and start-up activities, and the potential for accidents and emergency situations. This may seem redundant; after all, aspects have been identified for these varying conditions (see chapter 2). It is a critical step here because of the possibility that an aspect may be constant regardless of normal or abnormal operating conditions, but the impact may differ considerably.

Environmental impacts can be evaluated in a number of ways. There are as many schemes for evaluating environmental impacts as there are companies with evaluation procedures. A company must select some combination of evaluation criteria that are appropriate for its own operations and activities.

Criteria commonly used are presented in this section, along with a sampling of definitions. Interestingly, virtually all evaluation criteria employ a three-point or five-point rating scale. The drawback to such scales is the tendency for evaluators to select the midpoint or neutral position when there is some question about whether a particular attribute is slightly more negative or positive than neutral. If this is likely to be a concern, establish a four-point scale and force evaluators to commit themselves on one side of neutral (harmful) or the other (harmless). Some organizations may find it preferable to use nonnumerical scales, such as *minimal, low, moderate,* and *high*. There is nothing wrong with a nonnumerical approach; however, the use of numerical scales may simplify the determination of significance.

The nine scales presented here are five-point scales. These scales are generic; that is, they reflect the concepts embodied in numerous company procedures. Companies should not feel compelled to evaluate their environmental impacts on the basis of nine (or six or 12) factors. Rather, each organization must decide for itself what factors are important considerations. Select a combination that is appropriate for you.

Nor should companies feel compelled to use these scales as written. Both the range of scores and accompanying definitions can be modified to better suit a particular organization.

The three most common criteria for evaluating environmental impacts are severity, likelihood, and frequency of an impact. Severity refers to the degree to which a company's surroundings (including air, water, land, natural resources, flora, fauna, and humans) are affected by an impact.

Severity Scale

5 = Severe/catastrophic—very harmful or potentially fatal; great effort to correct and recover

4 = Serious—harmful but not potentially fatal, difficult to correct but recoverable

3 = Moderate—somewhat harmful, correctable

2 = Mild—little potential for harm, easily correctable

1 = Harmless—no potential for harm, correctable

Likelihood serves as an indicator of probability. It attempts to rate impacts on the probability of their occurrence.

Likelihood Scale

5 = Very likely—high probability (90 percent or more) that an aspect will result in a detectable impact

4 = Likely—strong probability (68 percent to 89 percent) that an aspect will result in a detectable impact

3 = Moderate—reasonable probability (34 percent to 67 percent) that an aspect will result in a detectable impact

2 = Low—low probability (11 percent to 33 percent) that an aspect will result in a detectable impact

1 = Remote—very unlikely (10 percent or less) that an aspect will result in a detectable impact

Frequency addresses how often an impact could occur. If it is very likely that an impact will occur, how often is it likely to happen—daily, monthly, once a year? Definitions can vary widely and should reflect the nature of a company's operations. For example, repeated occurrences in a manufacturing company are likely to be defined differently than in a services setting.

Frequency Scale

5 = Continuous—occurs three times per week (on average) or more often

4 = Repeated—occurs one to two times per week (on average)

3 = Regular—occurs monthly (on average)

2 = Intermittent—occurs quarterly (on average)

1 = Seldom—occurs two times per year (on average) or less often

Other common criteria are geographic boundaries, controllability, and regulatory status of an impact. Geographic boundaries reflect the physical area in which the impact occurs.

Boundaries Scale

5 = Global—impact migrates outside region in which company is located

4 = Regional—impact migrates outside local community in which company is located

3 = Local—impact migrates off-site into surrounding community

2 = Confined—impact migrates off-site, but is contained in small, adjacent area

1 = Isolated—impact is contained on company's site with no migration

Controllability is a key concept because ISO 14001 refers explicitly to the environmental aspects of a company's activities that it can control and influence.

Controllability Scale

5 = Uncontrollable—process and materials are not controlled

4 = Indirectly influenceable—processes and materials controlled by independent third party

3 = Influenceable—processes and materials controlled by customer or supplier

2 = Indirectly controllable—company controls supplier contract, mandates use of materials and/or processes

1 = Directly controllable—company controls processes and materials, no requirements imposed by customers

Regulatory status identifies whether an impact is associated with government requirements. Some companies treat this as a yes-no rating; that is, there is a government regulation or there is not. A more comprehensive rating system considers self-imposed requirements, including any requirements described as "other" in ISO 14001 sections 4.2 (environmental policy) and 4.3.2 (legal and other requirements).

Regulatory Status Scale

5 = Regulated—mandated by a federal, state, or local government agency

4 = Regulated in future—not currently mandated by a government agency, but either under consideration or has the potential to become regulated in future

3 = Company policy—industry standard, code of practice, or other initiative that has been adopted and formalized into a company-wide policy

2 = Company practice—industry standard, code of practice, or other initiative that guides established practice, but is not formally codified

1 = Unregulated—no guidance

Some companies have expanded the concept of regulatory status to include the criterion of reportability. This refers to any governing bodies that must be notified about the impact in question. In many cases, this may be more applicable to impacts that result from abnormal operating conditions or emergency incidents. Depending on organizational structure, this scale should be modified to reflect relevant levels of ownership and responsibility.

Reportability Scale

5 = Government authorities—reporting to federal, state, or local authorities

4 = Corporate management—reporting outside the facility responsible for the impact and its immediate company to the corporate owner

3 = Company management—reporting outside the facility responsible for the impact, but within the immediate company that owns the facility

2 = Facility management—reporting within the facility responsible for the impact

1 = Not reportable—no reporting required beyond documented procedure for monitoring and measuring key characteristics of activities that can have a significant environmental impact (per ISO 14001, section 4.5.1)

Additional considerations include stakeholder concerns and duration of impact. Stakeholder concerns reflects how external interested parties, typically defined in terms of customers, regulators, residents in proximity to the organization, and special-interest groups, perceive an environmental impact. Thus, an impact that is not severe but is of primary concern to external interested parties might be rated as equally significant as a severe impact that is of secondary concern to few external interested parties.

Stakeholder Concerns Scale

5 = primary concern to all/most interested parties

4 = primary concern to a few/one interested parties

3 = secondary concern to all/most interested parties

2 = secondary concern to a few/one interested parties

1 = little/no concern to interested parties

Duration pertains to the length of time that the environmental impact will be felt by affected entities. The rating scheme used can be modified to include time frames that reflect the kinds of impacts created by a company's activities. To ensure consistency among company staff tasked with assessing duration, it is necessary to quantify what is meant by terms such as *short-term*. Such definitions often differentiate acute and chronic impacts. An acute condition typically results from an episode in which the associated damage or harm is corrected. An acute impact can be likened to the common cold; the condition can be treated (usually with aspirin and chicken soup) and after a relatively short period of time, all adverse symptoms are eliminated.

A chronic impact presents a situation in which the associated damage is controlled but not corrected. Chronic impacts are analogous to arthritis; associated discomfort can be controlled but the cause of that discomfort cannot be eliminated.

Duration Scale

5 = Irreversible—controllable but not correctable

4 = Three years or more—great effort to correct and recover

3 = One to three years—difficult to correct but recoverable

2 = Three to 12 months—correctable

1 = Short-term—impact can be corrected in three months or less

Some organizations also include factors such as cost of remediation and effect on production. Although an organization can employ any criteria that it deems appropriate, cost, effect on production, and other similar considerations are more appropriate in determining which impacts will be addressed through environmental objectives and targets.

The evaluation factors presented here and in chapter 5 focus on adverse environmental impacts. Very few organizations have established evaluation criteria that compare beneficial impacts. Typically, such impacts are identified without any attempt to determine whether one is more beneficial (that is, more significant) than another.

Regardless of the number and type of factors to be considered, the construct that is conveyed by any evaluation criterion must be clearly defined. There are two types of definitions. In the first type, a word can be defined by other words. For example, we can define *weight* as the *heaviness* of an object. Such a definition simply substitutes one concept for another. The second type, referred to as an operational definition, assigns meaning to a word by specifying the manner in which it can be measured. Thus, an operational definition for *weight* might be *number of pounds*.

A key consideration in impact evaluation is inter-rater reliability; that is, the ability of different evaluators to make the same, correct determination about an impact as it reflects a specific criterion. Inter-rater reliability is enhanced by a clear, concise operational definition for every score within a particular scale.

Consider two employees who are asked to evaluate an impact for frequency. The choices available to these raters are: 1–seldom, 2–intermittent, 3–regular, 4–repeated, 5–continuous. Depending on their professional experience and facility with language, the words on the scale may connote very different things to these raters. This increases the likelihood that each rater will assign very different scores (for example, 2 and 4). When an operational definition is added (see the Frequency Scale earlier in this chapter), variability in scoring should decrease because the raters have been told the basis for assigning any number on the scale.

Because different teams of employees may be evaluating environmental aspects, it is critical to develop operational definitions that are meaningful to all participants.

Evaluating Environmental Impacts

Once a rating scheme has been determined and underlying constructs defined, each impact must be evaluated according to the selected criteria. Every identified impact (delineated in Figure 3.2) must be assigned a number that reflects its position for any given criterion. For example, if an impact is to be evaluated for severity, and a five-point scale is used to define degrees of severity, then the impact will be assigned a number (from 1 to 5) that depicts its severity rating. If the impact is to be evaluated according to seven factors, then seven numbers must be assigned—one for each criterion of interest.

Typically, this information is summarized on a worksheet such as that presented in Figure 3.3. Note that the figure reflects all nine criteria for which scales appear earlier in this chapter. Obviously, it should be modified to reflect the evaluation criteria chosen by a company. Because answers to the questions require quantification, scores entered onto this summary form are taken from the rating scale definitions. Additional examples of rating scales and summary forms appear in chapter 6.

After the rating numbers have been assigned, simple mathematics can be used to determine a cumulative score for each impact. The most common approaches involve addition or multiplication—the higher the number, the more significant the impact.

Both approaches introduce a bias to the total significance score. Addition reflects the assumption that all rating factors are equally important. Multiplication introduces a different bias. Rating criteria are not equivalent with this method. Any factor with a low rating score contributes less to the total significance score than those factors with high rating scores. To illustrate these biases, consider two impacts that are rated on the basis of likelihood and severity (see Figure 3.4).

Although Impact 2 is very likely to occur, it is easily correctable and there is no potential for harm. Impact 1 is less likely to occur than Impact 2 (34 percent to 67 percent as compared to 90 percent or more), but will be somewhat harmful. In the first example, the two impacts are equally significant. However, when rating scores are multiplied instead of added (see example 2), Impact 1 yields a higher significance score than Impact 2.

Such differences also occur when multiple evaluation criteria are used (see Figure 3.5). For example, suppose a company decides to evaluate its impacts for four factors—severity, likelihood, frequency, and duration.

Figure 3.3. Environmental impact ratings.

Aspect (from Figure 2.2)	
Impact (from Figure 3.2)	
Form Completed by:	Date:
Questions/Data	Score*
1. Can the impact be corrected? If yes, how is it corrected? How long (on average) does such correction take? What kind of harm (if any) occurs to people, animal life, water, air, land?	
2. If no, can the impact be controlled? How? How long (on average) does such control take? What kind of harm (if any) occurs to people, animal life, water, air, land?	
3. What is the percentage likelihood that this impact will occur?	
4. In the course of one year, how many times (on average) does this impact occur?	
5. Is the impact contained on our site or does it migrate off-site? If it migrates, how large an area is affected?	
6. Who, if anyone, has control over the cause of this impact? If control is inside our company, indicate the department or functional area. If outside our company, provide as much detail as possible.	
7. Is the impact regulated? If yes, by what agency? If no, is it likely to be regulated anytime soon?	
8. Is the impact addressed by company policy or practice? If yes, provide details.	
9. Are there any reporting requirements related to this impact? If yes, how often and to whom are reports submitted?	
10. Is this impact of concern to any of our stakeholders? If yes, which ones? How much concern?	
11. What is the duration of the impact when it occurs? How long does it take to correct/control the impact?	
Total Score (indicate whether numbers are to be added or multiplied to achieve the total)	

* from applicable rating scale (scales should be attached to this form or otherwise provided to evaluators)

Figure 3.4. Examples of rating bias.

Impacts	Likelihood	Severity	Significance
Example 1 (added)			
Impact 1	3	3	$3 + 3 = 6$
Impact 2	5	1	$5 + 1 = 6$
Example 2 (multiplied)			
Impact 1	3	3	$3 \times 3 = 9$
Impact 2	5	1	$5 \times 1 = 5$

In this example, significance is determined by *adding* the assigned rating for each criterion. Thus, in Figure 3.5, Impacts 2 and 4 are the most significant. Although both impacts have a total score of 13, Impact 2 will occur far less often (no more than twice annually) than Impact 4 (monthly). However, Impact 2 is irreversible, while Impact 4 can be corrected in less than a year. With a score of 12, Impact 5 is almost as significant—it is more likely to occur than Impact 2, but will be far less severe when it does.

If we determine significance by *multiplying* the assigned ratings, the results change dramatically (see Figure 3.6). Impacts 2 and 4 are no longer equal in significance. Impact 4 has a significance score that is half again as large as the score for Impact 2.

How, then, does one decide whether to add or multiply assigned values?

The scales employed in evaluating environmental impacts are attribute scales; that is, they identify characteristics associated with inanimate objects. These attributes are considered continuous variables because they are measured using a numerical system (in this workbook, 1 through 5) where the numbers designate more or less of the attribute in question.

Figure 3.5. Multiple evaluation criteria, added.

Impacts	Severity	Likelihood	Frequency	Duration	Significance
Impact 1	3	3	1	2	9
Impact 2	4	3	1	5	13
Impact 3	2	2	4	2	10
Impact 4	3	5	3	2	13
Impact 5	1	5	3	2	12

Figure 3.6. Multiple evaluation criteria, multiplied.

Impacts	Severity	Likelihood	Frequency	Duration	Significance
Impact 1	3	3	1	2	18
Impact 2	4	3	1	5	60
Impact 3	2	2	4	2	32
Impact 4	3	5	3	2	90
Impact 5	1	5	3	3	45

Without devoting extensive space to a statistical discussion, suffice it to say that scores should be *multiplied* when the values assigned to measured attributes (for example, severity, likelihood, and so forth) are unrelated to each other. Let's return to Figure 3.6—for impact 1, severity is assigned a score of 3. Likelihood also has a score of 3; however, it could just as easily have a score of 1 or 5. The likelihood of occurrence is unrelated to severity. Scores should be *added* when the values of attributes are related to each other.

Generally speaking, the criteria employed in impact evaluation are unrelated. Therefore, multiplication should be used to determine the total significance score.

Pulling It All Together

Although the process flow diagram, aspect identification forms, and impact identification and evaluation forms are excellent tools, the number of pages involved can be cumbersome when quick reference is required. Thus, companies often summarize

Figure 3.7. Environmental aspects and impacts summary.

Source/ Activity	Aspect	Impact	Medium	Potential Emergency	Related Documents
Receiving dock— unloading	Oil leaks	Run-off to storm sewer	Water	None	WI-3-02
Paint booth— spray paint	VOCs	Emission of particulates*	Air	Venting	WI-7-06 EP-3

*Denotes significant impact.

their aspects and impacts in a way that affords employees, auditors, and others a quick overview. Figure 3.7 offers one example of how aspects and impacts can be consolidated. Note that information is organized according to specific operations and activities.

CHAPTER 4

DEFINING SIGNIFICANCE

ISO 14001 limits its focus to environmental aspects that have or can have *significant* impacts on the environment. Interestingly, the writers of ISO 14001 provide no insight as to their perception of what renders an impact significant. According to *Webster's Third New International Dictionary* (Unabridged), *significant* is defined as *having meaning; having or likely to have effect*. It is up to individual companies to decide the point at which an impact has meaning or is significant.

Assigning significance relies on the results of impact evaluation. As explained in chapter 3, once evaluation criteria are established and numerical values assigned, an impact score is derived for every identified aspect. Typically, a high impact score denotes a significant impact. The challenge is determining where to draw the line that separates significant impacts from the trivial. Suppose that impact scores range from 1 to 10. How does one organization decide that a score of 7 or higher is significant while another includes everything with a score of 6 or more?

Based on two five-point scales for likelihood and severity, all possible significance scores for impacts are presented in Figure 4.1. Two scores are shown in each cell: the first is obtained by multiplying the likelihood value times the severity value; the second by adding those values.

Multiplied scores range from a low of 1 (1×1) to a high of 25 (5×5); added scores range from 2 ($1 + 1$) to 10 ($5 + 5$). Another way of looking at the significance scores is to list them on a continuum from highest to lowest numerical value.

- Continuum of multiplied scores (14 scores possible)

  25 20 16 15 12 10 9 8 6 5 4 3 2 1

- Continuum of added scores (9 scores possible)

  <u>10   9   8   7   6   5   4   3   2</u>

Figure 4.1. Significance scores for two evaluation criteria.

Likelihood	Severity				
	5	**4**	**3**	**2**	**1**
5	25/10	20/9	15/8	10/7	5/6
4	20/9	16/8	12/7	8/6	4/5
3	15/8	12/7	9/6	6/5	3/4
2	10/7	8/6	6/5	4/4	2/3
1	5/6	4/5	3/4	2/3	1/2

The example presented in Figure 4.1 uses only two evaluation factors. As the number of evaluation criteria increases, the number of possible scores and the maximum value of those scores also increase. If five five-point scales are used to evaluate impacts and scores are multiplied, the maximum value for a single impact jumps to 3,125!

Conceptually, the task is the same no matter how large the number of possible scores or the maximum value. Companies must decide where they will draw the line that denotes significance. The following three factors are often used to make this judgment credible:

- Regulatory status: Some companies define all regulated impacts as significant. Others argue that some regulated entities pose relatively little harm to the environment and, therefore, are not significant on the basis of actual harm engendered.

- Stakeholder interest: Impacts that are of concern to external parties with a legitimate interest in a company's operations often are defined as significant.

- Percentile ranking: Percentile rank refers to the relative position of a score in a distribution of scores. Specifically, it identifies the percentage of scores equal to or less than the given score. A percentile rank is always a number representing a percentage. Thus, if 80 percent of impact scores have a value of 15 or less, the percentile rank for the score of 15 is 80.

Some companies define as significant those impacts with scores higher than the score with a percentile ranking of 80. Other companies may use a percentile ranking of 75 or 90. Conceptually, what they are saying is that impacts with scores in the top 20 (or 25 or 10) percent are of interest.

Such methods can be used in combination. Such an approach would define an impact as significant under the conditions depicted in Figure 4.2.

Figure 4.2. Conditions for significance, combined approach.

	Impact Score Exceeds Percentile Ranking of _N_	**Impact Score Equals or Less Than Percentile Ranking of _N_**
Impact is Regulated	Significant	Significant
Impact not Regulated	Significant	Not Significant

Any approach for defining significance will be somewhat subjective. Who is to say that a percentile ranking of 80 is more appropriate than one of 70? Ultimately, a company must rely on the professional experience and judgment of those charged with this task. Regardless of the method used, it should be clearly defined so that the assignment of significance to different environmental impacts is done in a consistent manner.

CHAPTER 5

A FINAL WORD

The process flow approach presented in this workbook eliminates much of the frustration that can arise when organizations attempt to identify and evaluate their environmental aspects and impacts. It allows examination of information across three separate screenings to ensure that a full array of elements with actual or potential environmental effects is fully explored. The screening process quickly and effectively narrows the list of aspects to those most critical to a pollution prevention strategy on the basis of selection criteria developed by the organization.

The initial screen enables any organization to delineate the full array of environmental aspects associated with core business and ancillary operations and activities. The second screen evaluates the environmental impact of every identified aspect. The third screen provides an elimination function—by determining which impacts are significant, a company narrows the focus of environmental objectives and targets, thereby saving time and money.

However a company chooses to identify environmental aspects and impacts, the most important consideration is establishing a procedure that is suited to its core business and internal culture. Readers should not lose sight of the fact that this workbook is printed on paper, not carved in stone. The sample procedures in chapter 6 are just that—examples. Although each employs a similar approach, actual steps in the procedures, assigned responsibilities, and manner of reporting results differ from company to company.

This workbook provides information to enhance understanding. It is incumbent upon you, the reader, to transform that understanding into your own procedure for effectively addressing your organization's environmental aspects and impacts.

CHAPTER 6

SAMPLE PROCEDURES

The role of an ISO 14001 auditor is to determine whether established procedures conform to the requirements stipulated in the standard and to verify that such procedures are being followed. Therefore, the approach selected for identifying environmental aspects, evaluating their impacts, and assigning significance must be applied consistently throughout the organization.

This section presents procedures that have been implemented in companies from five business sectors: automotive, electronics, industrial gases, utilities, and service.

BOC Gases Americas—manufacture and supply of industrial gases and gas handling technology

Consolidated Edison Company of New York—electric, gas, and steam utility

First Environment—strategic management and environmental engineering services

MKA-Matsushita Kotobuki Electronics Industries of America—manufacture of combination television/VCRs

Panasonic-Matsushita Communication Industrial Corporation of U.S.A.—manufacture of automotive electronics and telecommunication products

Purolator/Arvin Industries—manufacture of automotive oil, air, and fuel filters and filter housings

In addition to the procedures themselves, several companies also have provided tables of aspects and impacts identified by their procedures.

The author's purpose in presenting these examples is to illustrate how companies in different sectors have chosen to identify and evaluate their environmental aspects and impacts. These procedures are not intended as templates. Any organization that implements ISO 14001 must develop its own procedure to reflect internal processes and activities.

BOC Gases Americas
Murray Hill, New Jersey

BOC Gases is a worldwide leader in the manufacture and supply of industrial gases and gas handling technology. The company's gas products are essential to almost all modern industries, including chemicals, fabrication and welding, food, electronics, glass, iron and steel, and medical. BOC Gases' primary gas products include cryogenic and non-cryogenic nitrogen and oxygen, as well as argon, carbon dioxide, helium, hydrogen, and a variety of medical rare and special gases.

BOC Gases is the industrial gases business of The BOC Group, the worldwide industrial gases, vacuum technologies, and distribution services company operating in more than 60 countries with sales in excess of $7 billion.

The Kittery, Maine, site of BOC Gases Americas was registered to ISO 14001 in July, 1997, by Lloyd's Register Quality Assurance.

In addition to its environmental aspect identification and significance evaluation procedure, BOC Gases has provided three tables of data.

- Section One, Table S1-3 presents the facility-wide environmental aspect inventory with evaluation scores and designation of significance.

- Section A—Air Separation Plants presents impacts associated with the facility's air separation plants for which pollution prevention activities (best management practices) have been identified.

- Section G—Truck Maintenance presents impacts associated with truck maintenance for which pollution prevention activities (best management practices) have been identified.

BOC Gases Americas
Murray Hill, New Jersey

This procedure was used for ISO 14001 registration at BOC's Kittery, Maine site.

Environmental Aspect Identification
and Significance Evaluation Procedure

ENVIRONMENTAL ASPECTS

Kittery will establish and maintain procedure(s) to identify the environmental aspects of its activities, products, or services that it can control and over which it can be expected to have an influence, in order to determine those which have or can have significant impacts on the environment. The Kittery site will ensure that the aspects related to these significant impacts are considered in setting our environmental objectives. This information will be kept up to date.

Table S1-3 identifies Environmental Aspects related to facility activities and evaluates the significance of those Environmental Aspects. Environmental Aspects are defined as, An element of an organization's (facility's) activities, products, or services that can interact with the environment.

1. Identification of Environmental Aspects

The methodology used to identify environmental aspects at this facility is provided below:

Step 1   The site Pollution Prevention Team will conduct a review of the Process Flow Diagrams (See Tables S1-3, S1-4, and S1-5). These tables provide useful pictorial flow diagrams for **Air Separation Plants and Distribution Operations** to identify environmental aspects at this location. Best Environmental Management Practice Tables (see EMS Manual Appendix 12A) will also be reviewed to further identify applicable environmental aspects for this facility.

Step 2   Site-specific environmental aspects (both direct and indirect) related to site equipment and features, neighbors, environmentally sensitive areas, ecologically significant resources, and abnormal/emergency conditions will be identified by the Pollution Prevention Team in a brainstorming session.

Step 3 Environmental Aspects, estimates of quantities generated/released (when applicable), and potential environmental impacts will be listed in Table S1-3 for this facility.

Step 4 Review/update the identified Environmental Aspects at least annually or whenever there is a change in facility processes, surroundings, or applicable regulations.

2. Evaluation of the Significance of Identified Environmental Aspects

The methodology used to evaluate the significance of the identified Environmental Aspects is provided below:

Step 1 The Pollution Prevention Team will use the following factors to evaluate the significance of the Environmental Aspects. They include:

A. **Toxicity/Hazard**—The relative toxicity of the environmental aspect or the relative impact (for example, ozone depletion) it may have on the environment/community.

B. **Quantity**—Generally the amount of the environmental aspect (waste quantity, kilowatts, and so on) produced/used per year. When the environmental aspect is measured in other terms (such as, noise decibels) the evaluation will be based on site-specific criteria. Hazardous waste manifests, waste bills of lading, Form Rs, fuel usage records, purchasing records, flow records, and so on, are used to estimate these quantities.

C. **Probability/Exposure**—The likelihood of the environmental aspect causing an exposure with significant environmental damage.

D. **Regulatory**—The environmental aspect is regulated under a federal, state, or local environmental requirement.

E. **Liability/Cost**—The potential estimated liability or costs for taking corrective actions if the environmental aspect is not managed properly.

F. **Stakeholder Concerns**—Identifies whether the environmental aspect has been a legitimate concern of any stakeholder.

Step 2 Each factor is evaluated by the Pollution Prevention Team using the following criteria to determine the significance of each Environmental Aspect and record the results in Table S1-3. A consensus can be obtained informally or can be accomplished through more formal (for example, nominal group) techniques. As appropriate, a representative of the Corporate Environmental Affairs Department may facilitate this evaluation. Note that energy usage is considered a significant environmental aspect at all BOC Gases ASUs.

CRITERIA FOR EVALUATING ENVIRONMENTAL ASPECT SIGNIFICANCE

A. Toxicity/Hazard

1 = Process/Activity generates primarily municipal (garbage) and relatively inert industrial waste, noncontact cooling water, components of air, and inert compounds. Sound levels generated by activity at property line are less than **50** decibels.

2 = Process/Activity generates special wastes such as petroleum product wastes, criteria pollutants (such as products of combustion), and conventional water pollutants (BOD, COD, suspended solids, oil, and grease). Sound levels generated by activity at property line are greater than **50** but less than **65** decibels.

3 = Process/Activity generates listed hazardous air pollutants, Toxic Release Inventory chemicals, hazardous waste, PCBs, asbestos, priority water pollutants, ozone depleting substances, or other wastes generally acknowledged to be toxic/hazardous to the environment. Sound levels generated by activity at property line are greater than **65** decibels.

B. Quantity

1 = Process/Activity generates releases less than 1000 pounds/year. Noise source(s) generates sound levels less than **50** decibels at property line.

2 = Process/Activity generates releases greater than 1000 pounds but less than 10,000 pounds per year. Noise source(s) generates sound levels greater than **50** decibels but less than **65** decibels at property line.

3 = Process/Activity generates releases greater than 10,000 pounds per year. Noise source(s) generates sound levels greater than **65** decibels at property line.

C. Probability/Exposure

1 = There is a low likelihood (0–10%) that the activity/aspect will result in an exposure over a 10-year period that causes significant environmental damage or complaints.

2 = There is a moderate (11–30%) likelihood that the activity/aspect will result in an exposure over a 10-year period that causes significant environmental damage or complaints.

3 = There is a high (> 30%) likelihood that the activity/aspect will result in an exposure over a 10-year period that causes significant environmental damage or complaints.

*Note: When the score for A. Toxicity x B. Quantity x C. Probability/Exposure is **greater than 8**, the environmental aspect and associated potential environmental impacts are considered to be significant.*

D. Regulatory

Insignificant = Activity/aspect not regulated at federal, state, or local level.

Significant = Activity/aspect regulated at federal, state, or local level.

E. Potential Liability/Cost Impact

Insignificant = Cost liabilities associated with potential environmental impacts from the activity/aspect are estimated to be less than $5,000.

Significant = Cost liabilities associated with potential environmental impacts from the activity/aspect are estimated to be greater than $5,000.

F. Stakeholder Input

Insignificant = No legitimate concerns identified by stakeholders related to environmental aspect.

Significant = Legitimate concerns identified by stakeholders related to environmental aspect.

Activity or Process[1]	Environmental Aspect[2]	Potential Impact	Annual Amount Released (lbs.)	Toxicity/Hazard (1)	Quantity (2)	Probability/Exposure (3)	Significance Points (1 × 2 × 3)[3]	Regulatory Compliance S/I	Stakeholder Concerns S/I	Cost/Liability S/I	Significant Aspect/Impact Yes/No
Cooling tower	Blowdown—Warm water with low levels of pollutants	POTW/Piscataqua River	24.3 million	1	3	1	3	S	I	I	Y
Cooling tower	Water use	Surface water resource depletion	304.4 million	1	3	1	3	I	I	S	Y
Cooling tower	Water treatment chemicals (use and storage)	Stormwater/soil/surface water contaminant	16,000	2	3	1	6	S	I	S	Y
Cooling tower drift	Water vapor	Aesthetic	280 million	1	3	1	3	I	I	I	N
Compressors/equipment	Oils from leaks	Stormwater/soil/surface water contaminant	1750 lbs	2	2	1	4	S	I	I	Y
Compressors	Compressor condensate	POTW/Piscataqua	1.0 million	1	3	1	3	S	I	I	Y
Compressors/expanders	Noise	Noise to neighbors	85 dBA at property line	3	3	3	27(s)	S	I	I	Y
Compressors/expanders	Oily rags, pigs	Soil/ground/surface water contamination	375	2	1	1	2	S	I	I	Y
Plant maintenance	Equipment used oil	Soil/ground/surface water contamination	None	2	1	1	2	S	I	I	Y
Oxygen service equipment cleaning	Solvent emissions	Soil/ground/surface water/air contamination	80	2	1	1	2	I	I	I	N
Stormwater runoff	Oils, disolved solids, suspended solids, solvents, metals, etc.	Soil/ground/surface water contamination	Not available	1	3	3	9(s)	S	I	I	Y

SECTION ONE TABLE S1-3

Facility-wide Environmental Aspect Inventory and Evaluation (cont.)
BOC Gases Kittery Site Environmental Plan

Activity or Process[1]	Environmental Aspect[2]	Potential Impact	Annual Amount Released (lbs.)	Toxicity/ Hazard	Quantity	Probability/ Exposure	Significance Points $(1 \times 2 \times 3)$[3]	Regulatory Compliance S/I	Stakeholder Concerns S/I	Cost/ Liability S/I	Significant Aspect/ Impact Yes/No
Industrial waste generation (nonroutine)	Spent catalyst, molecular sieve, etc.	Landfill impacts	None	1	1	1	1	I	I	I	N
Sanitary wastes	Sanitary wastes	POTW/Piscataqua River	3 million	2	3	1	6	I	I	I	N
Municipal solid waste	Waste paper, cardboard, scrap metal, food, aluminum cans, etc.	Landfill impacts	60,000	1	2	1	2	S	I	I	Y
Freon air chiller	Freon 22 fugitive emissions	Ozone layer destruction	145	2	1	1	2	S	I	I	Y
Freon liquifier	Freon 12 fugitive emissions	Ozone layer destruction	725	3	1	1	3	S	I	S	Y
Off spec. product	Waste nitrogen, oxygen, argon	Energy/resource use	31,795	1	3	1	3	I	I	I	N
Product storage (N2)	N2 flash loss	Energy/resource use	78 million	1	3	1	3	I	I	S	Y
Underground diesel storage tank	Leaks to soil/groundwater	Soil/groundwater/ surface water contamination	None	2	1	1	2	S	I	S	Y
Underground diesel storage tank	Spills due to fueling/ tank filling	Soil/groundwater/ surface water contamination	35	2	1	2	4	S	I	S	Y
Underground diesel storage tank	Fugitive air emissions	Ambient air quality impacts	Minimal	2	1	1	2	I	I	I	N

SECTION ONE TABLE S1-3

Facility-wide Environmental Aspect Inventory and Evaluation (cont.)

BOC Gases Kittery Site Environmental Plan

Activity or Process[1]	Environmental Aspect[2]	Potential Impact	Annual Amount Released (lbs.)	Toxicity/ Hazard	Quantity	Probability/ Exposure	Significance Points $(1 \times 2 \times 3)$[3]	Regulatory Compliance S/I	Stakeholder Concerns S/I	Cost/ Liability S/I	Significant Aspect/ Impact Yes /No
Electricity use for production	Indirect impacts	Indirect impacts	108 mm kwhrs	2	3	1	6	I	I	S	Y
Electricity use not for production	Indirect impacts	Indirect impacts	<1 mm kwhrs	2	2	1	4	I	I	I	Y
Oil demisters	Oil emissions	Oil emissions/soil contamination	5	2	1	1	2	I	I	I	N
Hazardous material liquid storage (potential spills)	Oil, cooling tower chemicals, antifreeze, etc.	Soil, groundwater, surface water contamination	None	3	1	2	6	S	I	S	Y
Boiler	Boiler blowdown	POTW/Piscataqua River	30,000	2	3	1	6	S	S	I	Y
Boiler	TSP, SO2, NOx, VOC, CO emissions	Ambient air quality	72, 5140, 724, 8, 181	2	1	1	2	I	I	I	N
Above ground oil tank	Oil spills/leaks	Soil, groundwater, surface water contamination	None	2	1	2	4	S	I	S	Y
Waste oil tank (garage)	Oil spills/leaks	Soil, groundwater, surface water contamination	None	2	1	2	4	S	I	S	Y
Kerosene tank (compressor building)	Oil spills/leaks	Soil, groundwater, surface water contamination	None	2	1	2	4	S	I	S	Y
Underground heating oil tank	Oil leaks to soil/groundwater	Soil, groundwater, surface water contamination	None	2	1	2	4	S	I	S	Y
Underground heating oil tank	Fugitive emissions	Ambient air quality impacts	Minimal	2	1	1	2	I	I	I	N
Emergency diesel generator (nonroutine)	Emissions of particulate matter, SO2, CO, VOCs, NOx	Ambient air quality	Minimal	2	1	1	2	I	I	I	N

SECTION ONE TABLE S1-3

Facility-wide Environmental Aspect Inventory and Evaluation (cont.)
BOC Gases Kittery Site Environmental Plan

Activity or Process[1]	Environmental Aspect[2]	Potential Impact	Annual Amount Released (lbs.)	Toxicity/ Hazard	Quantity	Probability/ Exposure	Significance Points $(1 \times 2 \times 3)$[3]	Regulatory Compliance S/I	Stakeholder Concerns S/I	Cost/ Liability S/I	Significant Aspect/ Impact Yes/No
Vehicle maintenance	Used motor oil	Soil, groundwater, surface water contamination	8,295	2	2	1	6	S	I	S	Y
Vehicle maintenance	Used ethylene glycol	Soil, groundwater, surface water contamination	1,620	3	1	1	3	I	I	S	Y
Vehicle maintenance	Oily rags/ uniforms/mats	Landfill usage	1000	2	1	·	2	S	I	I	Y
Vehicle maintenance	AC freon losses	Ozone layer	Minimal	3	1	1	3	S	I	S	Y
Vehicle maintenance	Used batteries	Soil, groundwater, surface water contamination	30	3	1	1	3	S	I	I	Y
Vehicle maintenance	Used solvents– terpene based	Soil, groundwater, surface water contaminat on	240	2	1	1	2	S	I	I	Y
Vehicle maintenance	Used tires	Landfill usage	9,500	1	2	1	2	I	I	S	Y
Truck washing	Washwaters containing detergents, solids, oils, grease, etc.	Soil, groundwater, surface water contamination	44,000	2	3	2	12	S	I	S	Y
Truck washing	Oily solids (grit tank)	Soil contamination/ landfill impacts	Minimal	3	1	1	3	I	I	I	N
Truck washing	Heater emissions	Ambient air quality impacts	Minimal	3	1	1	3	I	I	I	N
Vehicle emissions	TSP, S02, VOC, CO, NOx	Ambient air quality impacts	156,000 gal	2	1	1	2	S	I	I	Y
Garage sump (sand trap) and drains	Oils, greases, antifreeze, etc.	POTW/Piscataqua River	12,000	3	3	2	18	S	I	S	Y
Painting (non-routine)	VOC emissions	Ambient air quality	Minimal	3	1	1	3	I	I	I	N
Paint removal (nonroutine)	Waste paint	Soil contamination/ landfill impacts	Variable	2	2	1	4	I	I	I	N
Deriming (non-routine)	CO_2, H_2O	None	Variable	1	1	1	1	I	I	I	N
Deriming (non-routine)	Noise	Noise to neighbors	N/A	3	3	3	27	S	I	I	Y

SECTION ONE TABLE S1-3

Facility-wide Environmental Aspect Inventory and Evaluation (cont.)
BOC Gases Kittery Site Environmental Plan

Activity or Process[1]	Environmental Aspect[2]	Potential Impact	Annual Amount Released (lbs.)	Toxicity/Hazard	Quantity	Probability/Exposure	Significance Points $(1 \times 2 \times 3)$[3]	Regulatory Compliance S/I	Stakeholder Concerns	Cost/Liability S/I	Significant Aspect/Impact Yes/No
Transformer mineral oil (substation)	Mineral oil (non-PCB)	Soil, groundwater, surface water contamination	None	1	1	1	1	I	I	S	Y
Painting (nonroutine)	VOC emissions	Air quality impacts	Minor	2	1	1	2	I	I	I	N
Paint removal (nonroutine)	Waste paint & blasting grit	Soil/surface water contamination	Nonroutine	3	1	1	3	I	I	I	N
On-site and adjacent wetlands	Presence	Potential degradation due to site activities	NA	1	1	1	3	S	S	I	Y
Fire fighting	Fire water	Soil, surface water, groundwater contamination	NA	2	2	1	4	I	S	I	N
Tractor operation	Diesel emissions	Air quality impacts	Minor	1	1	1	1	I	I	I	N
Switchgear batteries	Potential acid release	Soil, surface water, groundwater contamination	NA	3	1	1	3	I	I	I	N
Air conditioner operation	Potential freon release	Ozone layer destruction	Nil	3	1	1	3	I	I	I	N
Emergency diesels generator (gasoline)	Combustion emissions	Air quality impacts	Minor	1	1	1	1	I	I	I	N
Parts degreaser	Used solvent	Soil, surface water, groundwater contamination	720	2	1	1	2	S	I	S	Y
Floor drains	Chemical spills	POTW/Piscataqua River contamination	Spills only	3	1	2	6	S	I	S	Y

SECTION ONE TABLE S1-3

Facility-wide Environmental Aspect Inventory and Evaluation (cont.)
BOC Gases Kittery Site Environmental Plan

Activity or Process[1]	Environmental Aspect[2]	Potential Impact	Annual Amount Released (lbs.)	Toxicity/ Hazard	Quantity	Probability/ Exposure	Significance Points $(1 \times 2 \times 3)$[3]	Regulatory Compliance S/I	Stakeholder Concerns	Cost/ Liability S/I	Significant Aspect/ Impact Yes/No
Air chiller	Ethylene glycol cooling system	Soil, surface water, groundwater contamination	Spills only	3	1	2	6	S	I	S	Y
Boiler chemical storage	Boiler chemicals	Soil, surface water, groundwater contamination	Spills only	3	1	2	6	S	I	I	Y
Deriming	H$_2$O and CO$_2$	CO$_2$ emissions	Nonroutine	2	1	1	2	I	I	I	N
Deriming	Noise	Noise	Nonroutine	2	2	1	4	I	I	I	N
Compressors/ expanders	Catastrophic leaks	Oil discharge to POTW	Spills only	2	2	1	4	S	S	S	Y
Cold box–decommissioning/repairs	Rockwool disposal	Landfill use	Nonroutine	2	3	1	4	I	I	S	Y
Cooling tower sump cleaning	Cooling tower sludge	Soil, surface water, groundwater contamination	Nonroutine	2	3	1	6	S	I	S	Y
Plant start up	Off-spec product	Indirect impact from energy use	Substantial	1	3	1	3	I	I	I	N
Plant shut down	Off-spec product	Indirect impact from energy use	Substantial	1	3	1	3	I	I	I	N
Storage tank decommissioning/ repair	Perlite disposal	Landfill use/perlite emissions	Nonroutine	2	3	1	6	I	I	S	Y
Cooling tower fan gearbox	Oil leak to cooling tower	Oil discharge to POTW	Spills only	2	1	1	2	I	I	I	N
Compressor oil coolers	Oil leak to cooling tower	Oil discharge to POTW	Spills only	2	2	1	4	S	I	S	Y

SECTION ONE TABLE S1-3

Facility-wide Environmental Aspect Inventory and Evaluation (cont.)
BOC Gases Kittery Site Environmental Plan

Activity or Process[1]	Environmental Aspect[2]	Potential Impact	Annual Amount Released (lbs.)	Toxicity/Hazard	Quantity	Probability/Exposure	Significance Points $(1 \times 2 \times 3)$[3]	Regulatory Compliance S/I	Stakeholder Concerns	Cost/Liability S/I	Significant Aspect/Impact Yes/No
Production	Oxygen gas loss	Indirect impacts from energy use	219 MMSCF	2	3	3	18	I	S	S	Y
Facility aesthetics	Facility aesthetics	Aesthetic impact	N/A	1	1	1	1	I	S	I	Y
Propane heating equipment–sales office	Air emissions (CO_2, NOx, VOCs)	Impact to air quality	Minimal	2	1	1	2	I	I	I	N
Propane HE163B process equipment	Air emissions (CO_2, NOx, VOCs)	Impact on air quality	Minimal	2	1	1	2	I	I	I	N
Propane heating equipment–truck wash	Air emissions (CO_2, NOx, VOCs)	Impact on air quality	Minimal	2	1	1	2	I	I	I	N
Utility pole transformer	Oil spills	Soil, surface water, groundwater contamination	Spills only	2	1	1	2	I	I	I	N
Salting parking lot	Salt release	Soil, surface water, groundwater contamination	9,000	2	2	1	4	I	I	I	N
Weed removal	Pesticide use	Soil, surface water, groundwater contamination/ecological impacts	Minimal	3	1	1	3	S	I	I	Y

1 Indicate from which activity this environmental aspect is generated.

2 Review facility waste flow diagrams, Best Management Practices (EMS Manual Appendix 12A), waste generator reports, Form R, NPDES Discharge Monitoring Reports, groundwater monitoring compliance reports, quarterly air emissions reports, waste manifests, and/or hazardous and waste release reports, electric bills, fuel bills, noise studies, review of site and surroundings, etc. to identify and quantify facility wastes and environmental aspects.

3 Note: When the score for Toxicity × Quantity × Occurrence/Exposure is greater than 8, the environmental aspect/impact is considered to be significant.

Section A—Air Separation Plants

Pollution/Impact Source	Agent	Impact	Best Management Practices
Cooling tower and direct cooler blow-down	High temperature water, chlorine, corrosion inhibitors, biocides, and acids	Surface water/ groundwater contamination	Use nonchromate corrosion inhibitors and obtain approval/permit to discharge to 1. POTW or 2. surface water body. Air-cooled (closed loop) systems, if practical, might be an option.
Compressor-used oil and lubricating oils	Used oil	Surface water/ groundwater/soil contamination, waste disposal	Minimize leaks and oil changes to the extent possible through PM, and 1. Recycle used oil (separate from solvents) through a permitted (EPA I.D. Number) recycling company or 2. Dispose of used oil through a permitted hazardous waste disposal firm particularly if oil is contaminated with freon.
Freon use (refrigeration)	Freon	Impact on ozone layer, greenhouse effect, groundwater contamination	1. Minimize leaks from valves, flanges, etc., through PM, using Enviroseals, etc. 2. Use purging systems designed to minimize CFC releases. 3. Recover CFCs and HCFCs to the maximum extent possible during maintenance/servicing by certified technicians, through receivers and EPA-approved recovery and recycling equipment. 4. Recycle CFCs and HCFCs in equipment or through permitted recycling companies. 5. Consider using alternative refrigerants or alternate measures for refrigeration.
Building, floor drains	Solvents, oils, detergents, chemicals	Surface water/ groundwater/soil contamination	Keep solvents, oils, and other hazardous materials out of floor drains through proper storage and handling, and obtain approval/permit to discharge to 1. POTW or 2. Surface water body.

Section A—Air Separation Plants (continued)

Pollution/Impact Source	Agent	Impact	Best Management Practices
Solvent/chemical use and disposal	Terpene solvents, detergents, 1,1,1 trichloroethane, mineral spirits, other solvents/ chemicals	Hazardous waste, surface water, and groundwater impacts; air pollution; personnel exposure	Minimize solvent/chemical purchases (small containers) and use. Keep containers closed when not in use, use proper handling procedures and drip pans to prevent spills/leaks. Clean up spills immediately and conduct inspections of storage areas at least monthly. Train employees on the importance of pollution prevention. Use terpene-based or other relatively harmless solvents when possible. Use Safety Kleen solvent recycling benches when possible. When using 1,1,1 trichloroethane or similar solvents/chemicals (e.g., oxygen equipment), collect waste solvent in approved closed container and dispose of as hazardous waste through incineration. *Do not dispose of solvents in any drains or on the ground.*
Stormwater runoff	Oils, dissolved solids, suspended solids, metals, acids, caustics, solvents	Surface water/ groundwater contamination	Minimize and consolidate chemical inventories and avoid storage of incompatible materials near each other. Store hazardous materials in proper containers on impervious material, and prevent exposure to rainfall. Secondary containment of liquid hazardous materials should also be provided. Keep containers closed when not in use, use proper handling procedures and drip pans to prevent spills/leaks. Conduct appropriate PM on equipment. Clean up spills immediately and conduct inspections of storage/equipment areas at least monthly. Train employees on the importance of stormwater pollution prevention. Obtain stormwater permit when appropriate, and develop stormwater pollution prevention plan using Site Environmental Plan and Emergency Plan template. Portable plastic containment pallets and diked areas with covers are an option for secondary containment. Clean up spills/leaks immediately.
Noise (ASU, compressors, traffic, etc.)	Noise	Noise	Design and install nonreversing units. Design and install compressors, expanders and other "noisy" equipment with appropriate noise-attenuation measures (sound insulation, noise curtains, buildings, walls). In addition, select sites with adequate land and distance to buffer noise. Install "noisy" equipment on site in a location that will minimize the noise impact to neighbors. Minimize nighttime "noisy" activities.

Section A—Air Separation Plants (continued)

Pollution/Impact Source	Agent	Impact	Best Management Practices
Water treatment and other chemical storage (e.g., chlorine, sulfuric acid, ethylene glycol, oil, and solvents)	Chlorine, sulfuric acid, biocides, ethylene glycol, corrosion inhibitors, oil	Surface water/groundwater contamination, accidental spillage/release, waste disposal	Minimize and consolidate chemical inventories. Store hazardous materials in proper containers on an impervious material with secondary containment, and prevent exposure to rainfall. Plastic containment pallets and diked areas with covers are also an option.
Compressor blow-down (condensate)	Oil, water emulsion	Surface water/ groundwater/soil contamination, waste disposal	Install "oil-less" compressors. For reciprocating compressors, use oil/water separator (ultrafiltration) to separate oil from water. Recycle reclaimed oil. Obtain approval to discharge blow-down to 1. POTW or 2. surface water body.
Truck/equipment washing	Detergents, oils, greases, suspended solids, dissolved solids (salts), and metals	Surface water/ groundwater/soil contamination, disposal	Wash trucks on a contained pad with a cover, and treat washwater with oil/water separator and solids removal for washwater recycling or prior to approved/permitted discharge to 1. POTW or 2. surface water body.
Vehicle maintenance, distribution/transportation	Fuel, oil, grease, noise, Freons, antifreeze, batteries, detergents	Surface water/ groundwater/soil contamination, air pollution, noise	Purchase and maintain vehicles to be fuel efficient and minimize air pollutant emissions. Collect and segregate all waste fluids in appropriate, labeled containers and store properly (e.g., secondary containment, protection from weather). Recycle used oil, antifreeze, batteries, and Freons. Individuals working on air conditioning systems must be EPA-certified technicians and use EPA-approved Freon recovery equipment. Use Safety Kleen bench for cleaning parts. Conduct truck washing off site unless truck washwater discharges are treated and permitted. Avoid truck routes through residential neighborhoods, and minimize nighttime trucking through residential areas.

Section A—Air Separation Plants

Pollution/Impact Source	Agent	Impact	Best Management Practices
Underground and aboveground storage tanks (USTs and ASTs)	Diesel oil, fuel oil, and acetone	Surface water/groundwater/soil contamination	An aboveground tank with secondary containment (Petrovault, Ecovault, etc.) and rain protection are preferred. Obtain approval from the Fire Marshal. If installing USTs, install double-walled USTs with double-walled piping. Fiberglass, steel with cathodic protection, or fiberglass-clad steel USTs may be appropriate. Include interstitial monitoring, overfill protection, and spill containment manhole. Use "deadman" or concrete slab to stabilize the UST when appropriate. Design fueling area to contain spills. Cover fueling area with canopy and/or provide containment with berm and discharge to oil/water separator. Require personnel fueling tractors to hold nozzle when fueling. Provide spill cleanup kit in tank area and clean up spills/leaks immediately. Conduct appropriate inventory control/release prevention procedures to meet regulatory requirements particularly with USTs. Work with Environmental Affairs on tank removals and installations.
Nitrogen, oxygen, argon storage and transfer	Nitrogen, oxygen, argon	Accidental release/visibility, efficiency loss	Design and maintain storage and transfer equipment and implement procedures to minimize losses.
Boiler air emissions	Smoke, particulate matter, carbon monoxide, hydrocarbons, nitrogen oxides, sulfuric dioxide	Air pollution	Operate and maintain boiler to be efficient and minimize smoke, hydrocarbons, and carbon monoxide emissions. Use fuel with low sulfur and solids content.
Boiler blow-down	Biocides, corrosion inhibitors	Surface water/groundwater contamination	Use nonchromate corrosion inhibitors and obtain approval/permit to discharge to 1. POTW or 2. surface water body.

Section A—Air Separation Plants (continued)

Pollution/Impact Source	Agent	Impact	Best Management Practices
Deriming	Concentrated industrial pollutant, including oils and other hydrocarbons (older ASUs)	Surface water/ groundwater contamination, waste disposal	Obtain approval to discharge wastewaters to 1. POTW or 2. surface water body.
PCBs	PCB oil	Surface water/ groundwater/soil contamination, personnel exposure, disposal	Test equipment for presence of PCBs. If present, replace equipment or retrofill equipment. Dispose of PCB equipment according to EPA regulations. If cost of PCB equipment replacement/retrofill is prohibitive, significant efforts (quarterly monitoring, records, etc.) must be taken to prevent leaks of PCB liquids. Work with Environmental Affairs on all PCB-related projects.
Painting/paint removal	Paints, solvents, paint dust (heavy metals)	Surface water/ groundwater/soil contamination, solid/hazardous waste disposal, personnel exposure, air pollution	Use water-based paints to the extent possible. Waste solvent–based paints and thinners typically should be disposed of as hazardous waste. Collect sand-blasted wastes with tarps and dispose of as solid or hazardous wastes, depending upon analysis results. Using CO_2-based blasting equipment is a preferred paint-stripping method.
Oil-contaminated debris	Oily rags, leak/spill cleanup materials, oily soils	Soil, surface water and groundwater contamination	Collect large quantities in drums or dumpster (separate from garbage) and dispose of through an approved industrial waste disposal firm. For large amounts of contaminated soil, on-site bioremediation or off-site recycling through asphalt batching or brick/cement manufacturer plant might be more appropriate.

Section A—Air Separation Plants (continued)

Pollution/Impact Source	Agent	Impact	Best Management Practices
Industrial solid waste	Silica gel, molecular sieve, alumina, rock wool, perlite, etc.	Solid waste disposal	Collect waste material and dispose of as industrial waste at an approved facility. If available, recycling through original manufacturer, cement manufacturer, brick manufacturer, etc., is usually preferred.
Asbestos-containing materials and buildings	Asbestos	Air pollution, waste disposal	Notify EPA at least 10 days in advance of any demolition/renovation and use OSHA-approved asbestos removal contractors. Remove asbestos materials according to OSHA/EPA requirements and place waste in double-lined plastic bags or in drums with proper labels. Dispose of asbestos in an EPA-approved landfill.
Electricity use	Indirect	Indirect impacts: air, water, solid waste	Design, purchase, and maintain equipment to operate efficiently and minimize electricity use. Conduct energy audits to identify potential opportunities to improve energy efficiencies. Train employees to conserve energy.
Spent catalysts	Heavy metals (e.g., palladium)	Solid/hazardous waste	Return to catalyst manufacturer for reclaiming. If this option is unavailable, dispose of through licensed industrial/hazardous waste contractor.
Halon fire suppression systems	Halon	Depletion of ozone layer	Maintain system to avoid leaks. As suitable halon replacements are identified, recover halon and place in halon banks. Design new systems without halon.
Compressor oil mists	Oil	Air pollution, stormwater	Install oil demisters to collect oil mist emissions. Air permits may be necessary for these units. Recycle the collected oil through approved recycling companies.
Garbage	Garbage	Waste disposal	Dispose of waste through a licensed solid waste hauler or at a licensed sanitary landfill.
Waste paper, aluminum cans, scrap metal, cardboard, wood pallets	Garbage	Waste disposal	Recycle these materials to the extent possible.
Sanitary wastes	Sanitary waste	Surface water/ groundwater pollution	Dispose of sanitary wastes through POTW. Do not dispose of chemicals down sinks, drains, or toilets. If POTW is unavailable, discharge to on-site approved treatment system or septic system may be acceptable.

Section G—Truck Maintenance

Pollution/Impact Source	Agent	Impact	Best Management Practices
Oil changes	Used oil, filters	Surface water/ groundwater/soil contamination, waste disposal	Minimize leaks and oil changes to the extent possible through a proper PM program. Store used oil in labeled aboveground containers with secondary containment and weather protection. 1. Recycle used oil (separate from solvents) through a permitted recycling company or; 2. Dispose of used oil through a permitted hazardous waste disposal firm. In addition, drain oil filters to extent possible, and recycle/dispose of filters according to state requirements.
Antifreeze changes	Used antifreeze	Surface water/ groundwater/soil contamination, waste disposal	Minimize antifreeze changes to the extent practicable through a proper PM program. Collect used antifreeze and store in a labeled drum protected from weather. If possible, reuse antifreeze in BOC Gases trucks. Otherwise, recycle antifreeze through a licensed antifreeze recycler (e.g., Safety Kleen) or dispose of through a licensed hazardous/industrial waste disposal company.
Parts washing-degreasing	Solvents/ degreasers	Surface water/ groundwater/soil contamination, waste disposal	Conduct cleaning/degreasing on Safety Kleen/Zep or similar parts-cleaning bench. Recycle used solvents through Safety Kleen or other BOC Gases-approved recycler/waste disposal contractor. Only use 1,1,1 trichloroethane or similar approved solvents for oxygen equipment cleaning, and purchase in small containers. Store waste solvents in properly labeled and DOT-approved containers. Dispose of solvents as hazardous waste through BOC Gases-approved, licensed disposal company. *Do not dispose of solvents through drains or on the ground.*

Section G—Truck Maintenance (continued)

Pollution/Impact Source	Agent	Impact	Best Management Practices
Cleaning agents, chemicals—storage, handling and using	Detergents, terpene-based solvents, mineral spirits, chlorinated solvents	Surface water/ groundwater/soil contamination	Minimize quantity of solvent/chemical purchased and size of container. Segregate different chemicals/wastes in separate, compatible, labeled containers in good condition. Store on impervious surface, use secondary containment, and protect from weather. Keep containers closed when not in use, use proper handling procedures and drip pans to prevent spills/leaks. Clean up spills immediately and conduct inspections of storage areas at least monthly. Train employees on the importance of pollution prevention. Minimize amount used for cleaning. Collect for reuse, or use Safety Kleen type of solvent recycling benches to recycle and collect solvent. Use detergent or terpene-based cleaning agents if possible. Collect used solvent in good containers with proper labels. Recycle/dispose of used solvent through EPA-licensed and reputable industrial/hazardous waste haulers. Collect solvent-contaminated rags and dispose of properly. Train employees to use and handle solvents/chemicals properly. *Do not dispose of solvents down drains, sinks, or on the ground.*
Stormwater runoff	Oils, dissolved solids, suspended solids, metals, acids, caustics	Surface water/ groundwater contamination	Minimize and consolidate chemical inventories. Store hazardous materials in proper containers on impervious material with secondary containment, and prevent exposure to rainfall. Avoid storage of incompatible materials near each other. Keep containers closed when not in use, use proper handling procedures and drip pans to prevent spills/leaks. Clean up spills immediately and conduct inspections of storage areas at least monthly. Train employees on the importance of stormwater pollution prevention. Obtain stormwater permit when appropriate, and develop stormwater pollution prevention plan using Site Environmental Plan and Emergency Plan template when necessary. Portable plastic containment pallets and diked areas with covers are an option for secondary containment.

Section G—Truck Maintenance (continued)

Pollution/Impact Source	Agent	Impact	Best Management Practices
Underground and aboveground storage tanks (USTs and ASTs)	Diesel fuel, lubricating oil, waste oil	Surface water/groundwater/soil contamination	Aboveground tank meeting appropriate fire codes with secondary containment and rain protection is preferred. When installing USTs, install double-walled UST with double-walled piping. Fiberglass, steel with cathodic protection, or fiberglass-clad steel USTs can be appropriate. Include interstitial monitoring, overfill protection, and spill-containment manhole. Use "deadman" to stabilize tank when appropriate. Design any fueling areas to be impervious and contain spills. Cover fuel area and/or discharge to oil/water separator Require personnel fueling tractors to hold nozzle when fueling. Clean up spills/leaks immediately. Conduct appropriate inventory control/release prevention procedures to meet regulatory requirements particularly with USTs.
Building floor drains	Solvents, oils, detergents	Surface water/groundwater/soil contamination	Keep solvents, oils, and other hazardous materials out of floor drains through proper storage and handling. Obtain approval/permit to discharge drains to 1. POTW or 2. surface water body.
Air conditioner maintenance	Ozone-depleting substances (CFCs and HCFCs)	Stratospheric ozone reduction, greenhouse effect, groundwater contamination	Use certified mechanics and EPA-approved recovery/recycling equipment to collect CFCs. Reuse CFCs in BOC Gases trucks or sent to EPA-approved CFC recycling company.
Vehicle washing	Oils, greases, detergents, suspended solids, dissolved solids (salts), and metals	Surface water/groundwater/soil contamination	Wash trucks on a contained pad with a cover, and treat washwater with oil/water separator for washwater recycling or prior to approved/permitted discharge to 1. POTW or 2. surface water body.
Oil-contaminated soil/debris	Oil	Surface, groundwater contamination, waste disposal	Collect large quantities in drums or dumpster (separate from garbage) and dispose of through an approved disposal firm. For large amounts of contaminated soil on site, bioremediation or off-site recycling through asphalt mixing or brick manufacture might be more appropriate.

Section G—Truck Maintenance (continued)

Pollution/Impact Source	Agent	Impact	Best Management Practices
Truck emissions (fuel economy)	Carbon monoxide, nitrogen oxides, hydrocarbons	Air pollution	Purchase energy-efficient vehicles and vehicles that meet EPA emission standards. Maintain vehicles to operate efficiently while minimizing emissions. Purchase "clean" fuels. Minimize trips and distances traveled to extent possible.
Trucking, maintenance, and loading/unloading operations	Noise, exhaust emissions	Noise, air pollution	Select sites that are buffered from surrounding populations. Provide sound reduction measures when necessary. Minimize nighttime operations when surrounding community might be affected.
Trucking noise	Noise	Noise	Select transportation routes that avoid residential neighborhoods.
Stormwater runoff	Oils/greases/sediments	Surface and groundwater contamination	Store hazardous materials on impervious material with secondary containment, and prevent exposure to rainfall. Portable plastic containment pallets with covers are an option. Obtain stormwater permit and develop stormwater pollution prevention plan, when necessary. Clean up spills/leaks immediately. Provide containment of fueling operations.
Battery recycling/disposal	Lead and sulfuric acid	Solid/hazardous waste	Return batteries to dealer when purchasing new batteries or recycle through licensed recycling facility. Protect batteries from severe cold to prevent freezing and release of battery acid.
Asbestos-containing materials and buildings	Asbestos	Air pollution, waste disposal	Notify EPA 10 days prior to conducting demolition/renovation. Hire a certified asbestos removal contractor to remove asbestos materials according to OSHA/EPA requirements and place waste in double-lined plastic bags or drums with proper labels. Dispose of asbestos in an EPA-approved landfill.
Electricity use	Indirect	Indirect impacts: air, water, efficiency loss	Design, install, and maintain equipment to operate efficiently and minimize electricity use.

Section G—Truck Maintenance (continued)

Pollution/Impact Source	Agent	Impact	Best Management Practices
Halon fire suppression systems	Halon	Depletion of ozone layer	Maintain system to avoid leaks. As suitable halon replacements are identified, recover halon and place in halon banks. New systems must be designed without halon.
Sanitary wastes	Sanitary wastes	Surface water and groundwater pollution	Dispose of sanitary wastes through POTW. Do not dispose of chemicals down sinks, drains, or toilets. If POTW is unavailable, discharge to on-site approved treatment system, or septic system may be acceptable.

Consolidated Edison Company of New York Transportation, Stores and Technical Services Group Queens, New York

Consolidated Edison Company of New York (Con Edison) is one of the nation's largest utility companies, with more than $7 billion in annual revenues and approximately $14 billion in assets. Con Edison provides electric, gas, and steam service to more than three million customers in New York City and Westchester County, New York.

The Transportation and Stores operation consists of 650 employees. It is chiefly responsible for the transportation and storage of all Con Edison materials, equipment, and waste streams. Its environmental management system is applicable to warehousing, waste management, fleet operations, rigging, fleet services, garage services, materials testing, and equipment/instrument calibration and repair.

Con Edison's Transportation and Stores operation was registered to ISO 14001 in April, 1998, by Lloyd's Register Quality Assurance.

Con Edison's environmental aspect evaluation procedure is accompanied by worksheets A and B. Worksheet A delineates the aspects and impacts associated with specific activities. Worksheet B presents the numerical scoring data for each aspect. Worksheets A and B are provided for two functions: garages, fleet administration, engineering; and stores.

**Consolidated Edison Company
Transportation and Stores Operation
Queens, New York**

*Environmental Aspect Evaluation
February 10, 1998 (ISO 4.3.1.0, Rev. 2)*

---

1. Scope

Those environmental aspects that Consolidated Edison Company's Transportation and Stores Department can control or be expected to control.

2. Objective

To ensure that all activities carried out or controlled by Transportation and Stores (T&S) are effectively reviewed and all significant environmental aspects are identified.

3. Responsibility

Operations Personnel

It is the responsibility of operations personnel (that is, Managers and Supervisors) to inform Environmental Operations of any new work activities or unique conditions (that is, a remediation project) in their work area. Operations Personnel will also assist Environmental Operations as needed in the evaluation of significant aspects.

Environmental Operations

It is the responsibility of Environmental Operations to evaluate the significance of the environmental aspects related to the activities performed by T&S and to monitor new developments in law, procedures, technology, and so on, to ensure that the Environmental Aspects Register is kept up to date.

4. Procedure

4.1   Environmental Operations will compile a listing of all activities performed by T&S. All activities will then be broken down into discrete aspects, and the associated impacts for each aspect will be noted. This information will be recorded in "Aspect Evaluation Worksheet A" of the T&S Environmental Aspects Register. Should Environmental Operations need assistance in preparing Worksheet A, operations personnel will be consulted. The operations personnel consulted should be noted on the worksheet in these cases.

4.2 Environmental Operations will then calculate the relative environmental significance of each activity, based on the scoring criteria listed in Attachment A. The relative significance of each activity will be reflected in the Environmental Aspect Score. Information relative to the scoring of each aspect will be recorded in "Aspect Evaluation Worksheet B" of the T&S Environmental Aspects Register. Should Environmental Operations need assistance in preparing Worksheet B, operations personnel will be consulted. The operations personnel consulted should be noted on the worksheet in these cases.

4.3 Environmental Operations will then make a determination as to what score will be used to separate significant environmental aspects from all others. Once this score is determined, all items that scored at that level or above will be considered to be "Significant Environmental Aspects" as defined by ISO 14001, and will be listed in the "Significant Aspects Worksheet" of the Environmental Aspects Register.

4.4 Significant Environmental Aspects will be considered when addressing the following:

- Objectives and Targets (see ISO 4.3.3.0)
- Training Requirements (see ISO 4.4.2.0)
- Communications with the Public (see ISO 4.4.3.2)
- Operational Controls (see ISO 4.4.6.0)
- Monitoring and Measurement (see ISO 4.5.1.0)

4.5 In light of legislative changes, audit findings, policy changes, and so on, the list of aspects which T&S can control or can be expected to have a significant influence on, and their associated significant environmental effects, is kept up to date through periodic review of all activities performed by T&S (approximately every 12 months). Should Environmental Operations be notified of a major change in operations or new project being undertaken by T&S, they will review the activities associated with these operations or project within three months of notification.

4.6   Should an operating unit be added to the T&S EMS, all activities associated with that operating unit will be reviewed for significance within three months from the effective date that the operation has been determined to fall within the scope of the T&S EMS. Results of these reviews will be maintained in a "Supplemental Environmental Aspects Register" that pertains only to these new operations, projects, and/or operating units.

4.7   Should an operating unit be removed from the T&S EMS, all significant aspects that were associated solely with that operating unit will be removed from the T&S EMS. All related management system items, such as objectives and targets, operational controls, monitoring and measuring, and so on, will also be removed from the overall EMS.

4.8   Upon completion of any aspects review, Environmental Operations will notify all applicable operating areas as to what their Significant Environmental Aspects are, and provide each location with a listing of these activities.

5. Reference Documents

5.1   Attachment A—"Significant Environmental Aspects: Scoring Criteria."

5.2   Environmental Aspects Register (master copy maintained by the ISO 14001 Management Representative).

ATTACHMENT A
Significant Environmental Aspects: Scoring Criteria

Environmental Effect Criteria

A   Event Probability

1—Extremely low likelihood of event occurring

2—Low likelihood of event occurring

3—Moderate likelihood of event occurring

4—High likelihood of event occurring

5—Event guaranteed to occur

B1   Severity of Impact
B2

1—Extremely low

2—Low

3—Moderate

4—High

5—Critical

C1   Scale of Impact
C2

1—Trivial

2—Small

3—Moderate

4—Large

5—Very large

D   Duration of
    Release

1—Impact likely to reverse itself naturally

2—Impact reversible with minor effort

3—Impact reversible with moderate effort

4—Impact reversible with substantial effort

5—Impact irreversible

E   Legal and Public
    Exposure

1—Little to no interest, little reaction likely

2—Minor interest, little reaction likely

3—Normal interest, moderate reaction likely

4—High interest, moderate reaction likely

5—High interest, large reaction likely

Environmental Aspect Score = $A^*((2B1+B2)/3)^*((2C1+C2)/3)^*D^*E$

Notes on Environmental Effect Criteria

Probability of Occurrence

This scoring criterion is fairly straightforward—it represents the relative likelihood that an aspect is likely to cause its associated impact. An item with a probability of 1 is very unlikely, such as the air emissions from a fire occurring, as fires in the T&S operation are extremely rare. Conversely, an item with a probability of 5 *will* occur, such as emission to the air from the operation of a motor vehicle.

Severity of Impact

This scoring criterion has two components—B1 and B2. B1 is the most likely impact and B2 is the worst case impact. In the scoring formula, B1 is assigned twice the relative weight of B2, since it is more likely to occur. In looking at the severity of the impact, the primary considerations are the toxicity of releases or scarcity of resources consumed.

For Releases:

1—Material is non-toxic and biodegradable (example = paper)

2—Material is basically non-toxic, but non-biodegradable (example = oil)

3—Material is normally non-toxic, but could be toxic under some instances (example = Dielectric fluid, which usually does not have PCBs, but may on occasion)

4—Material is toxic over an extended period of time (example = asbestos)

5—Material can be immediately toxic (example = hydrochloric acid)

For Resources:

1—Resource is easily renewed (example = grass)

2—Resource is moderately renewable (example = paper or metal parts)

3—Resource is depletable (example = oil)

4—Resource is already scarce (example = water in a drought period)

5—Resource is critically scarce (example = uranium)

Scale of Impact

This criterion also has two components—C1 and C2. C1 is the most likely impact and C2 is the worst case impact. In the scoring formula, C1 is assigned twice the relative weight of C2, since it is more likely to occur. In looking at the scale of the impact, the primary considerations are the size of releases or relative quantity of resources consumed.

For Releases:

1—less than 1 gallon or pound released

2—1 to 5 gallons or pounds released

3—5 to 10 gallons or pounds released

4—10 to 100 gallons or pounds released

5—greater than 100 pounds or gallons released

For Resources:

All scoring for resources is relative, and considers the amount of the resource consumed relative to the available quantity, as well as considering the impacts associated with obtaining the resource. For example the depletion of resources needed to make the automotive parts used would score relatively low, while the depletion of resources needed to fuel the entire fleet would be relatively high.

1—High resource/usage ratio, little impact in obtaining resource

2—High resource/usage ratio, moderate impact in obtaining resource

3—Moderate resource/usage ratio, moderate impact in obtaining resource

4—Low resource/usage ratio, moderate impact in obtaining resource

5—Low resource/usage ratio, large impact in obtaining resource

Duration of Impact

This criterion focuses on how long the duration of any impacts associated with an activity are likely to last, and/or how difficult it would be to correct these impacts. The scoring is self-explanatory.

Legal and Public Exposure

This criterion focuses on the relative interest in the aspect or impacts that governing agencies, the public, or other interested parties have shown, or are expected to show. It also considers the expected outcome of any notice (positive or negative) that is received by T&S from these entities. For example, an item that is non-regulated, and which the public is not expected to care about how T&S is addressing, is likely to score a 1. Conversely, items that are closely regulated and for which we know there is likely to be a large governmental and/or public reaction to any action we take (for instance, an asbestos release on the streets of Manhattan) would likely score a 5.

General

In some cases, the aspect being reviewed may not fit well into the categories discussed up to this point (that is, releases or resources). In these cases, the evaluator should simply apply the relative scales for each scoring item to the aspect, using his/her best professional judgment.

Aspect Evaluation Worksheet A
Garages, Fleet Admission, Engineering

Activity	Aspect(s)	Impact(s)
Perform emissions testing	Air emissions from engines	Contamination of air
	Energy usage for equipment	Depletion of natural resources
Operate vehicles	Spillage/leakage from vehicles	Contamination of soil or water Damage to flora/fauna/humans from toxic materials
	Air emissions from engines	Contamination of air
	Fuel usage from vehicles	Depletion of natural resources
	Noise from vehicles	Disruption to fauna/humans
	Air emissions due to fire	Contamination of air
Perform vehicle painting	Spillage/leakage of paints	Contamination of soil or water Damage to flora/fauna/humans from toxic materials
	Air emissions from spills	Contamination of air Damage to humans from toxic materials
	Air emissions from grinding/ paints/solvents	Contamination of air Damage to humans from toxic materials
	Paint/solvent usage in painting and cleanup	Depletion of natural resources
	Incidental use of other materials while painting	Depletion of natural resources
	Noise from painting operations	Disruption to fauna/humans
	Energy usage to operate painting equipment	Depletion of natural resources
	Air emissions due to fire	Contamination of air

(continued)

Aspect Evaluation Worksheet A
Garages, Fleet Administration, Engineering (continued)

Activity	Aspect(s)	Impact(s)
Supervise fuel deliveries	Spillage/leakage during deliveries	Contamination of soil or water Damage to flora/fauna/humans from toxic materials
	Air emission due to fire	Contamination of air
Store used vehicles/equipment for auction	Spillage/leakage from vehicles/equipment	Contamination of soil or water
Store/handle hazardous wastes	Spillage/leakage from waste drums	Contamination of soil or water Damage to flora/fauna/humans from toxic materials
	Air emissions from spills	Contamination of air Damage to humans from toxic materials
	Management of wastes	Contamination of soil/water/air from improper disposal Reduction of landfill space needed from pollution prevention Conservation of resources from recycling
	Air emission due to fire	Contamination of air
Operate/maintain garage oil/water separators	Discharges from operation	Contamination of water
	Use of energy to operate	Depletion of natural resources
Maintain/manage fuel pumps	Spillage/leakage from pump malfunction	Contamination of soil or water Damage to flora/fauna/humans from toxic materials
	Air emissions from fuel vapor	Contamination of air
	Oil/solvent/chemical usage from operations	Depletion of natural resources
	Parts usage from operations	Depletion of natural resources

(continued)

Aspect Evaluation Worksheet A
Garages, Fleet Administration, Engineering (continued)

Activity	Aspect(s)	Impact(s)
Maintain/manage fuel pumps (continued)	Energy required to operate pumps	Depletion of natural resources
	Air emission due to fire	Contamination of air
Maintain/manage USTs	Leakage from tanks	Contamination of soil or water Damage to flora/fauna/humans from toxic materials
	Air emission due to fire	Contamination of air
Store and handle oils and chemicals	Spillage/leakage from materials	Contamination of soil or water Damage to flora/fauna/humans from toxic materials
	Air emissions from spills	Contamination of air Damage to humans from toxic materials
	Air emission due to fire	Contamination of air
Perform vehicle inspections	Health/safety concerns reviewed during inspection	Damage to humans/environment prevented
Perform vehicle/equipment PMs	Spillage/leakage of oils/chemicals from operations	Contamination of soil or water Damage to flora/fauna/humans from toxic materials
	Air emissions from spills	Contamination of air Damage to humans from toxic materials
	Air emissions from asbestos containing materials (brakes/clutches)	Contamination of air Damage to humans from toxic materials
	Air emissions from air conditioning systems	Contamination of air
	Oil/solvent/chemical usage from operations	Depletion of natural resources

(continued)

Aspect Evaluation Worksheet A
Garages, Fleet Administration, Engineering (continued)

Activity	Aspect(s)	Impact(s)
Perform vehicle/equipment PMs (continued)	Reduction in future spills from proper maintenance	Reduction of contamination to soil/water/air
	Noise from operations	Disruption to fauna/humans
	Energy required to perform PMs	Depletion of natural resources
	Parts/materials usage from operations	Depletion of natural resources
Perform vehicle/equipment repairs	Spillage/leakage of oils/chemicals from operations	Contamination of soil or water Damage to flora/fauna/humans from toxic materials
	Air emissions from asbestos-containing materials (brakes/ clutches)	Contamination of air Damage to humans from toxic materials
	Air emissions from air conditioning systems	Contamination of air
	Oil/solvent/chemical usage from operations	Depletion of natural resources
	Parts/materials usage from operations	Depletion of natural resources
	Noise from operations	Disruption to fauna/humans
	Energy required to perform repairs	Depletion of natural resources
Store/handle used oil	Spillage/leakage from tanks	Contamination of soil or water Damage to flora/fauna/humans from toxic materials

(continued)

Aspect Evaluation Worksheet A
Garages, Fleet Administration, Engineering (continued)

Activity	Aspect(s)	Impact(s)
Store/handle used oil (continued)	Management of wastes	Contamination of soil/water/air from improper disposal Reduction of landfill space needed from pollution prevention Conservation of resources from recycling
	Air emissions due to fire	Contamination of air
Vehicle engineering activities	Choice of coatings to be used on vehicles	Air emissions from painting/repainting vehicles Depletion of natural resources based on durability of coatings used
	Expected life of vehicles	Depletion of natural resources when vehicles must be replaced
	Specification of chemicals used in vehicles	Contamination of soil/water/air from ultimate use of vehicles Depletion of natural resources from chemicals used Conservation of resources from recycling
	Containment/leak protection systems in oil/chemical hauling vehicles	Prevention of pollution/contamination associated with vehicles
	Determination of number of alternate fuel vehicles in Con Ed fleet	Reduced air emissions from alternate fuel vehicles
	Provide support for AFV programs to others in NYC area	Reduced air emissions from alternate fuel vehicles

(continued)

**Aspect Evaluation Worksheet A
Garages, Fleet Administration, Engineering (continued)**

Activity	Aspect(s)	Impact(s)
New vehicle storage and commission	Spillage/leakage from equipment	Contamination of soil or water Damage to flora/fauna/humans from toxic materials
Store/handle industrial debris	Spillage/leakage from waste drums	Contamination of soil or water Damage to flora/fauna/humans from toxic materials
	Management of wastes	Contamination of soil/water/air from improper disposal Reduction of landfill space needed from pollution prevention Conservation of resources from recycling
	Air emission due to fire	Contamination of air
Store/handle solid waste	Management of wastes	Contamination of soil/water/air from improper disposal Reduction of landfill space needed from pollution prevention Conservation of resources from recycling
Administrative work from repairs	Management of paper	Contamination of soil/water/air from improper disposal Reduction of landfill space needed from pollution prevention Conservation of resources from recycling
	Paper usage	Depletion of natural resources

(continued)

Aspect Evaluation Worksheet A
Garages, Fleet Administration, Engineering (continued)

Activity	Aspect(s)	Impact(s)
Facilities usage	Energy usage in occupying building	Depletion of natural resources
	Incidental water usage	Depletion of natural resources
	Incidental water/sewage discharges	Contamination of water/soil
Spill response	Spillage/leakage of materials from improper/insufficient response	Contamination of soil or water Damage to flora/fauna/humans from toxic materials
	Parts/materials usage from operations	Depletion of natural resources
	Energy required to respond to spill	Depletion of natural resources
Supervise vehicle washing	Discharges from operation	Contamination of water
	Water usage in washing	Depletion of natural resources
	Materials usage in washing	Depletion of natural resources
Operate hydraulic lifts	Leakage of oils from hydraulic lifts	Contamination of soil or water Damage to flora/fauna/humans from toxic materials

Aspect Evaluation Worksheet B

Garages, Fleet Administration, Engineering

Activity	Aspect(s)	Prob	Sev 1	Sev 2	Scale 1	Scale 2	Dur	Exp	Score
Perform Emissions Testing									
	Air emissions from engines	5	3	4	4	4	5	3	1000
	Energy usage for equipment	5	3	3	2	2	3	2	180
Operate Vehicles									
	Spillage/leakage from vehicles	5	3	4	1	4	3	5	500
	Air emissions from engines	5	3	4	4	4	5	3	1000
	Fuel usage from vehicles	5	3	3	3	3	3	3	405
	Noise from vehicles	5	1	3	1	3	3	2	83
	Air emissions due to fire	1	4	5	2	4	5	3	173
Perform Vehicle Painting									
	Spillage/leakage of paints	3	3	4	1	4	3	5	300
	Air emissions from spills	2	3	4	1	2	5	4	178
	Air emissions from grinding/paints/solvents	5	2	4	4	5	5	4	1156
	Paint/solvent usage in painting and cleanup	5	3	3	5	5	3	3	675
	Incidental use of other materials while painting	5	2	3	1	2	3	1	47
	Noise from painting operations	5	1	3	1	3	3	2	83

(continued)

Aspect Evaluation Worksheet B (continued)

Activity	Aspect(s)	Prob	Sev 1	Sev 2	Scale 1	Scale 2	Dur	Exp	Score
Garages, Fleet Administration, Engineering									
Perform Vehicle Painting (continued)									
	Energy usage to operate painting equipment	5	3	3	2	2	3	2	180
	Air emissions due to fire	1	4	5	4	5	5	5	469
Supervise Fuel Deliveries									
	Spillage/leakage during deliveries	3	3	4	1	5	3	5	350
	Air emissions due to fire	1	3	5	3	5	5	3	202
Store Used Vehicles/Equipment for Auction									
	Spillage/leakage from vehicles/equipment	5	3	3	1	4	3	5	500
Store/Handle Hazardous Wastes									
	Spillage/leakage from waste drums	2	4	5	1	4	3	5	260
	Air emissions from spills	2	3	4	1	2	5	4	178
	Management of wastes	5	2	5	3	5	4	5	1100
	Air emission due to fire	1	4	5	4	5	5	5	469
Operate/Maintain Garage Oil/Water Separators									
	Discharges from operation	3	3	4	2	4	4	5	533
	Use of energy to operate	5	3	3	2	2	3	2	180

(continued)

Aspect Evaluation Worksheet B (continued)

Garages, Fleet Administration, Engineering

Activity	Aspect(s)	Prob	Sev 1	Sev 2	Scale 1	Scale 2	Dur	Exp	Score
	Maintain/Manage Fuel Pumps								
	Spillage/leakage from pump malfunction	2	3	4	1	5	3	5	233
	Air emissions from fuel vapor	4	2	3	3	5	5	3	513
	Oil/solvent/chemical usage from operations	5	3	3	1	1	3	3	135
	Parts usage from operations	5	2	2	1	2	3	1	40
	Energy required to operate pumps	5	3	3	1	1	4	2	120
	Air emission due to fire	1	3	5	3	5	5	3	202
	Maintain/Manage USTs								
	Leakage from tanks	2	3	3	4	5	4	5	520
	Air emission due to fire	1	3	5	3	5	5	3	202
	Store and Handle Oils and Chemicals								
	Spillage/leakage from materials	4	2	3	1	4	3	5	280
	Air emission due to fire	1	4	5	3	4	5	5	361
	Perform Vehicle Inspections								
	Health/safety concerns reviewed during inspection	5	1	5	1	5	5	2	272

(continued)

Aspect Evaluation Worksheet B (continued)

Garages, Fleet Administration, Engineering

Activity	Aspect(s)	Prob	Sev 1	Sev 2	Scale 1	Scale 2	Dur	Exp	Score
	Perform Vehicle/Equipment PMs								
	Spillage/leakage of oils/chemicals from operations	5	2	4	1	4	3	5	400
	Air emissions from spills	2	3	4	1	2	5	4	178
	Air emissions from asbestos-containing materials (brakes/clutches)	3	4	4	1	2	5	5	400
	Air emissions from air conditioning systems	3	4	4	1	3	5	4	400
	Oil/solvent/chemical usage from operations	5	3	3	5	5	3	3	675
	Reduction in future spills from proper maintenance	5	3	4	1	4	5	2	333
	Noise from operations	5	1	3	1	3	3	2	83
	Energy required to perform PMs	5	3	3	2	2	3	3	270
	Parts/materials usage from operations	5	2	3	2	3	3	1	82
	Perform Vehicle/Equipment Repairs								
	Spillage/leakage of oils/chemicals from operations	5	2	4	1	4	3	5	400
	Air emissions from spills	2	3	4	1	2	5	4	178
	Air emissions from asbestos-containing materials (brakes/clutches)	3	4	4	1	2	5	5	400
	Air emissions from air conditioning systems	3	4	4	1	3	5	4	400

(continued)

Aspect Evaluation Worksheet B (continued)

Garages, Fleet Administration, Engineering

Activity	Aspect(s)	Prob	Sev 1	Sev 2	Scale 1	Scale 2	Dur	Exp	Score
	Perform Vehicle/Equipment Repairs (continued)								
	Oil/solvent/chemical usage from operations	5	3	3	5	5	3	3	675
	Parts/materials usage from operations	5	2	3	2	3	3	1	82
	Noise from operations	5	1	3	1	3	3	2	83
	Energy required to perform repairs	5	3	3	2	2	3	3	270
	Store/Handle Used Oil								
	Spillage/leakage from tanks	2	3	4	1	4	3	5	200
	Management of wastes	5	2	2	5	5	4	5	1000
	Air emissions due to fire	1	3	5	3	5	5	3	202
	Vehicle Engineering Activities								
	Choice of coatings to be used on vehicles	5	3	3	3	3	4	4	720
	Expected life of vehicles	5	2	2	3	3	2	3	180
	Specification of chemicals used in vehicles	5	3	3	3	3	3	3	405
	Containment/leak protection systems in oil/chemical hauling vehicles	5	3	4	2	4	3	3	400

(continued)

Aspect Evaluation Worksheet B (continued)

Activity	Aspect(s)	Prob	Sev 1	Sev 2	Scale 1	Scale 2	Dur	Exp	Score
Garages, Fleet Administration, Engineering									
Vehicle Engineering Activities (continued)									
	Determination of number of alternate fuel vehicles in Con Ed fleet	5	3	3	5	5	4	4	1200
	Provide support for AFV programs to others in NYC area	5	3	3	5	5	4	4	1200
New Vehicle Storage and Commission									
	Spillage/leakage from equipment	2	3	4	1	4	3	5	200
Store/Handle Industrial Debris									
	Spillage/leakage from waste drums	2	3	4	1	4	3	5	200
	Management of wastes	5	2	2	5	5	4	4	800
	Air emission due to fire	1	3	5	3	5	5	3	202
Store/Handle Solid Waste									
	Management of wastes	5	2	3	3	4	4	4	622
Administrative Work from Repairs									
	Management of paper	5	1	1	5	5	2	4	200
	Paper usage	5	2	2	3	3	3	4	360

(continued)

Aspect Evaluation Worksheet B (continued)

Garages, Fleet Administration, Engineering

Activity	Aspect(s)	Prob	Sev 1	Sev 2	Scale 1	Scale 2	Dur	Exp	Score
Facilities Usage									
	Energy usage in occupying building	5	3	3	3	3	3	3	405
	Incidental water usage	5	2	3	3	4	3	3	350
	Incidental water/sewage discharges	5	2	3	3	4	3	3	350
Spill Response									
	Spillage/leakage of materials from improper/insufficient response	3	3	4	1	5	4	5	467
	Parts/materials usage from operations	5	2	2	3	3	3	2	180
	Energy required to respond to spill	5	3	3	2	2	3	2	180
Supervise Vehicle Washing									
	Discharges from operation	5	2	3	1	4	4	5	467
	Water usage in washing	5	1	4	4	5	3	3	390
	Materials usage in washing	5	2	3	2	3	3	2	163
Operate Hydraulic Lifts									
	Leakage of oils from hydraulic lifts	3	3	4	2	4	4	5	533

Aspect Evaluation Worksheet A
Stores

Activity	Aspect(s)	Impact(s)
Operate vehicles	Spillage/leakage from vehicles	Contamination of soil or water Damage to flora/fauna/humans from toxic materials
	Air emissions from engines	Contamination of air
	Fuel usage from vehicles	Depletion of natural resources
	Noise from vehicles	Disruption to fauna/humans
	Air emissions due to fire	Contamination of air
Store and handle hazardous waste	Spillage/leakage from waste drums	Contamination of soil or water Damage to flora/fauna/humans from toxic materials
	Air emissions from spills	Contamination of air Damage to humans from toxic materials
	Management of wastes	Contamination of soil/water/air from improper disposal Reduction of landfill space needed from pollution prevention Conservation of resources from recycling
	Air emissions due to fire	Contamination of air
Store and handle used electrical equipment	Spillage/leakage from equipment	Contamination of soil or water Damage to flora/fauna/humans from toxic materials
	Management of equipment	Contamination of soil/water/air from improper disposal Reduction of landfill space needed from pollution prevention Conservation of resources from recycling

(continued)

Aspect Evaluation Worksheet A
Stores (continued)

Activity	Aspect(s)	Impact(s)
Store and handle virgin oils and chemicals	Spillage/leakage from materials	Contamination of soil or water Damage to flora/fauna/humans from toxic materials
	Air emissions from spills	Contamination of air Damage to humans from toxic materials
	Air emissions due to fire	Contamination of air
Store and handle new electrical equipment	Spillage/leakage from equipment	Contamination of soil or water Damage to flora/fauna/humans from toxic materials
Store and handle industrial debris	Spillage/leakage from waste drums	Contamination of soil or water Damage to flora/fauna/humans from toxic materials
	Management of wastes	Contamination of soil/water/air from improper disposal Reduction of landfill space needed from pollution prevention Conservation of resources from recycling
	Air emissions due to fire	Contamination of air
Store and handle universal waste	Spillage/leakage from waste drums	Contamination of soil or water Damage to flora/fauna/humans from toxic materials
	Air emissions from spills	Contamination of air Damage to humans from toxic materials

(continued)

Aspect Evaluation Worksheet A
Stores (continued)

Activity	Aspect(s)	Impact(s)
Store and handle universal waste (continued)	Management of wastes	Contamination of soil/water/air from improper disposal Reduction of landfill space needed from pollution prevention Conservation of resources from recycling
	Air emissions due to fire	Contamination of air
Clean network transformer pans	Spillage/leakage from cleaning process	Contamination of soil or water Damage to flora/fauna/humans from toxic materials
	Energy use from cleaning operation	Depletion of natural resources
Store and handle oil-filled equipment	Spillage/leakage from equipment	Contamination of soil or water Damage to flora/fauna/humans from toxic materials
Store and handle "other" materials	Asbestos releases from asbestos-containing materials	Contamination of air Damage to flora/fauna/humans from toxic materials
	Spillage/leakage from equipment	Contamination of soil or water Damage to flora/fauna/humans from toxic materials
	Air emissions due to fire	Contamination of air
Administrative work associated with picking and shipping materials	Management of paper	Contamination of soil/water/air from improper disposal Reduction of landfill space needed from pollution prevention Conservation of resources from recycling
	Paper usage	Depletion of natural resources

(continued)

Aspect Evaluation Worksheet A
Stores (continued)

Activity	Aspect(s)	Impact(s)
Store/handle solid waste	Management of wastes	Contamination of soil/water/air from improper disposal Reduction of landfill space needed from pollution prevention Conservation of resources from recycling
Store and handle asbestos	Asbestos releases from waste bags/drums	Contamination of air Damage to flora/fauna/humans from toxic materials
	Management of wastes	Contamination of soil/water/air from improper disposal
Repair capital tools	Spillage/leakage of oils/chemicals from operations	Contamination of soil or water Damage to flora/fauna/humans from toxic materials
	Air emissions from spills	Contamination of air Damage to humans from toxic materials
	Oil/solvent/chemical usage from operations	Depletion of natural resources
	Parts/materials usage from operations	Depletion of natural resources
	Noise from operations	Disruption to fauna/humans
	Energy required to perform repairs	Depletion of natural resources
Facilities usage	Energy usage in occupying building	Depletion of natural resources
	Incidental water usage	Depletion of natural resources
	Incidental water/sewer discharges	Contamination of water/soil

(continued)

Aspect Evaluation Worksheet A
Stores (continued)

Activity	Aspect(s)	Impact(s)
Spill response	Spillage/leakage of materials from improper/insufficient response	Contamination of soil or water Damage to flora/fauna/humans from toxic materials
	Parts/materials usage from operations	Depletion of natural resources
	Energy required to respond to spill	Depletion of natural resources

Aspect Evaluation Worksheet B

Stores

Activity	Aspect(s)	Prob	Sev 1	Sev 2	Scale 1	Scale 2	Dur	Exp	Score
	Operate Vehicles								
	Spillage/leakage from vehicles	5	3	4	1	4	3	5	500
	Air emissions from engines	5	3	4	4	4	5	3	1000
	Fuel usage from vehicles	5	3	3	3	3	3	3	405
	Noise from vehicles	5	1	3	1	3	3	2	83
	Air emissions due to fire	1	4	5	2	4	5	3	173
	Store and Handle Hazardous Waste								
	Spillage/leakage from waste drums	2	4	5	1	4	3	5	260
	Air emissions from spills	2	3	4	1	2	5	4	178
	Management of wastes	5	2	5	3	5	4	5	1100
	Air emissions due to fire	1	4	5	4	5	5	5	469
	Store and Handle Used Electrical Equipment								
	Spillage/leakage from equipment	3	4	4	1	4	4	5	480
	Management of equipment	5	2	5	3	5	4	5	1100

(continued)

Aspect Evaluation Worksheet B (continued)

Stores (continued)

Activity	Aspect(s)	Prob	Sev 1	Sev 2	Scale 1	Scale 2	Dur	Exp	Score
	Store and Handle Virgin Oils and Chemicals								
	Spillage/leakage from materials	4	2	5	1	4	3	5	360
	Air emissions from spills	2	3	5	1	5	5	4	342
	Air emissions due to fire	1	4	5	4	5	5	5	469
	Store and Handle New Electrical Equipment								
	Spillage/leakage from equipment	3	2	2	1	4	4	5	240
	Store and Handle Industrial Debris								
	Spillage/leakage from waste drums	2	3	4	1	4	3	5	200
	Management of wastes	5	2	2	5	5	4	4	800
	Air emissions due to fire	1	3	5	3	5	5	4	269
	Store and Handle Universal Waste								
	Spillage/leakage from waste drums	2	3	4	1	4	4	5	267
	Air emissions from spills	2	3	4	1	2	5	4	178
	Management of wastes	5	2	5	3	5	4	4	880
	Air emission due to fire	1	3	5	3	5	5	4	269

(continued)

Aspect Evaluation Worksheet B (continued)

Stores (continued)

Activity	Aspect(s)	Prob	Sev 1	Sev 2	Scale 1	Scale 2	Dur	Exp	Score
Clean Network Transformer Pans									
	Spillage/leakage from cleaning process	3	3	4	1	4	3	5	300
	Energy use from cleaning operation	5	3	3	1	1	3	2	90
Store and Handle Oil-Filled Equipment									
	Spillage/leakage from equipment	3	2	2	1	4	3	5	180
Store and Handle "Other" Materials									
	Asbestos releases from asbestos-containing materials	3	4	4	1	3	4	5	400
	Spillage/leakage from equipment	3	2	2	1	4	4	5	240
	Air emissions due to fire	1	3	5	3	5	5	4	269
Administrative Work Associated with Picking and Shipping Materials									
	Management of paper	5	1	1	5	5	2	4	200
	Paper usage	5	2	2	3	3	3	4	360
Store/Handle Solid Waste									
	Management of wastes	5	2	3	3	4	4	4	622

(continued)

Aspect Evaluation Worksheet B (continued)

Stores (continued)

Activity	Aspect(s)	Prob	Sev 1	Sev 2	Scale 1	Scale 2	Dur	Exp	Score
	Repair Capital Tools								
	Spillage/leakage of oils/chemicals from operations	4	2	3	1	4	3	5	280
	Air emissions from spills	2	3	4	1	2	5	4	178
	Oil/solvent/chemical usage from operations	5	3	3	3	4	3	3	450
	Parts/materials usage from operations	5	2	2	2	3	3	3	210
	Noise from operations	5	1	3	1	3	3	2	83
	Energy required to perform repairs	5	3	3	2	2	3	2	180
	Facilities Usage								
	Energy usage in occupying building	5	3	3	3	3	3	3	405
	Incidental water usage	5	2	3	3	4	3	3	350
	Incidental water/sewage discharges	5	2	3	3	4	3	3	350
	Spill Response								
	Spillage/leakage of materials from improper/insufficient response	3	3	4	1	5	4	5	467
	Parts/materials usage from operations	5	1	2	2	3	3	1	47
	Energy required to respond to spill	5	3	3	1	1	4	2	120

First Environment
Riverdale, New Jersey

First Environment provides strategic management and environmental engineering services. Services include risk-based remediation, expert testimony, environmental litigation support, and environmental management system development and training. Environmental engineering services include Phase I and Phase II site investigations, soil and groundwater remediation, and air-source testing.

First Environment was the first strategic management and environmental engineering organization in the United States to attain ISO 14001 certification. The company received a German DAT/TGA certificate issued by TÜV Rheinland of North America, in November 1997.

Two procedures are presented. The first addresses identification of environmental aspects. The most significant impact, taken from the list of significant impacts referenced in Section V of this procedure, also is included. The second procedure describes how significance is determined. The actual rating matrix for First Environment's most significant impact illustrates how the procedure is applied.

First Environment
Riverdale, New Jersey
Identification of Environmental Aspects and Impacts
October 17, 1997 (EM4314.DOC, Rev 1)

1. Purpose

To identify the environmental aspects of First Environment's activities, products, and services that we can control or over which we can be expected to have an influence, in order to determine those which may have a significant impact on the environment.

2. Scope

This procedure is used to identify all of First Environment's activities, products, and services that we can control or over which we can be expected to have an influence. For purposes of evaluation, activities, products, and services with similar characteristics will be grouped. Significant environmental impacts identified through this process are considered in the setting of environmental objectives and targets.

3. Responsibilities

3.1   It is the responsibility of the ISO 14000 Steering Committee to provide overall direction and support and to act as a resource for Function Area Representatives (FARs).

3.2   It is the responsibility of the ISO 14000 Steering Committee to engage FARs in the identification of aspects and impacts associated with the activities, products, and services of First Environment.

3.3   It is the responsibility of the ISO 14000 Steering Committee to review and provide final revisions to the aspects and impacts identified by the FARs.

3.4   It is the responsibility of the FARs to identify environmental aspects associated with new equipment or changes within the respective function area which is not related to specific project work.

3.5   It is the responsibility of the Project Managers to identify environmental aspects associated with new projects at kick-off and existing projects at changes to the scope of work.

4. Procedure

4.1   The ISO 14000 Steering Committee, a cross-functional team, has been assembled by senior management and has been assigned the responsibility for performing the evaluation. The ISO 14000 Steering Committee designates the FARs. The ISO 14000 Steering Committee may call upon other individuals in the organization, as necessary.

4.2   The activities, products and services of First Environment are broadly categorized into function areas as follows:

- Office functions, including administrative duties and report preparation, accounting, marketing, and human resources
- Remediation
- Field work (health & safety)
- Laboratory
- Project execution/technical
- Building & equipment maintenance/housekeeping

Each function area is evaluated in terms of aspects and potential impacts. Aspects are identified by evaluating (1) inputs associated with the functional area that have an environmental component; and (2) outputs that have potential environmental consequences. FARs meet with individuals familiar with each of the functional areas to ascertain information, as necessary.

4.3   The FARs ensure that the findings of their respective function areas are documented in a form such that the ISO 14000 Steering Committee can review them.

4.4   The ISO 14000 Steering Committee reviews the findings of the function areas and if they determine that additional information is needed to evaluate a specific functional area, the ISO Management Representative assigns the responsibility for collecting that information to an appropriate team member and/or the function area representative.

4.5   The Steering Committee defines impacts associated with each aspect. These include both positive and negative potential impacts. The impacts are documented.

5. References/Related Documentation

- Product/services/activities and associated aspects and impacts (master list)
- Process flow chart
- Significance procedure
- Function area assignments (structure & responsibility)
- Significant impacts
- Project startup guidelines

Significant Impacts

Significant Impact	Aspect	P/S/A(s)	Function Area
Degradation of GW quality	Discharge to septic	Bathroom/kitchen use	Building operation & maintenance
Degradation of GW quality	Discharge to septic	Warehouse/workshop activities	Building operation & maintenance
Degradation of GW quality	Potential chemical spill discharged to septic	Warehouse/workshop activities	Building operation & maintenance
Degradation of GW quality	Potential chemical spill discharged to septic	Office cleaning	Building operation & maintenance
Degradation of GW quality	Discharge to septic	Office cleaning solutions disposal	Building operation & maintenance
Degradation of GW quality	Potential chemical spill discharged to septic	Liquid sample/reagent disposal	Laboratory
Degradation of GW quality	Potential chemical spill discharged to septic	Lab equipment cleaning activities	Laboratory
Degradation of GW quality	Potential reagent/extract/sample spill discharged to septic	Sample analysis activities	Laboratory
Degradation of GW quality	Cross contamination	Boring/well drilling	Field investigation
Degradation of GW quality	Improper purge water disposal	Well sampling/developing	Field investigation
Degradation of GW quality	Improper decon. solutions disposal	Equipment decontamination	Field investigation

(continued)

Significant Impacts (continued)

Significant Impact	Aspect	P/S/A(s)	Function Area
Degradation of GW quality	Potential chemical spill in field	Equipment calibrations Decontamination Fueling of equipment	Field investigation
Degradation of GW quality	Potential contaminant expansion	Remediation system operation	Remediation
Degradation of GW quality	Contaminant removal	Remediation system operation	Remediation
Degradation of GW quality	Potential spill or discharge from collection/treatment system	Remediation system installation and operation	Remediation
Degradation of GW quality	Potential spill or discharge during maintenance/monitoring	Remediation system installation and operation	Remediation
Degradation of GW quality	Potential cross contamination	Remediation system installation	Remediation
Degradation of GW quality	Potential spill or discharge from construction equipment	Remediation system installation	Remediation
Degradation of GW quality	Potential contaminant expansion	System design	Project execution/technical
Degradation of GW quality	Contaminant removal	System design	Project execution/technical
Degradation of GW quality	Discharge to septic	Pilot/bench scale testing	Project execution/technical
Degradation of GW quality	Potential spill discharged to septic	Pilot/bench scale testing	Project execution/technical

First Environment
Riverdale, New Jersey

Significance
October 17, 1997 (EM4315.DOC, Rev 1)

---

1. Purpose

To determine the most significant environmental impacts and their associated environmental aspects, activities, products, and services.

2. Scope

This procedure is used to evaluate the environmental aspects and impacts for significance and determines which are most significant to First Environment. The significant environmental impacts identified through this process are considered in the setting of environmental objectives and targets.

3. Responsibilities

It is the responsibility of the ISO 14000 Steering Committee to define and implement the significance criteria.

4. Procedure

4.1   The Steering Committee developed Significance Criteria (see Table 1) and ran each of the potential impacts through the criteria to assign numerical ranking. The Steering Committee determined the total number of impacts to be defined as significant and designated the highest ranked as significant.

4.2   Significant environmental impacts identified are considered in setting objectives and targets for the organization.

4.3   The results of the most recent environmental aspect/impact identification are found on the List of Significant Impacts. The Steering Committee is responsible for ensuring that the significant aspects and impacts are reviewed as part of the Management Review Process (see Management Review Procedure). Based on this review, First Environment's management determines the need to update the environmental impact evaluation. Factors such as major changes to the organization's mission, activities, products, or services are considered in determining the need to update the assessment.

5. References/Related Documentation

- Identification of environmental aspects and impacts
- Significant aspects & impacts process flow chart
- Significant impacts
- Significance criteria
- Significance matrix
- Objectives and targets
- Management review

Table 1. Significance Criteria
(Excerpt from 5/14/97 Meeting Minutes)

Based on discussions between committee members and the potential impacts to First Environment, the surrounding environment and the extent to which First Environment can control these influences, the following criteria were used to assess significance:

- Client interest—How our clients would view the various impacts.

- Ecological factors—How the impact would affect the surrounding ecology (flora and fauna) either positively or negatively.

- Resource conservation—How the impact would affect natural resources, either enrichment or depletion.

- Low cost of implementation—Potential cost to First Environment associated with each impact and inversely scored (a low cost to First Environment was ranked high and a potential high cost for First Environment was ranked low).

- Potential costs—Potential cost to First Environment should the impact occur (e.g., what would be the potential cost for First Environment should there be degradation of the surface water quality?). The potential cost could be high; therefore, this criterion was given a high rank.

- Concerns of interested parties—How interested parties (e.g., Sierra Club, Greenpeace, and so on) would view the impact.

- Risk of regulatory exposure—First Environment's potential to receive fines and negative public relations based on regulatory exposure resulting from the impact.

The criteria were then weighted, based on the potential impact to First Environment either operational or capital. The criteria were weighted as follows:

- Client interest (2×)

- Ecological factors (1×)

- Resource conservation (1×)

- Low cost of implementation (2×)

- Potential costs (2×)

- Concerns of interested parties (1×)

- Risk of regulatory exposure (1×)

Each impact was then individually ranked either high (3 points), medium (2 points), or low (1 point) against the criteria using a matrix format. The resulting point totals were used to determine significance to First Environment.

Attached is a copy of the results of the significance analysis based on the weighing of the individual criteria and the ranking of the individual impacts against those criteria.

Significance Matrix

Rank No. 1	High	Medium	Low
Impact: Degradation of Groundwater	**3**	**2**	**1**
Client Interest (2×)	2(3) = 6		
Ecological (×)	3		
Resource Conservation (×)	3		
Low Cost of Implementation (2×)		2(2) = 4	
Potential Cost (2×)	2(3) = 6		
Concerns of Interested Parties (×)	3		
Risk of Regulatory Exposure (×)	3		

TOTAL POINTS = 28

Matsushita Kotobuki Electronics Industries of America
Vancouver, Washington

Matsushita Kotobuki Electronics Industries of America (MKA) is a wholly owned subsidiary of Matsushita Electronic Industrial Company of Japan.

MKA is located near the Columbia River in Vancouver, Washington and is a tenant of the Port of Vancouver. It employs more than 500 people.

MKA is a manufacturer of combination television/VCRs. Processes at the facility include injection molding, painting, cabinet assembly, and electrical assembly/completion.

MKA obtained ISO 14001 registration from Underwriters Laboratories in February, 1999.

MKA's environmental aspects procedure is accompanied by aspect identification/evaluation charts for nine departments: molding; painting; cabinet assembly; final assembly/technical support; warehouse/customer service; product renewal; facilities engineering; quality assurance/quality control; and administration/purchasing/janitorial.

Matsushita Kotobuki Electronics Industries of America
Vancouver, Washington

Environmental Aspects Identification
October 1, 1998 (EMS-PR-001, Rev. 3)

---

1. Purpose/Scope

1.1   Purpose: To identify the environmental aspects of MKA's activities, products, and services.

To determine which aspects will be considered significant by MKA management.

1.2   Scope: The identified environmental aspects will be limited to those activities, products, and services that MKA can control and over which it can have an influence.

This procedure is written to address the criteria established by Section 4.3.1 of ANSI/ISO 14001-1996, and section 3 of MKA's EMS Manual.

2. Related Procedures and Reference Documents

Procedure No.   **Title**
EMS-PR-012   Environmental Records Procedure

Documents
Aspect Identification/Evaluation Worksheet (Appendix EMS-AP-001-01)
Significance Evaluation Worksheet (Appendix EMS-AP-001-02)
Management Review Committee (Appendix EMS-AP-014-01)

3. Procedure

3.1   The ISO Representative will establish an Environmental Aspect Team (EAT) for each department/group.

3.2   Each EAT will review all activities, services, and processes related to its department/group. Each EAT team must also consider aspects it can control related to product.

3.3   Each EAT will complete the Aspect and Impact sections of the appropriate Aspect Identification/Evaluation Worksheet.

3.4   The ISO Representative and the respective Management Review Committee members will review the worksheets.

3.5   The Management Review Committee will determine the significance of each aspect and assign a rating accordingly. Regulatory requirements and scale of impact will be considered in order to determine the significance of the environmental aspect. Scoring is done on a scale of 1 to 5, with 5 meaning highest, and 1 the lowest.

3.6   The Management Review Committee will determine the control that MKA has over each aspect, and assign a rating accordingly.

3.7   Once the Significance and Control ratings have been assigned, the ISO Representative will plot the ratings on the Significance Evaluation Worksheet. The aspects for which the product of (significance × control) that exceeds a threshold specified by the Management Review Committee will be considered significant.

3.8   The Management Review Committee may determine at its discretion whether additional aspects are significant.

3.9   The Aspect Identification/Evaluation Worksheet will be reviewed and updated at least annually by the appropriate Environmental Aspects Team and Management Review Committee in order to keep the information up-to-date.

3.10   The aspects identified as significant will serve as a basis for establishing MKA's environmental objectives and targets. Environmental aspects which have or can have a significant impact on the environment will be considered first in setting environmental objectives and targets.

4. Responsibilities

4.1   Environmental Aspect Team

    4.1.1   Meet at least annually to identify and review environmental aspects for their department/group.

4.2   ISO Representative

    4.2.1   Establish Environmental Aspect Teams.

    4.2.2   Review and approve the significant environmental aspects.

    4.2.3   Provide instructions and/or training to the Environmental Aspect Teams for completing the Aspect Identification/Evaluation Worksheets.

    4.2.4   Maintain file of completed Aspect Identification/Evaluation Worksheets and Significance Evaluation Worksheets. These completed worksheets will be filed and maintained in accordance to the Environmental Records Procedure (EMS-PR-012).

    4.2.5   Review Aspect Identification/Evaluation Worksheets.

    4.2.6   Complete Significance Evaluation Worksheets.

4.3   Management Review Committee

    4.3.1   Review Aspect Identification/Evaluation Worksheets and determine the Significance and Control ratings.

MKA ISO 14001
Aspect Identification/Evaluation

Department

MOLDING–11110

FUNCTION Activity, Product, Service	Aspect #	ASPECT	IMPACT Air, Soil, Water	Concerns				
				Regulatory (1–5)	Scale of Impact (1–5)	Significance (sum)	Control (1–5)	Significance × Control
PRODUCTION								
Energy consumption	M1	Electricity	Consumption of natural resource.	1	2	3	3	9
Water consumption	M2	Cooling Tower—recycle water	Conserve natural resource. Potential for spill contamination (oil into sewer).	2	3	5	2	10
Air emissions	M3	Degassing purge material	Reduces air quality.	1	2	3	2	6
Water disposal	M4	Recycle cardboard	Reduce landfill volume and conserve natural resources.	1	3	4	3	12
	M5	Recycle paper	Reduce landfill volume and conserve natural resources.	1	2	3	4	12
	M6	Recycle purge material	Reduce landfill volume and conserve natural resources.	1	1	2	4	8
	M7	Landfill purged material on cardboard	Increase landfill volume resources and conserve natural resources.	1	3	4	4	16
	M8	Recycle waste oil	Conserve natural resources. Potential for spill contamination.	2	4	6	3	18
	M9	Grease to Waste Management	Reduce landfill volume and conserve natural resources, potential for ground water contamination.	2	3	5	3	15
	M10	Landfill waste packaging	Increase landfill volume and destruction of natural resources.	1	2	3	3	9
	M11	Landfill paper towels	Increase landfill volume and destruction of natural resources.	1	1	2	3	6
	M12	Recycle Cheil bags	Reduce landfill volume and conserve natural resources.	1	1	2	4	8
	M13	Reuse and landfill gloves	Increase landfill volume and destruction of natural resources. Reuse to reduce landfill volume. Wash water contributes to public sewer.	1	2	3	4	12

MKA ISO 14001
Aspect Identification/Evaluation

MOLDING—11110

FUNCTION Activity, Product, Service	Aspect #	ASPECT	IMPACT Air, Soil, Water	Concerns				
				Regulatory (1–5)	Scale of Impact (1–5)	Significance (sum)	Control (1–5)	Significance × Control
	M14	Recycle waste cabinets	Reduce landfill volume and conserve natural resources.	1	3	4	4	16
	M15	Reuse fabric towels	Reduce landfill volume and conserve natural resources. Wash water contributes to public sewer.	1	2	3	2	6
	M16	Recycle stretch wrap	Reduce landfill volume and conserve natural resources.	1	3	4	4	16
	M17	Landfill aerosol cans	Increase landfill volume resources and potential for ground water contamination.	1	2	3	5	15
	M18	Recycle molds	Reduce landfill volume and conserve natural resources.	1	3	4	5	20
	M19	Used/contaminated absorbent	Potential for ground/water contamination.	3	4	7	4	28
Hazardous material	M20	Handling of hazardous material	Potential for spill contamination.	2	4	6	3	18
CHEMICALS	M21	Usage (Approved Chemical List)	Reduce air quality.	2	4	6	2	12
MATERIAL STORAGE	M22	Silo—storage of plastic pellets	Potential for spill contamination.	1	1	2	3	6
	M23	Rail car—storage of plastic pellets	Potential for spill contamination.	1	1	2	3	6
	M24	Cheil bags—storage of plastic pellets	Potential for spill contamination.	1	1	2	4	8
	M25	Gaylords—storage of plastic pellets	Potential for spill contamination.	1	1	2	4	8
Piping distribution system	M26	Plastic pellets from silo and rail cars	Potential for spill contamination.	1	1	2	3	6
Chemical storage areas	M27	Flammable storage cabinet	Potential for spill contamination.	2	4	6	3	18
(refer to approved chemical list)	M28	Small quantities stored throughout department	Potential for spill contamination.	2	4	6	3	18
Material transport	M29	Forklift use	Reduce air quality. Potential for spill/leak of fluids. Potential for propane release to environment.	1	2	3	3	9

MKA ISO 14001
Aspect Identification/Evaluation

Department: PAINTING

FUNCTION Activity, Product, Service	Aspect #	ASPECT	IMPACT Air, Soil, Water	Concerns				
				Regulatory (1–5)	Scale of Impact (1–5)	Significance (sum)	Control (1–5)	Significance × Control
PRODUCTION								
Energy consumption	P1	Electricity	Consumption of natural resource.	1	2	3	2	6
	P2	Natural gas	Consumption of natural resource.	1	3	4	2	8
Water consumption	P3	Water filtration in paint booths	Consumption of natural resource.	1	1	2	2	4
Air emissions	P4	Fugitive air emissions	Reduce air quality.	4	3	7	4	28
	P5	Emissions processed through oxidizer	Reduce air quality.	5	4	9	4	36
Waste disposal	P6	Landfill paint sludge	Increase landfill volume. Potential for spill contamination.	3	3	6	3	18
	P7	Landfill used filters	Increase landfill volume and destruction of natural resources.	3	3	6	2	12
	P8	Recycle small parts	Decrease landfill volume and destruction of natural resources.	1	2	3	4	12
	P9	Recycle paper	Decrease landfill volume and destruction of natural resources.	1	2	3	4	12
	P10	Use of fabric towel	Decrease landfill volume and destruction of natural resources.	1	2	3	5	15
	P11	Landfill latex gloves	Increase landfill volume and destruction of natural resources.	1	2	3	4	12
	P12	Landfill tyvec suit	Increase landfill volume and destruction of natural resources.	1	2	3	5	15
	P13	Recycle stretch wrap	Decrease landfill volume and destruction of natural resources.	1	3	4	4	16
	P14	Landfill paint cans	Increase landfill volume and destruction of natural resources.	1	3	4	3	12

MKA ISO 14001
Aspect Identification/Evaluation

PAINTING

FUNCTION Activity, Product, Service	Aspect #	ASPECT	IMPACT Air, Soil, Water	Concerns				
				Regulatory (1–5)	Scale of Impact (1–5)	Significance (sum)	Control (1–5)	Significance × Control
	P15	Reuse/recycle waste packaging	Decrease landfill volume and destruction of natural resources.	1	2	3	4	12
	P16	Recycle cardboard	Reduce landfill volume and conserve natural resources.	1	3	4	4	16
	P17	Recycle waste cabinets	Reduce landfill volume and conserve natural resources.	1	3	4	4	16
	P18	Still bottoms	Potential for spill contamination.	4	2	6	3	18
	P19	Reuse and landfill gloves	Increase landfill volume and destruction of natural resources. Reuse to reduce landfill volume. Wash water contributes to public sewer.	1	2	3	4	12
Hazardous material	P20	Handling of hazardous materials/waste	Potential for spill contamination.	4	4	8	3	24
CHEMICALS	P21	Usage (Approved Chemical List)	Reduce air quality.	1	4	5	2	10
Process	P22	Paper filter usage	Remove particulate from air.	1	3	4	2	8
	P23	Wipe down cabinets with Anti Stat	Potential for spill, reduce air quality.	1	4	5	3	15
	P24	Water filtration	Remove particulate from air.	1	3	4	2	8
	P25	Lacquer coating	Generate air pollutants. Create hazardous and non-hazardous waste.	3	4	7	3	21
	P26	Still	Reduce hazardous waste. Potential for spill contamination.	2	3	5	4	20
	P27	Oxidizer operation	Reduce VOCs. Produce CO & NO_x. Increase global warming.	5	5	10	4	40
MATERIAL STORAGE								
Above ground tanks	P28	Paint Booth water tanks	Potential for spill contamination.	1	3	4	3	12
Chemical storage areas	P29	Paint storage building	Potential for spill contamination.	3	3	6	3	18

MKA ISO 14001
Aspect Identification/Evaluation

PAINTING

FUNCTION Activity, Product, Service	Aspect #	ASPECT	IMPACT Air, Soil, Water	Regulatory (1–5)	Scale of Impact (1–5)	Significance (sum)	Control (1–5)	Significance × Control
	P30	Paint booth	Potential for spill contamination.	2	3	5	3	15
	P31	Repair area	Potential for spill contamination.	2	3	5	3	15
	P32	Flammable storage area	Potential for spill contamination.	3	3	6	3	18
	P33	Mixing room	Potential for spill contamination.	2	3	5	4	20
	P34	Small quantities stored throughout	Potential for spill contamination.	2	3	5	4	20
Hazardous waste storage	P35	90-day storage area	Potential for spill contamination.	4	3	7	3	21
	P36	Satellite accumulation	Potential for spill contamination.	4	3	7	3	21
Material transport	P37	Forklift use	Reduce air quality. Potential for spill/leak of fluids. Potential for propane release to environment.	1	1	2	3	6
	P38	Cart transport from paint storage building	Potential for spill contamination.	2	2	4	4	16

MKA ISO 14001
Aspect Identification/Evaluation

Department

CABINET ASSEMBLY

FUNCTION Activity, Product, Service	Aspect #	ASPECT	IMPACT Air, Soil, Water	Concerns				
				Regulatory (1–5)	Scale of Impact (1–5)	Significance (sum)	Control (1–5)	Significance × Control
PRODUCTION								
Energy consumption	CA1	Electricity	Consumption of natural resource.	1	2	3	2	6
Air emissions	CA2	Fugitive air emissions	Reduce air quality.	3	3	6	3	18
	CA3	Emissions processed through oxidizer	Reduce air quality.	5	4	9	4	36
Water disposal	CA4	Recycle cardboard	Reduce landfill volume and conserve natural resources.	1	3	4	4	16
	CA5	Landfill used filters	*Increase landfill volume and destruction of natural resources.*	1	3	4	2	8
	CA6	*Reuse/recycle waste packaging*	*Decrease landfill volume and destruction of natural resources.*	1	2	3	4	12
	CA7	Landfill paper towels	Increase landfill volume and destruction of natural resources.	1	1	2	2	4
	CA8	Empty ink/thinner/chemical containers	Increase landfill volume and destruction of natural resources.	2	3	5	4	20
	CA9	Reuse cardboard w/ foam	Recycle to reduce landfill volume and conservation of natural resources.	1	1	2	1	2
	CA10	Landfill tape	Increase landfill volume and destruction of natural resources.	1	1	2	1	2
	CA11	Recycle waste cabinets	Reduce landfill volume and conserve natural resources.	1	3	4	4	16
	CA12	Reuse fabric towels	Wash and reuse to reduce landfill volume and conservation of natural resources. Increase contribution to public sewer.	1	2	3	2	6
Hazardous materials	CA13	Handling of hazardous material	Potential for spill contamination.	4	4	8	3	24

MKA ISO 14001
Aspect Identification/Evaluation

CABINET ASSEMBLY

FUNCTION Activity, Product, Service	Aspect #	ASPECT	IMPACT Air, Soil, Water	Regulatory (1–5)	Scale of Impact (1–5)	Significance (sum)	Control (1–5)	Significance × Control
						Concerns		
CHEMICAL	CA14	Usage (Approved Chemical List)	Reduce air quality.	1	4	5	2	10
Process	CA15	Cleaning ink trays/3405 on cart	Potential for spill contamination. Reduce air quality.	3	3	6	3	18
	CA16	Wash tank	Potential for spill contamination. Reduce air quality.	3	3	6	4	24
MATERIAL STORAGE								
Chemical Storage areas	CA17	Ink stored on racks in departments	Potential for spill contamination.	2	2	4	3	12
	CA18	Acetone drum on dock	Potential for spill contamination.	2	3	5	3	15
	CA19	Flammable storage cabinets	Potential for spill contamination.	3	2	5	3	15
Hazardous waste storage	CA20	90-day storage area/3405	Potential for spill contamination.	4	3	7	3	21
	CA21	Satellite accumulation/still bottom	Potential for spill contamination.	4	3	7	3	21

MKA ISO 14001
Aspect Identification/Evaluation

Department

FINAL ASSEMBLY/TECHNICAL SUPPORT

FUNCTION Activity, Product, Service	Aspect #	ASPECT	IMPACT Air, Soil, Water	Concerns				
				Regulatory (1–5)	Scale of Impact (1–5)	Significance (sum)	Control (1–5)	Significance × Control
PRODUCTION								
Energy consumption	FA1	Electricity	Consumption of natural resource.	1	2	3	2	6
Air emissions	FA2	Fugitive air emissions	Reduce air quality.	2	3	5	5	25
Waste disposal	FA3	Recycle cardboard	Reduce landfill volume and conserve natural resources.	1	3	4	4	16
	FA4	*Recycle plastic VCR frames*	*Decrease landfill volume.*	1	2	3	4	12
	FA5	*Landfill used waste solder from solder extractor*	*Increase landfill volume. Potential contamination of natural resources.*	2	2	4	5	20
	FA6	*Landfill used batteries from remotes*	*Increase landfill volume. Potential contamination of natural resources.*	2	1	3	5	15
	FA7	Landfill waste packaging	*Increase landfill volume and consumption of natural resources.*	1	2	3	3	9
	FA8	Recycle styrofoam	Reduce landfill volume and conserve natural resources.	1	3	4	3	12
	FA9	*Recycle stretch wrap*	Reduce landfill volume and conserve natural resources.	1	3	4	4	16
	FA10	Recycle cathode ray tubes	Reduce landfill volume and conserve natural resources.	1	3	4	5	20
	FA11	Landfill electrical components with solder	Increase landfill volume and consumption of natural resources.	2	2	4	3	12
	FA12	Recycle circuit boards	Reduce landfill volume and conserve natural resources.	2	2	4	3	12

MKA ISO 14001

Aspect Identification/Evaluation

FINAL ASSEMBLY/TECHNICAL SUPPORT

FUNCTION Activity, Product, Service	Aspect #	ASPECT	IMPACT Air, Soil, Water	Concerns				
				Regulatory (1–5)	Scale of Impact (1–5)	Significance (sum)	Control (1–5)	Significance × Control
Hazardous materials	FA13	Handling of hazardous materials	Potential for spill contamination.	2	4	6	3	18
CHEMICALS	FA14	Usage (Approved Chemical List)	Reduce air quality.	2	2	4	2	8
MATERIAL STORAGE								
Chemical storage areas	FA15	Flammable storage cabinet	Potential for spill contamination.	2	2	4	3	12
	FA16	Small quantities stored throughout department	Potential for spill contamination.	2	2	4	3	12

MKA ISO 14001
Aspect Identification/Evaluation

Department

WAREHOUSE/CUSTOMER SERVICE

FUNCTION Activity, Product, Service	Aspect #	ASPECT	IMPACT Air, Soil, Water	Concerns				
				Regulatory (1–5)	Scale of Impact (1–5)	Significance (sum)	Control (1–5)	Significance × Control
DISTRIBUTION								
Energy consumption	W1	Electricity	Consumption of natural resource.	1	2	3	1	3
Transportation	W2	Transportation of finished goods	Reduce air quality. Potential for spill/leak of fluids. Consumption of natural resources. Contribution to global warming.	1	2	3	1	3
	W3	Forklift use	Reduce air quality. Potential for spill/leak of fluids. Consumption of natural resources. Contribution to global warming.	1	2	3	4	12
Waste disposal	W4	*Recycle stretch wrap*	*Reduce landfill volume and conserve natural resources.*	1	3	4	4	16
	W5	*Recycle pallets*	*Reduce landfill volume and conserve natural resources.*	1	3	4	3	12
	W6	*Recycle styrofoam*	*Reduce landfill volume and conserve natural resources.*	1	3	4	3	12
	W7	*Styrofoam coffee cups to landfill*	*Increase landfill volume and consumption of natural resources.*	1	2	3	5	15
	W8	*Recycle waste packaging*	*Reduce landfill volume and conserve natural resources.*	1	2	3	4	12
	W9	*Recycle cardboard*	*Reduce landfill volume and conserve natural resources.*	1	3	4	4	16
	W10	*Recycle cathode ray tubes*	*Reduce landfill volume and conserve natural resources.*	1	3	4	5	20
	W11	Recycle electrical components with solder	Increase landfill volume and consumption of natural resources.	2	2	4	2	8

MKA ISO 14001
Aspect Identification/Evaluation

WAREHOUSE/CUSTOMER SERVICE

FUNCTION Activity, Product, Service	Aspect #	ASPECT	IMPACT Air, Soil, Water	Concerns				
				Regulatory (1–5)	Scale of Impact (1–5)	Significance (sum)	Control (1–5)	Significance × Control
	W12	Recycle circuit boards	Reduce landfill volume and conserve natural resources.	2	2	4	2	8
	W13	Landfill batteries	Potential for release to environment. Hazardous material, increased landfill volume.	2	2	4	5	20
	W14	Transportation batteries (tractor)	Hazardous material, potential negative impact to environment.	2	2	4	5	20
Chemical storage areas	W15	Propane tank	Potential for release to environment.	2	3	5	3	15
CHEMICAL	W16	Usage (Approved Chemical List)	Reduce air quality.	1	4	5	2	10
Hazardous materials	W17	Handling of hazardous material	Potential for spill contamination.	3	4	7	3	21

MKA ISO 14001
Aspect Identification/Evaluation

Department

PRODUCT RENEWAL

FUNCTION Activity, Product, Service	Aspect #	ASPECT	IMPACT Air, Soil, Water	Regulatory (1–5)	Scale of Impact (1–5)	Significance (sum)	Control (1–5)	Significance × Control
Energy consumption	PR1	Electricity	Consumption of natural resource.	1	2	3	2	6
Waste disposal	PR2	Recycle electrical components with solder	Decrease landfill volume and conserve natural resources.	2	2	4	5	20
	PR3	Recycle circuit boards	Reduce landfill volume and conserve natural resources.	2	2	4	2	8
	PR4	Recycle cardboard	Reduce landfill volume and conserve natural resources.	1	3	4	3	12
	PR5	Recycle waste packaging	Decrease landfill volume and conserve natural resources.	1	2	3	4	12
	PR6	Recycle styrofoam	Reduce landfill volume and conserve natural resources.	1	3	4	3	12
	PR7	Styrofoam stretch wrap	Decrease landfill volume and conserve natural resources.	1	3	4	4	16
	PR8	Landfill plastic parts (VCR front)	Increase landfill volume and consumption of natural resources.	1	2	3	5	15
	PR9	Landfill batteries from remotes	Increase landfill volume and consumption of natural resources.	2	2	4	5	20
Transportation	PR10	Forklift use	Reduce air quality. Potential for spill/leak of fluids. Consumption of natural resources. Contribution to global warming.	1	2	3	4	12

MKA ISO 14001

Aspect Identification/Evaluation

Department									
FACILITIES ENGINEERING				Concerns					
FUNCTION Activity, Product, Service	Aspect #	ASPECT	IMPACT Air, Soil, Water	Regulatory (1–5)	Scale of Impact (1–5)	Significance (sum)	Control (1–5)	Significance × Control	
Energy consumption	FE1	Natural gas usage	Consumption of natural resource.	1	2	3	2	6	
	FE2	Electricity	Consumption of natural resource.	1	3	4	2	8	
Water consumption	FE3	Water usage	Contribute to public sewer.	1	3	4	2	8	
Stormwater runoff	FE4	Storm drains	Potential for polluted water sent to public sewer. Contribute to public sewer.	3	3	6	2	12	
Chemical storage areas	FE5	Flammable storage cabinets	Potential for spill contamination	2	2	4	3	12	
	FE6	Small quantities stored throughout factory	Potential for spill contamination.	2	2	4	3	12	
Maintenance	FE7	Oil/water separator	Potential for polluted water sent to public sewer.	2	2	4	3	12	
	FE8	Equipment	Create waste for disposal.	2	2	4	3	12	
Landscaping	FE9	Weed killer	Potential pollution of groundwater.	1	1	2	4	8	
Waste disposal	FE10	Reuse fabric towels	Wash and reuse to reduce landfill volume and conservation of natural resources. Increase contribution to public sewer.	1	2	3	2	6	
	FE11	Recycle waste oil	Conserve natural resources. Potential for spill contamination.	2	4	6	2	12	
	FE12	*Grease to Waste Management*	*Reduce landfill volume and conserve natural resources, potential for groundwater contamination.*	2	3	5	3	15	
Hazardous materials	FE13	Handling of hazardous materials	Potential for spill contamination.	3	4	7	3	21	
CHEMICAL	FE14	Usage (Approved Chemical List)	Reduce air quality.	1	4	5	2	10	

MKA ISO 14001
Aspect Identification/Evaluation

Department

QUALITY ASSURANCE/QUALITY CONTROL/PED/MRB

FUNCTION Activity, Product, Service	Aspect #	ASPECT	IMPACT Air, Soil, Water	Regulatory (1–5)	Scale of Impact (1–5)	Significance (sum)	Control (1–5)	Significance × Control
Energy consumption	QA1	Electricity	Consumption of natural resource.	1	2	3	2	6
Waste disposal	QA2	Recycle cathode ray tubes	Reduce landfill volume and conserve natural resources.	1	3	4	5	20
	QA3	Recycle electrical components with solder	Reduce landfill volume and conserve natural resources.	2	2	4	5	20
	QA4	Recycle circuit boards	Reduce landfill volume and conserve natural resources.	2	2	4	3	12
	QA5	Recycle cardboard	Reduce landfill volume and conserve natural resources.	1	3	4	4	16
	QA6	Landfill waste packaging (polysheeting)	Increase landfill volume and consumption of natural resources.	1	2	3	3	9
	QA7	Recycle styrofoam	Reduce landfill volume and conserve natural resources.	1	3	4	3	12
	QA8	Recycle stretch wrap	Reduce landfill volume and conserve natural resources.	1	3	4	4	16
	QA9	Recycle paper	Reduce landfill volume and conserve natural resources.	1	1	2	4	8
	QA10	Recycle plastic parts	Reduce landfill volume and conserve natural resources.	1	2	3	5	15
	QA11	Recycle roll staples and hand staples	Reduce landfill volume and conserve natural resources.	1	1	2	5	10

MKA ISO 14001
Aspect Identification/Evaluation

QUALITY ASSURANCE/QUALITY CONTROL/PED/MRB

FUNCTION Activity, Product, Service	Aspect #	ASPECT	IMPACT Air, Soil, Water	Concerns				
				Regulatory (1–5)	Scale of Impact (1–5)	Significance (sum)	Control (1–5)	Significance × Control
	QA12	Styrofoam cups	Increase landfill volume and consumption of natural resources.	1	2	3	5	15
Process	QA13	Environmental chamber	Consumption of natural resources.	1	1	2	2	4
	QA14	Landfill video tapes	Increase landfill volume and consumption of natural resources.	1	1	2	4	8
Hazardous material	QA15	Handling of hazardous material	Potential for spill contamination.	2	2	4	2	8
Product design	QA16	Not based on environmental impact	Potential for unnecessary use of natural resources and hazardous material.	1	2	3	3	9
Product end of life	QA17	Customer disposal	Potential for increased landfill volume.	1	2	3	1	3
	QA18	End user packaging	Potential for increased landfill volume.	1	2	3	2	6
CHEMICAL	QA19	Usage (Approved Chemical List)	Reduce air quality.	1	2	3	2	6

MKA ISO 14001
Aspect Identification/Evaluation

Department

ADMINISTRATION/PURCHASING/JANITORIAL

FUNCTION Activity, Product, Service	Aspect #	ASPECT	IMPACT Air, Soil, Water	Concerns				
				Regulatory (1–5)	Scale of Impact (1–5)	Significance (sum)	Control (1–5)	Significance × Control
Energy consumption	AD1	Electricity	Consumption of natural resource.	1	2	3	2	6
Water consumption	AD2	Janitorial purposes	Consumption of natural resource.	1	1	2	2	4
	AD3	Cafeteria/restroom	Increase landfill volume and destruction of natural resources.	1	2	3	3	9
Recycled material usage	AD4	Packing cases	Reduce landfill volume and conserve natural resources.	1	3	4	3	12
	AD5	Foam cushions	Reduce landfill volume and conserve natural resources.	1	2	3	3	9
	AD6	In-house use of scrap paper	Reduce landfill volume and conserve natural resources.	1	1	2	3	6
	AD7	Fan bags	Reduce landfill volume and conserve natural resources.	1	1	2	3	6
	AD8	Aluminum cans	Reduce landfill volume and conserve natural resources.	1	1	2	4	8
	AD9	Cardboard	Reduce landfill volume and conserve natural resources.	1	3	4	4	16
Non-recycled material usage	AD10	Paper use in mass print jobs	Consumption of natural resources.	1	2.	3	5	15
	AD11	Printer cartridges and toner	Increase landfill volume and destruction of natural resources.	1	1	2	5	10
Material selection	AD12	Not based on environmental impact	Potential for unnecessary consumption of natural resources.	1	2	3	3	9
	AD13	Paint/thinners	Potential for damage to air, soil.	2	2	4	3	12

MKA ISO 14001
Aspect Identification/Evaluation

ADMINISTRATION/PURCHASING/JANITORIAL

FUNCTION Activity, Product, Service	Aspect #	ASPECT	IMPACT Air, Soil, Water	Regulatory (1–5)	Scale of Impact (1–5)	Significance (sum)	Control (1–5)	Significance × Control
	AD14	Ink 1999 models	Potential for damage to air, soil.	2	2	4	3	12
	AD15	Paper type of parts 1999 models	Increase landfill volume and destruction of natural resources.	1	1	2	3	6
	AD16	Plastic resin 1999 models	Potential for damage to air, soil.	1	2	3	3	9
Supplier evaluation	AD17	Not based on supplier's EMS	Potential for support of non-environmentally friendly suppliers.	1	2	3	3	9
CHEMICAL	AD18	Usage (Approved Chemical List)	Reduce air quality.	2	3	5	3	15
Waste disposal	AD19	Styrofoam cups	Increase landfill volume and destruction of natural resources.	1	2	3	5	15
	AD20	Fax cartridges/typewriter and printer ribbon	Increase landfill volume and destruction of natural resources.	1	1	2	5	10
	AD21	Paper towels in bathroom	Increase landfill volume and destruction of natural resources.	1	3	4	5	20
Parking lot	AD22	Employee parking	Potential contamination of storm sewer. Encourages use of natural resources.	2	3	5	1	5
Employee transportation	AD23	Commute trip reduction	Less air emissions/less global warming and less use of natural resources.	1	2	3	5	15
Emergency Preparedness	AD24	Spill kit materials and procedures	Protection of water and land from contamination.	2	3	5	5	25
Perimeter	AD25	Rubble and waste	Potential water and land contamination.	1	1	2	5	10
	AD26	Modification due to	Air and water pollution potential.	1	2	3	3	9
	AD27	Truck loading docks	Spill potential.	2	2	4	2	8
Train tracks	AD28	Rail cars stored/delivered on	Increased spill potential.	1	1	2	1	2
I.S./computers	AD29	Reuse/sale/archival of used or outdated or broken hardware	Reduce landfill volume and conserve natural resources.	1	2	3	5	15

MKA ISO 14001
Aspect Identification/Evaluation—Addendum

Department

ADDENDUM

FUNCTION Activity, Product, Service	Aspect #	ASPECT	IMPACT Air, Soil, Water	Concerns				
				Regulatory (1–5)	Scale of Impact (1–5)	Significance (sum)	Control (1–5)	Significance × Control
Maintenance	X1	Subcontractor equipment maintenance	Spill potential, ground and water contamination.	1	3	4	3	12
Chemical Usage	X2	Rodenticide	Spill potential, ground and water contamination.	2	2	4	5	20
	X3	R22 used in HVAC	Spill potential, ground and water contamination.	1	4	5	2	10
	X4	3M Super 77 spray adhesive	Spill potential, ground and water contamination.	1	2	3	5	15
Metal Usage	X5	Metal shavings	Increase landfill volume and destruction of natural resources.	1	1	2	5	10
	X6	Razor blades and Dr. Blades	Increase landfill volume and destruction of natural resources.	1	1	2	5	10
Chemical Storage	X7	Storage of paint at West	Spill potential, ground and water contamination.	1	2	3	5	15
Facility Operations	X8	Air compressors	Spill potential, ground and water contamination.	1	2	3	2	6
	X9	Air compressor condensate	Spill potential, ground and water contamination.	3	3	6	4	24
Materials Storage	X10	Storage and salvage of equip. at West	Spill potential, ground and water contamination.	1	1	2	5	10

Panasonic
Matsushita Communication Industrial Corporation of U.S.A.
Peachtree City, Georgia

Matsushita Electric Corporation of America, a principal North American subsidiary of Matsushita Electric Industrial Company of Osaka, Japan, introduced the Panasonic name to the U.S. market in 1961. Today, there are 150 business locations and 23 manufacturing sites in North America, each with its own objectives and responsibilities.

Matsushita Communication Industrial Corporation of America manufactures automotive electronics and telecommunication products. It was awarded ISO 14001 registration by KPMG in November 1998.

Three documents are presented:

- The procedure for identification and evaluation of environmental aspects and impacts

- Aspect identification/impact rating worksheet, referenced in step 5.4 of the procedure

- Definition chart for ratings

Actual aspects and impacts are not provided.

Panasonic
Matsushita Communication Industrial Corporation of U.S.A.
Peachtree City, Georgia

Identification & Evaluation of Environmental Aspects & Impacts
October 23, 1998 (E4.03.01.R02)

---

1. General Provisions

1.1   Purpose: To identify the environmental aspects of MCUSA's activities, products, and services. Also, to determine impacts these aspects have or can have on the environment.

1.2   Scope: Identified environmental aspects will be limited to those activities, products, and services that MCUSA can control and over which it can have an influence.

2. Authority

This procedure is proposed by the EMS Adminstrator and is authorized by the Vice-President and Personnel Manager.

3. Responsibility

The EMS Administrator is responsible for executing this procedure.

4. Revision/Abolishment

This procedure may be revised or abolished by EMS Administrator in compliance with document control procedures and with the approval of the MCUSA Vice-President and Personnel Manager.

5. Procedure

5.1   The EMS Administrator and a selected cross-functional team meet at least annually to identify and review environmental aspects and impacts of MCUSA activities, products, services, and operations. This cross-functional team is made up of employee representatives from various disciplines, organizational levels, and areas of responsibilities throughout the plant.

5.2   The EMS Administrator provides instruction and/or training to needed personnel for the aspect identification and significance determination process, coordinates the related activities, and records and retains results. The Significance Rating Matrix for Aspect Identification/Impact Rating Form (R14003) is used as a tool for training.

5.3   The EMS Administrator directs the team in the effort to compile and review a list of process, product, service, and related activities with known or potential environmental interaction, and may include both positive and negative aspects. Information for this listing is obtained from the cross-functional team to insure correctness and completeness. The methods used to identify aspects may include, but are not limited to, process flow, bill of materials, fixed asset lists, and facility/site maps.

5.4   The aspect identification and impact rating worksheet (F14001) is used to compile the aspects and impacts.

5.5   Upon completion of the list, a selected cross-functional team reviews and assigns rating values for frequency, severity, regulation, controllability, and likelihood (see R14003—Significance Rating Matrix for Aspect Identification Rating) to each aspect/impact. A total score for each aspect and impact is calculated and then the spreadsheet is sorted in ascending order by total score. A cross-functional team then determines "significant" aspects and impacts of MCUSA activities, products, services, and related activities (R14005—Significant Aspect and Impact List). Those aspects with scores falling within the top 10 percent of the highest actual total in normal conditions are determined to be significant.

5.6   The aspects identified as "significant" serve as a basis for establishing targets and objectives (E4.03.03). Environmental aspects that have or can have a significant impact on the environment are considered first in setting environmental targets and objectives. The EMS Administrator directs efforts to improve significant aspects. The significant aspects with negative impacts are presented to Management Review. The management then determines and approves which aspects will have targets and objectives. The approval is documented in the form of meeting minutes (E4.03.03). The EMSA then assigns ETAP (Environmental Target Action Plan) task teams, using the Objectives and Targets Action Plan form (F14006).

5.7   The EMS Administrator ensures that all controllable significant aspects and impacts are addressed in the relevant functions (that is, work instructions, procedures, training, and so on).

6. Revision History

R01 9/22/98—clarified cross-functional team (5.1). Added related documents to text body, indicated positive and negative aspects and impacts (5.3), clarified cross-functional team's role and significant aspect criteria (5.5), linked significant aspects with objective and targets (5.6). R02—Revised Significant Aspect List (R14005.R01).

7. Records

Records are retained as stated in P4.16.1.

8. Related Documents

See body text.

9. Attachments

None.

Aspect Identification/Impact Rating Worksheet F1401.R00
(Referenced in Procedure Step 5.4)

Area	Aspect	Impact(s)	Condition	Significance Rating					Accumulated Ratings
				Frequency 1 2 3 4 5	Severity 1 2 3 4 5	Regulated 1 2 3 4 5	Controllable 1 2 3 4 5	Likelihood 1 2 3 4 5	
			Normal = N Abnormal = A	How often does the impact occur?	To what degree and/or extent will the impact effect the environment?	"Regulated" (safety/environmental) to what extent?	To what extent can the impact be controlled or influenced?	Probability that an impact will occur.	Totals from each column.
(ex: Production, Purchasing, Marketing, Warehouse, S&R)	Activity, Product, Service that can interact with the environment.	List areas of environmental impact: air, water, soil, landfill, noise, odor, energy usage, flora, fauna, humans, etc.	If abnormal condition could change impact, then repeat the aspect with an "A" marked in this column and indicate the new ratings.						

Definition Chart for Ratings

	Frequency 1 2 3 4 5	Severity 1 2 3 4 5	Regulated 1 2 3 4 5	Controllability 1 2 3 4 5	Likelihood 1 2 3 4 5
	How often could the impact occur?	To what degree can the impact effect the environment?	What kind of regulation is required?	To what extent can the impact be controlled or influenced?	What is the probability that an impact will occur?
1 =	Seldom (rarely; 6 months or more)	Not likely to effect	Non-regulated	Easily controlled or influenced; requires very few resources	Improbable
2 =	Intermittently (from time to time; 1 to 6 months)	Minor—easily correctable, short-term, clearable	Voluntary	Requires some resources to address	Remote
3 =	Regularly (recurring; 1 week to 1 month)	Moderate—correctable	Company policy	Requires moderate resources to address	Moderate
4 =	Often (1 day to 1 week)	Serious—More difficult to correct; recoverable	Potential to become regulated in future	Difficult to control or influence; requires many resources	Likely
5 =	Repeatedly (happening again and again; daily)	Severe—complex effect with complicated solution and great effort to correct and recover	Regulated (permitted or requires following government programs)	Very difficult to control or influence; requires extensive resources	Very likely

Purolator/Arvin Industries
Fayetteville, North Carolina

Arvin Industries is a leading worldwide manufacturer and supplier of vehicle exhaust systems and ride control products for both the original equipment and replacement markets. With over $2.2 billion in sales, Arvin has approximately 14,000 employees at 60 facilities in 16 countries. The company sells its exhaust systems and ride control products in more than 65 countries around the world.

Arvin's Purolator facility in Fayetteville, North Carolina, manufactures a complete line of automotive oil, air, and fuel filters and filter housings for use in virtually all automobiles and light-duty trucks currently operating in North America.

The Fayetteville plant, which has earned quality awards such as Chrysler's Gold Pentastar Award for supply excellence, AutoAlliance's Supplier Recognition Award, Ford Q1, Mazda Zero Defect, Navistar Preferred Supplier, and the Department of Defense Supplier Quality Award, achieved ISO 14001 registration from BVQI in May, 1999.

Purolator's procedure for identifying environmental aspects and impacts is accompanied by a rating form template and a checklist for proposed objectives and targets. Actual aspects and impacts identified by the procedure are not included.

Purolator/Arvin Industries
Fayetteville, North Carolina

Environmental, Health and Safety (EH&S) Planning
December 3, 1998 (OPP-02-001)

---

1. Purpose

1.1   To describe the process used to establish and maintain EH&S aspects and impacts, legal and other requirements, objectives and targets, and programs for achieving the objectives and targets.

2. Scope

2.1   Purolator Products, Fayetteville, NC

3. Definitions

3.1   Prevention of Pollution Team—Cross-functional team operating under the guidance of the Environmental Manager. The activities typically represented on the team include manufacturing, maintenance, and quality. The membership and activities represented can vary dependent upon the area/aspects under consideration.

3.2   Safety Team—Cross-functional team operating under the guidance of the Health & Safety Manager. The activities typically represented on the team include manufacturing, maintenance, and quality. The membership and activities represented can vary dependent upon the area/aspects under consideration.

4. Responsibility

4.1   As defined in the text of this procedure.

5. Related Procedures

5.1 Business Plan: BUP-01-001.

5.2 Request for Quote (RFQ) and Quality Planning: BUP-02-002.

5.3 Business Plan: OPP-01-003.

5.4 Document and Data Control: OPP-05-001.

5.5 Control of Management System: QSP-16-001.

6. Applicable Forms and Exhibits

6.1 ISO 14001 Planning: Exhibit I—Process flow diagram.

6.2 Aspects and Impacts Form: QSF-98-004.

6.3 Objectives and Targets Form: QSF-98-005.

7. Procedure

7.1 EH&S aspects and impacts are identified by the Prevention of Pollution and Safety Teams. The aspects and their potential impacts are identified based upon inputs considerations listed in the following table.

The list of aspects and impacts is maintained per QSP-16-001.

The aspects and impacts are kept up-to-date by the following means:

- Annual Prevention of Pollution and Safety Team meetings

- BUP-02-002, including the Team Feasibility Commitment and Capital Appropriation approval processes

- MEP-09-004, including the Chemical Approval process

Applicability		Considerations
Environmental	Health & Safety	
X	X	Process flow charts
X	X	Facility layouts
X	X	Legal & other requirements (e.g., environmental, health, safety, and community issues)
X		Emissions to air
X		Releases to water
X		Waste management
X	X	Use of raw materials and natural resources
	X	Job safety analysis

Significant aspects and the associated significant impacts are determined by the Prevention of Pollution and Safety Teams. The criteria for the determination of significance are given on the Aspects and Impacts form (QSF-98-004). The aspects/impacts with the highest risk impact rating are considered significant.

The Environmental Manager will review the identified aspects and impacts as presented by the Prevention of Pollution and Safety Teams for viability by utilizing his experience, training, and education prior to submission of consideration for significance.

7.2   EH&S legal and/or other requirements are identified:

- By the manager(s) of environmental, health, and safety activities

- Based upon inputs from applicable CFRs, state codes, OSHA standards, industry codes of practice, agreements with public authorities, non-regulatory guidelines, and Arvin programs and directives

Access to these requirements can be by hard copy or electronic media, and currentness of the information is maintained per OPP-05-001 Document and Data Control Procedure.

7.3　EH&S objectives and targets are considered and established as part of the Business Planning process (BUP-01-001 and OPP-01-003). When setting objectives and targets consideration is given, but not limited, to the significant aspects and impacts. The Prevention of Pollution and Safety Teams can recommend objectives and targets to the Business Planning staff.

The Objectives and Targets form (QSF-98-005) is initiated and dispositioned (by all listed on the form) to ensure the objectives and targets are consistent with the EH&S policy, the commitment to prevention of pollution, and the other considerations required by ISO 14001. After consideration of the feasibility inputs, final disposition of the proposal is made by the Operations Director or Manager. These objectives and targets become part of the business plan.

7.4　As part of the Business Planning process, management assures designation of responsibility, allocation of resources, deployment of time-based action plans, and progress monitoring in support of the established objectives and targets.

7.5　Maintenance of EH&S planning activities is assured as listed in 7.1 whenever the following occur:

- New or changed products or processes
- Introduction of new or modified materials or services (for example, contractors)

Identification of Aspects and Impacts (QSF-98-004, Rev. 1)

1 = Low Impact—Impacts that are manageable and operations are easily within the scope of permits. Minor health and safety risks.

2 = Moderate Impact—Moderate risks for potential compliance issues. Moderate health and safety risks.

3 = High Impact—Higher probability for compliance issues, notices of violation, mitigation, increased liabilities. Higher level of health and safety risks.

ID #	Process	Env. Aspect	Env. Impact	Job Title/JSA	Health/Safety Aspect	Health/Safety Impact	Env. Rating	H&S Rating

Purolator Environmental, Health & Safety Objectives and Targets (QSF-98-005, Rev. 1)

Site:	Proposed by:	Date:

Proposed Objective:

Proposed Target:

Consideration has been given to the factors below in order to determine the feasibility of the proposed objective and target. All responses should include some explanation.

Applicability		Consideration	Explanation
Yes	No		
		Does inaction pose a risk in satisfying legal or other requirements?	
		Does this objective affect a significant environmental, health, or safety aspect/impact? If yes, then list or reference aspect & impact in "explanation" column.	
		Is the technology available to address this objective?	
		Does this objective fit our business directives and operational requirements?	
		Are the views of other interested parties affected by this objective?	
		Is this objective consistent with our EH&S policy?	
		Does this objective support our commitment to prevention of pollution?	
		Does this objective support our strategy for clean: process, product, plant, planet, & profit?	
Estimated Cost of Proposal:			

Definitions:
Feasible	Objective and target accepted as submitted
Conditional	Objective and target accepted with modifications, as explained below
Not Feasible	Objective and target not accepted at this time, as explained below

Sign-Off:

1. Manufacturing or Area Manager & Date	Feasible	Conditional	Not Feasible
Explanation:			
2. Environmental Manager & Date	Feasible	Conditional	Not Feasible
Explanation:			
3. Occupational Health & Safety Manager & Date	Feasible	Conditional	Not Feasible
Explanation:			
4. Operations Director or Manager & Date	Feasible	Conditional	Not Feasible
Explanation:			

Signed-off copy distribution: Initiator, signer, business plan update, management representative

INDEX

Tools for Engagement

Tools
for
Engagement

Managing Emotional States
for Learner Success

THE BRAIN STORE
Resources for Growing Minds ®

Eric Jensen

Tools for Engagement: Managing Emotional States for Learner Success

Eric Jensen

 ©2003 The Brain Store®

Designer: Tracy Linares
Project Editor: Karen Graves

Printed in the United States of America
Published by The Brain Store®, Inc.
San Diego, CA, USA

ISBN #1-890460-38-9

Library of Congress Cataloging-in-Publication Data

Jensen, Eric
Tools for Engagement
Includes biographical references and index.
ISBN: #1-890460-38-9
I. Education—Teaching.

For additional copies or bulk discounts contact:

The Brain Store®, Inc.
4202 Sorrento Valley Blvd., #B • San Diego, CA 92121
Phone (858) 546-7555 • Fax (858) 546-7560 • www.thebrainstore.com

Table of Contents

A List of Activities
by Chapter

Chapter 3

- Anticipatory Rituals • Breathing • Stretching • Chair Movement • Directions that Evoke Anticipation • Goal Setting • Musical Deadlines • Graphic Organizers • Stand and Listen • Hypothesis Generation • Identify the Person Who… • Mind Map® • Mind Your Ps and Qs (Prompts and Questions) • Quiz in Advance • Return Responses • Ripple Call • Role Model • Send to a Spot • Taking the Stage • Teasers • Unfinished Sentences • Universal Questions • Voting on a Topic • Write Now! • Written Questions

Chapter 4

- BPM is Up! • Call-Response Psych-Ups • Commercial Breaks • Competitive Games • Dance • Deadlines • Jump! • Keystone Rally Walk • "Launch Pad" Directions • Marching • Massage • Seat Switching • Match Your States • Mixer Walks • Movement Bursts • Peer Suspense • Quick Breaths • Relays • Simon Says • Standing • Touch Gold • Triangle Tag

Chapter 5

- Accountability • Circle Run-Ons • Deadlines • Group Quizzes • Group Review • Limited Resources • Look at Your Neighbor's Paper • Novelty • Read-Arounds • Teach a Partner • Think-Pair-Share • Turn-To • Universal Questions • Walkabouts • Whips

Chapter 6

- Agree or Disagree? • Brain Breaks • Cars in Motion • Seat Switching • Clapping Games • Creative Handshakes • Cross Laterals • Finger Math • Humor • Imaginary Object Pass • Macarena • Musical Chairs • Pass a Face • Visualization • Stretching • Voting on a Topic

Chapter 7

- Affirmations • Birthdays • Brain Gym • Call-Response Wrap-Ups • Compliments • Grateful Reflection • Group Reviews • Mental Relaxation • Sustained Movement • Music • Pleasure Questions • Recognition • Responsibility •Stretching • Support Teams

Chapter 8

- Ad Madness • Agree or Disagree? • Air Writing • Anniversary Party • Audience Reviews • Ball Toss • Balloon Review • Bingo • Brainstorming • Calling Cards • Group Quizzes • Circle Add-Ons • Compare and Contrast • Divide and Conquer • Fairy Tales • Feedback • Filling Potholes • Fishing for Gems • Graphic Organizers • Group and Regroup • If-Thens • Jigsaw • Ketchup Catch-Up • Lyrical Learning • Musical Messages • Nonlinguistic Representation • Paper Airplane Follow-Up • Point to the Place • Quick Draw • Read and Share • Repeat After Me • Resident Expert • Ring of Fire • Sentence Affirmations • Snow Ball • Think-Pair-Share • Summarize Learning • Timeline Review • Topic Tag Lines • Wacky Words • Write Now!

Chapter 9

- Acknowledgements • Body Relaxers • Breathe through the Nose • Environment • Focusing Strategies • Journaling • Music and Drawing • Mental Vacation • Reflection and Planning • Settling Time • Storytelling • Stretching

Chapter 10

- Celebrations • Praise • Problem-Solving Success • Repetitive Gross Motor Movement • Social Bonding • Winning or Achieving Success • Prediction of Reward

Preface

We often think of learning as either active or passive. Passive learning clearly has its place. We effortlessly absorb all kinds of knowledge just by watching and listening, often paying minimal or no attention. But if you care about the results of your students you'll be interested in active learning. With the right tools in hand, you can create engaging, non-threatening learning that also feels good. How? Research shows that people who do the most talking, thinking, reflecting or moving do the most learning. Additionally, the research clearly shows that when learners feel good about what, how and with whom they learn, they're more likely to want to do it again. The next time you see someone in your audience grading papers, talking to others or reading the newspaper, take heart.

> ### Let's raise the bar because "good enough" is no longer good enough.

This book is a practical, comprehensive resource that explains how to elicit better learning states and help your audience become more engaged, focused and successful. It is for anyone who teaches elementary, adolescent or adult learners and its premise is that there are no unreachable students. This unflinching attitude combined with the right skills can help you succeed with every learner. My message is simple: It's time to raise the bar of your teaching or training standards. There

are limits to how much your audience can absorb and limits to their patience. Education is neither a game nor an opportunity for personal pontification. Don't waste your audience's time. Today they expect more from you as a presenter.

This book is *not* a guide to smart lesson planning, creating relevant, meaningful curriculum or establishing positive personal relationships. If these strategies are missing from your toolbox, you have little chance of success with your audience. Many other sources address those critical ingredients of the learning process. Nor is this a book of things to do *to* the audience; rather, it's chock full of tools to use *with* them—things in which they actively participate. The "dean" of active learning once said, "You can tell students what they need to know very fast. But they will forget what you tell them even faster" (Silberman, 1996). That's why *every single suggestion or strategy* within these pages is one that engages most or all of your audience. Keep in mind that with a simple tweak, *any activity* can be adapted to *any age*. This book will work for your students once you think through what adaptations are necessary to optimize it for them.

You may be a bit skeptical that you can have such influence over your student population. After all, years of your experience suggest that you can lead a horse to water, but you can't make it drink. Well, you're right. You can't make a horse drink —but you can make it thirsty. Experienced trainers take the horse out for a quick run or even salt the oats to encourage its thirst. My point is that you are not helpless. And though I would never say that you can *control* your students the way you might want to, I will say this:

> **You have far more influence over your students than you have ever, ever imagined.**

Everything you do as a teacher or trainer in some way influences the brains of your students. Recent scientific data supports the relationships between talking and changes in the brain, physical activity and changes in the brain, and learning strategies and changes in the brain. You may not be up to date on the very latest discoveries in neuroscience, but research has come a long way. We now know that humans can influence their own heart rate, brain chemistry and stress levels. "There is [even] firm evidence that any single neuron or any population of neurons [in your brain] can come to be voluntarily controlled (with practice)…in about ten minutes" (Baars & McGovern, 1996). This evidence suggests that what goes on inside the heads of your students is not completely inaccessible. Certainly things like food, trauma, drugs and neurofeedback are among the most powerful modulators of brain activity, but they aren't appropriate for an educator like you to use. This book, instead, is full of realistic, practical things you can do to really make a difference in the lives of your audience.

If you're good at what you do, you have learned to *involve and engage*, not show and tell. And you don't just entertain your audience in the kind of engagement I'm talking about. Humor has its place and we all like to put smiles on faces, but getting an audience to laugh every thirty seconds is not the sign of a good trainer or educator. It may be instead a sign that you have missed your calling as an entertainer. I have heard far fewer *funny* presenters who were effective, than *effective* speakers who were funny. Personally, I focus on activating my audience physically, emotionally and mentally. If they're not actively learning, I'm doing a poor job and no sob story or lame excuse can disguise it.

Believe and expect that the strategies in this book will work. Not only are they highly practical and learner-tested, but evidence also suggests that if you honestly believe in the efficacy of the strategies you are using, your chances of success rise dramatically (Dossey, 1993). That's why this book was written for truly caring presenters who want to serve and engage their learners by making their presentations come alive.

As an educator, I never had any formal training in these tools. I was unprepared to deal with the challenges of teaching and training without re-tooling myself professionally. We are all expected to somehow "pick up" these presentation tools "somewhere." Well, this book you've picked up is full of great ideas. I'm trusting you'll appreciate how my background in neuroscience brings a potent and fresh approach to your challenge of reaching every learner. Whether you think this book is pure genius or full of baloney, I'd like to hear from you. Send me an email at *info@jlcbrain.com* with your feedback. Thanks! Now, read on…

Chapter 1
"What Are States?"

Have you ever done something just because you "felt like it"? Did you ever have someone tell you that you weren't acting like yourself? Have you ever done something a little crazy and later admitted that you didn't know what had come over you, that it was so unlike you? Have you ever reminded yourself to put on a good face for a meeting? Do you have friends who make you laugh a lot? These experiences are nearly universal. When you aren't exactly "yourself," you can be said to have entered an "altered state."

States Are Weather in Your Brain

Our many selves and other feeling-moments are called "states." A major revelation in the history of neuroscience was the discovery that all external behaviors somehow correlate to the brain's internal processes. All states of consciousness, from sleeping, imagining, hoping and dreaming to thinking, are the results of electrical and chemical activity in our brain. Not only that, each individual electron generates its own activity, both electrical and chemical. Millions of neurons cooperate to form complex, web-like signaling systems that represent the behaviors we call states just as the wind, sunshine and moisture collectively form the complex atmospheric patterns we call weather. States create "weather" conditions in our brains at every moment. In your brain, though, this weather usually changes every few seconds. Knowing today's weather outside does not allow you to predict the weather very far in the future; knowing this moment's brain weather or state does not help you predict future states more than a few moments in advance. But there's a bright side! Unlike the weather in the outside world, you have some say-so and control over the weather in your own brain. To a larger degree, you can control the quality of your life.

Here's another analogy: If our personalities are like long-running TV shows, our states are just quick scenes or snapshots from one episode. You've probably observed that *we all* go through changes of states (unless we're in a coma—only in extreme medical conditions do we have stable states). States change as our sensations (hungry, tired, itchy, etc.), feelings (guilty, happy, worried, etc.) and thoughts (optimistic, gullible, focused, etc.) combine and recombine simultaneously. But states are not intangible, as we once thought; instead, *they are highly quantifiable, very real and definitely cognitive* (Damasio, 1994) and we're more conscious of them than you might think. When you remark that you don't feel like doing something, what you're really saying is that you aren't in a state in which it seems like a good idea. Think about it. We've all done something that we later explained to ourselves "seemed like a good idea at the time." Again, your feelings, actions and thoughts all combined into a recognizable state. In fact, each physical and mental aspect of your body "contributes a content that is part and parcel of the workings of the normal mind" (Damasio, 1994).

What we feel is what is real— it's the link to how we think.

Why should you care about states and why is this book focused on them? For one, states combine our emotional, cognitive and physical interactions to make all our decisions. We can call our emotional states "action sets" because they prepare "the organism *[us]* to act in some ways rather than in others" (Frijda, 1986). If we put our learners into particular action sets, we can better orchestrate the conditions that will optimize their learning. But don't think of learning as a fixed, stimulus-response relationship between teacher and student; evoking specific emotional states allows learners more freedom, not less, to make new discoveries. Once you learn to evoke a greater variety of learner states, you will begin to *uncouple the learner's rigidity.* You'll open up enormous flexibility in the interaction between the learner and the environment because you've artificially decoupled the narrow, stereotyped set of behaviors to which the learner may have become accustomed. But we will study emotional states for these reasons, too:

Frequent State Changes Uncouple Learner "Rigidity"

| Extended, "stuck" states are self-reinforcing. | Eliciting more states leads to greater learner flexibility and fewer stuck states. |

❖ *Emotions involve cognitive appraisals.*

❖ *States can involve conscious awareness.*

❖ *Emotions and cognition activate overlapping response systems.*

❖ *Our cognition is shaped by emotions.*

❖ *Our activities are shaped by sensations and emotions.*

We can use the same principles and processes to study states that we have used to study cognitive psychology (Lane et al., 2000). Therefore, we are interested in a wide variety of state-change indicators, including heart rate, activity level, stress levels, posture, hunger level and more. Although we could say that there will always be some randomness in our brains—at the micro-level, changes from one state to another occur through generalized electrical and chemical activations —for the most part, states obey reliable rules. Understand these rules about states and you'll be living the presenter's high life! Let's look at these rules and see if we can piece this all together.

First of all, states are what we live for. We live to feel satisfied; we live to have a body in which we feel confident; we live to have sensations of pleasure at play-time. In fact, we like pleasure states so much that some of us abuse drugs, overeat, gamble or have sexual affairs. Others enjoy state changes in simpler ways, with hot fudge sundaes, shopping sprees, new cars or going to the theater. The bottom line is that states mean so much to us they are the only (absolutely *only*) things we ever pay money for! Think of the last few times you spent money for any reason at all. Did you...?

❖ *Pay bills? That rid you of a state of anxiety about being in debt or under obligation.*

❖ *Buy new clothes? That helped you feel better in a new, well-dressed state.*

❖ *Give to a charity? Now you feel satisfied for helping another person.*

❖ *Go out to eat? Food helps you enjoy the state of being "full" and the pleasure of being served a meal is relaxing.*

❖ *Pay someone to clean your house? Having the work already done relieves your stress about a cluttered home and makes you feel a little bit spoiled and delightfully indulgent.*

Harvard neuroscientist Allan Hobson says, "The basic action that the brain-mind takes to keep itself fit is to change its state" (1994). My point is simpler. We run our lives (in a funny kind of way) based on what states our actions will produce. You bought this book because, although you dislike parting with hard-earned cash, you realized that if you master some of

these tools, you'd be in a more confident, happier state during your next presentation and would therefore succeed with more students. In other words, you traded your money for the chance to change your state from uncertainty to hope and, later on, self-confidence. If I haven't quite made my case that states are important to everyone, consider this: When babies cry, we comfort them into a better state; when teenagers complain, we tell them to "snap out of it" and get into a better state; if our spouses whine, we (hopefully) give them hugs of support to make them feel better. It's pretty easy to conclude that positively affecting students' states can and should be a big part of an educator's role.

Motivation & Loved Ones

States influence our motivation. Every state that you enter increases the probability that you'll engage in a particular behavior because certain behaviors are attracted to certain states. If you are tired and have the opportunity, you're likely to take a nap. But if you are not in a state of fatigue, having a couch and the luxury of time will not trigger sleep. If I come home after a long day at work and put my feet up to relax on the sofa, then I enter a relaxed state. If my wife asks me to do a favor while I am in this state, I probably won't feel much like doing it. Not because I don't love her (I do, of course), but because of the state I'm in. If I were already walking around the house looking for something to do, that would be a much better time for her to ask me to help her. So what, you may ask, does all this about my wife and me have to do with you? Plenty, my friend!

States Provide a "Pool of Choices" from Which All Behaviors Emerge

silly, happy, crazy, fun states

lead to...

behaviors like this

serious, mindful, intellectual, thoughtful states

lead to...

behaviors like this

If you ask someone for a favor when he or she is not in the right state of mind, you'll likely be ignored or turned down; if that person does the favor at all, it will probably be with great reluctance. If you're smart, however, you'll wait until that person is in a "doing favors" state. If you're even smarter, you'll prompt them to enter that positive state and then ask for a favor. (Perhaps a hot cup of tea or a kind word would move things along?) For example, don't ask your teenager to take the trash out when he's kicking back playing video games. He's probably in a

"veg-out, do-no-chores" state and will grumble about helping you. Wait until he's in an upright, vertical position—preferably walking—and then ask him. "Hey, son!" you might say. "On your way out the door, be sure to grab the garbage. Today is trash day." He may still grumble about it, but he'll do that chore and with much less resistance.

Now, I can hear those wheels spinning inside your head; you're thinking about all those times people gave you grief over the simplest tasks. Remember how you quickly you tired of all the groaning and whining and just did those tasks yourself? Well, here's some hope for the future!

All States Precede Behaviors—Change the State So the Behavior Can Follow

There's a complex interplay going on inside our heads between states and behavior. We act our way into some states and behave according to the state we're in at the moment (Grigsby & Stevens, 2000). Think about this: Even if you prefer to eat at home, sometimes you really start to enjoy the act of going out to dinner once you are seated at the restaurant. The reverse also happens. We'll get hungry and think of a favorite place to eat, and we find ourselves ready to go there! In short, we influence our states and our states influence us. Research at Stanford University has demonstrated that even the simplest act of moving our facial muscles can change our state (Ekman & Davidson, 1993). And what could be easier than a smile?

Differences Between Two States Can Be Subtle or Dramatic

States Are Always in Motion Because They Are Real-Time, Shifting, Neural Networks

Now that I've introduced state "basics" (and hopefully put you in the state of wanting to learn more), we can explore the science behind them. States are frequently activated, fast-changing, specific neural networks that typically incorporate multiple areas of the brain. Thousands, often millions, of neurons comprise the integrated combinations of mind, body and feelings that are states. These internal systems cannot be separated. The mind influences the body in a way similar to the way a sore muscle or upset stomach influences the mind. Even the sensorimotor system is packed with cognitive representations (Jeannerod, 1999)—you have to think to move! Picture states

as global mind-body experiences that dominate your life, shift quickly and provide most of your joy (or misery) on a daily basis.

Surprisingly, states are neither concrete nor reliable "things," even though we often refer to them as such. Technically, they are moving targets, constantly fluctuating because of their high sensitivity to both the internal and external environment. It makes sense to describe states as "emergent properties" of our self-organizing brains because they are *always* in a state of flux (Grigsby & Stevens, 2000). Even though you may experience your own state as stable at any particular moment, it is always in the process of strengthening, diminishing or changing to another state. Most of these implicit changes are subtle but they are encoded into the cortex as part of our ongoing stream of consciousness (Vaughan, 1997). In fact, the majority of our states are more like background moods, occupying secondary positions of which we are hardly conscious. Nonetheless, they are noticeable when we are able to stop, listen and feel for them.

Keep this concept in mind as you read this book: States are normally subtle and shifting (Clore & Ortony, 2000), but, as presenters, we will make them more overt in order to manage them methodically. And even though we'll talk about changing another person's state, remember that it was going to change anyway. We merely guide, influence or nudge it in the direction of our choice. But how does that happen?

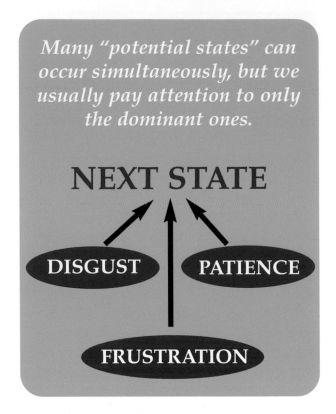

Many "potential states" can occur simultaneously, but we usually pay attention to only the dominant ones.

NEXT STATE

DISGUST   **PATIENCE**

FRUSTRATION

States Are Patterns

States are self-organized. Our brain is fundamentally a "pattern-forming, self-organized system governed by nonlinear dynamical laws" (Kelso, 1997), which suggests that all the behaviors you and I see are the result of states that arise from patterns of spatiotemporal (space-time) brain activity. These patterns are actually cooperative neural clusters, activated by both chemical and electrical energy. If one enters a state again and again, the neurons involved tend to *coalesce into cooperative groups*, self-organizing into a collective behavior we call "stable states." Imagine it this way: Our neurons may be busy all day doing many different tasks, but can arrange themselves into specialized clusters or "neural mobs" within a split second just to help you begin an important action, react to something hot or take a stand on an issue (or on a

table!). Then, as quickly as they temporarily assembled and connected themselves, they can disassemble like a falling house of cards. There are a few rules that guide the formation, stability and instability of these predictable, spatiotemporal, neuronal assemblies. Some of the ones we've introduced so far are:

❖ *States are like weather in your brain.*

❖ *States run your lives.*

❖ *States regulate motivation.*

❖ *States precede behaviors.*

❖ *States are shifting neural networks.*

❖ *States are always in motion.*

❖ *States are self-organized.*

States Are Self-Organized Patterns Governed by Non-Linear Laws

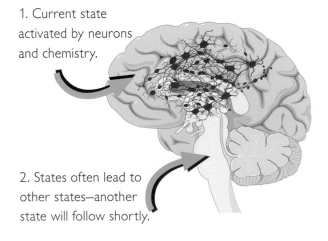

1. Current state activated by neurons and chemistry.

2. States often lead to other states—another state will follow shortly.

Another rule is that all learning takes place at the synaptic level and all states are collections of attracted, recruited and activated synapses. It sure sounds like states are pretty significant, doesn't it? Well, they are. We could even go so far as to say that:

> *Learning is the process by which spatiotemporal assemblies are "memorized" by our system.*

States are so strong, in fact, that we rarely unlearn anything. Instead, we create newer, more attractive states to enter (Grigsby & Stevens, 2000), which happens both consciously and unconsciously all of the time. Learning, which we could say is the physical "rewiring" of our synapses, requires just the right balance of neurotransmitter chemicals (released at the synapses where axons talk to dendrites) and neuromodulator chemicals (which travel through the bloodstream).

If you're skeptical about your ability to influence the brain chemistry of other people, ask yourself the following questions. Have you ever stressed out your class? Have you ever relaxed and calmed your audience? Have you ever initiated a classroom celebration of success? Do you organize social groupings within your audience? Have you ever created a sense of urgency to spur groups to take action? If you can answer "Yes" to any of these questions, then you have influenced the brain chemistry of other people. Since you do have some influence over these biological phenomena, you might as well learn how to use it skillfully.

If you're worried that this seems a lot like mind control, I have two things to say to you:

1. It is. (But you're being paid to influence other minds, aren't you?)
2. Most people need some initial support to manage their own states.

Ideally, you'd like to empower your audience to manage all of their own states. At the outset, you will probably be the only "manager" of states in your classroom or training session, but your long-term goal should be to help others learn how to manage their own states by themselves. Realizing this goal, though, takes a while. In the meantime, I never feel guilty about successfully manipulating the states of others around me. Good parents guide their children. Kids influence classmates. A comedian or a singer manipulates a crowd for a living. I've induced you to read this book. Managing someone's state of mind doesn't seem sneaky and underhanded to me   but how does one really do it?

It Takes Practice to Get to the Promised Land: The Law of State Stability and State Flexibility

In general, states originate in the brain stem, the hypothalamus, the thalamus, the cingulate cortex and the somasensory cortex (Damasio, 2000). States are monitored and maintained by a different set of structures in both the dorsal area of the frontal lobes and the orbitofrontal cortex (Damasio, 1999). Trying to suppress all other potential variations of our states uses a lot of our resources. What we think of as concentration is actually our effort to keep constant our fluctuating, emerging neural networks. People who do this very well are able to perform at high levels again and again, a skill richly rewarded by our society. You may recognize some of their names: Michael Jordan, Oprah Winfrey, Wayne Gretsky, Carol Burnett and Robin Williams. If you can stay in a productive, focused state—which is hard to do—you have an excellent chance of achieving professional success.

> *Intelligence building is enhanced by managing two key state variables:*
>
> ## CONTINUITY
> *(strength and persistence of previous, useful states)*
>
> ## FLEXIBILITY
> *(capacity for variability and responsiveness to context demands)*

Highly adaptable and successful learner systems exhibit state continuity and state flexibility, or the ability to stay in the same state or change it at will. This talent comes from a combination of genetics, environment, personal will and maturing frontal lobes, all of which are required for most school-based learning tasks. Individuals with low adaptability and chaotic patterns find it very hard to learn and are often looked upon as discipline "handfuls." These individuals have difficulty managing their own states and will *always* have the proverbial cards stacked against them. Internally, these students

may not be good at reading other's states, regulating their own or managing the states of those around them. State management, as you now know, is a very important life and learning skill.

One Grain of Sand Can Destabilize the Entire Pile and Change Its Shape

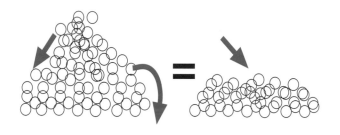

States Are So Subtle That a Grain of Sand Changes Our World

Here's another way to think about states: If you continually add one grain of sand to a sand pile, eventually you'll get a sand landslide that transforms its shape. But imagine a constant stream of sand falling onto a pile, building it higher than the point of stability. It will inevitably collapse. States are like that. Although one minor event usually won't change our state, there are exceptions. Over time, after many grains of sand have formed the pile that represents our mental state, even a minor event (like an ill-timed comment) can cause our state to slide into another. Consider how a day in which nothing goes well can put us into a crabby state. Once we are in that state, it takes only a small event like a friend's criticism to destabilize us further and we lash out in anger at someone who doesn't deserve it.

In one scenario, a particular event may have no effect on a state but in another scenario, the same event may change a state completely. This observation about states leads us to further define them as non-linear, which means that they are not predictable on a small scale (within just one person at a given time). We can also say that they are contingent on a number of internal dynamic factors, among them hunger, age, menstrual cycles, thirst, body temperature, moods, sleep-awake cycles and stress levels. At any given moment, a snapshot of these factors playing themselves out could be thought of as a portrait of our state. Some of these factors are genetic and some are environmental (Siever & Frucht, 1997), but all of them are the result of complex subsystems in our bodies that power and identify our "signature states." Many of these signature states are so common in us that others learn to rely on us going into them in certain emotional or physical situations.

There Are Countless Possible States, Each Consisting of Neural Networks with a Unique Electro-Chemical Signature

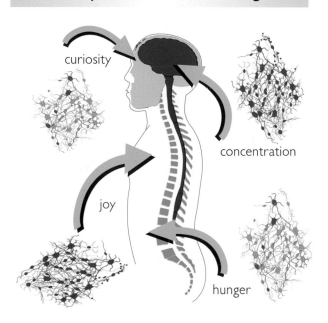

Learning Requires Attractor States for Receptivity, Understanding and Retrieval

The signature states that we enter most often are called attractor states. Our brain strengthens those neural networks and integrates the emotions and sensations specifically for that state. Soon, those states become even easier to enter. In other words, we are attracted to those states by our internal environment (homeostasis) according to *how often we're in them.* Some people laugh a lot because that's their primary attractor state. Others are angry a lot—that's their strongest attractor state. Some signature states, like depression, mania, violence or delirium, might never or rarely occur in one person while frequently plaguing another. People who are often angry will find that anger becomes their attractor or most stable state. That state becomes their allostatic (adjusted stress load) state, instead of the healthier homeostatic state. The result is that they will often pick fights with others just to feel "like themselves" by re-entering that familiar state.

When others observe and identify our signature states, they label those states as part of our personality. Our personalities stick because they are amalgamations of states we find very easy to enter and stay in. States that never occur or might occur only for an extremely short time are called repeller states. Our systems naturally repel these states when we move towards them. We tend to avoid them because the complex interplay of our intent (frontal lobes) and the myriad of our other subsystems (emotions, hunger, high-low energy cycles, heart rate, etc.) indicate that we'll find no good maintaining in those states.

Wide Range of States

Variations include intensity, duration and specificity.

Our learning is the process by which our system memorizes these neuronal assemblies (our states) until they become attractor states. Now can you see why it is essential to keep audience members in the right state? It regulates their learning! Over time, new states prompt different behaviors and eventually create new minds and personalities. For so many people, school and learning states are repeller states because of their experience with frustration, boredom, anxiety or other negative factors. As educators, we should be helping our students turn their learning states into positive, attractor states.

State stability is managed partly with practice and partly by our frontal lobes. To look at it from the flip side, state instability is triggered internally by a separate host of factors. Since not all brains and bodies are the same, many people have more internal stability while others have stronger fluctuations. I mentioned earlier that hunger, age, monthly cycles, moods, thirst, body temperature and sleep-awake cycles are state changers. But other things influence them, too.

Our amygdala, thalamus and hypothalamus are constantly responding to outside stimuli. Our stomach sends us messages. Our pain centers might tell us that we have a stiff back. Our eyes may feel dry or our skin itchy. In other words, many complex factors, both internally regulated and externally stimulated, "conspire" to keep our states in flux. Given all these factors and their range of intensity, it's a wonder we stay in any state for more than a few seconds. That's one reason I find writing books so hard; staying in that relatively "foreign" state of focus for long enough requires enormous frontal lobe discipline. But I take great pleasure in the rewards (a finished book), so I endure the intense state required of the effort. People can (and do) enter foreign states all the time for a variety of reasons. Think of all those news stories about supposedly sane people who enter states so unusual that they actually kill another human.

A Murderous State

So far, we have seen that we have both attractors that attract us to certain states (which form much of the personality that others attribute to us) and repellers that prevent us from entering certain states. Nonetheless, almost any of us can be pushed into extreme states. Twice in my life I have plotted to kill another person. No, I'm not an extremist or a pathological killer. Once I was a desperate child planning to poison my extremely abusive stepmother. I'm glad I didn't do it, but it seemed like a good idea at the time. Years later, while traveling, I was kidnapped by two thugs. I seriously considered killing my abductors before I eventually figured out how to negotiate my way out of captivity. These represent two wildly varied circumstances but in both cases, because my life was at risk, I maintained an intense state strong enough and long enough to consider murder.

In one way, it's just a variation of the state that inspires a person to enlist in the military and go off to war. The United States Marine Corps can make the idea of killing an enemy seem very patriotic or like a reasonable act of defense. But extreme states can also be triggered in the most ordinary environments, and not necessarily during an emergency on the scale of the September 11, 2001 disaster at the World Trade Center. School snipers can trigger this state, as can the suicide of a well-liked classmate, a romantic break-up or an athlete's tension about the outcome of a play-off football game (remember the grains of sand falling onto a pile?). States are indeed the scaffolding that structures our lives.

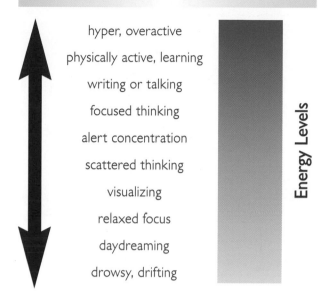

States Are the Primary Determinants of Behavior

hyper, overactive
physically active, learning
writing or talking
focused thinking
alert concentration
scattered thinking
visualizing
relaxed focus
daydreaming
drowsy, drifting

Energy Levels

We Can Pay Attention to Only One State at a Time!

States are typically so consuming, you might have guessed that there are limits to manipulating them. In fact, consider it a blessing that you can only pay attention to one single state at a given time. Now, I didn't say you couldn't *experience* more than one state at a time (which is admittedly hard to do); I said you could only *be aware of* one state at a time. That's because each dynamic, emergent state requires a unique signature, or trigger set of activators. These activators may include synaptic activity (connectivity of neural networks), hormonal activity (maybe an increase or decrease in cortisol or estrogen), physiological activity (posture changes or movement) and neurotransmitter activity (maybe a lowered level of serotonin or dopamine). Activating this complex set of attractors

How Students Regulate Their States

• talking • social contact • hydration
• medications • movement/fidgeting • music
• sports • drug abuse • romance
• sleeping • lighting variations • food choices

all at once is a very specific and highly dynamic process. There is no separation of the mind, body and feelings. In short, it's not easy to stay in a state for very long and it's not easy to be in two states at once. You can feel hungry but then be immediately distracted by curiosity. You may enter two or three different states within ten seconds. While hungry, you might say yes to the idea of spaghetti for dinner. But later on, a state of boredom with Italian food might tempt you to try out a new Greek restaurant in town. Again, different states prompt different behaviors.

If you put on a frown, slump down in a chair and shake your head back and forth in the classic "no way" pattern, it's difficult to think positive, uplifting thoughts. (Nor do we write very good love letters when we are angry.) But when we're happy, we rarely honk our horn at careless drivers on the road. Why? States contain their own

guidelines and constraints involving not just the neural networks we mentioned earlier, but also the various chemicals known more specifically as neuromodulators. These chemical groups travel through the bloodstream and enter the brain as peptides, interleukins, hormones and cytokines. While neurotransmitters are the primary stimulus between neurons, neuromodulators influence this interaction. It's not an automatic process; how you feel constantly changes the quality of your brain's interactions. While you are focused on a particular state, only one fixed set of thoughts, behaviors and feelings are available to you. Until you change your state, the thoughts, feelings and actions of other states are unavailable. That means that you cannot easily activate the behaviors of one state when you are in another.

> *Manage states well and the learning will take care of itself.*

In short, states are complex. But remember—anytime you want to change the behavior of your audience, begin first with a change of state. New states create new attractors for memory, emotions, information and behaviors and that may be just what is necessary to make presentations and activities work.

Where in Our Brains Do States Occur? What's in Charge of My Brain?

There is no one area in the brain that is functionally equipped to process all three sources for our states (emotions, sensations and thoughts). States can occur anywhere; it just depends on which state we are referring to at the moment. In general, the representation of body states that are more sensory-based occurs in the insula and parietal regions. These sensations often compete with other input. We experience feelings that are mediated by the hypothalamus, amygdala, the dorsal frontal lobes, ventromedial frontal lobes and orbitofrontal cortex. We experience thoughts (which may be verbal) originating in the superior temporal lobes and dorsal frontal cortex. On top of all that, information in the brain moves in multiple directions—there are no "one-way" signs in your head! We have multiple, parallel and converging information streams. Still, without exceptions, all states include emotions, activity and cognition (Schulkin, 2000). Remember, states are activating entire neuronal assemblies, so their presence will be felt across the whole brain.

The fast-moving world inside your body and brain turns everything—every idea, feeling, action, belief, sensation or decision you've ever named—into a state. Three physical qualities define them:

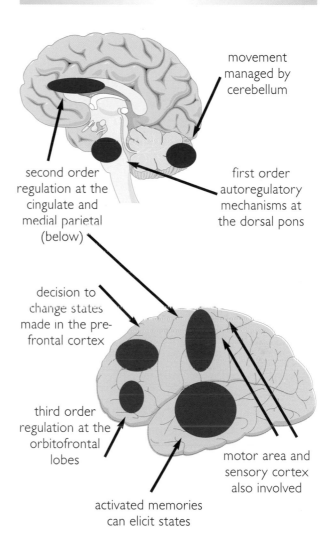

Brain Areas Involved with Regulation of States

movement managed by cerebellum

second order regulation at the cingulate and medial parietal (below)

first order autoregulatory mechanisms at the dorsal pons

decision to change states made in the pre-frontal cortex

third order regulation at the orbitofrontal lobes

motor area and sensory cortex also involved

activated memories can elicit states

The *amount* of activity: From semi-consciousness to dreaming, brainstorming sessions or even seizures, the sheer number of neurons firing (from thousands to millions) influences states.

The *source* of activity: The source of information continually shifts from being primarily *external* while you're awake, alert, and conscious to mostly *internal* while you dream or indulge in fantasies.

The *mode* of the activity: Chemical activity shifts from acetylcholine-dominated (restorative, low-volition encoding of memories) to amine-dominated (activity-dominated, high volition creation of new memories). Amines include serotonin, dopamine and epinephrine. Other modes are influenced by neuromodulators like epinephrine and cortisol.

Thus, we could characterize our brain-based states by their activity, or how they are activated and by the source of their activation (Hobson, 1994). The behavioral explanation for a state could be, "I was hungry," "I stubbed my toe," or, "I received bad news." Yet there may be a multitude of other reasons behind it. For example, even subtle exposure to an offensive word, picture, person or memory could trigger a state without any understanding or realization on your part. States are, indeed, nearly infinite and often full of surprises.

The Most Popular Populations of States

What states are the most common? That depends on where you are. Go to a mental institution and get one answer; go to a prison and get another. Go to a soccer match and get a third answer and go to a local happy hour to get yet another. In short, transient populations (like people spending the day at an amusement park,

traveling on an airplane, waiting for treatment in an emergency room or attending school) come together partly because they have common needs and hopes. Commonalities attract people with common states. But a state is only partly a function of the external environment; it is also a function of an individual. If you are a passenger who travels rarely, you might experience more states of anxiety, frustration and boredom than an experienced traveler who has worked out the nuances of an airport and who probably undergoes fewer states of frustration (unless there are flight delays). States also vary by culture, with one major exception: emotions.

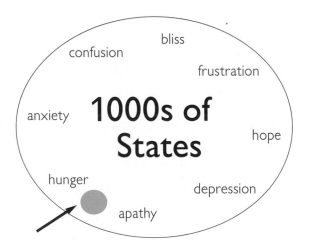

The primary emotions are joy, fear, anger, disgust, surprise and sadness.

These six emotions are a subset of all possible states and are the only states biologically "hard-wired" into the brain.

Which States Are Universal? Are Any States Hard-Wired?

A small subset of states is known as our emotions. Emotions are also biological; think of them as "hard-wired" responses common to *all* cultures. Surprisingly, they have a genetic basis (Johnston, 1999), although many researchers believe there are only a few cross-cultural, context-independent emotional states. These include anger, disgust, fear, sadness, surprise and joy (Pert, 1997). Anywhere in the world, you can give a man a piece of rotting food and he'll show the common facial expression of disgust. Anywhere in the world, you can sneak up behind someone to scare her and she'll display the universal "startle" response. But with the exception of these hard-wired, emotional states, the expression of other states is culturally learned and far less stable.

growing international population

Now that you understand what states are and do, we'll explore why it is so critical to manage states. As with all good teaching and training, understanding why you should use them is just as important as knowing how to use them.

Chapter 2
"Why Bother?"
The Rationale Behind Managing States

In the first chapter, we explored what states are and how much they influence us (all the time!). Hopefully, I made my case for the potency and value of them as a learning construct. This chapter addresses your next few questions. Now that you have a better idea of what states are, why should you bother managing them in others? Why shouldn't learners just manage *their own* states? Is it the responsibility of the educator, trainer or the learner? These are important questions both from a philosophical and pedagogical basis, but also from a practical basis. Obviously, I'm already sold on the process, but when I reflect upon it, the reasons to manage others' states seem even more compelling. There are at least five good reasons why you ought to make it your job to manage the states of your audience.

Learning Is Both the Package and the Process

Your role as an instructor is to facilitate learning and you cannot separate the content of what you offer from the social environment it is offered within. They form a complex, unified "package" that is delivered to the learning brain. If you send a package through the mail, what is the most important part of the process? The answer is that the package *and* the

delivery process are essential; one is useless without the other. Is the role of a mail carrier to travel all the routes just to meet the customers? Not without delivering packages, too! Unless the delivery process is good, the content of a package will *not be received* by a customer. Is the role of a mail service just to pick up

packages and take your money? No, it still has to deliver them. Neither the process nor package is valuable in itself.

A presenter may deliver content, but unless the learning process is completed, the package is wasted. How much of a one-hour lecture do you think the average audience member could remember, share and teach to a partner? The answer is that most audiences would be hard-pressed to remember more than five minutes (or about eight and a half percent of the lecture). Of those few minutes, it's questionable how much of would be dead-on accurate. Remember, while creating content is the mandated part of your job, the process of ensuring delivery is just as important.

Learning Requires Purposeful Layering

The human brain is not generally designed to get things right the first time. About the only exception to this rule is trauma, which takes effect in the brain immediately. Trauma smothers its sensory systems and, as a survival mechanism, our brain says, "I must remember this so I will avoid it in the future." Once we learn something new, the best way to ensure accuracy with it is through trial and error, not one-time, one-way input. Why? Because complex learning means we involve more neurons, connections and hence, larger networks. Learning not to touch a hot stove requires far fewer resources in our brains than understanding the abstract complexity of concepts like "states," "democracy," "composition" or "gravity."

Trial and error is the way to begin. Learn from mistakes because it's no sin!

To really learn, we must not only activate the right neurons in a complex neural network but also train other neurons *not* to activate. What produces good learners is not just turning the necessary switches "on" but turning some "off," too. We must get feedback for wrong answers so our brain can eliminate them from its bank of possible future answers.

We don't get smart by hearing or memorizing what someone else tells us. We get smart by eliminating poor choices through feedback-driven trial and error. After all, negative feedback mobilizes our responses better (Taylor, 1991) and creates a better change in the output of our learning systems (Cacioppo et al., 1997). Learning activities with high levels of both positive and negative feedback built into them further the learning process *far better* than *any* "sit and git" lecture. These activities include (but are not limited to):

❖ *peer teaching*
❖ *brainstorming*
❖ *discussion*
❖ *checking work against a model*
❖ *competition*
❖ *cooperative games*
❖ *team assignments*
❖ *peer editing*

If anything, our brain is designed to allow most learning to disappear from memory. Why? Because explicit learning and memory systems are governed by a "surge protector" known as the hippocampus.

Hippocampus in the Human Brain

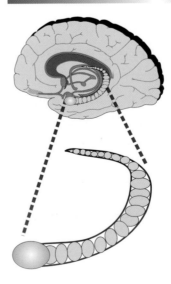

The hippocampus is a small, C-shaped structure buried deep in the temporal lobes (we have one on each side) that serves as a "surge protector" for incoming explicit information.

These two small, C-shaped structures are buried deep in each of our temporal lobes and learn fast. But the hippocampus has a small capacity and can be easily overloaded. If content exceeds capacity, it simply "rewrites" new material over old material (Kelso, 1997). This protective rewriting process prevents a destabilization from massive amounts of irrelevant input (a "slow trauma"). So, the phrase to remember as a presenter is:

Too much, too fast won't last.

It's really a form of sanity protection; we are best adapted for survival, which only represents a very narrow band of all possible learning. Note that we are good at remembering specific things like:

❖ *bad or dangerous foods (reflexive);*

❖ *extreme pain or pleasure (derived from anything from people to foods);*

❖ *locations (of home, food sources, safety and social contacts); and*

❖ *procedural survival skills (eating, walking, self-defense, grooming, etc.).*

When was the last time you forgot your way home, the name of a restaurant that served bad food or someone who said hurtful things to you? Chances are you still recall those memories. Notice that classroom lecture is absent from this list; abstract knowledge is not a high priority for a brain with survival in mind. Any time you lecture for more than five or ten minutes, you run the risk that the material will not be thought of as relevant, not be heard right or not be remembered.

All Learning Engages Brain Systems

- All experiences influence both wholes and parts.
- All parts are pieces of the larger system.
- All systems interact with other systems.
- All other systems influence their parts.
- Repetition and variation strengthen content.

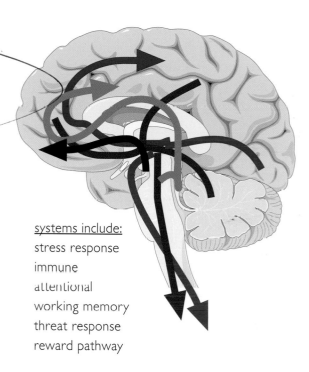

systems include:
stress response
immune
attentional
working memory
threat response
reward pathway

Bottom Line: The more systems that are engaged over time, the greater the strength and resiliency of the connections and memories. **The greater the variety of learning activities, the better.**

Humans Are Fundamentally Social Animals

Humans develop primarily within complex relational webs at work, home and play. Many primatologists now believe that social problem-solving was the force that drove human evolution, not, as earlier believed, tool-making (Whiten, 1991). Much of what we learn is learned socially, especially in school environments. Interactive, social contexts appear to be fundamental to driving healthy, quality learning. Humans are born less developed than most other mammals and require a huge amount of social and maternal investment to survive. Individuals who live in isolation are less likely to survive and certainly less likely to reproduce. While any one animal may be stronger, faster or better fighters than humans, we form the most complex social communities of any species.

The prior notion of human learning, motivation and behaviors was far simpler than today's current understanding. The older, prevailing thought was that a master set of genes activated the DNA necessary to produce the proteins that activated the neurons to produce behaviors. Clearly, everyone knew that environmental stimulus was a factor, with its own separate path of influence. This model is not only old-fashioned, it is dead wrong. How much do we know about how the environment (especially the social one) influences learning? A good deal, it turns out. We have what many refer to as a "social brain" (Dunbar, 2002). Recent neuroscience has explored a wide range of the substrates of other-generated behavior (generated by other people, that is!).

Many more things influence behavior (including many under your control) than we previously thought. For one, we now know that the specific effects of a particular gene associated with behavior vary widely, *depending on environment* (Crabbe et al., 1999). Change the environment and we suddenly switch on a gene that had not been expressed before! In other words, environment changes us and we change the environment. Our brains are not passive containers of an increasing amount of knowledge and (hopefully) wisdom. They are instead very dynamic, active, changing structures, greatly dependent on our learning, social, behavioral and health levels. One reason that many of the activities in this book are social is to harness the powerful positive effects of person-to-person contact.

The Social Climate Matters

Photo courtesy of Mary Penzenik.

"What?"
"This is so confusing!"
"That doesn't make sense."

Photo courtesy of Mary Penzenik.

"Yes!"
"Call on me!"
"I want to contribute."

There is substantial research that suggests positive affiliation and other social behaviors are mandatory for healthy and cognitively developed learners. Remember that your audience often has close social contacts among peers. For many people, going to school and sitting in isolated rooms in separate chairs, doing individual work most of the time (versus working alone only the optimal twenty to forty percent of their time) is very discouraging. In fact, after being separated from their peers, same sex companions show a marked and dangerous increase in cortisol levels, from as little as eighteen percent to as much as eighty-seven percent (Levine et al., 1999). One way for presenters and teachers to address this issue is to strengthen social ties by cultivating academic aspects to social relationships rather than separating participants for discipline reasons. Setting up a social environment may sound like a lot of work, but there is convincing evidence that social influences affect our biology, health and learning (Cacioppo et al., 2002). That's a tremendous pay-off for your efforts.

ideas / tattle / box.

How effective is a highly social learning environment? Won't students give each other misinformation? Many presenters worry that learners may mislead each other. They worry that incorrect information will get passed from participant to participant if they don't directly teach their audiences themselves. I admit, this is a possible risk, but keep these three things in mind:

❖ *Direct lecturing does not ensure accuracy, either. What you put into a learner's brain is not necessarily remembered correctly or even at all! You have nothing to lose by implementing active learning strategies.*

❖ *Multiple groupings and multiple methods will improve the accuracy of the information you are trying to teach. Never rely on just one group arrangement if you want your audience to process quality information. Always mix up the media and mix up the partners.*

❖ *If you have even the slightest concern about what you are doing, get audience feedback. Use written quizzes (which can be learner-generated). Then, have learners review, refresh and re-teach each other if necessary. Sometimes I present a think-pair-share challenge. If I see learners having a hard time repeating the material, I'll stop, review key information and (while they are still standing) have them re-do the activity correctly.*

Social Brains Influence Learning

Social contact shapes our learning through fears, hope, attraction or companionship.

- **manage relationships**
- **support connections**
- **structure social groupings**

We now also know that social climate strongly effects brain processing (Cacioppo, 1994; Cacioppo et al., 1999). Why does this matter? Social isolation is becoming a serious issue! We expect thirty-one million Americans to be living alone by 2010. In fact, social isolation is just as great a *risk factor for mortality* as cigarette smoking (House et al., 1988). We know that restriction of tactile contact in animals negatively influences stress reactivity (Meaney et al., 1985). But just as important are the pathological impacts of restricting the tactile contact of humans (Carlson & Earls, 1999). You may also know that positive social contexts appear to improve immune responses (Padgett et al., 1998). Trainers and teachers wanting learners sitting isolated in long rows, unable to speak to their neighbors, defies both common sense and current research.

With social learning, three principles are at work. The principle of *multiple determinism* specifies that a single targeted event (like an activity) will have multiple effects within or across the system. (Cacioppo & Berntson, 1992). Activities can affect genes and social contact can affect immune systems. The principle of *nonadditive determinism* means that the properties of the whole are not predictable by the properties of the parts. Amphetamines increase dominant behavior among primates in *higher* social circles but increase submissive behavior among those *lower* in the social hierarchy (Haber & Barchas, 1984). This study and others suggest a different response to exogenous influences *depending on social status.* Finally, the principle of *reciprocal determinism* suggests that there can be mutual influences between seemingly disconnected factors. For example, studies by Dolf Zillmann (1984) suggest that what we read influences our behavior and our behavior influences what we read.

I often hear teachers say that some students don't like activities and some don't like social contact. We all know from experience that with certain students, this observation is true. But if you throw out of your repertoire *every activity* or instructional method that one or more students don't like, you'd do absolutely nothing! A more likely explanation is that *the teacher, trainer or professor is uncomfortable* with more physical or social activities. Any teacher that worries about some students not liking an activity has probably never asked students how much they like being bored by a lecture.

> ## Social Climate Influences:
>
> ### Our brain chemistry and activations which influence...
>
> ### Our mindset, safety and states which influence...
>
> ### Our cognition and joy of learning which influence...
>
> ### Our interest, motivation and recall

The difference between an average teacher and a great one is easy to identify. An average teacher may be reaching, at any given time, fifty to seventy percent of the audience. A great teacher may be reaching, at any given time, fifty to seventy percent of the audience, *but a different fifty to seventy percent* each time! In other words, the great teacher uses a variety of activities and instructional methods to ensure that they reach different learners at different times. Over the course of a week or a month, the great teacher will eventually reach all the learners. The average teacher, however, will still be reaching the same learners over and over again. The average teacher, too, will lump learners by ability into a bell curve at grading time, convinced that the differences among learners are because of differences in effort or ability, not because of the teaching!

State Management Empowers Students

Over time, you'll be able to share with your audience information about how they can manage their own states. The ultimate end point of this process is to empower students to continually adjust their own states and maximize their own learning. In general, learners believe they have little control over their own states. I'm sure you've had the experience of students commenting on how others make them feel a certain way. While there's always some truth to statements like that, the reality is that state changing involves *multiple* parties. Others don't *make* you feel a certain way, but they *can* create plausible opportunities for you to do so. As a result of this interplay, most students under the age of fifteen really believe that the world is full of things that happen to them and that states are just something you have to deal with.

Why is triggering certain states important? Because almost everybody will say, "Yes!" to what you ask *if* they are in the right state. Start seeing your audience as humans in the full range of possible states, with some in more productive states than others. People in counterproductive states will learn next to nothing. Why? Because the "machinery" of learning

Always Move Learners from Their Present State to Your Target State

present state

target state

requires the right neuronal connections and the right neurotransmitters to create the right assemblies working in the right systems. The brain doesn't care *what* you're trying to learn and remember. It only knows whether the right mixture of ingredients for that "learning state" is present or not. That's why getting students into the right state is so important.

Too much talking makes them blue — more of them and less of you.

In general, states are either appetitive (positive, towards the object or event) or aversive (unpleasant, defensive, away from the object or event). If your students are in negative or counterproductive states, only negative behaviors are likely. If you take the time to put them in more positive states first, you've got a whole wide range of options available, and all of them are possible. Always be asking yourself, "What state are they in? What are my target states? How will I get there?" In time, it will become automatic to you and more productive and joyful for your students.

The longer a student stays in a counter-productive state, the chances increase that non-productivity will become an attractor state, one they'll enter easily and often. Time reinforces the states we are in, for good and bad states alike. On the bright side, they are self-reinforcing, so the more you engage your audience by using the tools of this book the more likely it is your audience will become thinking, learning and growing human beings. Gradually, your ability and commitment to influence the state of others will grow and make longer-lasting differences in your audience's lives. Be persistent!

What are some easy ways to do this? The following chapters of this book are full of them. Physical movement and activity are quick and strong influencers of student states. More activity increases the motivational brain chemicals. Walking at only two miles per hour increases norepineph-rine levels by one thousand percent, compared to remaining in a resting state (Krock & Hartung, 1992). In fact, the benefits of an activity will last for at least five more minutes after it has run its cycle, even as the students calm down. This helps explain why you want learners to stand, walk, or move as part of an assignment. Instead of passing out class materials yourself, set them on a table and let participants come get them. Better yet, put on a recording of the *William Tell Overture* (by Gioacchino Rossini), announce that you aren't sure if there are enough copies for everyone and watch how fast those learners move!

When you first demonstrate that states can be influenced (notice I avoid the word "controlled"), it gets attention. Your audience will enjoy coming to your learning experience when they have strong, positive emotional memories, feel successful and feel competent. But that's just the tip of the iceberg. There are many more benefits.

More Than 50 Chemicals Circulate Throughout the Brain, Influencing Behavior

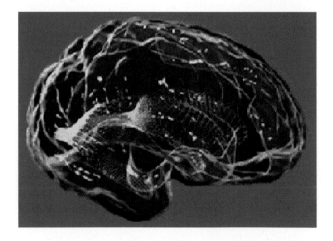

Your Job Will Be Easier

There are several positive effects of the activities that are suggested in this book. The more effectively you influence learner states, the fewer discipline problems you will experience and the more your audience will learn. In short, the better you get at using active learning, the easier your job will become. Consider these examples and discover how social experience, physical activity and rapid movements change a learner's brain and increase his or her success, with very little effort on your part.

To captivate and educate, put learners in states that invigorate.

First, any learner who is not in the appropriate brain state for an assignment, activity or directive will offer you (the illusion of) resistance. If a learner is not eager, anticipating and mobilized, he or she will be sluggish or inert. This behavior is frustrating and even demotivating to the instructor. But remember what I said in Chapter 1 about states *preceding* behavior: Put that student in a motivated state first, and your request for a state change via a new assignment or activity will be met with accommodation and even enthusiasm. This puts a smile on the faces of both teacher and student. You *can* influence your students and that influence on their states can make your job harder or easier. Nothing is set in stone; the way a class behaves is neither determined by random mood swings nor predictable only by horoscopes and current events.

You Can Positively Influence Your Learners

Nearly every activity in this book is either social or physical. Why? Because an increasing body of evidence suggests that social environments can influence everything from cardiovascular function to genetic expression, immune activity, disease, personality disorders, trauma and possibly even genetic constitution (Cacioppo et al., 2002). Increased social support is well known to decrease the blood pressure of people with hypertension (Uchino et al., 1996). Research also suggests that social experiences can modulate brain circuits that, in turn, modulate neurotransmitters (like serotonin) that, in turn, affect behavior (Yeh et al., 1996). Serotonin is a common neurotransmitter that helps regulates attention, learning, mood, neurogenesis and memory. Low serotonin is implicated in depression, which now affects five percent of all school-aged children and up to fifteen percent of all adults. You create social experiences that change the brain, which influences learning. Positive social contact can be a part of your instructional strategy; it is well known to ameliorate symptoms of depression.

WOW!

Additionally, there is a large amount of data supporting the premise that learned helplessness causes depression (Alloy & Abrahamson, 1979). Physical activity can prevent behavioral depression and learned helplessness by acting on the serotonin circuits (Greenwood et al., 2003). This research supports the idea that, when done well, games, physical activities, recess and physical education can play a significant part in improving cognition in the school climate. Plenty of studies have shown that these exercises can help students learn better (Jensen, 2000).

Never think that activities and games are too childish for your audience. When presented correctly and framed well, learners of all ages enjoy them. Adults enjoy games like charades, board games, amusement parks and recreation. Never believe that competition, costumes or social learning are too silly. We see adults participate in those all the time on television game shows. But will they do it in a learning experience? You bet!

You can empower learners of any age to practice this "therapy" on themselves. Teach them some of the factors that can influence their own states. Chances are that the lesson will resonate with them. Talk to them about how foods can influence their brain, how a brisk walk can be therapeutic or good friends can heal. The more they try out the state-changing activities you suggest and discover that they work, the better. People who feel a sense of control over their life are more likely to feel competent as learners.

> **There is no such thing as an unmotivated student. There are, however, students in unmotivated states.**

Ultimately, your goal is to empower learners to manage their own states. You can teach the basics of states management as early as kindergarten. First, teach learners to recognize their own states, even with labels as simple as color names (with an elementary school audience, for example): "Red" states could mean to pause, freeze or stop; "yellow" states perhaps indicate that you should slow down or expect a calm activity with quiet conversation; "green" states possibly represent high speeds like clean-up activities or relay games. When you call out "red state" or "green state," your class will know what that means and that they can choose to move into it at will. In time, you can introduce the more refined and subtle states. At every educational level, the students who can best manage their own states tend to be the most academically successful and have high emotional intelligence.

In sum, there are many good reasons to be the person who manages state changes within your learning environment. I've always thought that the person who knows the most, is the most responsible for teaching it to everyone else. If you're a college professor and believe that your students should come to you highly motivated since they have achieved this level of education, you're right. But being right doesn't mean that you always get your wish. Deal with the reality that many students are *not* motivated to learn and *do* need your support. If you aren't managing the states of your students in your class, they might as well stay home and take it over the Internet. If all you can offer is the delivery of content, you are fast becoming a modern-day dinosaur. Why? Because content is cheap, easy to find and, in many cases, nearly free. Take a look at the writing on the wall (or, better yet, the digital highway)! In school after school, the trend is to lower costs by reducing the need for teachers and by disbursing information electronically. If you do not create strong relationships and make your learning environment a great place to be, why would someone need to attend your class in person? Hopefully, the next eight chapters will help you become irreplaceable!

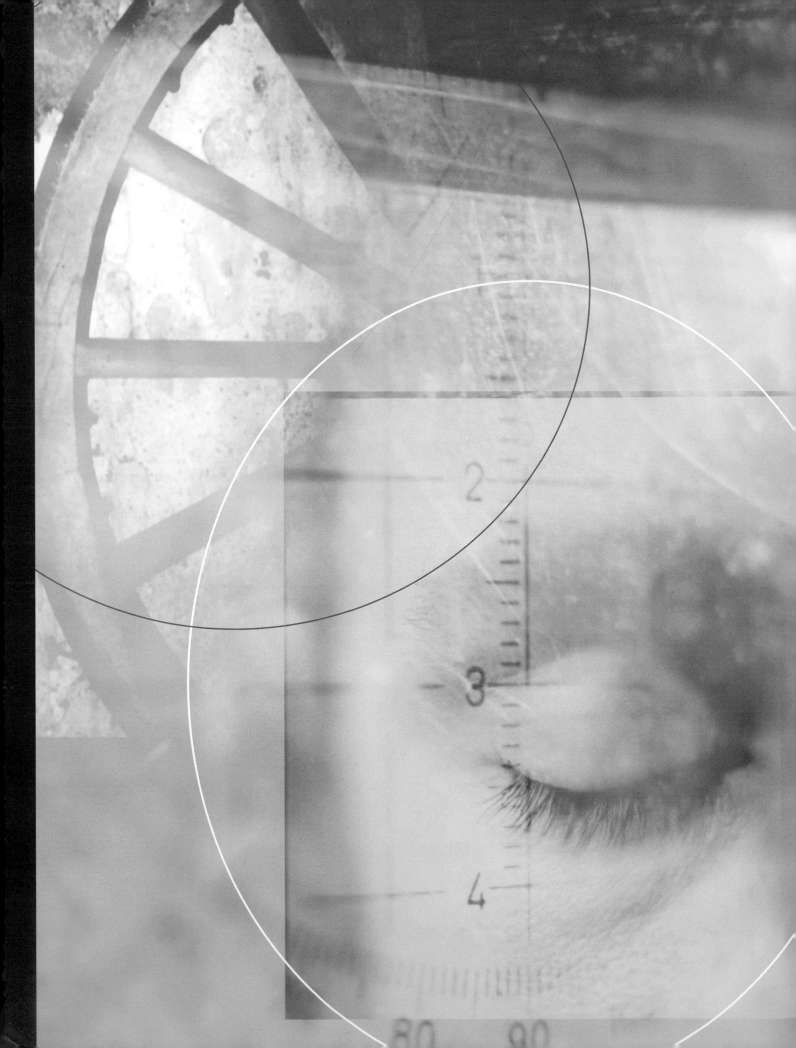

Chapter 3
"Huh?"
Arousal States for Learning (Anticipation, Curiosity and Confusion)

Normally, a resting brain is on "idle chatter." Millions of low-level communications go on inside learners' heads but that doesn't necessarily mean they are paying attention to you or your presentation. Why? Because brains need an attentional bias for learning to avoid being distracted by the sights and sounds of a chaotic classroom environment. Getting and keeping a student's attention may seem like a dignified pursuit, but the problem is that *too* many things will capture a student's attention before you do. Besides, attention alone is not specific enough of a state for learning. You want more focused and avid learning states like curiosity or anticipation. Both of these useful learning states, as well as confusion, are explored in this chapter because they affect your audience in ultimately the same way. That is, they all increase learner readiness.

Why? Curiosity and anticipation are incomplete states of waiting, of hungering for more and desiring to experience something expected. Curiosity and anticipation are known as appetitive states because they stimulate the mental appetite. They are highly motivating states that drive hungry organisms toward their goals; in this case, the goal is to satisfy their hunger to learn more (Bradley & Lang, 2000). Now, don't these states sound like things you'd like to know more about?

What Is This State?

Anticipation is the presence of an associated expectation in a preparatory manner (LaBerge, 1995). It is usually concerned with the timing of an event or with *when* something will happen. Often you already know what to expect—you just don't know how soon it will come. Anticipation is a highly useful state for learning that displays the *physiology of wanting or waiting with positive expectancy.* For low-level attention we might engage hundreds of thousands of neurons; for the high levels of attention we dedicate to our anticipatory states, we engage millions of neurons.

Anticipation could also be an example of the body's reaction to a potential (but not yet realized) threat. After all, there are legitimate types of "almost-threats" that teachers and presenters already use sparingly and appropriately in narrow circum- stances (like where immediate safety is at risk). Arne Ohman's lab at the Karolinska Institute in Stockholm, Sweden, showed that evolutionarily relevant threat stimuli are highly effective in engaging attention (Ohman et al., 2000). His lab studied facial displays (ever heard of the "evil eye"?), but other common "threat" strategies include peer pressure, serious deadlines with significant consequences if they are missed and being forced to stay after school, make reparations or give public apologies.

The state of curiosity manifests as either a content or process issue. It is typically a state of wanting something which is temporarily unfinished or unanswered. It's a state of wanting to know more about a topic—the Who, What, When, Where, Why or How of something. You can evoke student curiosity easily by tapping into existing interests. For example, some students are very interested in Golden Globe and Emmy nominations but others are far more curious about who's dating who or when football season begins.

PET Scan Reveals Areas of Brain Activated for Sustained Attention

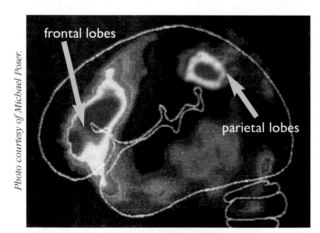

Photo courtesy of Michael Poser.

Note high activity in parietal lobes and some activity in frontal lobes.

Confusion as an Arousal State

Although you might find exceptions to this rule, confusion is typically a healthy state for learning. Confusion indicates that a learner is engaged in the learning process despite feeling slightly frustrated. It is far better to have your audience "hooked" and confused than not interested at all. Learners in this state will usually try to move out of it by clearing up their confusion. If they cannot do so (by asking a question, talking to a neighbor or reflecting on new knowledge), they may go from the productive state of cognitive and intellectual confusion and frustration to a counterproductive state of visceral and angry frustration, or, just as likely, into a state of apathy—neither of which is good for learning!

The source of confusion is straightforward. The most likely culprits are any of three precursors. First, confusion could arise from data overload—too much information coming in too fast. Second, confusion may originate in the complexity of a lesson; the concepts and ideas, new vocabulary or needed prior knowledge are simply too much for the learner to comprehend all at once. Finally, a learner can become confused during dissonance. Perhaps your audience holds very strong, conflicting values. In a history class, one learner may have intense, controversial, environmental or political feelings about a certain government policy and constantly debate it. But dissonance is not always academic; one learner could be confused by his or her attraction to another member of the group because the object of affection is unavailable in some way.

EEG Arousal Readings

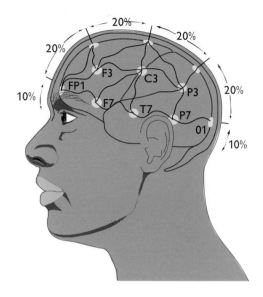

The brain's arousal and attentional states can be measured by electrode placements and the electrical activity readings of an EEG.

Why Is This State Important?

Anticipation, confusion and curiosity bring resources to an upcoming learning activity. They arouse the brain's attentional neurons and activity chemicals so it can prepare itself for something relevant and of value (like your presentation). Additionally, there is strong evidence that positive expectancy robustly and consistently influences the formation of new knowledge. That is to say, when we anticipate and are curious about a subject matter, our learner response goes up (Kirsch, 1999). Without careful orchestration of a learning environment, however, these productive states can quickly dissipate. Although we could describe the human brain as naturally curious, schools and offices are very artificial environments that can kill off any natural curiosity in a learner's brain.

Attention is good to focus the brain, but limit the strain 'cause it can't maintain.

How Long Do These States Last?

Anticipation, confusion and curiosity rarely last long. These states require so many attentional resources that we can only hold them for a very short while— thirty to ninety seconds perhaps, or a few minutes straight at the most. If we don't get resolution, we move on to other states. (One form of resolution is when an anticipated event occurs.)

Daily Highs & Lows

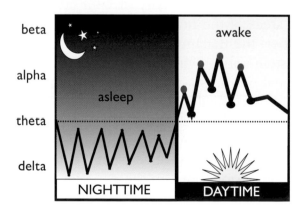

Ultradian: 90–110 min. High-low cycles are consistent for all learners. The attentional peaks are marked with red dots; low arousal points are marked with blue.

For example, a child may anticipate a trip to Disney World for just a few moments before getting distracted, but will probably come back to the state of anticipation later. You've heard expressions like, "Maria has been looking forward to this for six months," but the reality is she's been in a state of anticipation for maybe three minutes a day over a period of six months. If we anticipate something and then actually get it, we may move into a state of satisfaction or self-congratulation; if we don't, we may become frustrated, disconnected or apathetic. Most often, however, we just move on to other states because of the inherent instability of these states. They are simply too difficult to maintain.

What Brain Activity Is Involved?

Curiosity, confusion and anticipation each involve many systems of the brain. No one state is best for the arousal and activation of any particular area of the brain. Increases in the activity of your attentional areas of the brain include the frontal lobes, the thalamus, reticular activating system and pulvinar nucleus. Visual attentional prompts activate the sensory areas of the occipital cortex, the entire visual system and the LGN (lateral geniculate nucleus), the brain's visual "switchboard." Auditory stimulus triggers extra activity in the auditory cortex in the superior temporal lobes. Somatic (or touch) attentional prompts activate the motor or sensory cortex as well as areas like the cerebellum. Chemically, anticipation can enhance the alertness and arousal catecholamines such as dopamine and its metabolic products, epinephrine and norepinephrine.

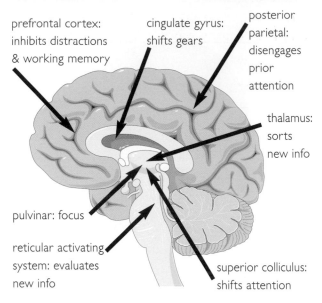

Brain Systems for Arousal

prefrontal cortex: inhibits distractions & working memory

cingulate gyrus: shifts gears

posterior parietal: disengages prior attention

thalamus: sorts new info

pulvinar: focus

reticular activating system: evaluates new info

superior colliculus: shifts attention

shifting attention

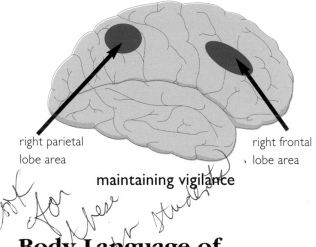

right parietal lobe area

right frontal lobe area

maintaining vigilance

Body Language of These States

The body language of curiosity and arousal is distinctive. You commonly display anticipation by leaning forward with unblinking eyes that are wide open in expectancy. Curiosity usually involves a slight head turn (rotation to the left or right), a wrinkling of brow or bringing your hand your the chin. Confusion manifests itself with a tilted head, furrowed brow or hand to the head or mouth. There are, however, cultural variations and well as varied circumstances that might change what you see and hear.

Generalizations

Primarily, all three of these states are states of arousal, in the casual "What's up?" sense instead of alarm. To trigger anticipation, give your audience the "what" of an upcoming event and let them sweat out the "when." For example, announce, "In a few moments we'll have a drawing for a special privilege. When I call your name, be ready to answer correctly so you can enter the drawing." Just follow these simple steps:

❖ *Provide participants with an expectation of a clear, perceived benefit. Some presenters refer to this as W-I-I-F-M, or the "What's in it for me?" state.*

❖ *Hint at a positive event that would create uncertainty or expectancy without threat, such as a group celebration or playing music during class.*

❖ *Offer something to participants of personal value or for personal gain, tapping interests in areas such as health, safety, pride, security or relationships. Even announcing, "We are going to try something new!" can be perceived as valuable to an audience that appreciates novelty.*

❖ *Establish a sense of immediacy for a positive, expected outcome within the next few seconds or minutes.*

The activity classifications described below will fuel your students' curiosity. Remember that this state is driven by the discovery of Who, What, Where, Why or How elements (the "When" being set more or less at "Now"). These discoveries are prompted by unfinished thoughts, incomplete phrases or half-completed activities and events that evoke a desire to see the remainder (like a TV promo or movie trailer). General activities that elicit curiosity include:

❖ *displaying strong emotions in yourself to arouse a student's attention or wonder;*

❖ *teasing or revealing only part of something so that a student wants the other part;*

❖ *leaving movements, gestures, or activities unconcluded or abruptly and visibly halting them;*

❖ *purposely leaving students in a confused state right before a class is over and asking them to resolve the "problem" as part of a homework assignment; and*

❖ *providing a change or contrast in existing sounds, visuals or touch.*

[handwritten note: ASK H?]

What Food Affects These States?

Glucose is your brain's primary fuel, although there are no known dietary changes that directly augment the state of curiosity. Indirectly, you can ready the brain for arousal with an increase in amines. Amines are the brain's "uppers" and they help support a state of positive vigilance or a readiness to learn. The world's most popular amine by far is caffeine. When used occasionally and in moderation, this metabolic accelerant has minimal negative effects on the body.

One study of school-age children suggests that the moderate ingestion of caffeine (75 mg to 150 mg, or the amount in one cup of regular coffee) enhances visual systems in tests of attention (Bernstein et al., 1998). Another study found that caffeine improved attention, problem-solving and delayed recall (Warburton, 1995). A third found that, among prepubertal boys, moderate caffeine ingestion improved reaction time, increased speech and decreased reaction times compared to a group of college age men who were also given caffeine (Rapoport et al., 1981). The effect of caffeine on adults seems to vary widely, however, possibly because of baseline changes to our arousal systems brought about by living in a complex world. Although each person should find his or her own tolerance for the potential side effects of caffeine use, researcher consensus is that moderate amounts (75 mg to 100 mg) support improved mental performance and greater amounts (150 mg to 200 mg) support physical exertion (Bennet & Bealer, 2002). Do not

sustain this level for days on end, though—it diminishes your brain's natural ability to produce its own amines.

For general arousal, glucose is your primary fuel. It can be metabolized from nearly all energy sources, such as fructose, fats, carbohydrates and proteins. Also important is norepinephrine, one of the neuromodulators of arousal. It is made from tyrosine, which is found in many animal and vegetable proteins. Tyrosine eventually metabolizes into dopamine, which is essential for maintaining short-term memory, planning, alertness and coordinating our thoughts. Additionally, copper, zinc, magnesium and the B vitamins are essential for cognition. Finally, hydration can support alert states, too. Encourage participants to stay hydrated! And remember: In the short run, a sweet snack treat may increase a student's energy, but that energy is likely to dissipate within an hour (Thayer, 1987). You need strategies other than food to keep an audience's attention over the long haul.

What Music Affects These States?

Selected music may elicit the states of anticipation and curiosity, particularly selected pieces from movie soundtracks. Try *Peter and the Wolf* (by Sergei Prokofiev) or the *Theme from Pink Panther* (by Henry Mancini). Funny, suspenseful or unusual movie clips work, too. Still, if I'm going to show a video clip to my audience, first I'll get them up for a brief physical activity, such as a short walk around the room, before letting them settle down to a darkened room and passive activity. I want my participants alert. Better yet, I want them anticipating and curious! Additionally, music played too quickly to understand or introduced completely out of context can create confusion states in your audience.

Key Basic Concepts

To elicit these states, you must involve and engage your audience, not preach to them. The biggest obstacle to creating a successful learning environment will be your audience's habituation to clichéd attention-getters. It is essential that that you begin each session consistently and predictably but then, over time, add enough novelty to your state-changing techniques to avoid a "ho-hum, been-there-done-that" atmosphere. Curiosity often comes from a desire to know the unknown, usually by answering the questions Who, What, When, Where, Why or How; the expectancy of relevant behavior creates anticipation. Think about this: You may know that many stretching or yoga postures can increase arousal states while decreasing stress and muscle tension. But instead of telling your students you're going to introduce yoga postures and movements, simply say, "Let's try something different. Follow along with me." Why? Their curiosity about what or how you're doing it will drive their attention. If you announce that the upcoming activity is yoga, the label may turn some students off. Even the ones that like yoga will think that they already know about it and won't be very curious. Why take that risk? Don't explain yourself—just move ahead!

Strategies of Arousal (Huh?) Typically Move from Theta to Alpha or Beta States

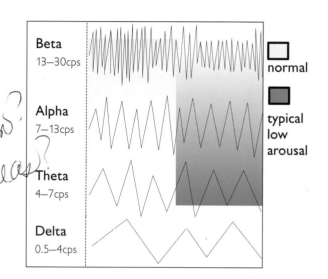

Understanding Specific Brain Wave States

Beta High Activity: excitement, debate, exercise, complex projects, competition

Alpha Focused: in control, reading, writing, watching, drawing, problem-solving, talking

Theta Slow: spacy, unfocused, drowsy, dreamy, more receptive to suggestions

Delta Nonconscious: deepest sleep time, very slowed down, no reactions

Strategies for Arousal

Many things compete for your participants' attention. This segment of Chapter 3 focuses on activities that prompt their participation instead of activities allowing only you (the presenter) to participate. It is far more engaging and powerful for your audience to respond to you as a group than for you to perform in front of them while they sit and watch. In the first case, they are active learners; in the second case, they are passive receptors. In the end it boils down to the choice between ringing a bell to get an audience's attention or having participants make sounds themselves. I'm not going to give you any generic, wake-up-the-brain energizers; I'm going to give you targeted strategies that elicit the anticipation and curiosity that drive quality learning.

1 Anticipatory Rituals

Surprising your audience with something once is okay, but establishing a ritual by creating a positive, predictable and practical tool is even better. Every teacher or facilitator needs to get a group's attention at some point. How you get attention can either build relationships and add fun to the day or introduce stressors to your students and increase their sense of being controlled. You may want to develop a ritualized (automated, stimulus-response) attentional device that is easy to perform to which your audience can respond quickly. There are endless variations; many are as simple as raising your hand when you want the group's attention and asking them to raise their hand and stop talking once they see your hand is up. When participants see other hands go up,

they raise their hands, too. Soon, the entire audience has a hand in the air and the room is quiet.

VARIATIONS

Clap patterns

★ Clap once and say, "If you can hear me, clap twice." Then, clap twice and say, "If you can hear me, clap three times." Then, clap three times and say, "If you can hear me, clap four times." Finally, clap four times. By this time, all your audience will be clapping with you, ready with their complete attention for you to jump in and start talking.

★ Stomp your foot once and say, "If you can hear me, stomp your feet twice." Then, stomp twice and say, "If you can hear me, stomp your feet three times." Then, stomp three times and say, "If you can hear me, stomp your feet four times."

Although many other strategies, like sounding a bell, gong or whistle, changing the room lighting or changing your location, can get a group's attention, they engage only you—not the participants.

2 Breathing

Did you know that breath is powerfully connected to our states? Taking a deep breath is often a precursor to tackling a challenge or anticipating something significant. Prompted, whole-group breathing is an excellent tool for engaging curiosity or attention, aligning the group into a unified state or boosting oxygen levels in the brain. The higher the oxygen levels in the brain, the better it can focus and stay alert. To establish this breathing pattern, you might say, "Let's pause for a minute. Take a slow, deep breath." Take a deep breath of your own to get them started. Then, guide them by saying, "Inhale and hold it. Now, slowly exhale." Again, model how they should do it. Then, continue by saying, "Very good. One more time. Breathe in slowly, as if you're taking in a divine gift. A little more. Very good. Now, hold it. Finally, slowly exhale and release all the stress of the day."

VARIATIONS

★ Use the release of the breath to prompt an if-then scenario. You might ask the group to inhale slowly and then tell them, "If you feel ready to begin, breathe out." Use the release of the breath for an additional release by saying, "If you're ready to learn (or feeling more relaxed), exhale slowly." Acknowledge their decision to move on with a simple "Good" or "Great!"

★ Stand up before beginning a deep breathing activity. Say, "Everybody, stand up. Now, inhale as we all raise our arms above our head. Now, exhale as we all lower our arms like we're doing a swan dive." Be sure to model the physical motions as you request them.

★ Lead the audience in a short period of quick breath bursts. Have everyone stand and then breathe in and out quickly for ten seconds. Pause, repeat the breathing pattern for twenty seconds and finally, pause and repeat it for thirty seconds. This will flush the brain with oxygen. Finish up with a slow inhale and even longer slow exhale so the audience can wind down from their rapid breathing.

❸ Stretching

Say to your group, "We're going to do something very interesting in just a moment. But first, let's get up and stretch." Getting participants up raises heart rates and triggers arousal states; being vague about what interesting thing awaits them sparks curiosity. Ask your audience to take a deep breath and exhale completely. Ask them to stand up and have the team leaders move their teams through a round of stretches. When everyone is done with stretching but still standing, you summarize the key points of your talk.

VARIATIONS

★ Lead the audience through a thirty-second set of slow stretching exercises.

★ Ask a volunteer to lead the whole group in stretching to music.

★ Have volunteers lead the group in a dance step to blow off (or generate) some energy.

4 Chair Movement

Asking participants to move chairs or rearrange the room will commonly create anticipation and curiosity, especially if you do not explain what you're going to do next. For example, you might say, "I just thought of the perfect thing! But we'll need a different chair arrangement. Please stand up. Great. Now, our goal is to have seven groups total. So here's where to move...." Put a little "tease" at the front of your statement ("I just thought of the perfect thing!") and act quickly and confidently towards a common goal. You could also introduce it with, "I have an idea, but it'll take a bit of adjustment. Everyone please angle your chair so you are facing the windows. Great. Now, find a partner."

VARIATION
★ Use chair movements to create new groups. Say, "Please stand up and grab your own chair. Good. In just a moment, when I say 'Go,' carry that chair to the nearest group of five others. If you meet a group of six, keep walking around with your chair until you find a group to join. If it gets tough, stop, stand on your chair and advertise. Ready? Get set. Go!'"

5 Directions that Evoke Anticipation

Many teachers miss the state of anticipation because of a bit of class confusion that sometimes accompanies their directions, but they don't have to. They can learn the secrets of how to give directions correctly (Allen, 2002). Follow these simple guidelines to make them work:

❖ *Announce the time that the group will start an activity: "In just 30 seconds...."*

❖ *Select a trigger word: "When I say the word 'Go,'...."*

❖ *Give the actual directions: "Walk ten steps and find a partner."*

❖ *Check for readiness by noting body language, listening for chit-chat, et cetera.*

❖ *Determine when everything and everyone is ready and give the trigger word: "Ready? Get set. Go!"*

VARIATIONS
★ Have participants repeat directions to a partner.

★ Use a visual cue, like an overhead transparency, with your directions.

★ Put your directions on a piece of paper and let group leaders read them to the group—they'll listen better to a peer!

★ Break the directions into chunks and have participants silently read only their chunk. When everyone is finished reading, each person shares his or her chunk and the whole group discusses and agrees on the order of the steps.

6 Goal Setting

A goal is the specific possibility of a desired future event. The simple act of setting goals can change a student's outlook on learning (Carver & Scheier, 2001). Create states of anticipation by expressing the possibility of and desire to reach challenging goals. Give your audience time to figure out what they want and to write it down. Remind them to make the goals specific, positive and attainable in the time available. Make sure that learners explain *why* reaching these goals is good—many people set goals so boring that there is no personal value to be gained even upon accomplishing them. Check on participant goals at a half-way point and note their progress. If participants are reaching their goals, have them congratulate each other. If they aren't, have them devise a quick plan of action to correct the lapse. No rewards are necessary except those of fun and satisfaction!

VARIATIONS

★ Have participants write their goals down and share them with a neighbor for immediate feedback on how to refine them.

★ Have participants share goals aloud in front of a small group and get affirmations and applause.

★ Have participants create group goals or team goals and post them. Then, every day or once a week, they revisit their goals and mark and celebrate their progress.

★ Use group leaders to check daily or weekly on each learner's progress towards their goals. If group members need help with something, they tell the group leader. If a learner needs help refining or accomplishing a goal, he or she can ask for it then.

7 Musical Deadlines

A musical deadline creates anticipation for the start-time of an activity or an activity change. Use a set-up song, otherwise known as a cue-signal or "call-back" song, that meets the following criteria:

❖ *It's short—less than three minutes long.*

❖ *It has positive lyrics or no lyrics at all.*

❖ *It ends with a clear, predictable finale instead of trailing off or fading away.*

Remember the music you use should match the generation you're working with. For experienced (older) audiences, two songs that meet these criteria are *Rock Around the Clock* (by Bill Haley and the Comets) and *Chantilly Lace* (by The Big Bopper). For youngish audiences, use songs from the 1980s (The Cars recorded many songs that meet these criteria). Lots of tunes work for all audiences. Make an agreement that everyone will be in their seats and ready to move on to the next activity when the song ends. Encourage this habit by walking around the first few times you play the song to "round up" the class so they know you mean it. Tell participants that they'll get have more fun or get "extra credit" if they pat their thighs, stomp their feet, hum or sing along with the music. Individual or team participation encourages more overall learner involvement.

VARIATIONS

★ Create musical anticipation and curiosity by having teams compose homemade call-back music. The participants themselves will become a temporary ensemble (no talent required) and use their desktops or thighs for drum rolls, stomp their feet or clap their hands, and bring in harmonicas or whistles. Rotate the schedule so each team has the chance to play.

★ Ask participants to compose a class song after two to four weeks of hearing your choice of music. If they don't want to write the music and lyrics themselves, let them suggest a new song that meets the criteria and your approval.

8 Graphic Organizers

Graphic organizers use words and short phrases to arrange information about a topic in a very visual, non-linear way. They can be used to help your audience identify what they would like to know about an upcoming topic as well as what prior knowledge they have about new material. Matrices, flow charts, idea webs, Mind Maps® and Venn diagrams are all examples of graphic organizers that are quick and easy to make. Encourage participants to enhance their graphic organizers with color and non-linguistic symbols to make them even more memorable.

VARIATIONS

★ Assign to a team of participants a chapter or section of the total content to be learned. Give them twenty to twenty-five minutes to first read it, organize it and finally create a team graphic organizer of the material. To help them stay productive, give verbal milestones at five-minute intervals of time so they get feedback on their progress.

★ In pairs, one participant talks through the material while the other organizes it as he or she hears it. When this is finished, they switch roles. Once both participants have created graphic organizers, give them three to five minutes to clean up and finalize them.

Simply Standing Up for a Moment Can Raise Focus and Concentration

9 Stand and Listen

Sitting down for too long (fifteen minutes or more) may cause postural stress, loss of blood flow to the brain and attentional lag (Grieco, 1986). The longer you let your audience sit, the more activities you'll have to plan to keep them focused while sitting in their chairs. It's easier, instead, to plan frequent stretch breaks. Simply ask your audience to take a deep breath, exhale and then stand up. Once they're on their feet, speak for one to three minutes, but no longer. While standing, participants share with a partner what they've just learned. Within a couple of minutes, reseat the group.

⑩ Hypothesis Generation

If you give participants time to identify a theory about upcoming topics, they may learn it better (Lavoie, 1999). Generally, making either inductive (creating new conclusions about existing content) or deductive (using a rule to predict the future) predictions will work. Aside from the learning that results, the value of generating predictions is that the learners now want to know how accurate their own predictions were. Learning is driven by error correction and prediction is a useful operational tool for enhancing it. One fringe benefit of making a successful prediction is a surge in dopamine, which gives the learner the reward of feeling good (Schultz et al., 2002). This strategy lets you enhance learning by generating curiosity and anticipation all at once. Give your participants a defined body of content, like the last fifteen minutes of a lecture, a chapter in a book or a website. Then, give them five minutes to synthesize a prediction or hypothesis about the material. Allow them to work in pairs. They can share their results with others when they finish or turn in a paper to you.

VARIATIONS ★ ★ ☆

★ Teams create a step-by-step process for devising a hypothesis and then divide up the work to make one or do it together. One team can later share their work with another team. When you are finished with the learning segment, have participants go back to their notes and check their hypothesis against what they actually learned.

★ Have one person come to the front of the group and walk through the steps of devising a hypothesis. Let that individual call on the others for help. Then, have the whole group write out what the hypothesis was. Later, have everyone check on the results. Was their hypothesis accurate? How should it be changed? Participants can write about it and share.

★ Participants work on a hypothesis with a partner of their choice.

★ You (the presenter) generate three hypotheses about the new topic, each two to four sentences long. Put them on paper and pass them out to the group. Let them discuss each of your predictions, noting the strengths, weaknesses and likelihood of each. Then, have the group rank the hypotheses for their overall strength and functionality.

⑪ Identify the Person Who...

This simple activity works with teams or groups only, but they can be temporary groups or teams that you establish for the week or even only a day. You'll want to create a pattern of having something happen the person who gets chosen. Be sure to always have a task ready and waiting for the people identified by their groups. It works like this: You might say, for example, "Please identify in your group the person who has laughed the most today. Great. Will those people please raise their hands? Perfect. When I say 'Go,' they will head over to the supply table and get two index cards for every person in their groups. Ready? Get set. Go!" The simple acts of discovery and choosing a delegate creates active, curious and often humorous states.

VARIATIONS

★ Have groups identify the person who has taken the most detailed notes. That person will remain seated while everyone else on their team takes their own notes with them as they disperse around the room to sit with another group for five minutes. Each of the note-takers left behind will share what they have with the people from the other groups who will in turn add to their own notes. It's like a reverse Jigsaw grouping strategy (see Chapter 8 for a detailed description of a Jigsaw activity). Many of the following variations can be mixed and matched to suit a particular age group, so be flexible.

★ For K–12 Students:
Let the team leader pick someone at random or have the group identify the person:
- who has seen the movie... (*popular movie title*)
- who has eaten ice cream the most recently
- who has laughed the most today
- who is the tallest (or shortest)
- who has the most freckles
- who has the longest (or shortest) first name (or middle or last name)
- who has the messiest (or cleanest) desk/study area
- who is wearing the most white (or red, blue or black, or the most number of colors)
- who has the curliest (or longest or shortest) hair
- who is sitting closest to (or farthest from) the door
- who has the most (or fewest) pets
- whose home phone number sums to the highest (or lowest) number

★ For Adults:
Have the team leader pick someone at random or with a quick contest (like odds-even or rock-scissors-paper). You could also have the group identify the person:
- who has the longest (or shortest) commute
- who is wearing the least (or most) jewelry
- who is wearing most white (or red, blue or black, or the most number of colors)
- who has the curliest (or longest or shortest) hair
- who is sitting closest to (or farthest from) the door
- who has the most (or fewest) pets
- who has worked in education for the longest (or shortest) amount of time
- who comes from the biggest (or smallest) school
- who has the most children
- who is sitting closest to the clock in the room
- who has moved the greatest (or least) distance from their home town

- who was born during spring (or fall, winter or summer)
- whose last four digits of their Social Security Number total the greatest (or least) number
- who has lived in their current house the longest (or shortest) amount of time
- who comes from the smallest (or largest) state

❖ *Start by writing the topic in the center of your paper.*

❖ *Add branches to hold key sub-topics.*

❖ *Add details to the branches and establish hierarchies and numerical order.*

❖ *Personalize it for the right brain with symbols, pictures, colors and shapes.*

12 Mind Map®

Mind Map is a trademarked term for a specific learning and note-taking format developed by Tony Buzan and Barry Buzan. A Mind Map is a creative pattern of connected ideas. It is similar to a sentence diagram, a road map or a blueprint. Although Mind Mapping is often referred to as "clustering" or "mapping," you will discover that there are some important differences from the familiar classroom activity. While any note-taking system can store material, the unique value of a Mind Map is that it will help you understand your material far better and boost your recall of it dramatically. One significant benefit is that Mind Mapping can reach almost all types of learners. Why? When done properly, Mind Maps *appeal powerfully to both sides of the brain* (the left side processes words and right side processes colors, relationships, pictures and symbols). When done with a colleague or partner, Mind Maps can also appeal to the auditory, visual and kinesthetic learners. Use them for taking personal notes, planning, review, problem solving, speeches, studying, making decisions or more. The steps to making Mind Maps are simple:

13 Mind Your Ps and Qs (Prompts and Questions)

Evidence shows that prompts and questions support greater learning for the simple reason that the more you know about a topic, the more interest you tend to have in it. This interest (read: arousal and anticipation) often translates into better learning (Alexander et al., 1994). The secret is to provide or elicit enough substance learning (not frivolous, gee-whiz data) so that learners become naturally curious about getting more details. You can both enhance learning and generate some curiosity and anticipation with prompting and questions.

On your end, provide prompts and cues to alert learners to upcoming content. Their job will be to formulate questions that focus on higher-level thinking (if appropriate). At first, participants may write fairly simple questions but, as they become more experienced (and with your encouragement), they'll be ready for more challenging ones. Ensure that participants have plenty of time to create these and allow them to work in pairs. Identify a specific body of content, like the next fifteen minutes of class lecture, a chapter in a book or a particular website. Then, give them about five minutes to generate, for another group's use, three cues (hints) and three questions about the material.

VARIATIONS

★ Teams develop a step-by-step process for creating topical cues and questions and then divide up the work or do it together. One team can later share their work with another team. At the conclusion of the learning segment or unit, go back and check the questions.

★ Participants pair up and select a manageable passage of text from the unit. Each partner writes out a list of prompts and cues to help him or her recall it later. Then, partners go back through their lists and create a few questions that, if they could answer, would help them understand the material better. Finally, the pair shares their prompts and questions with the rest their small group so everyone can learn from it.

14 Quiz in Advance

Over the years, we've all seen audiences that already "know it all" and are hesitant to engage in any new learning or discussions. In some cases, they may actually know a lot, but other times they just assume they know a lot because they've been disappointed by the poor quality of content in presentations they've seen in the past. In this situation, one of the best tools for creating anticipation and curiosity about your presentation is to generate dissonance. The more uncomfortable you can make the audience, the more likely they are to be drawn towards your material with a genuine hunger to figure it out (or prove you wrong!). To implement this, write an opening quiz of ten to twenty questions on the topic you're about to present. Put in some questions that almost everyone will answer correctly but also include some that almost no one will know. Include controversial questions, too. Give participants about five minutes to complete the quiz. To take away the stigma of cheating, I even give the audience the option of consulting with their neighbor (very few people, however, take me up on this offer). Go over the answers to the quiz as a group. This will give you the opportunity to help the audience members affirm what they already know while still realizing that they have a lot more to learn.

★ Participants create a quiz and give it to a partner to take.

★ Teams create a ten-question quiz and give it to another team to take. Then, teams switch papers and grade them. Individuals from each team pair up to discuss how they did.

★ Students take the quiz and check their answers. Then, they create a list of questions for you about the answers they didn't know.

15 Return Responses

Return responses are simple devices that are used the moment the group returns from an absence of any duration, including lunch, a short break, or the day or week that has passed since the previous class. Return responses align the group, reorient the audience to you and their social structure and quiet them for a couple of seconds. Almost any tool, vehicle or group response activity can be used if it is:

❖ *short;*

❖ *solves the "return to your seats" problem;*

❖ *ends in a positive state;*

❖ *engages everyone; and*

❖ *is used with absolute consistency.*

For example, upon your group's return, say, "If you made it back on time, raise your hand please and say, 'Yes!' Now, turn to your nearest neighbor and say, 'Welcome back!'" Naturally, you'll need to jump in with your presentation right after that moment and begin the class before the noise starts up again.

★ A volunteer, assigned delegate or class team uses the return response to get the rest of the group to quiet down and prepare to learn.

★ Avoid using noisemakers like train whistles, slide whistles, horns, squeeze toys or gongs unless as part of an active group ritual. Otherwise, the noisemakers are merely passive, not active, attention getters.

★ Have group or team leaders create a return response for their own small group and enact it whenever they meet.

16 Ripple Call

Our brains have an attention bias for certain words, especially our own names. There is no better way to arouse attention, anticipation or focus than to use participant names. But if you single out just one name, it defeats the purpose of whole-group engagement! The secret here is simple. Don't use any name unless you do a ripple call. Then, use names half a dozen at a time, rippling your way through the group in one or two sentences. This strategy puts the entire group on alert that they may be next. Here's one example:

"Today, Samantha, we'll be, Travis, exploring, Kim, two of, Jeff, the most critical decisions, Karen, of the Supreme Court, Britney, since, Jason, the turn of the century, Diego." Now, I agree that's a mouthful, but, by using as many names from the group as you can, you put everyone on notice that no one can hide from your attention. Additionally, calling out multiple names removes the stigma of having the entire group's attention turned to one student because his or hers was the only name you called.

17 Role Model

Tell your group to get their "Sherlock Holmes" caps on because something is about to happen that will take a detective's eye to spot. Statements like this can create curiosity, but only if they are set up properly. Choose an activity or behavior that your audience will need to learn (or is in the process of learning) and perform it, but omit some key distinctions or elements. Then, ask them to put their heads together and identify three things they learned by watching you.

VARIATION
★ Ask participants to role model within a small group or in front of the whole group. Remember, the steps to successfully using this strategy are to set up the activity, model the activity, provide sufficient discovery and reflection time, and finish by having participants discuss conclusions about the activity and sharing their thoughts with the group.

18 Send to a Spot

Set up in advance some interesting spots in the room. For example, you might display an unusual magazine article or book, a flip chart with provocative ideas, a learning station, a pet or plant, a hands-on manipulative, a powerful picture, or physical demonstration. Your audience will be curious about the spots you have chosen and what will happen there. Send everyone to different stations by picking a unique way to sort them, such as asking all people with January birthdays to go to station number one.

VARIATIONS
★ Allow learners to choose which station they want to visit; have them set the goal of bringing back to their group one new insight or piece of learned information to share.

★ Ask participant "experts" (one from each group) to visit a station. They will announce their topic to their group and then go study it. The group members remaining in their seats will come up with questions to ask the "expert." Finally, the group visits their "expert" at the station to ask the questions.

★ Send everyone to all of the stations; give them seven minutes or so in one place before having them rotate to the next one.

19 Taking the Stage

Create anticipation with anyone who "needs the floor" before speaking. When someone is ready to speak to your group or class (excluding you), they should use an established ritual. Any call-response pattern can work; it just has to be fun, short and consistent. For example, before saying a word, a speaker might stand up, clap three times and wait. The audience, realizing someone is ready to speak, responds with three claps and sends with their hands and voices a big "whoosh" of positive energy towards the speaker. This back and forth exchange tells the audience when someone ready to speak and tells the speaker that the audience is giving him or her both attention and support.

VARIATIONS

★ The speaker starts with a popular rhythm, like the stomp-stomp-clap from the opening bars of Queen's *We Will Rock You*. The audience responds with the same stomp-stomp-clap.

★ The speaker leans over and pats his or her thighs quickly. That's the signal for all participants to repeat the motion, letting the pat-slaps on their knees build to a crescendo and adding foot stomps to build an even greater crescendo.

★ The speaker stands with both arms out and then moves them straight up and down, as if they're doing "the wave." The audience follows along until everyone is involved.

★ The speaker says his or her first name out loud and then everyone chants it back ("Jer-ry, Jer-ry") until the speaker signals them to stop.

⓴ Teasers

"A man is coming home. He's in a hurry, but is stopped by another man, who is wearing a mask. The first man never gets home, although the man in the mask didn't harm him in any way. Why didn't the first man make it home?" Are you intrigued?

A long-standing way of engaging a group is by asking questions and letting the group discuss them with each other to figure them out. Unusual questions, demonstrations, displays or tasks are perceived by the audience as worth pursuing, challenging, or mind-boggling in a healthy, curious way. By the way, the man coming home in a hurry was a baseball player rounding third base and the man in the mask was the catcher on the opposing team, guarding the plate!

Notice the Body Language of Curiosity

★ Display an optical illusion on an overhead projector for participants to identify.

★ Present a puzzle to be solved and an incentive, like extra-credit, to solve it.

★ Make available a set of manipulatives that begs to be handled, like a metal ring or horseshoe puzzle.

★ Give the participants an unidentified quip or quote and have them find the correct source of the quote from among a list of famous people.

21 Unfinished Sentences

Unfinished sentences are particularly effective for auditory learners. Purposefully leave off the last word of a... (sentence). Many participants will be driven to finish it for you by supplying the missing word out loud. Only use this as a reliable strategy for engaging the whole group's attention if you meet three conditions:

❖ *You have a good relationship with the group.*

❖ *Your group knows the drill because of you've already practiced and prompted them.*

❖ *The missing word or phrase is obvious.*

Bad example: "Yesterday we explored topics such as...." This unfinished sentence has too many possible endings. A statement like this better sets up a group recall activity or brainstorming session.

Good example: "We've talked about the importance of reading states and changing states. So, the next time a student is not responding appropriately, you probably just need to change their..." (state).

★ Use hand gestures, (à la *Charades*) to prompt the group to fill in the correct word.

★ Prompt the desired word with visual clues, like pointing to the actual word posted on the wall or a picture of its meaning.

★ Use word stems to help participants figure it out. For example: "What part of the brain deals with emotions? It starts with the letters A-M-Y." (The word that finishes this sentence is "amygdala.")

22 Universal Questions

Universal questions are questions that nearly everyone will respond to quickly. Ask, "How many of you have seen a bad movie in the last six months?" Or, "How many of you have had this happen? You hear about an event—maybe it's a theater, a concert or sporting event coming up. It's something you're really, really excited about. You want to go so badly you're almost drooling and are willing to pay for best available seats, no matter what they cost?" Raise your own hand to model the response you want. Learners will wonder how this question relates to the upcoming topic even as they enjoy the sensation of a group consensus or shared experience. The answers to these questions may seem like no-brainers to you, but that's the point. Compelling questions create universal participation and curiosity.

One important suggestion: If you ask a question that you expect your audience to answer (rather than a rhetorical question to prompt thought), *always* indicate to the audience *how* you want them to respond. If you want a show of hands, *you* raise your hand. If you want them to say the answer out loud, gesture with your hands to encourage verbal answers. If you don't give them direction, two things will happen. First, you'll get fewer answers because your audience is confused about how to respond. Second, you'll eventually lose the "active contract" you created with your group and they'll quit responding to other things because you have accepted their passivity or silence.

Variations

Use questions that create anticipation specific to your topic. Some possible questions and follow-up questions are listed below.

★ "How many of you have seen an article on the brain in a magazine or newspaper, or on TV lately?" Or, "Who would like to know how we can apply brain science in our classrooms?" After a pausing for a response, follow up with the statement, "As you can see, the brain has been getting a lot of press lately. Today we're going to see if we can make some connections between research and real life and find practical applications to our work."

★ "How many of you have heard of the book, *Teaching with the Brain in Mind*, or the idea of brain-compatible or brain-based learning?" After a pausing for a response, follow up with the statement, "It looks like a few of you have. Today we're going to see if we can make some connections to these strategies and find some practical applications to our work."

★ "Who would like to learn some cut-to-the-chase strategies that help you set up the best student learning environments?" After pausing for a response, follow up with the statement, "Good, because that's what we're here to do today."

★ "How many of you have had students who take up a lot of your time and don't understand new ideas or topics?" After pausing for a response, follow up with the statement, "As you can see, that happens often. Today we're going to discuss some great ideas to make their learning easier."

★ "Who has had the experience of teaching something one day but the next day hardly any of your students remember it?" After a pausing for a response, follow up with the statement, "As you can see, that happens often. Today we're going to learn some practical steps you can take to reverse that trend."

★ "How many of you have felt physically exhausted and emotionally drained at the end of your day?" After pausing for a response, follow up with the statement, "As you can see, that happens often. Today we're going to learn some practical things we can do about it."

★ "Who has had that nagging feeling that a student was slipping through the cracks but you didn't know how to reach him or her?" After pausing for a response, follow up with the statement, "As you can see, that happens often. Today we're going to learn some tools to help those students."

23 Voting on a Topic

Offer your group a choice between two or more arguable positions, perhaps to take a stand on an issue like the death penalty or a constitutional amendment to ban handguns. Introduce your discussion with words like the following: "Class, let's find out where you stand on this topic. You have three choices. You can vote for [choice #1], which means that you believe.... If you vote for [choice #2], that means.... Voting for [choice #3] means...." Have the audience vote as individuals or discuss the topic in a small group first and allow one vote per team. Finally, conduct the vote or poll. Go through each of the choices and have its proponents raise their hands or otherwise identify their support for that position.

VARIATIONS

★ Have participants vote with their feet. Point to places in the room for audience members who take a particular stance. Ask them to physically move to that spot to cast their vote. This simple voting option ensures everyone walks to the "polling" place and that everyone expresses an opinion. For example, learners who want to have two ten-page papers due during the semester can stand by the chalkboard; learners who want one twenty-page paper can stand by the windows. You could also have them

express opinions about subject content. "If you believe the Korean War was a mistake for America and can say why, go stand by the bookshelf."

★ Allow participants to vote verbally with a simple "Yea" or "Nay" to the options you present.

★ Don't force participants to cast a vote right away, especially with opinions about content. After more confident participants have moved to their spots, ask them to share the reasoning behind their opinions. As the undecided participants listen to the evidence, they can make a decision about which group to join (and those who took one position can move to another if so persuaded). If time permits, let the undecided participants question those already in place. Alternately, if they can come up with a new position or stance, let them start their own group.

24 Write Now!

We can quickly create a state of anticipation by simply telling learners (in an excited way) to write something very important down. Build suspense by adding steps to the directions one at a time. For example, say, "Please get something to write with," and pause. Continue with, "Show your neighbor your writing implement. If theirs is as nice as yours say 'Wow!' Now, find something to write on (or turn to page whatever), and write this down. The first word is...." Telling others to write something will get their attention, but avoid overuse. For best effect, use this tool only when you have something really important for students to capture.

25 Written Questions

You supply the topic but participants write all the questions. Let's say the topic is recycling. Let the learners' curiosity generate questions like, "How can we recycle more of our trash?" or, "Why can't we recycle everything?" Engaged learning will generate its own questions. Have participants jot them down in their notes as you deliver instruction and challenge them to answer their own questions as their learning about this topic progresses.

VARIATIONS
★ Learners work with partners to write three questions about what they think might be important in the upcoming topic or material.

★ Learners create five questions as a team or group. At the conclusion of the unit or topic, two teams will pair up and quiz each other.

★ Before a unit or topic begins, learners create possible test questions. Stop occasionally during your instruction so they can pair up and see if any of their questions have already been answered.

VARIATIONS
Increase curiosity or anticipation with set-up statements such as:

★ "I haven't asked you to write down anything all day but this is a biggie, so grab your pen."

★ "Write this down even if you only write down one thing all day."

★ "Write this down even if you have to borrow a pen from a neighbor."

★ "There's only one thing that I can guarantee will be on the test. But, before I tell you what it is, grab your pens."

★ "Take a deep breath. Good. Now, please identify the person nearest you. Great. Now, switch pens with them. Good. Now, write this down with your borrowed pen. [Make your statement.] Good. Now, if your partner did a good job of writing with your pen, congratulate them."

Chapter 4
"Yikes!"
High Energy States

What Is This State?

"Yikes!" Have you ever felt that rush of energy when you were "racing against the clock" to get ready for a party or "risking it all" for something very important, like a new job or a special relationship? This high-energy state of excitement is the positive aspect of the "fight or flight" defensive mechanism, a burst of extra energy to help you meet an urgent challenge or accomplish some risky task.

Norepinephrine (the neuromodulator also known as noradrenaline) is released into your bloodstream and reaches the brain during the thrill of riding a roller coaster or during the terror of a car crash—any situation for which there are some "stakes" in the game. It's released whenever it makes sense for you to try to "fight" your way out of a conflict; you might be faced with possibility of failure, but you also have the potential to escape or triumph. If your chances look bleak, your body slows down and kicks into a "flight" or "play dead" state. Skilled teachers and presenters know the art of triggering an audience's competitive instincts without scaring or inhibiting them, and can evoke this state at will. More important, they know how to channel the resulting productivity towards learning and fun.

Many presenters are terrified to get students up and going. They're afraid that they'll never be able to calm them down again (Chapter 11 addresses these concerns). Others wonder if any state that triggers too much movement is actually good for learning. Yet there is convincing evidence that well-organized physical activities can and do boost academic achievement (Dwyer et al., 1996; Jensen, 2000). Whether they are blended into an academic class or taught within their own discipline, movement and physical education can be a very positive experience for learners from ages two to ninety-five. Never assume that adults don't like to get up and move. If you meet adults that don't, realize that they are usually:

❖ *exceptions to this rule;*

❖ *abstract learners (versus concrete, hands-on learners);*

❖ *dealing with personal health issues; or*

❖ *simply not used to the idea (it will take a bit of time before they "buy in" to your strategies).*

If I see someone in my group that *may* have physical difficulty moving around, I'll approach them *before* I begin my workshop and talk to them privately. Generally, if they know you're being empathetic instead of nosy and if you give them additional "permission" not to participate in the physical activities, these participants will be very appreciative of your consideration.

Why Is This State Important?

The high-energy "Yikes!" state brings all of your audience's urgency and resourcefulness to the table (LeDoux, 1996). It is not a state of delicate relationship interactions but rather a state of go! go! go!. In this state, students can:

❖ *get lots done;*

❖ *get it done in a hurry;*

❖ *get excited about doing it; and*

❖ *remember doing it longer.*

How Long Does This State Last?

This state typically lasts for only a few minutes, though it can last longer. We feel urgency for a limited period of time because the triggering incident usually resolves or concludes itself rapidly (which is why we were so urgent in the first place), or else because we burn out on the excitement and take a break from it. Only in rare cases, such as war, sustained trauma or long athletic events, will this state last for hours. Many students, though, crave the rush and like the excitement.

Note: A teacher might consider activating a state of excitement no more often than once or twice an hour. Deactivating this state takes time.

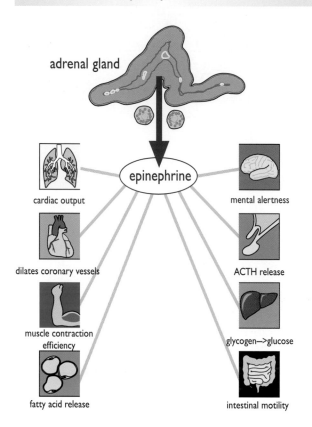

Epinephrine and adrenaline are different names for the same hormone, which is released by the adrenal gland.

What Brain Activity Is Involved?

Two primary systems of the brain are at work in this state: orienting and taking action. Epinephrine is one of our arousal chemicals. It is part of the family of chemicals known as amines or "uppers." It both serves as a neurotransmitter (it is present in the synapses of the brain) and a hormone (it is released into the bloodstream). Released by the cells of the medulla (located in the upper area of the adrenal gland) when the sympathetic nervous system is aroused, epinephrine acts within seconds to gear up your body and focus your brain so you can deal with urgent, acute situations (see illustration on facing page). Epinephrine concentrations in the central nervous system are fairly low, although they do vary depending on circumstances like diet, fatigue, age or health (Cooper et al., 2001).

Your brain gets a thrill when your body's not still.

Whenever epinephrine is released, levels of its sister chemical, norepinephrine, also rise. Norepinephrine enables the body to "get up and go" when action is required. This hormone is secreted by sympathetic nerve endings located throughout the body. Epinephrine originates in your adrenal gland; however, norepinephrine is released all through your body. It serves as both a neurotransmitter and hormone and kicks the body and brain into motion by stimulating the expansion of your capillaries, which fosters greater blood flow to the brain. This increase of blood in the brain facilitates its alertness.

There is evidence that norepinephrine modulates long-term memory by affecting the amygdala. At the University of California at Irvine, Larry Cahill and colleagues demonstrated that the narration of events that commonly evoke concern can also jumpstart the norepinephrine response in the body of a listener (1994). This discovery suggests that activities that boost epinephrine levels (and therefore norepinephrine levels) "fix" associated learning into a student's long-term memory. The actual engagement of a motion is initiated by the thalamus, the brain's central sorting station whose axons project to the prefrontal cortex. Finally, the basal

ganglia are also critical to your body's ability to take action; they organize and prompt neuronal assemblies for movement (Berridge, 1999).

Norepinephrine (Noradrenaline)

$$\text{HO} - \text{benzene ring} - \overset{\overset{\displaystyle OH}{|}}{\underset{\underset{\displaystyle H}{|}}{C}}\ \overset{\overset{\displaystyle H}{|}}{\underset{\underset{\displaystyle H}{|}}{C}} - NH_2,\quad \text{OH}$$

Norepinephrine is just slightly different from epinephrine (see formulas above and below). It is released by the peripheral nerve endings of the sympathetic nervous system. Amazingly, it also serves as a neuromodulator that helps "fix" new memories.

Epinephrine (Adrenaline)

$$\text{HO} - \text{benzene ring} - \overset{\overset{\displaystyle HO}{|}}{\underset{\underset{\displaystyle H}{|}}{C}}\ \overset{\overset{\displaystyle H}{|}}{\underset{\underset{\displaystyle H}{|}}{C}} - \overset{\overset{\displaystyle H}{\diagup}}{\underset{\underset{\displaystyle CH}{}}{N}},\quad \text{OH}$$

Body Language of This State

States of excitement put us in motion! Typically, when we enter a state of excitement our heart rate increases, pupils dilate, salivation decreases and digestion decreases, although our overall metabolic activity is increased. We often take a deep breath and hold it for a moment. Only when our bodies and minds are fearful that we have *no escape*

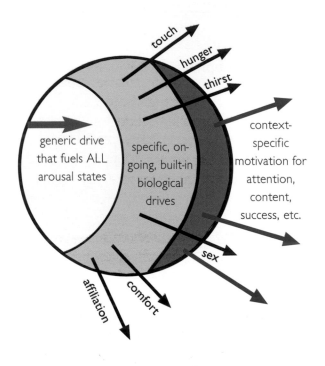

Epinephrine is One Key Source of Primary and Secondary Motivation

- touch
- hunger
- thirst

generic drive that fuels ALL arousal states

specific, on-going, built-in biological drives

context-specific motivation for attention, content, success, etc.

- sex
- affiliation
- comfort

from a dangerous or threatening situation will our heart rate actually drop and our motion decrease (so we can play dead). Still, there are cultural variations and varying circumstances of what sends people into states of excitement and which might change the body language and behavior you see and hear.

Generalizations

Neurotransmitters, like epinephrine and norepinephrine, are released into the bloodstream when there is a *perception* of risk or urgency, or both. Real danger isn't the only trigger for this state of excited behavior; riding a roller coaster or stealing a kiss while your parents are in the next room (remember those days?) could also throw you into this state. While it's true that under stress (good or bad) the

body releases *both* glucocorticoids (like cortisol) and sympathetic nervous system chemicals (epinephrine and norepinephrine), they all play different roles. Epinephrine is triggered in short-term "emergencies" and cortisol metabolizes energy during longer periods of time.

Movement Influences Both Brain and Body

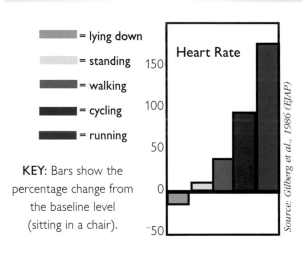

- = lying down
- = standing
- = walking
- = cycling
- = running

KEY: Bars show the percentage change from the baseline level (sitting in a chair).

Heart Rate

Source: Gilberg et al., 1986 (EJAP)

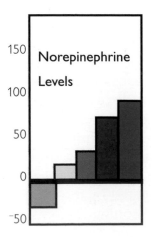

Advantage? Increased circulation means more blood flow and oxygen to the brain. Norepinephrine serves as a memory "fixative" and, in moderate amounts, will strengthen memories.

Norepinephrine Levels

What Food Affects This State?

The brain and body synthesize the chemicals necessary to maintain a state of excitement without much dietary help. Epinephrine is produced by the adrenal glands and norepinephrine is synthesized by nerve endings throughout the body. Ultimately, these chemicals are manufactured from proteins. It is not yet known if increased dietary levels of proteins will strengthen the adrenal response.

Understanding these fundamental brain-behavioral reactions can be quite empowering. With the right activities, your students will output more energy during their learning than you input to deliver it! How can that be? (Are teachers and presenters the only people in the world who can break the laws of physics?) Relax—it's neither voodoo nor perpetual motion; the secret is to use the high levels of stored energy in your students' bodies to begin with. The right catalyst will help you take advantage of it, and the right catalyst is easy to find.

Surprisingly, even the act of chewing gum will raise metabolism rates up to twenty percent (Levine et al., 1999). Although a small sugar treat like a candy bar will increase energy levels for about thirty minutes (Thayer, 1987), this temporary increase is followed by an extended energy decrease for the next hour or two. Excess sugar means that insulin kicks in and will depress the available glucose, often resulting in a net loss of energy. A quick physical activity is a better way to boost energy levels.

Raise Circulation & Boost Motivation with Music and Movement

What Music Affects This State?

People display a wide range of responses to music because of a diversity of variables (genre, volume, personal preference, etc.), but a meta-analysis of the studies of the effects of music on an audience does suggest some consistencies.

Music that's wrong will agitate; music that's right improves the state.

For example, when you play music with 110 to 160 beats per minute (BPM), there's a high likelihood you'll evoke an increase in heart rate (Bartlett, 1996). Music clearly affects our stress levels and, for most of us, high BPMs increase our sympathetic nervous system response (Charnetski et al., 1998). Prolonged exposure to higher-than-pulse-rate music creates arousal states (Darner, 1966; Standley, 1991). Music can also be used as a "pacing device" for when you want students to move faster (Hume & Crossman, 1992) or be more efficient at an activity.

Key Basic Concepts

To elicit the "Yikes!" state in your audience, add elements of urgency or uncertainty to assigned tasks. This means setting firm deadlines, limiting available resources to encourage competition, implementing physical activity, playing music with a fast tempo or adding to an ordinary activity the high stakes of risky failure or a huge payoff. By far the easiest of these triggers is getting students up and moving around. There is solid evidence that taking brisk walks can elicit this state of arousal (Saklofske & Kelly, 1992). Currently, the MEDLINE database shows more than 33,000 scientific articles on this topic and the vast majority of them confirm the value of exercise.

Strategies for High Energy

Keep in mind that many things will raise student's energy levels but, as in the previous chapter, this segment focuses on things that students can do themselves rather than activities you perform in front of them. Remember that the best learning occurs when students take an active instead of passive role. Our question about triggering high-energy states will be, "Does your audience hear you raise your voice or do they raise their voices themselves?"

Ideas for Easy Movement Activities

1	**2**	**3**
• Spin	• Quickly	• To a friend
• Jump	• Slowly	• Across the room
• Shuffle	• In a panic	• To a cool spot
• Hip-Hop	• Softly	• To a window
• March	• To a beat	• To the door
• Walk	• Out of synch	• For 25 feet
• Slide	• Gracefully	• While touching chairs
• Sneak	• Like an Egyptian	• In place
• Leap	• On one foot	• With a smile
• Saunter	• With style	• To a corner
• Slither	• Like a frog	• Until you drop
• Dance	• With a smile	• To a warm spot
• Cartwheel	• Leaning forward	• For 30 seconds
• Hopscotch	• With arms out	• With a partner
• Skip	• Laughing	• Ten steps and back

Participants choose an action from Column 1, a description from Column 2 and a direction from Column 3. When the presenter says, "Go!," they move around the room accordingly.

1 BPM is Up!

Our brain and body are tuned into the environment and will match internal rhythms to external ones. Fast music with a definite beat aligns the brain and body to its tempo and rhythm. This kind of music includes workout music (like you hear at fitness clubs) or music that gets us all up and moving. Music we happen to like will energize us better than music we don't, though, and music we find distasteful can even put us in a distressed state, despite its BPMs. I use the CD, *Transitions to Go!*, produced by The Brain Store® (author's potential conflict of interest is duly noted). It contains only musical selections of 120 beats per minute or more.

VARIATIONS

★ Play some high BPM music. Put participants into teams or groups and have them pick a leader. The leader demonstrates a few dance moves and the group members copy them. Have them take turns being small group leaders.

★ Set any classroom task against a high BPM musical background.

★ Organize a scavenger hunt (with musical backdrop) for participants (but don't let them disturb other classes!).

★ Participants dance as a group to a high BPM song. Consider having a volunteer lead the group through *YMCA* by the Village People, *Macarena* by Los Lobos, the Chicken Dance, Devo's *Whip It* and *Locomotion* (any artist's version) are all good examples of fun, action songs.

Movement Solves the "Binding Problem" in Learning

- *Young learners learn mostly through nonconscious acquisition and "binding."*
- *Binding is the integration of emotion, body and mind. It ensures that learning is meaningful and can be recalled.*

EXAMPLES:
*charades
manipulatives
role playing
learning by doing
games
kinesthetic learning
teacher-directed content links*

---

2 Call-Response Psych-Ups

Call-response psych-ups are auditory-kinesthetic routines that you set up with the class as preparations for learning. They get the whole group aligned in a common, excited state of "I can do it!" Before class, first prepare an overhead transparency or clear some space on a whiteboard or chalkboard. Draw two columns; label the one on the left "Me" and the one on the right "You." In the columns, write the pairs of calls and responses you'd like to perform. Make sure they are positive and motivational. You should have three to five call-responses on the list.

When you are ready to begin this activity, ask the whole group to stand and take a deep breath. Announce that you are going to give a call and they are going to answer with the matching response, vocally and with a physical sound (like a clap or a stomp). The best call-response routines are simple and quick; the first time you do one be sure to model it with lots of energy in your voice and your movements. See the table below for a sample set of call-response psych-ups.

Me	You
Who's here today?	I'm here!
Here for what?	To learn & have fun!
When do we start?	Right now!
How now?	Work hard, be smart!

VARIATION
★ After your class has learned the call-response ritual, rotate participants through the role of leader. Later on, they can prepare their own list of call-responses for the class.

3 Commercial Breaks

Commercial breaks are quick ways to review key ideas from specific content. Assign a topic to a team or let them choose one from the last segment, unit or theme. Give groups only five minutes to prepare; make it a quick review instead of a drawn-out re-examination of learned material (the looming deadline will spur them to action!). Have the teams "broadcast" a thirty second "commercial" to the rest of the class about the information they just reviewed. Their task is to make it fun, bizarre, cute or otherwise creative so they can capture the attention of their audience and make them want to buy their "service" or "product"— that is, make their audience remember the information and want to learn more.

VARIATIONS
★ Have individuals or partners, not teams, prepare a commercial to broadcast later. Throughout the rest of class, interrupt your lesson for commercial breaks. You could draw participant names from a bowl to determine the order; students could give their thirty-second commercials from the front of the room or their desks.

★ Choose a theme for the commercials to follow to make it easier for participants to focus their minds on the review. Try "Year-End Clearance Sale," "Latest CD Released by Popular Artist" or "New and Improved" for starters.

4 Competitive Games

Give participants a chance to win a competition, game or simulation. The thrill of victory coupled with possible agony of defeat is precisely what gets epinephrine flowing! Have groups or teams compete for points or tokens. Use short game periods as stand-up reviews at the end of a class or as warm-ups at the start of class.

Games and play forge the way.
Synapses buzz and brains say,
"Hooray!"

To get the epinephrine going, however, there have to be stakes for winning or losing and an activity must move fast. Your participants must care about the process (they want to win out of pride or for an early lunch pass, extra points or bragging rights). Make sure the competition can come to a quick and decisive outcome. It's better to spend more time preparing for the event than to scramble around with confused players during the game. And keep the directions and rules simple. You could, for example, host a relay race in which participants stand at one end of the room and have to transfer an answer on paper to a teammate standing at the other side of the room. Require that teams relay the information on foot.

VARIATIONS

★ Play fast-paced music to keep hearts pumping and bodies moving.

★ Encourage participants to cheer for teammates.

★ Appoint team scorekeepers to track points.

★ Celebrate a winner's victory with music like Billy Joel's *Big Shot*, Madonna's *Express Yourself*, Patti La Belle's *New Attitude*, Chic's *Good Times*, Rare Earth's *I Just Want to Celebrate* or the Pointer Sisters' *I'm So Excited*. Let them strut around a bit and enjoy it.

Movement Engages Our Cerebellar Learning System

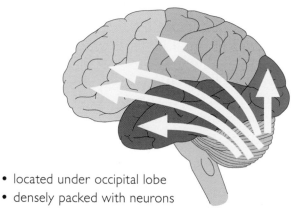

- located under occipital lobe
- densely packed with neurons
- strongly influences the other lobes
- contains 30–40% of all the brain's neurons
- plays a role in countless activities

5 Dance

Many educators believe that if *they* can't dance, then learners shouldn't dance. Others believe that dance has no place in an academic institution. And still others worry about chaos and control. Their concerns are valid in some respects, but so are observations that some students think school is boring, that they fall asleep in class and that they hate interminable lectures. I'm not here to take a side on the dance versus instruction debate because both have their proper place. But sometimes a two-minute dance can go a long way towards enhancing learners' mental sharpness for an upcoming lecture or class discussion. How? It gets their epinephrine going!

Start with something simple. You might post a sign-up sheet on your bulletin board and ask for volunteers. Participants who sign up will get four or five minutes with the rest of class to teach them a dance step. Have them bring in the music (but be sure to pre-approve it!). Provide extra credit if you think that's a necessary incentive. Once one participant does it successfully, however, others will want to follow.

VARIATIONS

★ Choose the music yourself and ask volunteers to sign up to teach a dance for one of the songs on your list. Pick music that many people already know from family reunions or weddings, like the *Macarena* (by Los Lobos), the *Electric Slide*, the *Hokey Pokey*, the *Bunny Hop* or the Chicken Dance, or let participants teach break dance or hip-hop routines—anything fun or silly.

★ Bring in someone from a dance class to teach your group "professional" moves.

★ Assign to each team the task of demonstrating and teaching one dance per school year. This can add up to many different dances, especially if you recombine teams every few months or each grading period.

6 Deadlines

Deadlines increase the surge of epinephrine but they can also incite panic or feelings of hopelessness so keep some critical caveats in mind. First, any goals that are set to meet deadlines need to be compelling enough—understandable, interesting, important—for learners to care if they ever reach them. Address the criteria of the goals before they even begin an activity. Second, your audience needs to have the necessary skills or resources to reach the goals. If they don't know how to do something or are lacking key information, teach it first. If meeting the goals requires three people on a team or having four colors of pens, they won't be very enthusiastic if they only have two people on their team or two colors of pens. If you don't do these things, you run the risk of students choosing the negative "flight" state of "Yikes!" instead of the positive "fight" state of this excitement, all because they don't have the minimum materials to be successful.

Have some high BPM music ready to accent and support the activity. Set it up with lots of energy. You need to demonstrate excitement and urgency before your audience will do the same. When you're ready, announce the goal and its deadline ("You have just five minutes to clean up your workstation, celebrate as a team and head back to your desks. Ready? Get set. Go!") and start up music like the *William Tell Overture* (by Gioachino Rossini) or the theme from the TV show *Hawaii Five-O* (by Morton Stevens).

VARIATIONS

★ Right before you announce the final, "Go!," have participants repeat the instructions to a partner.

★ Let participants know that you'll tell them when half the time has elapsed so they can pace themselves.

★ Give participants warnings as time runs out. Tell them things like, "You have two minutes left. Stay focused—it's just enough time!" Notice how these words will hurry them without causing panic.

7 Jump!

This activity is a group routine performed to the song, *Jump!*, by Van Halen. All participants walk briskly around the room (it's a high BPM song so they'll keep up the pace), following their own path or doing laps in the same direction. Whenever the vocalist sings the lyrics, "Jump," everyone jumps up in the air and points to another person before landing. If two participants happen to point to each other, both laugh. Make it the goal of each participant to point three times at someone who points back before the song ends.

★ Having a group walk and act out on cue can be done in many different ways. Experiment with other popular songs like *YMCA* (by the Village People), *Macarena* (by Los Lobos), *Whip It* (by Devo), *Dancing in the Street* (by Martha and the Vandellas) or *Hit the Road, Jack* (by Ray Charles).

8 Keystone Rally Walk

Think of this activity as a crazy fire drill. Tell your audience that it's time to wake up their brains. Send participants born during the first half of the year (January to June) to one side of the room and participants born during the second half of the year (July to December) to the other. At your signal (have high BPM music ready), both groups will exit the room to circle the building in opposite directions (weather and security rules permitting). They should walk briskly, but not run. Somewhere along this circuit the two groups will cross paths. Instruct them to high-five members of the opposite group as they pass each other. Set a time limit for the groups to return to the room (walk the distance yourself before your presentation begins so you'll know how much time it should take). Splitting your audience into groups and sending them in opposite directions makes them accountable to each other. They can see everyone go by (and see who tries to sneak off in a different direction!).

VARIATIONS
★ Use a Keystone Rally Walk as a relay game (relay activities are explained later in this chapter). Have each group station themselves evenly along the path. When signaled, participants pass a note around the entire building, without speaking.

★ Use participant teams. Send half the participant teams around the building clockwise and the other teams around the building counterclockwise. Team members must walk as a single unit and stay within an arm's length of each other for the entire trip around the building.

★ Invite participants to devise their own variations of the rally walk.

9 "Launch Pad" Directions

If you want learners geared up and ready to go like rockets on a launch pad, here are some secrets to giving focused directions that maintain high energy levels as well as generate curiosity about an upcoming activity. First, break them into chunks. Second, put and keep the learners in positive states while giving the directions. If you talk to them for too long, they'll get frustrated or tired. Follow these simple guidelines to make your directions really work:

❖ *Frame the activity before giving directions: "Everyone, please stand up. Let's try an unusual way to learn this upcoming section."*

❖ *Announce when the group will start an activity: "In just 30 seconds...."*

❖ *Select a trigger: "When I say the word 'Go,'..." or, "When the music begins, start walking."*

❖ *Give the actual directions: "Walk ten giant steps and find a partner."*

❖ *Check for readiness, noting body language, listening for chit-chat, et cetera.*

❖ *Determine when everything and every-one is ready and give the trigger: "Ready? Get set. Go!"*

VARIATIONS

★ Have each participant repeat your directions to a partner.

★ Use a visual cue, like an overhead transparency, with directions written on it.

★ Put your directions on a piece of paper and let group leaders read them to the group—they'll listen better to a peer!

★ Break the directions into chunks and have each group member read silently their chunk of the directions only. When everyone is finished reading, each person shares his or her chunk and the whole group discusses and agrees on the order of the steps.

Credit for this strategy goes to Richard Allen, the author of the book, *Impact Teaching.*

 10   Marching

This simple activity works best with younger (K–3) learners but with a lot of chutzpah you could make it work with an older crowd. Put on cheery marching music (something from John Philip Sousa or a military favorite like *Anchors Aweigh*) and have participants follow you in a march around the room. Lift your knees high and swing those arms in time to the music for about ninety seconds to get your heart rates going and epinephrine pumping.

VARIATIONS

★ Ask a participant to lead the marching.

★ Have small groups or teams march, following a designated leader.

★ Repeatedly stop and start the music; whenever the music begins again, have the groups choose and follow a new march leader.

11   Massage

Massage works with groups of any age but you have to be sure the group has a comfortable, friendly, open dynamic before implementing this strategy. Be careful to avoid embarrassments or inappropriate behavior by individuals. Rely on your professional judgment and personal instinct to decide if the time is right for this activity. I do it with adult groups, so peer pressure and peer approval influence its success (for the better). I introduce it in steps, so my audience gets used to the idea without any shock to their senses. When it's over, I move them quickly back to their seats and continue. Here's my favorite way to introduce a massage to a group:

❖ *First, I put on fast, upbeat instrumental music (The Brain Store® CD, Transitions to Go!, works well for this, too).*

❖ *Then, I add a little teaser: "How many of you are ready for a quick break to wake up the brain and body?" Pretty much everyone is always ready for this break. When they raise their hands I tell them, "Great!"*

❖ *I ask them to inhale deeply, hold it for a few seconds and then exhale slowly.*

❖ *I ask them to stand up and find a group of six to eight people. If they are already working in groups, I ask them to stand next to their other group members.*

❖ *At this point I turn up the music to medium volume.*

❖ *Once they are in groups, I ask them to form a circle about six feet in diameter (not in radius). A circle this size has everyone about two big steps from the person across from them.*

❖ *I ask them to stretch their arms to the sky and keep them up while they make a quarter turn to the right. They should turn until they see the back of the person next to them.*

❖ *To energize their hands I have them shake them out in the air above their heads. Then, I tell them to lower their hands onto the shoulders of the person in front of them and give them twenty-five "back pats" to wake them up. Don't discourage people who count out loud—the noise adds to the fun!*

❖ *On my cue I tell them to give each other ten seconds of stress-lowering shoulder massage. When the time has elapsed, tell them to put their hands in the air and do an about-face so they are facing the backs of the people who just gave them back rubs.*

❖ *They should give their new partner twenty-five pats to wake them up follow-ed by a ten-second, relaxing massage.*

❖ *Ooh and ahh aloud as you watch the groups massage each other. Tell them that they should ooh and ahh for each other, too.*

❖ *At the end have them drop their hands and turn to face the center of the circle to smile and say, "Thanks!" before returning to their seats.*

❖ *As soon as they are seated I get right to work with the next activity. Just as I kept up my encouraging patter and gave directions during the entire massage, this definite closure to the activity will give the group no time to talk about the massage or dwell on it in a positive or negative way. My only goal for this activity is to generate more energy and promote social bonding.*

VARIATIONS

★ Have partners trade off massaging each other instead of putting them into a big circle.

★ Choose upbeat music with lyrics that encourage participants to pat each other on the back. Michael Jackson's *Beat It!* and the Fixx's *One Thing Leads to Another* come immediately to mind, although there are many others.

Don't Sit—Move!

Too much chair time =
- **postural stress**
- **poor circulation and breathing**
- **musculoskeletal problems**
- **limits procedural learning**
- **students often feel subordinated in chairs**

BETTER:
slanted desks • foot rests • desk tops with rounded front edges

12 Seat Switching

Seat switching is a temporary change that invigorates quick activities like brainstorming sessions. Where a learner sits affects his or her hemispheric field of dominance and point of view. It's especially good to have them switch from the back of the room to the front or from the right side of the room to the left side.

VARIATIONS

★ Give participants a timed deadline to find new seats.

★ Play music while participants switch seats—it will be like Musical Chairs!

★ Have all the men (or boys) switch first and then all the women (or girls), or devise other groupings so participants take turns.

★ If participants are in teams or groups, call for everyone to stand and pick up their materials; then, they reseat themselves within the same groups but in different seats.

13 Match Your States

Find a partner and practice making three distinct faces and accompanying gestures: a silly face; a giggly and joyful face; and a wild celebration face. Then, stand back to back and mentally "tune in" to your partner—but don't talk aloud. On a cue, jump around and show each other one of the three faces. If the face you show matches the face your partner shows, you both win! Keep realigning yourselves back to back and jumping around trying to match faces. As soon as you have matched faces three times, congratulate each other and take a seat.

VARIATIONS

★ Ask partners to choose their own three faces to show to each other before the game begins. Insist that they pick positive states like surprise, joy or humor.

★ Turn pairs into foursomes and challenge participants to match all four faces.

★ Have participants walk around the room looking for temporary partners. They'll stand back to back and try to match faces. Once they've successfully matched their faces, they separate and look for another partner.

★ Play silly music in the background.

14 Mixer Walks

Sometimes an audience forms those all-too-common social cliques. If your audience becomes *too* familiar with each other, they'll stick up for a friend or cover someone's mistakes, often lowering an individual's accountability for their own thinking and learning. Upbeat music is a good vehicle for mixing up the group physically and for mental stimulation. Here's how it works: Say, "It's time for a change of pace. Take a deep breath, hold it for a moment and let it out. Great. Now, please stand up. In ten seconds, music will begin. When it does, walk around until it stops. Then, stop and wait for directions." Directions should be something like, "Introduce yourself to the person nearest you. You'll be partners for our next activity. If you need to find a partner, please raise your hand." A think-pair-share activity is a logical next step.

Your choice of music is important! To facilitate the mixer walks use familiar, age-appropriate music that puts everyone in the mood to move. Again, the CD, *Transitions to Go!*, has an excellent variety of upbeat tunes (author's potential conflict of interest once again duly noted) that work as quick, "get up and go" instrumental pieces for these mixer walks. With a little experience facilitating this activity, you'll be able to use many types of upbeat music, even just the first ten to fifteen seconds of a song before the vocals start.

VARIATIONS

You can mix up a group without the aid of musical accompaniment, too. The following list should give you some ideas for how to do so:

★ Touch seven tables and then stop.

★ Take as many steps as there are in the number of the month of your birthday plus ten (people born in April, the fourth month of the year, would walk fourteen steps: 4 + 10 = 14).

★ Circle the room one-and-a-half times from any starting point.

★ Walk during an instrumental introduction to a song and stop walking when the lyrics begin.

★ Shake hands with a close friend and then walk twenty-five steps away from each other.

★ Walk for approximately twenty-two seconds.

★ Spice up the walk with a skip, shuffle or salsa dance step.

★ Touch twenty-one chairs and then stop.

★ Shake hands with ten different people and then stop.

★ Walk around the room, exchanging affirmations ("You are a success!") with everyone you meet until the music stops.

★ Walk around the room until you find a partner with the same birth month as you, or someone who was born on the same day of a month as you. For example, someone born July 12 could partner with someone born July 30; someone born May 9 could partner with someone born December 9.

15 Movement Bursts

Any short burst of movement will raise our heart rate and epinephrine levels. That's all part of our arousal state. But sustained exercise, twenty to thirty minutes a day of extended gross motor activity (like jogging) performed three to five times a week, will help upregulate serotonin levels in the brain. Our long-term exposure to exercise benefits us in three ways:

❖ *It improves our physical and cognitive health.*

❖ *It helps stabilize and manage our moods.*

❖ *Voluntary gross motor activity is linked to increased neurogenesis, or the growth of new brain cells.*

Of course, in a classroom or a training session, it's not practical to mandate twenty to thirty minutes a day of sustained gross motor activity, three to five times a week. The best we can do is continually encourage students to exercise and give them a taste of its energy rush with some two to four minute samples, like active cross laterals to music or a march around the room (Chapter 6 has a description of cross lateral activities). The Learning Station CD, *Tony Chestnut*, has directions for other fun, total physical response activities.

16 **Peer Suspense**

Peer suspense certainly keeps epinephrine levels up! Put all your participants' names on slips of paper or 3" x 5" cards and keep them nearby in a bag, bowl or box. At some point during each class, let a participant come up to the container and draw out two names. The other participants do a drum roll on their tables to add suspense. One of the people whose name is drawn gets a standing ovation (Hooray!) and the other gets put on the

spot (Yikes!) to answer two questions in front of their peers. Whoever is called upon to answer the questions comes up to the front of the room while their team cheers for them. Give the participant one "lifeline" (an opportunity to call on someone for help or to use their notes or book to look up the answer) to use on either question. If the participant answers both questions correctly, he or she wins a silly prize or gets to enjoy a round of applause. This kind of peer pressure is both fun and stressful!

VARIATIONS

★ Participants can bring a buddy to the front to help answer questions.

★ Participants can bring their whole team to the front to answer questions.

★ The participant called upon to answer questions also has to make up (on the spot) a question to ask the rest of the class to answer.

★ The participant who answers questions this time gets to draw the names the next time.

17 **Quick Breaths**

Many quick breathing routines supercharge the body and brain with high energy. These activities do for the brain what exercising does for the body. Just because there is minimal physical movement, avoid thinking there is not much going on in your brain. Your brain's two primary fuels are glucose and oxygen—and it can survive a lot longer without glucose than it can without oxygen! To begin, ask your audience to stand while you demonstrate from the front of the room. With your hands at your sides, inhale and exhale short, quick breaths for ten seconds, then rest for five seconds. Repeat this breathing cycle three times.

VARIATIONS

★ Put on some active, instrumental music. Have everyone stand up and do cross lateral activators (like elbow to opposite knee) as they also do the quick breathing cycles. Move for fifteen seconds, rest and repeat. (Chapter 6 has examples of other cross lateral movements.)

★ While standing, extend both arms to the side, like you have wings and are about to fly (but don't flap your arms!). Inhale and exhale rapidly for fifteen seconds and repeat.

★ Stand with both arms held down to your sides. Inhale deeply through the nose. As you exhale, raise your arms straight up in front of you to all the way above your head (like you are doing the "wave" in slow motion) while saying the word, "Awe." Now, take another deep breath. As you exhale this time, let your arms drop all the way down to your sides (the reverse motion) while saying the word, "some." Repeat this cycle, inhaling and raising your arms on the "Awe" and lowering your arms on the "some." (Awesome!)

18 Relays

I get excited about any activity that combines learning *and* physical activity. Both elements are useful by themselves, but together they are a million-dollar event. Relays are simple. Teams compete to complete classroom or learning challenges. The required ingredients are few:

content from the course, participants, an object to transfer and deadlines or compelling goals. Music is optional, but I think it's a great addition to this list. Put your relay teams at one end of the room. Have team members take turns acting as messengers to retrieve and carry back something from the other side of the room. For example, have participants race to verify or discover academic information from a learning station, or bring back needed materials for a project they are building.

VARIATIONS

★ Teams write ten incomplete sentences (with the answers on the back) to review the most recent part of the course. Sentences might read, "Adrenaline is another name for the chemical [BLANK]" (epinephrine). Once they have ten sentences, teams pass them to the right for the use of another team. Place the papers across the room; during the relay, team members take turns crossing the room to answer one question.

★ Perform a relay completely without speaking.

★ Assign to one team the responsibility of setting up relays and officiating them for the other teams. Give them a few minutes to get organized before starting the game.

19 Simon Says

This favorite game requires a presenter who is willing to be a little silly. Tell your audience that you're going to challenge them in a fun way. Ask them to stand up and take a deep breath. Tell them that for this next activity, your name is "Simon" (or, if you wish, "Simone"). Remind them that they are to do whatever you (as Simon) tell them to do, as long as you preface your command with "Simon says...." For example, if you say, "Simon says jump three times," then the members of your audience jump up three times. Tell them to ignore any directions that do not begin with the words, "Simon says." On one hand, this is an elementary school game that many people played as children. On the other hand, you can make it as complicated and sophisticated as you wish in order to challenge an older audience. If you'd like to add an element of competition to the game (to raise the stakes and keep them excited), have people sit down for the rest of the game if they make a mistake.

VARIATIONS

★ Add a few incongruencies to your directions. When you say, "Simon says touch your shoulders," touch your knees instead (the audience should still touch their shoulders). Mix in real and false messages to ensure your group keeps listening and watching carefully.

★ Play fast, upbeat music in the background to add to the stress level. Instrumental music is best—some participants will be distracted by lyrics and vocals.

★ Incorporate subject matter content into your directions. Say, "Simon says point to a right angle in this room," or, "Simon says show with your fingers the sum of three times three."

★ Invite a student volunteer to lead the game.

20 Standing

Did you know that the act of standing increases your heart rate by five to ten percent compared to sitting? This increase means more blood (and oxygen!) flows to the brain. For a short time, maybe one to three minutes, standing can serve as an opportunity to change your posture or position, exercise a sore back or rump and stretch your legs. Say to your group, "We've been sitting too long. Let's boost our circulation with a quick stretch. Please stand up!" Then, use that time when everyone is on their feet to summarize the key points of the day or tell a short story that sets up the upcoming learning. If learners have to stand too long, though, they get tired or frustrated, so watch the clock.

VARIATIONS

★ Ask participants to stand on one foot for ten seconds while you discuss something really important.

★ Have participants hold an arm or ear or touch their head while you discuss something very important.

★ Participants march in place as you either summarize a few key points or play some fun, upbeat music for thirty seconds.

21 Touch Gold

Have high BPM music (like Rossini's *William Tell Overture*) ready to play and ask your audience to stand up and listen. Tell them that, when you give the signal, they are to locate and touch, in order, a list of particular items in the room. For example, when you say, "Go!," they might touch 5 things made of glass, 4 things made of metal, 3 things made of plastic, 2 things made of cloth and 1 thing made of paper. This activity works great as an instant scavenger hunt. A K–12 classroom is especially suited to having participants touch objects that reflect the current topic or unit. Keep your list of objects short so it is easy to remember.

Experiment with the following lists:

❖ *5 things that are recyclable, 4 things that are made in the U.S.A., 3 things that are made in a factory, 2 things that are opposites and 1 thing that is made of only one element.*

❖ *For a math class: 5 right angles, 4 cubes, 3 plane surfaces, 2 circles and 1 triangle.*

❖ *5 things that are spelled with five letters or more, 4 things that are pronounced with four syllables, 3 things that start with A, 2 things in alphabetical order and 1 thing in another language.*

22 Triangle Tag

This variation on the game of tag really generates energy. Divide your audience into groups of four. Some groups can have five people to accommodate extra players, but groups of three will *not* work. You'll need plenty of space (outdoors or a big, open room) to play this wild game. Three (or four) of the four (or five) players form a circle, holding hands. One of the four participants is "It" and stands outside the triangle with the goal of tagging a designated player—one of the people holding hands. The participants forming the triangle run in a circle, spinning so that the outside player cannot easily tag the target player. When "It" finally does, the tagged person becomes the new "It" and another participant is designated as the target. Play this game for a maximum of three to five minutes. It's very energetic!

VARIATION

★ Triangle Tag can be used to learn or review concepts, especially in science or math. For example, a biology class could play "Receptor Tag," in which the person who is called "It" represents the ligand (an information-carrying molecule, like a neurotransmitter or amino acid) and tries to "dock" with (tag) a receptor site (the person who is supposed to be tagged). Make the game content-meaningful and you can use it for all kinds of review.

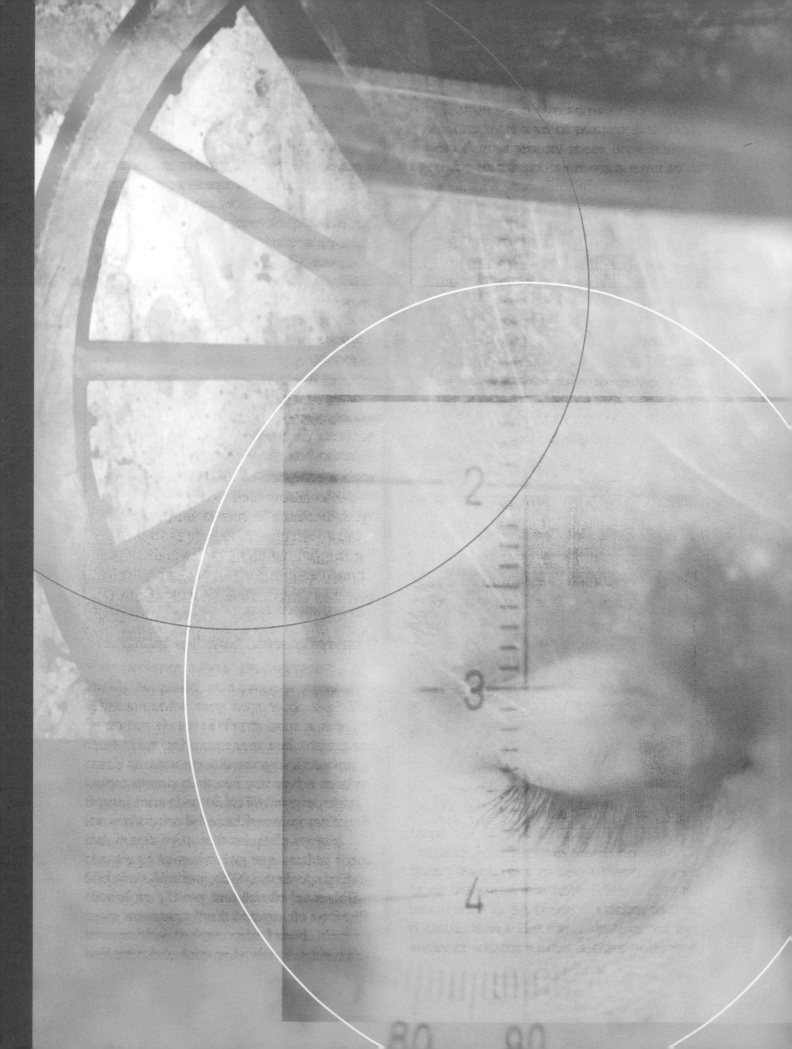

Chapter 5
"Uh-Oh!"
The State of Healthy Concern

What Is This State?

The usual negative connotations of the state "Oh, @#$%!" become positive when we rephrase its label to "healthy concern." In this "Uh-Oh!" state, you can orchestrate student concern, caring or hope for the outcome of their personal achievements. If you can't elicit this state you'll be in a lot of trouble because you'll instill very little motivation in your students.

Why Is This State Important?

A healthy state of concern prompts better student engagement, involvement and interest in the outcome of their learning. It's not very common for students to instinctively care about how to do algebra or to learn what the five longest rivers of South America are. One of the roles of a teacher in a school is to spark student interest in subjects that many have no inherent desire to learn. Triggering this state in students is at the heart of good teaching practices; it's absolutely critical to students' academic success.

How Long Does This State Last?

Like every other state, the state of healthy concern doesn't last very long. Typically, we can only care about one particular thing for so long because of the mental and physical resources required to maintain vigilance and emotional investment. Some people switch easily from one concern to another. Why? They might be genuinely more interested or curious about people, events or issues than others are. On the other hand, others are simply more anxious and worried about everything (which is only healthy if you're a safety engineer at a nuclear power plant). Differences in humans mean we have different homeostatic set points. Some are easily stressed and others are more resistant to it. There are advantages and disadvantages to each response. Having said this, keep in mind that some people maintain high levels of stress in their daily lives and very small events or new concerns can trigger more.

What brain activity is involved? People in a state of concern show a measurable increase in the release of stress hormones in their brain. In general, cortisol levels vary in all of us throughout the day; they are lowest at night, highest in the morning and moderate in the afternoon. (We are also more stressed when we are dehydrated (Levine & Coe, 1989).) Environmental stressors trigger the endocrine systems to release glucocorticoids (a category of neuromodulators that includes cortisol, vasopressin and ACTH) for short-term survival; glucocorticoids are released as coping chemicals and are generally considered positive for the human system. The occasional increase of this hormone will not harm the body. Over the long haul, however, cortisol is known to damage hippocampal neurons (Sapolsky, 1992). Prolonged exposure (at least four to six weeks) to elevated stress is dangerous. Therefore, teachers and presenters should keep in mind that the deliberate use of stressors is best done for short-term strategies rather than as a consistent, pervasive theme of instruction.

GOOD STRESS CAN:
- *increase focus*
- *mobilize energy*
- *dull pain*
- *increase acuity*
- *improve memory*

EXCESS STRESS CAN:
- *increase mistakes*
- *reduce spatial memory*
- *deplete energy*
- *reduce storage of energy*
- *impair reproduction*
- *kill brain cells*

Cortisol: The "Uh-Oh," Energy Releasing Hormone

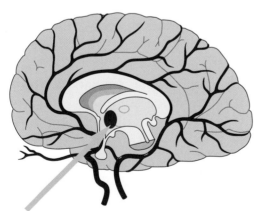

1. The hypothalamus is our thermostat for change and the origin of the stress response.
2. It produces CRF (corticotropin-releasing factor), which travels to the pituitary gland.
3. The aroused pituitary releases ACTH (adrenocorticotropic hormone) to your bloodstream.
4. Within seconds, it arrives at the adrenal glands.
5. Adrenal glands secrete glucocorticoids such as cortisol into the bloodstream.

Body Language of This State

A stressed body may tighten in areas that show stress, such as the neck, shoulders or back. The body may bend slightly forward. Breathing is often shorter, shallower or tighter. Keep in mind, however, that activities that are too stressful for one student may mobilize another. As always, cultural variations and varied circumstances among your students or audience might change what you see and hear. It's okay to vary the stress levels of the activities you use reaching order to reach, over time, all your students. Avoid becoming immobilized just because you are afraid to temporarily distress one or a few students. Even a great presenter cannot satisfy 100 percent of the audience at every moment. Let go of that hope; people are too different for that to happen.

Just make sure that by the end of your presentation, every participant enjoyed at least one thing in particular that seemed planned specifically for his or her benefit.

Cortisol: The Hormone of Concern and Negative Expectations

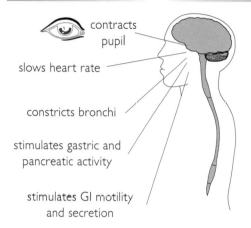

contracts pupil

slows heart rate

constricts bronchi

stimulates gastric and pancreatic activity

stimulates GI motility and secretion

Human response to stress is quite varied. Key factors include the person's own baseline stress levels as well as life experiences, coping skills, support available and perceived control over environmental variables.

What Food Affects This State?

There are no foods known to specifically increase or reduce stress. However, many people consume "comfort foods" during times of personal stress, most of which are not very good for the body. Comfort foods are usually high in fat or contain simple carbohydrates with little nutritional value. What the body really craves is a sense of calm, which may happen temporarily because eating a particular food is considered a reward. Additionally, carbohydrates may contain negligible amounts of tryptophan, a substance that gets converted to serotonin (a calming brain chemical).

Excess sugar and fats are converted to fatty acids and stored as triglycerides; during a stressful emergency, they are mobilized as glycerol, ketone bodies and fatty acids. Carbohydrates are converted to glucose, stored as glycogen and utilized as glucose during stress. Proteins are pretty straightforward; they are converted to amino acids without exception. They supply the raw materials (tyrosine, phenylalanine, etc.) that help focus the brain during arousal states (Sapolsky, 1998). Looked at this way, everything you eat can be considered "stress-relieving food," since most of it is converted to energy sources that deal with stressful events.

Stress and Cognition

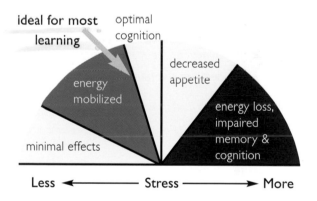

ideal for most learning

optimal cognition

decreased appetite

energy mobilized

energy loss, impaired memory & cognition

minimal effects

Less ← Stress → More

What Music Affects This State?

Music with poor auditory quality (like a song played on a badly tuned radio station), dissonant lyrics, a quick tempo or music that you simply don't like will generally increase stress levels. Although listening to music with qualities opposite to those just listed may not reduce your stress, it certainly won't increase it.

Distress and Learning

Stress Levels

High or sustained levels of stress (distress) or trauma: Strongly impaired or highly selective memory. Excess activation of the amygdala through trauma may inhibit hippocampal functioning. Excess and chronic stress commonly lead to neuronal death in the hippocampus.

Moderate stress: General facilitation of memory storage.

Very low stress: Neutral or minimal impact on memory; no excessive hormonal activation.

Key Basic Concepts

To elicit the state of healthy concern in order to enhance student learning, teachers and presenters can:

❖ *increase personal accountability;*

❖ *use appropriate novelty;*

❖ *occasionally limit class resources;*

❖ *enforce compelling deadlines; and*

❖ *implement episodes of minor unpredictability.*

Most of us know how we get stressed or how to stress others out. But as instructors, we want to create only "good" stress, or short-term stress. Therefore, we'll eliminate all forms of counterproductive stress such as that of clear or perceived physical danger, confusion over learning, subordinate social status (Carlson & Earls, 1999), loss of control, loss of predictability, loss of outlets for frustration, a perception of things worsening or a diminishing perception of power. Instead, we'll focus on other things that release cortisol in ways healthier in a learning environment.

Some social interactions can, by their very nature, be stressful. But why use social structures as part of learning? They add personal accountability even while building community. Social anthropologists call frequent, positive interactions "social play," something that *all* mammals do. Research suggests that social play and its subsequent bonding activate the opioid rewards in our brain (Panksepp et al., 1999). Opioids are neuromodulators that act as analgesics in the brain; one example is endorphins. These opioids are typically released during times of pain and can dull suffering or trigger pleasure. Still, some presenters still believe that social interaction during instruction is a waste of time, despite the considerable and mounting evidence that a great deal of learning takes place within a strong social fabric. In short, social activities have their place for promoting well-being and a little healthy stress, too.

Strategies for Healthy Concern

Keep in mind that *many things* will raise students' concern levels. This chapter focuses only on things that are healthy learning strategies, not strategies that create threat, distress or excess concern. In short, you have my permission to intentionally stress your audience in ways that may arouse them to learn. If you add stress to an activity that learners will have no control over, the stress needs to be temporary and positive (e.g., a change that precedes an improvement).

1 Accountability

Any time we feel that we will be held accountable for our actions, there's a pretty good likelihood that we'll stress about it. This pressure can be healthy stress if a presenter manipulates it well. You can add accountability in many ways, for things like doing what you promised, learning what is expected, behaving as requested and being back on time. Accountability also means implementing consequences for audience members who fail to accomplish what was required.

Caution: Make sure that you walk the fine line between concern and threat. You can increase concern without making threats. Threats are not appropriate for a learning environment unless there is a health, safety, personal property or survival issue at stake. Realize, too, that a consequence does not have to be a punishment—it can mean an absence of a reward that everyone else (who did perform the required behavior) gets to enjoy.

This Activity Started Out as "Yikes!" and Transistioned to "Uh-Oh!" as the Degree of Difficulty Increased

VARIATIONS
★ Establish consequences for being late by creating a brief ritual that acknowledges everyone who is back on time. For example, when your group returns from a break, say, "If you made it back on time, raise your hand and say, 'Did it!' Now, turn to the person seated nearest you and say, 'Welcome back, too!'"

★ Every fifteen minutes, have participants write three or four summary statements of what they just learned. Partner them up and ask them to trade and critique each other's statements. They should give their partners two compliments and one suggestion.

★ Participants pair up and respond to a question (orally or in writing) that you pose to the whole group. When they've had time to discuss it, call for volunteers to share their response.

② Circle Run-Ons

Circle Run-Ons are quick reviews that generate a moderate amount of stress. A group of four to eight participants stands in a circle. One person starts a run-on sentence about the subject or unit just completed. For example, he or she could say, "One thing we learned about evaporation today is…." The person to the left (or right) has to continue the sentence and leave off the ending for the next person. To continue the example, the second person could say, "…that evaporation happens more when it's windy, and then we learned…"

This extended run-on sentence keeps challenging participants to fill in the blanks, but they also get the fun of setting up a challenge for the next person. It is allowable for someone to not know an answer, but everyone in the circle will know if they don't. Of course, someone can always weasel out of knowing the correct answer by being creative! A wily participant might have answered the first statement with, "…that evaporation is important because…," inviting the third person to finish the sentence with a fact. The goal for the group is to keep the sentence going for two minutes.

VARIATIONS

★ Participant pairs play a game of "verbal tennis." One names an item from yesterday's lesson and the other immediately adds another item to the list. The last one to name an idea or concept is the "idea champ" for the day.

★ In groups of four to six, participants do a word association activity from the previous lesson.

③ Deadlines

In addition to keeping energy levels high (as you read in Chapter 4), deadlines will also elicit stress fairly consistently and are a good idea for class work in general. However, we all respond differently to deadlines, so pay close attention to each learner's response. Learners with ADHD or oppositional disorders typically aren't successful with deadlines, so when you have serious, important deadlines to meet it's a good idea to pair them up with another student. But everyone will be more successful if you keep the following guidelines for setting deadlines in mind:

❖ *Avoid overkill; assign no more than one or two deadlines per hour.*

❖ *Make the deadlines attainable and relevant.*

❖ *Ensure that participants have the necessary resources to meet the deadline.*

❖ *Announce when half the time before the deadline has passed to warn participants when there are only a few minutes left.*

VARIATIONS

★ Use music to countdown to a dead-line. Naturally, the theme song for *Jeopardy* is a humorous option, but it works best with the "over forty" crowd. For more universal appeal, try something like *Flight of the Bumblebee* (by Nicolai Rimsky-Korsakov).

★ Make announcements to foster stress, such as, "There are four minutes left. Turn to your neighbor; if they haven't started yet, tell them to get going!"

★ Moderate stress by boosting confidence while you announce time milestones. For example, tell participants, "You have seven minutes left but, if you stay focused, that will be enough time to complete your task."

Impact of Stress on Specific Types of Subject Content

Better for	Appropriate	Better for review
1) highly complex material with patterns such as language, math & music	for most other academic subjects	or for learning easy material with no complex patterns
2) learners with low tolerance for stress, or learning delays		

4 Group Quizzes

Break your audience into an even number of smaller groups. Each group creates a list of ten questions that can be answered in less than thirty seconds and with fewer than twenty-five words. Once they've made their lists, ask half the groups to remain seated and the other half to walk over to join one of the seated groups (and remain standing). The standing group quizzes the sitting one with their questions. A scorekeeper awards three points for a perfect answer, two points for a "close" answer and one point for making a stab at it. The goal is to score thirty points. When the first quiz is complete, the groups switch places. The standing group sits down to be quizzed by the group that just answered their questions (and the sitting group stands to deliver the quiz). As a whole group, celebrate high scores at the end of the second round.

VARIATIONS

★ On index cards, participants write two questions (with answers) that can be answered in thirty seconds or less. They take turns quizzing partners, then return to their small groups or teams to share what they learned.

★ Participants write two questions on one index card. Then, they write the answers to the two questions on a second card. Mix up all the cards in a big bowl or bin. Everyone draws out two cards. Then, they find the participants with the corresponding questions or answers to the cards they drew.

5 **Group Reviews**

Quick, unannounced reviews can raise stress levels depending on how ready learners are for an activity and whether or not they will be held accountable for more than just academic performance (like by having to present material to their peers). Without warning, tell participant groups that it's time for a quick review. Give them butcher paper or large sheets from a flip chart. Have them arrange all the concepts and terms they can remember from the lesson into some sort of graphic organizer for display. Post all the groups' review work around the room. Half the people in each group remain with their poster to explain it, while the other half walk around the room asking questions of the other groups. Then, they switch places.

VARIATIONS

★ Small groups of participants do graphic organizer reviews. Then, each group sends out all but one member to visit other groups and collect ideas from their graphic organizers; the remaining member of each group will share their own graphic organizer with visitors from other groups. Group members return from their visits and add new ideas to their group organizer. Post all the graphic organizers in the room for a gallery walk review later.

★ In groups, participants brainstorm everything they know about a particular topic and list it on paper. Then, they take those list items and arrange them in a discovery graphic organizer. Create these organizers at the end of each learning session. Have participants share them, add new items when appropriate and use them for review.

★ Put participants in groups of at least three people but no more than six. Individuals write three to five brief summary statements or a set of recap statements from the lesson, put their name on their paper and pass it to the left. Each participant takes a moment to read their neighbor's paper; on the back, he or she writes one compliment and one suggestion to make it better. Continue passing the papers around until each participant has his or her own again.

6 **Limited Resources**

Limited resources is a strategy that works easily and quickly to motivate an audience to get to work. First, identify resources that learners value, like time, supplies, friends, favorite activities, compliments, favors or tools that make their workload easier. (Anything of value that becomes scarce will increase cortisol levels if participants have to compete for its use.) Second, give your audience the opportunity to capture some of the diminishing resources for themselves. If they think that they have no control over the distribution or allotment of the resources, they'll slip into helpless immobility instead of jumping to capitalize on their chance to get stuff. Sound like gobbledygook? Think of Musical Chairs, the classic game of scarcity.

VARIATIONS

★ Spur participants to action by getting them to scramble for tools they need for an upcoming project. For example, say, "We're a bit short on colored markers, so if your table would like to use some for its brain poster, please pick a person to come up and grab no more than three."

★ Encourage promptness by adding mystery to scheduled events. Announce something like, "When you come in tomorrow, our room will be set up a bit differently for a fantastic guest speaker. Since she talks very softly, you may want to come early to get a seat up close."

7 Look at Your Neighbor's Paper

Many tools of engagement are also tools for increased accountability. It's very easy to have your participants check their neighbors' work; most people are curious about everyone else's work and will do their own just so no one can catch them with something lacking. You can have them emphasize either complete or missing aspects of their neighbor's paper:

❖ *"Look at your neighbor's paper. If they wrote down all three points that we just mentioned, congratulate them."*

❖ *"Look at your neighbor's paper. If they have written fewer than the last three items we've just reviewed, either raise your hand so I can come help them or tell them which items are missing."*

❖ *"Look at your neighbor's paper. If they haven't written anything yet, tell them to wake up and get going."*

❖ *"Look at your neighbor's paper. If they're only halfway done, raise your hand so I can come help them, because we need to finish up in a few moments."*

❖ *"Look at your neighbor's paper. If they're at least as far along as you, congratulate them, but then hop back to work."*

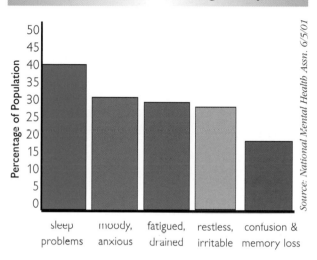

How Are Adults Doing Today?

Percentage of Population vs. sleep problems, moody/anxious, fatigued/drained, restless/irritable, confusion & memory loss

Source: National Mental Health Assn. 6/5/01

These data are from the general population. Does your specific group identify with these symptoms? This may suggest why there's value in stretching, reflection and social interactions.

8 Novelty

Predictable events and environments contribute to lower stress levels, even if the environment or events aren't necessarily good. Change is what concerns us— maybe not in a bad or "heavy" way, but it will make our cortisol levels rise. That means novelty is only novel if it is a variation from a predictable, baseline routine. Make sure you have embedded in your learners' brains consistent classroom patterns or behaviors before you try to introduce novelty to get them going. Only if you've always started lesson reviews at nine in the morning will there be any surprise or alertness if you one day start them at eight. Be sure to point out to learners that you are altering the routine to activate their anticipation and curiosity, too. Class routines you could vary include:

❖ *introducing a new song for the call-back signal;*

❖ *changing the way you review for a text or quiz (many ideas are listed in this book);*

❖ *assigning new tasks or chores to students; or*

❖ *rearranging the order of the day's activities.*

⑨ Read-Arounds

First, make sure everyone has the ability to read any material before you present it in this format (to avoid embarrassing anyone). Put in front of each participant a handout or assigned text material about one page in length. Have them form groups of three to five people and pick someone to start reading aloud the first paragraph (or the first five sentences, depending on how the text is broken up). Once the first person has read his or her section, the person to the right (or left) reads the next one. Each participant listens *without comment* while the others read. Rotate around the table until the entire paper has been read.

VARIATIONS
★ Once a group completes the document, have them either discuss it or raise their hands so you know when they are ready to move on.

★ While one participant reads, the others highlight material they don't understand or have questions about. When the document has been read completely, participants ask each other questions, discuss the answers and clarify confusion.

★ One group member reads the document aloud while the others create graphic organizers of the material.

⑩ Teach a Partner

Use an overhead transparency as a prompt for a quick lesson you deliver to the class; then, step aside so learners can put it into their own words. Have everyone stand and move around the room to find a partner. The pairs should remain standing. On cue, one partner will explain the concept you just taught, while using the displayed overhead transparency as a prompt. The partners then switch places so the other person gets a turn to teach. Listen to the pairs as they teach each other to ensure that everyone understands the material.

VARIATIONS
★ Split an assignment so each partner teaches half of what is shown on the overhead projector.

★ Put participants into groups of three and assign each a different role. One will summarize the material, the second will link it to past learning and the third will write two questions about it to present to the entire class.

11 Think-Pair-Share

This universal activity is a valuable tool for continually refreshing and revising our learning. It is also ideal for content review. Its basic steps are:

❖ *stand up and mentally reflect on your topic for a moment;*

❖ *move around the room to find a partner;*

❖ *share with each other your prior learning; and*

❖ *thank your partner and return to your seat.*

The trick is to create, innovate and explore fresh variations so the activity is always relevant to your learners. If your technique isn't updated constantly, it will get real old, real fast.

VARIATIONS

★ Participants turn to the person sitting next to them and teach him or her something they just learned.

★ One partner role-plays an adult; the other partner role-plays a five-year-old child. Each partner explains the last topic to the other as they think their character would do, using speech patterns and hand gestures. Simplicity is key.

★ One partner plays the role of a world-renowned expert on a topic and the other partner plays the role of a reporter who asks questions for two minutes. Give each person a moment to get into character.

★ One partner teaches a key point from the last ten minutes of instruction by using only the hands and body. Then, he or she reviews what was "said" using both gestures and words. Switch and have the other person do the same for a different topic. This strategy is great for embedding new learning into the right-side hemisphere of the brain.

Why Manage Student Stress? Many Underperform During Stress!

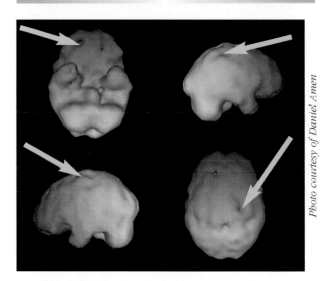

Photo courtesy of Daniel Amen

This SPECT scan usually shows smooth, even activation. Note the "holes" of underactivity when this particular subject is under stress.

12 Turn-To

In general, learners like interaction. Although some learners prefer to be left alone, the majority would talk to others all day long if they could. Turn-Tos take just seconds to accomplish and meet this common need to be social, as well as your need to induce a particular brain state for learning. To set up a state of healthy concern, use a Turn-To to introduce hesitation or worry about an activity. Introduce it by saying something like, "In just a moment we're going to play a three-level game that moves pretty fast. I hope everyone will be able to keep up because there's a short quiz after it about the content of the activity. So, before we get started, turn to your nearest neighbor and say, 'Good luck!'" "Good luck" is a positive sentiment, but in this case it carries a slightly ominous connotation to spur participants into action.

VARIATIONS
★ Use Turn-Tos to give well-deserved praise. Learners like praise and rarely get enough of it, although they are skeptical of praise that they think is shallow or unwarranted. Praise for something easy or routine is hollow. Make sure you only use praise when an audience would truly appreciate it. Wait until participants have just completed a task that they thought was challenging, time-consuming or complex. Then say, "Turn to your teammates and say, 'Great job!'"

★ Use Turn-Tos to relieve stress and induce relaxation by saying something like, "Turn to your neighbor and tell them it's time to relax."

★ Use Turn-Tos to motivate and encourage by saying, "Turn to your neighbor and tell them 'You can do it!'"

13 Universal Questions

Universal questions are questions to which *nearly everyone* will respond quickly. By eliciting healthy stress, they can be used to create a state of concern as well as anticipation (which is how they are used in Chapter 3). These questions can prompt a little "Uh-Oh!" inside the

minds of others because they precede the requirement of a learner having to show what he or she knows. Naturally, if a person is very confident of his or her knowledge, the stress is minimal. When you ask universal questions, raise your hand in the air to role model the kind of response that you want.

VARIATIONS
Use questions to create the desired stress:
★ "How many of you know we have a quiz on Friday?" followed by, "How many of you are not yet ready for it?" and, "How many of you have completed your assignment and are ready for the quiz?"

★ "How many of you are confident enough of what you know to teach it to another person?"

★ "How many of you know that we have only four class hours until the mid-term project is due?"

★ "How many of you know that your project is due Friday?" followed by, "How many of you know that the media center will be closed tomorrow?"

★ "How many of you know I use an Internet service that checks term papers to make sure they were actually written by you instead of downloaded from a website?"

14 Walkabouts

A walkabout is a walk-and-learn activity that makes sure each participant gets movement to maintain an active state as well as a chance to process new information cognitively. Try asking participants to stand, pick new partners and then take a three-minute walk together. While walking, partners explain to each other what they learned from the last unit or topic.

VARIATIONS

★ Participants walk with a partner in laps around the room as they do a topic review or key-points summary from the last ten to fifteen minutes of class.

★ Partners walk each other to their two favorite posters on display in the classroom. They will share with each other why they like the poster and what it means to them.

15 Whips

Whips are named for their quick pacing and the "snap" in their rhythm. They can be done within the entire class, but the time it takes to involve everyone slows the activity down and can bore participants. Whips are best done with a small group of participants (four to seven people in size) sitting in chairs. Whips go around the circle, with each person sharing one quick application, review a point or make a comment about what was just learned. The group leader might start by saying, "One thing I learned about *how* we learn today is that...." Participants have the option of "passing," but don't encourage too much of it.

VARIATIONS

★ When participants are finished summarizing what they have learned, they toss an object (like a ball) to another person. Whoever catches it speaks next.

★ Each participant finishes his or her comments with a question that the next person has to answer.

★ Participants have to use in their comments vocabulary words from a list that the instructor (you) posted. This gives them practice using these words in context.

Chapter 6
"Movin' On"
States of Transition

What Is This State?

Technically, there is no one state of transition. You need to know how to elicit transitions that don't contaminate or confuse units of learned material in students' minds and that also give them a little bit of mental "time off." This chapter is about creating physical, emotional and cognitive breaks from a prior activity. These "Movin' On" breaks can be activities as simple as energizers or as complex as journal writing, as long as they ensure smooth, plausible transitions from one activity to the next.

Why Is This State Important?

Human beings are generally not very good at going from zero to sixty miles per hour. Nor are we are very good at going from sixty to zero, or from excitement to patience or pleasure to danger. The "Movin' On" state is a moderate zone from which we can shift easily from one state to another.

Movement Facilitates State Changes

How Long Does This State Last?

Transition states don't have to last very long—they just have to be plausible. We really only want our audience to stay in the transition state until we can move them into the next activity.

What Brain Activity Is Involved?

During a transition, the brain switches from one definable state to another by using the prefrontal cortex, orbitofrontal cortex and cingulate gyrus. If you have the option, a physical activity like a brisk, ten-minute walk is often linked to increasing students' mental arousal and lowering their stress level (Ekkekakis et al., 2000). Brain changes like these are perfect preparations for new learning.

Body Language of This State

No particular body language will alert you to a learner in a transition state. However, people do get "stuck" in states and may have difficulty moving out of them. In general, stuck postures are more pronounced than the postures of other states—think of how much harder it would be to transition someone in an armchair recliner with her feet up than it would be to transition someone already standing. Finally, cultural variation and varied circumstances might change the body posture and language of what you see and hear among your audience.

Use State Management Strategies Whenever Groups Get Up and Move

What Food Affects This State?

There are no perfect foods that will help you transition from one state to another. However, some foods can influence our ability to change gears. When our serotonin levels are low, it can be difficult to alter our thinking and we are more likely to get stuck in a state. We can help our brains by consuming foods that are higher in tryptophan, which contributes to the body's synthesis of serotonin. These foods include turkey, milk, cottage cheese, poultry, eggs, red meats, tofu, avocados, almonds, walnuts, bananas, eggplant, plums and tomatoes. Energy to fuel transitions may come from amino acids such as phenylalanine or from vitamin B-6, both of which can be found in fish, liver or kidneys.

What Music Affects This State?

Selected music may help you "bridge" from one cognitive-emotional state to another. If your audience is in a calm state, you'll want play music with a snappy (not frenzied) tempo. Slowly bringing up the volume from quiet to audible will further help you make the transition; this gradual change is just as important as your choice of what you play. Abrupt changes are jarring, not helpful! Once learners are doing something in an active state, they can be moved to an even more energetic state. To transition your audience from a peppy state to a calmer state, slowly lower the volume instead. Any kind of music can transition learners as long as it is likely to change the current state and you slowly adjust its volume.

Key Basic Concepts

Transitions are typically prompted by "plausible novelty." Novelty can be almost anything, from changes in an activity to taking short breaks. The changes must be noticeable, but they must also make sense. A poor example of a transition is, "Class, you are all sitting down, but let's get up so we can transition to something else. Ready? Get up!" Transitioning learners without warning gives them no time to set aside one activity to make room for another. A better example of a transition is, "Oops! I just checked the clock and we're running a bit short on time. Let's shift gears now, so we can finish up when we're supposed to. Everyone take a slow, deep breath. Inhale and hold it.

Good. Now, exhale. Good. Let's get ready for the last thing for today. Everyone please stand up! Pick up your notes and find a partner." A deep breath allows your audience to mentally wrap-up what they've been doing before they are asked to move on to something new.

Strategies for Transitions

Keep in mind that many things can shift a student's energy levels but, as in previous chapters, this segment focuses on things that learners can do themselves rather than activities you perform in front of them. Remember that the best learning occurs when students take an active instead of passive role. Our question, then, about making smooth transitions will be, "Does an audience just hear you tell them to transition, or do they get to activate the transition for themselves?"

1 Agree or Disagree?

This simple engagement tool is used to elicit a confirming conclusion from your audience. You make a summary statement, then ask the audience directly, "Agree or disagree?" The idea is to set up some kind of closing point or finishing statement about what was just done or learned. This readies the audience to move ahead by providing closure to the last topic.

VARIATIONS

★ Ask who is ready for a quick quiz on the topic. If you get an affirmative response of fifty percent or more, move on; you don't have to do the quiz because learners already feel like they know the material—your goal to teach it has been accomplished. If fewer than half of your learners feel ready to take a quiz, you need to better clarify the material and answer some questions from the audience.

★ In small groups or teams, participants write conclusion statements on 3" x 5" cards (one per person). Collect the cards and read each one out loud to the whole group. The group can discuss or vote on the correctness or applicability of each statement or you can comment on each of them and solicit feedback from the whole group.

★ Give participants three index cards each. Have them write in big letters on each card, "GREAT," "OK" or "IFFY." They should keep their set of cards handy in a notebook or their desk. Anytime you want to quickly find out how well they comprehend a topic you just presented, ask them to show you their confidence level by holding up the card that best describes their knowledge and understanding. Once you get feedback, act on it.

2 Brain Breaks

Transitions may be needed for an emotional break after an activity during which participants expressed intense feelings. Likewise, they may need a mental break after an activity that was complex, extremely novel or heavy on content. The simplest break would be to give the class three to five minutes of personal time.

VARIATIONS

★ Have participants pair up and go for a short walk. During their walk, they perform a task completely unrelated to what they had been doing, like getting to know each other better.

★ Give students a few minutes to write in their journals.

★ Time your class so that the needed break comes up right before lunch or at the end of the day.

★ Give participants a stress-release moment, such as time for personal organizing. Let them consolidate notes, recopy anything they don't quite understand, review upcoming deadlines or clean up their desk area.

★ Play relaxing music and have students just listen to it, preferably with their eyes closed.

3 Cars in Motion

When it's a good time to take a brain break, tell the audience that you're all going to go for a drive. Have everyone pick a partner and adjust their chairs so they face each other (or so one person is sitting directly behind the other, like a passenger in the back seat of a car). Then, have one partner choose the letter D and have the other partner choose the letter P. Whoever chose D is the first Driver; the partner who chose P is the first Passenger. When you're all ready to start driving, put on very fast, upbeat music with a good rhythm. *Great Balls of Fire* (by Jerry Lee Lewis) is a good song to play; so is the track *Drag Racing* on the CD, *Energizers to Go*, produced by The Brain Store®. When you give the "green light," the Driver should "drive" like a maniac, leaning sideways through sharp turns, slamming backwards at sudden stops and being thrown forward when he or she steps on the gas. The Passenger has to hold on to keep up, copying the body moves of the Driver as they both zoom around in their "vehicle." After forty-five seconds, have the Driver "pull over" and switch roles with the Passenger.

Thinking is fun, learning is easy, but too much lecture makes us queasy.

VARIATIONS

★ Indulge the "backseat driver" impulse by having the Driver and Passenger on their feet and walking around the room. This time, though, the Driver is blindfolded (or simply closes his or her eyes) and the Passenger "steers." The Passenger stands behind the Driver with his or her hands on the Driver's shoulders. The partners have to maneuver through a room full of other "blind" drivers. Switch roles after forty-five seconds.

★ As in the previous variation, the Passenger directs a blindfolded Driver but this time with verbal commands only (no touching or shoulder-guiding), steering around obstacles and corners with commands like "turn left" or "back up."

4 Seat Switching

Have groups switch seats as a way to switch to a new topic, freshen up an old one or pump "new blood" into a brainstorming session. How you set up the activity is critical; some participants will enjoy the novelty and some will be a bit apprehensive. Avoid adding to resistance by saying things like, "In a moment, we're going to be changing seats. I know some of you might not like it, but give it a try."

Try this introduction instead: "We've all been sitting too long; it's a good time for a change. Please take a deep breath and hold it. Good. Now, exhale. Great. Let's stand up." Put on some marching music and start with a stretch. Have participants march in place as you direct them to collect their notebooks and other personal belongings. The whole time, model the movements you want them to make, with smiles and lots of energy.

To mix up the group, set them in motion by asking them to quickly touch the backs of sixteen chairs (they should march from chair to chair) and to stop as soon as they hear the music stop. When they all come to a stop, compliment their enthusiasm and cooperation with a "Great!" and ask them to take the nearest seat so you can all get started on the next activity. Tell them not to sit with anyone from their original tables.

VARIATIONS

★ Change participants' seats only within a single group, team or table.

★ Have participants routinely change seats once a day, at the cue of a student, a bell or the clock.

★ Have participants march around the room in a round of Musical Chairs, except that, in this variation of the game, there is a chair for everyone to sit in.

5 Clapping Games

Start a clapping rhythm for participants to pass around the room. You might do ba-dum, ba-dum, bum, bum, bum (two quick double claps followed by three regular claps). As the audience tunes into your rhythm, they imitate and clap it until everyone is involved.

VARIATIONS

★ A team leader, group leader or volunteer starts a clapping rhythm. The rest of the participants follow suit. As time goes on, the pattern should become longer or more complex. This is good for memory, listening and music skills as well as team-building.

★ Make patterns more complex by mixing handclaps with foot stomps.

★ Use a clapping pattern to create an end-of-the-day ritual that incorporates all groups or tables in your class. Give each group three minutes to brainstorm key ideas from the day's learning and decide which item they thought was the most important. They share their key item with the rest of the class through a clapping pattern. It might sound something like, "This is table number two. We learned how states work for you!"

6 Creative Handshakes

Get ready to turn on the high BPM music! Sometimes you need to shake up an audience if their energy level has dropped, they're stuck in passive states or need to get their blood circulating again. Ask everyone to stand; when you start the music have them walk around the room and touch the backs of twenty-one chairs as quickly as possible. When they finish, tell them to partner up with the person closest to them and to wait for your instructions.

When you say, "Shake!," their goal is to invent and use a wild, brand-new, totally creative handshake. Every ten to fifteen seconds, put them on the move to find a new partner and invent another handshake, until they've worked their way back to their original seats.

VARIATIONS

★ Instead of creative handshakes, ask partners to perform a celebration ritual; maybe they can improve on the High Five (with a Low Five or a Side Five, etc.).

★ Partners give each other auditory affirmations of confidence and support ("You're doing great today!").

★ One participant shows off a dance move and the partner repeats it.

 7 Cross Laterals

Cross laterals are activating movements, usually content-free. To perform a cross lateral, we "cross over" with our hands, arms or legs from one side of the body to the other. For example, use your right hand to pat yourself on the back of your left shoulder, or touch your right elbow to your left knee. Playing music with a steady beat can help establish a physical pattern. Alternate right-side, left-side motions for about ten seconds.

Some examples of cross-lateral movements are:

❖ *using your hands to touch opposite elbows*

❖ *using your hands to touch opposite hips*

❖ *using your hands to touch opposite knees*

❖ *using your feet to touch the backs of opposite heels*

❖ *putting one hand on your opposite earlobe, the other hand on your nose and switching, so each hand does what the other hand was doing*

 8 Finger Math

Have the audience break itself into small groups of three to six participants (ideally four per group). The members of each group face each other in a tight circle. They put one hand behind their backs and mentally choose a number to show, from zero (with a closed fist) to five (all their fingers spread out). You, as the presenter, pick a goal number—let's say, eleven. When you say "Go!," everyone shows their hands and the numbers they've picked. The group totals the numbers. If they hit the target, eleven, they all say out loud, "Got it!" Then, they can play again, aiming for a target number of their own choosing. If the group's hands don't total to eleven, they keep trying until they do.

VARIATIONS

★ Instead of adding the numbers on the hands, multiply the highest number by the lowest number to hit the target number.

★ Make the calculation more complex by adding the even numbers and subtracting the odd ones.

★ Play with pairs instead of groups.

9 Humor

Used well, humor can assist your transitions, although it's not a particularly useful state for learning on its own. (Of course, it's not a terrible state, either.) Laughing and learning can go together, just not exactly at the same second. Humor can *set up learning* by putting students in a more alert, cheerful or responsive state than they were before—especially if they are stuck in a tense or tired state. Humor can also reduce stress or eradicate perceptions of threat, if used well. You can incorporate humor in ways as simple as buying a joke book (with age-level appropriate material) and having a participant read one joke for each transition. Consider these suggestions by Doni Tamblyn, an expert trainer who uses humor well (2003):

❖ *Cut yourself some slack and lighten up.*

❖ *Don't depend on original material.*

❖ *Make positive humor choices.*

❖ *Focus on the learners, not yourself.*

❖ *Cheerfully acknowledge a "bomb" and move on.*

VARIATIONS

★ Participants write jokes on 3" x 5" cards and drop them into a big bowl. (Prescreen them, of course!) Once a day, pull out a card and read a joke.

★ Put participants in groups or teams. Then, tell everyone a joke but omit the punch line. Ask them to write a new punch line that includes some reference to the day's lesson.

★ At the same time each day, a participant team comes up with a daily joke. Be sure that everyone knows the criteria for acceptable jokes (short, clean, non-offensive and one that hasn't already been used in class). Encourage the joke-tellers to use as many gestures as possible.

★ Put up on an overhead projector a cartoon with the caption missing. Assign to each group to the task of writing a caption that includes a key point from the day's lesson. The whole group acknowledges the best caption with clapping or cheers.

What Is a State?

Physical movement changes mind/emotions/body, or "state."

States are combinations of emotions, posture, expectancies, activity, sensory input, opinions.

They are the primary modulators for all our attention, meaning, motivation and memory.

- *activity increases heart rate*
- *repetitive gross motor movement improves mood*
- *competition may increase norepinephrine levels*
- *celebrations may increase dopamine levels*
- *cooperative games and social structures influence stress levels*

⑩ Imaginary Object Pass

You can play this as a content-free game just for fun, or incorporate into it "objects" and ideas from the day's material. Participants form groups of five to eight people; each group stands in a circle of about ten feet in diameter. (Group size is important—too few or too many people in a group will cause problems.) Play some fun, upbeat music with positive lyrics, like oldies for an adult audience and hip-hop or Top 40 for kids and adolescents.

One person in a group starts by describing an imaginary object, like a canary with a broken wing, a greased piglet or a hot plate of pancakes. The group passes the "object" around the circle to the right, handling it appropriately. Cut the music after about thirty seconds and have everyone stop passing the object (without letting it "disappear"). Announce that the person opposite the current object-holder will begin passing a new object in the opposite direction as soon as the music starts again. Now there are two objects being passed around the circle, crossing each other every few seconds.

VARIATIONS

★ Every time someone "receives" an object, he or she must compliment the person who passed it.

★ When two objects hit one person at the same time, that person can call out, "Opposite!" to change the direction of the passing.

★ Introduce more imaginary objects to pass around the circle.

★ See which group can pass their objects around their circle the most number of times within a certain time limit (and without "mishandling" the objects). This works best if all your groups are the same size.

⑪ Macarena

For this activity, it is ideal to actually play the song, *Macarena* (by Los Lobos), although the dance has become such a popular standard many people know it well enough to perform without it. Add a little "salsa" to the dance to make it even more entertaining.

Caution: Some people will feel a bit awkward doing a dance routine. Be sure to:

❖ *model it for the class;*

❖ *make it safe to make mistakes;*

❖ *never isolate a person by making them dance solo—always let them be part of a group or team (unless they enjoy the spotlight); and*

❖ *make sure that having fun is number one!*

VARIATIONS

Here are a few ideas to spice up a dance:

★ Each group or team adds their own flair to the dance and presents a thirty to forty-five second segment of it to the larger group.

★ Tie new content or subject matter to the dance. For example, the *Macarena* is used well by master presenter Jean Blaydes-Madigan to present math concepts. With each move of the arms, her participants sing/say a number, word or math fact. Each choreographed move can represent a way to learn multiplication or addition tables (two times four equals eight, Macarena! two times five equals ten, Macarena!) or even parts of the body or brain. It can be used to practice geography or foreign languages, too!

12 Musical Chairs

Play classic game to fun, fast, familiar music. Arrange everyone's chairs in a circle so that the seats face outward. Remove one. There should be one more person playing the game than there are chairs. When the music starts, participants walk around the circle of chairs, giving positive affirmations to each other. When the music stops, everyone scrambles to sit in one of the chairs. The person left standing shares one thing he or she has learned so far that day.

VARIATIONS

★ When the music stops, participants have to find and sit in their chair from the first ten minutes of the day.

★ When the music stops, participants find a partner and two neighboring chairs for them both to sit in. Any partners left without places to sit next to each other have to share what they have learned so far that day.

★ When the music stops, participants have to either hop, skip or jump to a chair.

★ Arrange the chairs like a train car, in rows of four seats across. The "conductor" (perhaps the person who couldn't find a seat in the previous round) stands up and says, "New seats are being assigned. All passengers wearing socks must find a new row to sit in." During this shuffle, the teacher removes one more chair from the train. (Participants who are not wearing socks remain in their seats.) The next person to lose his or her seat is the new conductor who makes another announcement. "New seats are being assigned. All passengers with jewelry must now find a new seat!" If it turns out everyone finds a seat, remove enough chairs so they are one short at the next announcement.

13 Pass a Face

Participants form groups of six to eight people and stand in a circle. They designate someone to be the leader. He or she makes a funny face at the person to the right. Then, that person matches the face and "passes" it to the next person. The third person matches and passes the face to the right, and so on. At one point, the designated leader says out loud, "Switch!" Whoever has the face at that moment makes up a new face to pass. Play upbeat music during the game.

VARIATIONS

★ Start the game with a face and add a noise to pass in the opposite direction.

★ Start with a face, add a noise and then a gesture to pass in different directions.

★ Pass an imaginary object. The leader describes something unusual like a python and passes that object to the person on the right. Each person has to handle the imaginary object as if it were real.

★ While a group is busy passing things around the circle, the leader says, "Switch sounds!" or, "Switch objects!" The item called out by the leader will pass in the other direction. This variation can get very chaotic and fun!

14 Visualization

Visualization is a tool that can introduce, clarify or intensify a thought or feeling. It's an ideal way to make a smooth transition to a new topic. Most visualizations can be done in two to four minutes. The process is simple. Explain to your audience that you'd like them to prepare for an upcoming event. Ask them to close their eyes. Invite them to inhale slowly through their nose and exhale slowly through their mouth, relaxing comfortably. Next, ask them to create a mental picture of a goal as you describe it to them. Ask them to picture this goal fully accomplished. Walk your audience around that mental picture of this important thought, giving them time to build the sights, sounds and feelings that accompany the accomplished goal. Help them mentally adjust the picture by making it more colorful, intense, larger, attractive or detailed. When you are finished, give them time to slowly come back to present time before asking them to open their eyes again.

VARIATIONS

★ Let participants choose a partner. One partner has notes in front of him or her and talks through some key ideas. The other partner has his or her eyes closed while visualizing the material described. The goal of the talking partner is to be as descriptive and colorful as possible to make it more fun and more visual to the visualizing partner. After enough time has passed, let them switch places.

★ Ask participants to visualize the three things from the last topic or unit that they found the most memorable. They should give each of those items a label, a color or sound. Then, let them review those three things again before moving on to the next topic.

15 Stretching

The same stretching routine that raises heart rates and triggers arousal states makes an excellent transition activity. Start by saying something like, "We're going to do something very interesting in just a moment. But first, let's wake up the body and get ready for something new." Ask your audience to take a deep breath and slowly let it out. Then, ask them to stand up. Have team leaders lead their groups in a team stretch. When they are all done with stretching but while they're still standing, summarize the key points of your last subject or unit.

VARIATIONS

★ Lead the group through about thirty seconds of slow stretching exercises.

★ Have a volunteer lead the whole group through stretches to background music.

★ Have participant volunteers lead the group in a dance step to blow off steam or generate some energy.

16 Voting on a Topic

Before leaving one topic for another, it's good to gauge the confidence level of your audience about the newly learned material. (This activity varies from the version in Chapter 3 only in the types of issues they vote on.) Give them three choices. Participants select the first choice if they feel they understand the new material well enough to teach it. They vote for the second option if they pretty much understand all the key points but are fuzzy on the details (they'd ace an easy quiz but would stress about a big test on the material). The third choice is for learners who aren't confident that they know the topic at all, for whatever reason. Explain each option clearly and have participants show their hands in a vote. You could also put the choices on a paper ballot and have them vote privately or anonymously.

VARIATIONS

★ You can vote kinesthetically in any number of ways. By far the simplest method of voting with your body is putting two thumbs up ("I could teach this lesson myself!"), one thumb up ("I feel good about this topic!"), thumbs sideways ("I still have some questions") or thumbs down ("I'm not sure about this topic at all").

★ Perform a kinesthetic motivation when participants are already on their feet at the conclusion of some other activity (like a think-pair-share). You might say something like, "If you are ready for something new, take a deep breath, hold it and slowly exhale. Great! Now we can move on."

★ Everyone is familiar with auditory voting. Ask for a simple "Yea" or "Nay" vote of confidence of what was just learned. Add a "GQ" (got questions) option to the list.

Chapter 7
"Ah-hh"
The State of Well-Being

What Is This State?

"Ah-hh" is the sound of general well-being. This state is characterized by serenity, peacefulness, mild (not wild) joy and a smile. Overall, it may be the best state to elicit from students in your learning environment.

Why Is This State Important?

The state of well-being moderates our moods and actions. Well-being has been described with the seeming oxymoron, "calm energy" (Thayer, 2001). When our serotonin levels are just right we feel neither dominant nor subordinate. When our energy levels are just right we are neither bouncing off the walls nor drowsy. We are neither sad nor maniacally happy. We are, well, just fine.

How Long Does This State Last?

We can maintain a state of well-being for longer than just about any other state. It might quite possibly be the most stable state of all. (I'd say anxiety and depression run close seconds). A person who is healthy, stable and in good company can stay in this state on and off for hours. On the other hand, we can influence it adversely with distress, threats, emergencies, disappointments or other disruptions.

> **"Ah-hh" Is the State of Well-Being and Smiles**

What Brain Activity Is Involved?

It may surprise you, but positive emotions and thoughts predominately activate the left, not the right, hemisphere of the brain (Ahern & Schwartz, 1979). You could probably come up with a whole list of behaviors that stimulate mildly positive responses; here are a few to get you started: evoking positive memories, anticipating something wonderful, succeeding at something, having good friends, setting and reaching goals and maintaining a generally happy outlook on life. Another trigger for this state is the feeling of social connectedness; evidence suggests that personal attachment activates our brain's stress response and reward systems (Panksepp et al., 1999). That's why turning your classroom or training room into a social arena where positive social contact can be orchestrated is essential. Even drinking water (when we are dehydrated) will lower cortisol levels (Heybach & Vernikos-Danellis, 1979), thereby possibly decreasing consummatory behavior (the instinct to search for water or food) and increasing receptivity to learning!

The state of well-being is characterized by just the right balance of many different neurotransmitters. The neurotransmitter, serotonin, is one of the dominant chemical influencers of well-being. Some people are born with genetically higher or lower baselines of serotonin, which may influence their everyday moods. The picture of neurotransmitters is far more complex than we have the space to illustrate here. For example, there are more than fifteen different subtypes of receptors

for serotonin, making the reception and activation process quite complex (Gershon, 1998). As a rule, however, when we are low on serotonin, we often feel a bit down and sometimes depressed. Lower levels are even associated with higher levels of aggression (but not in a cause-effect relationship). Still, we can influence our serotonin levels in many ways, like with exercise, which is one known regulator.

Serotonin in the Brain

Serotonin is stored in vesicles of presynaptic axons as its precursor 5-hydroxytryptophan (5-HTP) and synthesized in the raphe nuclei area.

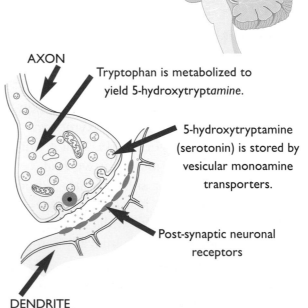

AXON

Tryptophan is metabolized to yield 5-hydroxytryptamine.

5-hydroxytryptamine (serotonin) is stored by vesicular monoamine transporters.

Post-synaptic neuronal receptors

DENDRITE

Body Language of This State

The body language of well-being exhibits comfort and general ease. It is characterized by normal breathing or slow, measured, easy breathing. The heart rate is neither high nor low. Often, well-being is accompanied by a smile and kind words for others. This is a state of happiness, not ecstasy, and of feeling good, not great. Cultural variations and well as varied circumstances might change the behaviors you see and hear.

What Food Affects This State?

Serotonin cannot be directly ingested but it is synthesized in the brain from the amino acid, tryptophan. Foods high in tryptophan include turkey, milk, cottage cheese, poultry, eggs, cheese, red meats, tofu, avocados, almonds, ham, walnuts, bananas, eggplant, plums and tomatoes. Lower levels of tryptophan are found in most carbohydrates, but complex carbohydrates are superior sources. Complex carbohydrates (whole grains, potatoes, rice and yams) break down slowly in our system. Simple carbohydrates (sweets, soft drinks, snacks, etc.) break down quickly, flooding the system with glucose which, in turn, triggers an insulin overreaction that counters the energetic "sugar high" and leads to a "roller coaster" cycle of energy surplus and shortage.

When we get stressed, we often turn to food to calm our nerves in a form of self-medication. Not surprisingly, among college-age students the most craved-for food is chocolate (Weingarten & Elston, 1991). Chocolate contains several ingredients that we know are used for self-regulation, like anandamine (mood regulation; also found in marijuana), theobromine (a stimulant), caffeine (mood elevation), sugar (satisfies a sweet tooth) and fats (a common comfort food with a smooth, filling taste).

Serotonin Stimulators

- *foods high in tryptophan (milk, turkey, complex carbohydrates)*
- *safety (or absence of threat)*
- *positive social status*
- *familiarity of surroundings (music, friends, etc.)*
- *regulated physical activity (exercise 3 to 5 times per week)*
- *certain agents (St. John's Wort, Selective Serotonin Reuptake Inhibitors — SSRIs)*

Serotonin is largely produced in the *raphe nuclei*, a cluster of neurons at the top of the brain stem. Serotonin is also synthesized at the point of usage in a presynaptic neuron. The amount of serotonin in us varies, but only one to two percent of our serotonin is found in the brain (Cooper et al., 1991); there are, in fact, more receptors for serotonin in your stomach (Gershon, 1998). The normal range for serotonin in the human blood-stream is quite wide (55 to 260 nanograms per milliliter) and levels vary during the day (Lesser, 2002). We cannot consume serotonin directly because it cannot cross the blood-brain barrier. Several commercially available products, however, can support serotonin levels in the brain. They do that by making more of the raw material, tryptophan, available. One such product is 5-hydroxytryptophan (5-HTP), a precursor to serotonin. When we consume 5-HTP, it gets converted into 5-hydrox-ytrypt*amine* (which is serotonin). St. John's Wort can also help maintain a higher level of serotonin in the brain. Of course, before stocking your shelves with any nutritional supplement, consult a health provider. Low levels of energy or a persistent depressed mood can be caused by physical conditions other than a lack of tryptophan in your diet; persistent symptoms should not be ignored.

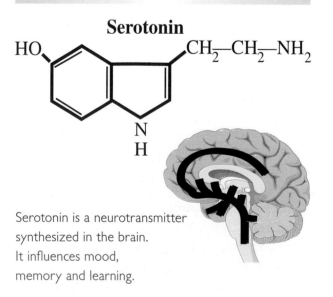

Serotonin = "Ah-hh"
Whistle While You Work

Serotonin

Serotonin is a neurotransmitter synthesized in the brain. It influences mood, memory and learning.

What Music Affects This State?

Music that is predictable, slightly calming and familiar has the best chance of helping you enter a state of well-being. Within this style of music, major keys are generally considered more upbeat and cheerful than minor keys (Millbower, 2000). Light, classical music soothes patients before, during and after surgery, coronary care or premature birth (Bonny, 1983; Barker, 1991; Lorch et al., 1994); music has also been found to influence positive changes in the brainwaves of children who were exposed to it an hour a day over time (Malyarenko, 1996). Furthermore, listening to soothing music was found to decrease blood sample cortisol levels (and therefore stress levels) during a dental procedure (Bartlett, 1996).

Key Basic Concepts

The state of well-being is more generalized and less specific than other states. Key factors that strengthen this state include positive social status, certain diets, a sense of safety, soothing music and regulated physical activity (Brownley et al., 1995; Ekkekakis et al., 2000). By stimulating mental arousal and decreasing stress and muscle tension, yoga postures contribute to a calm state of well-being, as does regular exercise, which you will remember helps upregulate serotonin in the brain. Well-being is also enhanced by the familiarity of friends, locale, music or family. For example, listening to oldies radio stations can elicit this state if they play songs from the era you grew up in, but it won't if you dislike that style of music or were born in a different time. Well-being is not perfection, just comfortable, easy moments.

Strategies for Well-Being

Keep in mind that many things will regulate students' well-being but, as in previous chapters, this segment focuses on things that they can do themselves rather than activities you perform in front of them. Remember that the best learning occurs when students take an active instead of passive role. Our question, then, about maintaining our students' well-being is, "Do they listen to you say something kind or do they get to give and receive positive affirmations from their classmates?"

1 Affirmations

Learners like to feel good. Saying positive things can improve their mood, but keep in mind they are far more receptive to affirmations in "open" states (like standing or shaking hands) versus "closed" states (like crossing the arms or slumping in a chair). Affirmations are worth doing at least once or twice a day (caution: too many affirmations can undermine their sincerity and effectiveness). In each of the following variations, start by writing the affirmations yourself but, over time, involve participants in their creation. Make sure your class is standing tall and ready for some fun before you begin.

VARIATIONS

★ *Individual affirmations:* Ask students to stand after successfully completing a task. Then, ask them to turn to a neighbor and say, "We did great!" to at least five classmates.

★ *Small group or team affirmations:* You or the participants create a list of twenty very positive affirmations. Put them on an overhead transparency or in a handout for everyone to keep in their notebooks. When you are ready to begin the affirmations, have every one stand up. Assign a group to read the first affirmation aloud (in unison) and establish a rotating order for the other groups or teams to read the rest. When you've gone through the whole list, have everyone applaud and then take a seat.

★ *Audience affirmations:* This simple engagement tool is used to elicit an affirmation from your audience. You make a summary statement, then ask the audience directly, "Agree or disagree?" When the audience agrees on the answer (and voices it in unison), people feel good and like they are really part of the group.

2 Birthdays

We operate in a complex social environment. Even the act of rising in social esteem (like going from a "nobody" to a "somebody" after winning an award for the school in a big competition) has a positive effect on the system. Celebrating a birthday can single out a person as special and award him or her some increased social status—but singling them out too much can backfire. The real trick here is to acknowledge one person's birthday while still including everyone. A quick way to do so is to ask the whole audience, "Compared to yesterday, who is a day older today? Please raise your hands. Now, let's give ourselves a round of applause! Great, now who is exactly *one year* older today?" Wait for hands to go down until only the people celebrating a birthday remain. Then, lead the group in cheering or applauding them, too.

VARIATION

★ If you have a K–12 class, ask students to write their birthday dates on 3" x 5" cards. During the first week of the school year, establish celebration teams of three students that will be responsible for organizing something special, like balloons, a cheer or a party favor, for each birthday. Change celebration teams monthly to involve everyone. Celebrate summer and holiday birthdays on the nearest school day. If that clumps too many summer birthdays in the last or first week of school, try celebrating "half-birthdays" exactly six months before or after the dates (like on January 20th instead of July 20th).

3   Brain Gym

The phrase "Brain Gym" has been widely used and often misused. It is critical to use Brain Gym activities properly, as they are taught by founders Paul Dennison and Gail Dennison or by certified Brain Gym instructors. Brain Gym is a series of postures and movements that have the specific purpose of relaxing, energizing, retraining or focusing the mind. Some of the movements are yoga-like and others more similar to T'ai Chi; active movements are similar to marching in place

with a cross-lateral approach. Before using this technique, attend official training and thoroughly read the Dennison's book, *Brain Gym,* to ensure that your use of the activities is accurate and effective.

Other resources for learning about Brain Gym include:

❖ *The Learning Gym* by Eric Ballinger

❖ *Learning with the Body in Mind* by Eric Jensen

❖ Training sessions by Brain Gym Certified Trainers. You can find a list of certified instructors in your area at the Brain Gym web site: http://www.braingym.org

4   Call-Response Wrap-Ups

Just as Call-Response Psych-Ups energized students in Chapter 4, Call-Response Wrap-Ups send students home with a feeling of pride, accomplishment and group unity. Before the activity, have your calls and responses written out on a board or an overhead transparency. The column on the left should be labeled "Me" and the column on the right should be labeled "You." End-of-day call-response rituals should be positive and affirming and use between three and five calls. When you first incorporate this activity, model both the calls and responses with lots of enthusiasm. See the table on the facing page for a sample set of Call-Response Wrap-Ups:

Me	You
Who participated today?	I did!
Who learned something new?	I did!
How did it feel?	Felt great!
What's our plan tomorrow?	Work hard and play fair!

Once students become familiar with this ritual, let them take turns leading the call-response or writing their own affirmations to use. You can also add choreography, like hand claps or foot stomps, for emphasis and kinetic reinforcement.

 ## 5 Compliments

Short but sincere compliments can elicit feelings of well-being. We are most receptive to compliments in open states (like when we are up on our feet or active), so before giving any make sure that participants' body language tells you they are ready. If students have finished a task particularly well, ask them to stand and pair up. Then, ask them to turn their bodies (the act of turning opens up their posture) to face their partners and say, "Great job!" If it is easier to keep them in chairs, ask them to physically rotate their bodies to look at each other before giving the compliment. Group or team compliments likewise should come out of motion. If your groups or teams are already standing, tell them to compliment every person in their group or team (or the whole class if time permits) by:

❖ *making eye contact;*

❖ *using their partners' names;*

❖ *shaking hands or giving high fives;*

❖ *vocalizing a positive affirmation; and*

❖ *performing these steps with enthusiasm.*

VARIATIONS

★ Put a "joy seat" in the center of a circle of five to eight students sitting in chairs. One person sits on the joy seat while the others spend sixty seconds sincerely complimenting him or her. At the end of the minute, another person from the group takes a turn in the joy seat.

★ Establish student mailboxes. Encourage students to write compliments to each other for you to post and deliver on a regular basis.

★ Assign anonymous student "buddies" and have them exchange written compliments on 3" x 5" cards though the student mailbox system.

6 Grateful Reflection

One way to change an external, anxious or unhappy mood to an internal, positive and calm mood is by actively feeling gratitude. At the beginning of a class, ask students if they'd be willing to participate in an experiment that might help them have a better day (most will say yes). Then, tell them that the experiment involves learning how to shift their thoughts to things that make them feel good about life. Begin the activity by having students find a partner and take a five-minute walk. For the outbound part of the walk (the first two and a half minutes), they make a point to get to know each other better. During the return half of their journey, they share things in their life for which they are grateful. Most people will be in a pretty good mood by the time they get back!

VARIATIONS

★ Students keep a daily journal; once a day they add an item to a list of things in their life for which they are grateful. Once a week have them share this list with a partner.

★ Students work with partners and ask each other questions to elicit a list of items for which they are individually grateful. They should encourage each other and see how many items they can come up with as a pair.

★ To set a positive tone for the day, ask volunteers to stand up each morning and read one or two items from their journal.

⑦ Group Reviews

By itself, prior knowledge can create in a learner a sense of either satisfaction or self-congratulation before they have to learn something new. Use group reviews in this context not as a source of healthy stress (like in Chapter 5), but instead as a way to reaffirm prior knowledge. Before new instruction begins, lead a brainstorming session. Have a note taker list the items that the group generates. Then, put participants into groups of three or four people and assign them the task of

arranging the list items within a graphic organizer. When the groups are finished organizing the material, have each group send out all but one member to collect ideas from other groups. When they return, they add the new ideas to their own. Post all the graphic organizers on the wall for a gallery walk later on.

When you are ready for the gallery walk, have the groups take one last look at the graphic organizers and identify the two most important items from their own. Play music and have everyone walk around the room, reading the other graphic organizers. If a student encounters one lacking either of the two important ideas from his or her own, that student has permission to add the idea to another group's work.

VARIATIONS

★ Participant pairs play a game of "verbal tennis." One names a remembered item from yesterday's lesson and the other immediately adds an item to the list. The last one to name an idea or concept is the "idea champ" for the day.

★ In groups of four to six, participants do a word association activity from the previous lesson.

⑧ Mental Relaxation

Mental relaxation can elicit or strengthen a state of well-being in order to facilitate learning. Most relaxation sessions can be performed in two to four minutes. The process is simple. Explain to your group that you'd like to give them a moment to prepare for your next activity. Ask them to close their eyes and relax comfortably;

invite them to inhale slowly through the nose and exhale slowly through the mouth. Next, ask them to imagine that they feel very calm and relaxed. Have them visualize a favorite place of calm or safety. Prompt them to imagine the sights, sounds and feelings that accompany the mental place they have gone to and allow them time to enjoy it. Suggest that they carefully note the details that make the place colorful, attractive or comfortable. Continually emphasize that they are really enjoying this vacation. When you are finished, give them time to bring their minds back to the present before asking them to open their eyes. Unlike the Visualization exercise in Chapter 6, this mental relaxation has the sole purpose of encouraging mental ease and harmony.

VARIATIONS

★ Play soothing music or nature sounds in the background.

★ Ask participants to lead the mental relaxation.

★ Have students describe their idea of a relaxing vacation to a partner (not necessarily their ideal vacation—sky diving in Peru may be fabulous, but it's not necessarily relaxing).

★ Read a story or travelogue about someone else's quiet vacation.

9 Sustained Movement

Short bursts of movement raise our heart rates and epinephrine levels (part of the arousal state). But twenty to thirty minutes a day of sustained gross motor activity (exercise), three to five times a week help upregulate serotonin levels in the brain. This long-term exposure to exercise benefits us in these ways:

❖ *It improves our physical and cognitive health.*

❖ *It helps stabilize and manage our moods.*

❖ *Voluntary gross motor activity is linked to increased neurogenesis, or the growth of new brain cells.*

Of course, in a classroom or a training session, it's not practical to mandate twenty to thirty minutes a day of sustained gross motor activity, three to five times a week. The best we can do is continually encourage students to exercise and give them a taste of its energy rush with some two to four minute samples, like cross laterals to music or a march around the room.

Music

Play music that appeals to a broad audience. Because music can clearly influence mood (for the better or for worse), focus on selections that please many people rather than trying to find the perfect tune for an activity. Music within the range of sixty-five to eighty beats per minute is the best choice for setting a positive mood. Use familiar tunes and songs in major keys that fit the age group of your audience. In general, soothing music at test time improves test scores (Cockerton et al., 1997) and, as a rule, soothing music can support the maintenance of high serotonin levels. Still, different age groups have different definitions of feel-good music. Depending on life experience and personal preferences, everyone has a different set of songs that make them happy. I've listed some of my favorites to give you a starting point for developing your own play list for classes and presentations:

Adult audiences:

❖ *Whistle While You Work* (from the Disney movie, *Snow White*)

❖ *Feels So Good* (Chuck Mangione)

❖ *Hot Fun in the Summertime* and *You Can Make It If You Try* (Sly & the Family Stone)

❖ *Born Free* (sung by Matt Monro, from the movie, *Born Free*)

❖ *Oh, What a Beautiful Mornin'* (from the musical, *Oklahoma*)

❖ *Fun, Fun, Fun* (Beach Boys)

❖ *What a Wonderful World* (Louis Armstrong)

Younger audiences:

❖ *Don't Worry, Be Happy* (Bobby McFerrin)

❖ *YMCA* (Village People)

❖ *Day-O (Banana Boat Song)*, *Matilda* and *Jump in the Line* (Harry Belafonte)

❖ *Zip-A-Dee-Doo-Dah* (from the Disney movie *Song of the South*)

❖ Songs by Hap Palmer

❖ Songs by Red Grammer (music for adult and child listeners)

11 Pleasure Questions

Pleasure questions are a sub-category of Universal Questions to which nearly everyone will respond quickly and in the affirmative. Ask only questions that will allow a unison answer and elicit a positive state. When you ask pleasure questions, always raise your own hand to model the type of response that you want. The following examples of pleasure questions should give you ideas for some of your own:

❖ *"How many of you would agree to shave five minutes off our break today if it meant we could all leave fifteen minutes earlier?"*

❖ *"Put your hands up if you've seen a good movie lately!"*

❖ *"How many of you enjoyed your lunch break?"*

12 Recognition

The state of well-being is heavily influenced by a sense of personal importance and positive social status. When we feel needed or special, we feel important; when we feel we are high on the social ladder or in the process of climbing it, we feel good. Teachers and presenters have countless tools to help students feel recognized and responsible. For example, Turn-Tos (from Chapter 5) can be used to recognize and affirm a peer's hard work or accomplishments. The best part about prompting peer affirmation and congratulations is that, over time, students will pick up the habit and do it spontaneously. What could be more rewarding or genuine than that?

VARIATIONS

★ Participants post their work on the walls for group recognition.

★ Track each team's points or score on the wall so everyone can acknowledge high achievement. (This doubles as an "Uh-Oh!" for teams falling behind the rest.)

★ Give a "Student of the Day" the opportunity to share a personal story or part of his or her history with the rest of the class.

★ Encourage participants to informally share their skills and hobbies with the rest of the class, during a casual demonstration of how to play the violin, for example, or an explanation of the importance of certain fossils in a collection.

★ Ask participants to do service work at home or in the community; spend some time in class sharing the results.

13 Responsibility

When we trust students, it's only natural to give them more responsibility. Responsibility comes in many forms, some as simple as trusting students with a chore or task that ordinarily older students would perform. Being assigned the role of team leader is also a responsibility, as is making routine announcements (like reading the daily bulletin) during class. With a sense of responsibility comes a sense of prestige and control over one's environment. Over time, you may be able to identify the more vocal and visible (but unofficial) group leaders. Win them over through your confidence, asking for their input or private meetings. When we are a part of a larger environment and perceive that we play an important role in it, we feel like we can make a difference and our well-being increases.

14 Stretching

Students commonly store in their bodies stress from the day's tension or from sitting awkwardly in uncomfortable chairs. Releasing that tension with slow, gentle stretches can be a powerful way to reconnect with their bodies as sources of well-being. Asking participants to stand *and* stretch, though, may elicit states of complaint or resistance (especially at the end of a long day). Set up the activity, then, by taking a quick survey of hands with the question, "How many of you get stiff or antsy after sitting in a chair too long?" Follow the question with something like, "Now, how many of you often get shoulder and neck tension that distracts you from learning?" Questions like these elicit states of curiosity and willingness to participate, especially if you've identified a problem that they'd like to fix.

If very few people put hands up in the air, either you and your audience are completely out of synch with each other (which is bad) or else your audience is not stressed (which is good). If you do get a good number of hands up in the air, however, that's your cue to move ahead with this stretching activity. Play relaxing music in the background and say, "I thought you might be ready for a little break!" Start with a few deep-breathing exercises and lead the group through one to three minutes of slow stretches. When they finally return to their seats, your students will experience a calm, de-stressed state of well-being.

VARIATIONS

★ Make a daily ritual of small group or team deep-breathing and stretching exercises to quiet, slow music. Have team members take turns leading their groups.

★ Show a meditation or stretching video that everyone can watch and follow as a class.

★ Have participants enrolled in a dance, yoga or gymnastics class or who play organized team sports take turns leading the group with special stretches they know from their disciplines.

15 Support Teams

Small groups and teams have the power to create stable but temporary social structures in which a person is at the bottom of the pecking order for only a short time. They also create small communities that keep self-conscious or shy people from getting lost and lonely in a crowd. Any time we're in a socially supportive environment instead of in a consistently subordinate role, our sense of well-being (and serotonin levels) is generally higher and our stress level (and cortisol levels) is generally lower.

Support teams should last long enough for students to settle into their relationships and cooperate but not so long that participants feel helplessly stuck in their roles. You should rearrange support team members every three to six weeks. Assign specific roles for each team member to play; depending on their purpose, the roles could be things like "Leader," "Note Taker," "Time Keeper," "Spokesperson," "Materials Gatherer" or "Cheerleader." Vary how you place students into these groups (refer back to Chapter 4 for Mixer Walk grouping ideas). Use support teams for academic purposes, but also for the team-building and state-eliciting activities detailed in this book.

Chapter 8
"I Got It!"
In-Depth Learning with Confidence

What Is This State?

The "I Got It!" state has both cognitive and emotional elements: awareness and recognition of the things you know and satisfaction in your accomplishment. These feelings are positive and reassuring, and augment the well-being that is so important to future learning.

Why Is This State Important?

This state is important because it helps learners gain confidence in their skills and abilities, which is absolutely necessary to the learning process. When people are given periodic opportunities to discuss and reflect upon new material, they absorb it better. Learners are sometimes surprised by how much they know after answering a question or explaining a tricky concept to a peer! When they are called upon to produce learned information and successfully do so, they enjoy the pride of accomplishment as well as the advantages of new knowledge.

If you only deliver instruction through lecture, you are doing very little for your audience. Why? Because you don't know what your audience already knows or has

learned. Feedback is required to achieve the "I Got It!" state. One form of feedback, error correction, is regulated in the brain by the anterior cingulate, a structure located in the upper back of the frontal lobes (Casey et al., 1997). Also beneficial is feedback that gives learners the opportunity to act on what they learn by trying it out for themselves—feedback only a living person (like you) can provide. One study showed that students who take a lecture-driven college course end up learning only eight percent more about a subject than students who don't take it at all. Attend a lecture class or take a vacation… it amounts almost to the same thing as far as gaining new knowledge is concerned (Rickard et al., 1988). Most professors would probably say their lectures were far more informative than that or blame students' failure on their own lack of motivation or effort, but there is another side to this story.

The State of "I Got It!" Is Enthusiastic Confidence

When students were given frequent breaks for processing new knowledge, however, their learning averaged a grade improvement of up to *two letters* over the control group of students who received information solely though lecture with no breaks (Ruhl et al., 1987). Giving learners time to talk over a lesson also allows you to informally assess how much they know and how certain they are about new information. Have you ever asked your children what they learned at school that day and gotten the frustratingly unspecific answer, "just some stuff"? Students who have confidence about what they know will reward their parents with answers like, "We learned that the brain releases dopamine from the frontal lobes!" (More on that in a few paragraphs...)

How Long Do These States Last?

Confidence and security in new knowledge typically last only a few minutes. Learners often get bored or mischievous if they realize that they already know what you are talking about. Once you give learners an adequate amount of time to experience and enjoy their learning, acknowledge its success but be ready with a break, settling time or another activity.

What Brain Activity Is Involved?

When you first enter the "I Got It!" state, your brain is quite active. Your frontal, temporal and parietal lobes will be busy processing the event. Dopamine, a reward-like neurotransmitter, is present in the frontal lobes to maintain working memory

and support information processing (Siever & Frucht, 1997). There is evidence that when we complete cognitive tasks, increased dopamine is released to reward the brain for learning (which inspires the brain to learn something else!). It's a useful cycle in this case; becoming addicted to the pleasures of learning will keep us coming back for more.

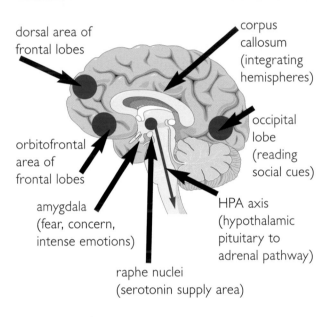

Social Brain Regulators

dorsal area of frontal lobes

corpus callosum (integrating hemispheres)

orbitofrontal area of frontal lobes

occipital lobe (reading social cues)

amygdala (fear, concern, intense emotions)

HPA axis (hypothalamic pituitary to adrenal pathway)

raphe nuclei (serotonin supply area)

Body Language of These States

The body language of confidence comes in as many varieties as learners do. Older learners may lean back and clasp their hands behind their head in a classic "I'm in control" posture (which is sometimes interpreted by others as "Know-It-All"). Visual learners light up with a big smile and good-natured creases on their faces. Auditory learners demonstrate it verbally with a "Yesssss!" or "Woo-hoo!" Kinesthetic learners typically clap their hands or high-five a friend. Almost everyone takes a deep breath and shifts their weight back as they puff out their chests in pride. Additionally, there are cultural variations and well as varied circumstances that might change what you see and hear.

Generalizations

Many people will know how to enter this state on their own, especially if they are hungry learners and really want to understand the world around them. We think of these people as self-confident when we like them (or as arrogant braggarts if we don't). Learners with difficulty accessing the "I Got It" state have a real problem—they are often reluctant to try something new or are hesitant to reward themselves with class activities or celebrations. Learners who too easily enter this state and think they know more than they already do have a problem, too; they may be unable to see what they still need to learn and may tune out or ignore your efforts to teach or train them. People can also be too gullible or too skeptical when faced with new information and make poor decisions about it, depending on the circumstances or the position they find themselves in. Flexibility is the key to everyone's success (yours and your audiences' alike).

What Food Affects These States?

Although there are no known foods that help elicit the "I Got It!" state, there is good evidence that many nutrients are responsible for general cognition. Necessary nutrients include folic acid, omega-3 and omega-6 oils, vitamins A, B and E and the minerals zinc, iron, magnesium, sodium and selenium. Foods that are detrimental to brain health are known as allergens. The seven most common food allergies are to soy, wheat, corn, dairy, chocolate, peanuts and shellfish. Finally, substances like saturated fats, excess caffeine, aspartame, excess sugars or bleached, enriched white flour—"pseudo-foods"—can react toxically with the body and the brain (Simontacchi, 2000). A good rule in general is to stick with foods from Mother Nature. If you don't know what the additives, preservatives and chemicals in the ingredients list will do to your body and brain, don't buy that package of food.

Finally, although small amounts of sugar can be helpful, avoid excess sugar for better learning. From candy bars to soft drinks, granola, sugary treats and non-healthy snacks, excess sugar wreaks havoc on the brain. We can track it through the body to better understand why it's a problem:

❖ *When a surplus of sugar enters the bloodstream, the pancreas is instantly activated. Its exaggerated reaction is to dump insulin directly into the bloodstream to help clear the excess sugars before they can damage the brain. Excess sugar is stored in the liver and may later be converted to fat.*

❖ *This overreaction of insulin means that soon the learner will have low blood sugar, so the brain sends a message to the body that it's hungry by exhibiting the symptoms of poor concentration, anxiety, headaches and lethargy.*

❖ *If there's no move to raise the blood sugar, the hypothalamus may signal the release of cortisol from the adrenal glands to raise energy. Now you have a stressed learner with low blood sugar!*

❖ *The learner overreacts, eats any food close at hand (often candy from a vending machine) and again dumps too much sugar into his or her system; the excess sugar activates the pancreas, causing another insulin reaction that…*

Well, you get the message. This nasty cycle of sugar, insulin, lethargy, stress, more sugar and finally, more insulin goes on all day long, in many people.

The Value of Trial and Error

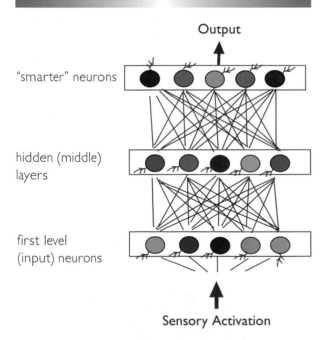

Output

"smarter" neurons

hidden (middle) layers

first level (input) neurons

Sensory Activation

Positive reinforcement during learning helps us sustain our states—we stay motivated. But we learn from our mistakes, too. They have a **greater impact** on our brain and are better remembered, helping us eliminate poor choices in the future. Optimal trial and error allows for both. Remember, we become smarter not by memorizing right answers but by **eliminating wrong ones**.

What Music Affects These States?

Certain types of music have a calming effect and lower student anxiety (Blood & Ferriss, 1993), making it easier for a group of participants to freely discuss and question what they have heard in lecture. In general, instrumental music is less distracting than music with lyrics, but we all have different sensory systems that influence our tolerance of novel environmental input. In one study, introverts struggled to concentrate when pop music played in the background, but extroverts enjoyed it (Furnham & Bradley, 1997). Pay close attention to how background noise affects your audience's productivity and stress levels, and use music carefully and with purpose.

Key Basic Concepts

It is absolutely critical that you trigger the "I Got It!" state in your students before sending them home at the end of the day, week or course. How much they actually know isn't nearly as important as their *perception* of how much they know. If learners don't perceive how much they've been able to learn, they could leave in a state of uncertainty, unwilling to use the information and possibly even feeling cheated. It's also worthwhile to remark that it is just as likely that a learner could not know something but still feel confident that he or she does, regardless of the reality.

There are only three triggers for this state, so pay attention:

❖ *First, new learning needs to be* repeated *before we are confident of it. Some people will cement their knowledge after one repetition; others will need to be drilled as often as twenty times. Make sure you have a wide variety of activities that allow students to practice the material as much as they need to without boring the ones who catch on faster than others.*

❖ *Second, the learning has to be of some* duration *before we are sure of it. As with repetition, some students will catch on in a few minutes; others will spend endless hours struggling with some concept. Be sure to offer lots of variety and choice in your assignments and curriculum (like optional extensions or remediation extra-credit points) so students can get what they need or move on when they are ready.*

❖ *Third, we need to learn material in our* dependent modality *to be truly convinced that we know it. That is, visual learners need to see it, auditory learners need to hear it and kinesthetic learners need to feel it or do it. Self-convincing is essential for self-confidence. It is also beneficial to apply new knowledge to real-life situations.*

To ensure that participants really know their stuff, you must implement a variety of strategies that will both expose a lack of understanding and confirm quality learning. Each one of the teaching tools described in this chapter will do exactly that. Maybe not all by itself, but when you combine it with other strategies and tools, you'll get a higher quality of learning.

Strategies for Learning and Understanding

Keep in mind that many things will improve learning and trigger self-confidence. This chapter focuses on how you can verify that your audience really knows what you taught them, so you can provide corrective feedback for gaps in their knowledge or reinforce and support their accomplishments. The activities in this chapter focus on repetition, duration and the use of specific learning modalities, the three aspects of learning that trigger the "I Got It!" state. The more of these activities that you do (within reason), the more likely it will be that you and the participants have a better handle on what they know or don't know. Finally, when they really do know it, the activities will help them feel confident about it.

Note: There are many ways to present these activities. Your tone, posture, sense of fun, vitality and passion for learning will influence your audience's attitude towards it. Assume that learners will need to process everything you teach. If it's not worth taking the time for them to really understand and remember something, why are you teaching it in the first place?

Malleable memories are the rule. Revise, review and you'll be cool!

Ad Madness

In groups, participants modify a magazine ad (you might provide samples of popular magazines for them to refer to) in order to "promote" an issue or concept of a newly learned topic. When their ads are finished, the groups will present them to the rest of the class. The ads should contain the following elements:

❖ *title, header or slogan*

❖ *picture or visual*

❖ *product or service to market*

❖ *features and benefits of that product*

VARIATIONS
★ Assign a theme to all the ads by dictating what type of magazine the ad would appear in (muscle car, bridal, science, video gaming, etc.). Alternately, assign each group a different theme so they create ads for different types of magazines.

★ Groups perform thirty-second radio ads, using difference voices or characters so every group member has a role.

2 Agree or Disagree?

This simple engagement tool works as more than just a transition; it can also informally assess how well your group as a whole absorbed new information. Make a summary statement and then ask everyone directly, "Agree or disagree?" If you get a minimal or hesitant response, try it again—it's possible that they were surprised by the question or just drifting. Add, "Let's try this again," and repeat

your statement, concluding with, "Agree or disagree?" Hesitation a second time will tell you that they probably are not confident about the new information. Why do this? Full awareness of new knowledge cannot come without repetition. This is one way to quickly repeat and review a fact or concept and give learners the satisfaction of success (within the non-threatening parameters of a group response).

VARIATIONS
★ Ask participants to stand up and carry their notes across the room to find a partner. In pairs, they will review each other's notes by identifying similarities and differences and then update their own notes to reflect what they've learned from each other.

★ Participants write five true summary statements and one misleading, false statement about a topic (in any order) on a 3" x 5" card. Then, they form groups of four (Mixer Walks in Chapter 4 describes lots of creative ways to form groups). In these groups, they take turns reading one statement at a time. At the end of each statement, the participant asks the other group members if they agree or disagree and why. Group members answer, "Disagree," if they think a statement is false, and restate it correctly. Once they have gone through all the statements, they switch cards with another group. This activity almost always generates a discussion within the group about the finer nuances of a subject.

3 Air Writing

Kinesthetic reinforcement is necessary for many people to convince themselves that they have really learned something new. For simple facts or concepts, like learning the first five letters of the alphabet or the name of a region in the brain, try air writing. Once participants have heard you say a term, ask them to stand and take a deep breath. Then, have them write it in the air as they say or spell it out, using their index fingers as pencils. For example, after discussing the three ways to trigger the "I Got It!" state, have everyone stand up and trace the letters R, D and M in the air as they recite "Repetition," "Duration" and "Modality."

VARIATIONS

★ Perform air writing to a soundtrack of funky music. Try the instrumental *Java* by Al Hirt or James Brown's *Make It Funky.*

★ Air write with elbows, knees, heads or feet instead of index fingers.

★ Let a volunteer lead the activity.

When Students Teach One Another, Learning Is Strengthened

4 Anniversary Party

Have everyone stand and listen to a brief review of the course learning. When you are finished, ask them to close their eyes and lead them through a visualization of themselves six months in the future. Have them visualize a scenario in which they remember everything they've learned and how they've been able to use it all successfully. Identify specific items from the review to keep them on track. Then, bring them one year into the future. Have them visualize attending an anniversary reunion of everyone in the room. Tell them that they are happy and excited to see each other again and to share how successful they've all been by using the knowledge they have gained. Ask them to open their eyes and circulate, re-introducing themselves and sharing a year's worth of imaginary success stories with each other. Set the stage with music that starts out quiet and soothing, builds with anticipation and then bursts into celebration for the "party."

VARIATIONS

★ Participants write a story about how successful they were using their new knowledge. Make sure the stories contain lots of details about the course.

★ Participants congratulate themselves for specific achievements. They write their message on the back of a post card and address it to themselves. Collect the postcards and mail them to the participants in either the near or somewhat distant (like a semester) future.

⑤ Audience Reviews

Put participants in groups of six to ten people. Each person picks one item for review from the last topic; every group member should pick a different item. Next, group members arrange themselves by the order in which the items were originally presented during the lesson. Finally, each group goes to the front of the room to present their recreated timeline for review.

VARIATIONS

★ A volunteer presents a brief (thirty seconds or less) review of an item, and then calls on another participant to briefly review the next item.

★ Link the learning to a set of playing cards, the four seasons of the year or the numbers on the face of a clock. Associate each learned item with a specific element of the prompt (like a particular playing card, the season of autumn or the hour of midnight). Have participants close their eyes and visualize the learned item against the backdrop of the prompt. For example, in a unit about the American Civil War, place "Battle of Gettysburg" on the back of the jack of hearts, "Battle between the Monitor and the Merrimac" on the two of clubs and "Signing at Appomattox" on the king of spades. When it is time for review, participants mentally picture the cards and events together.

⑥ Ball Toss

You'll need some upbeat music on hand for this question and answer game. For adults, try *Java* (by Al Hirt), *Tequila* (by the Champs) or *Take Five* (by Dave Brubeck). For kids, use hip-hop songs or Top 40 hits with positive lyrics. Put participants in groups of five to eight people. Have them stand in a circle about ten feet in diameter, facing each other. Give each group an object they can safely toss, like a bean bag, an orange, a Koosh ball or a crumpled piece of newspaper. Whoever tosses the ball asks a question; whoever catches the ball has to answer it. There are four simple rules to the game:

❖ *ask the question completely before tossing the ball;*

❖ *use a gentle, underhand toss that arches high in the air but doesn't go further than the perimeter of the circle;*

❖ *you must answer the question to catch the ball—if you don't know the answer, make up something silly and creative!; and*

❖ *when you have answered the question, ask another one and toss the ball to someone else in your group.*

VARIATIONS

★ Create a content-related, silly story; add one sentence with every ball toss.

★ Enhance the group's state of well-being by complimenting the person to whom you are tossing the ball. The person who catches it should be sure to say, "Thank you," before complimenting and tossing the ball to someone else.

★ The group reviews material by adding one word to a word association list with every toss.

★ Drill math facts, state capitals or foreign language vocabulary with every toss.

★ Use the ball toss as an ice-breaker so group members can get to know each other better. Every time they toss the ball, they give out one piece of personal information, like their names, state of birth or what grades they teach.

7 Balloon Review

In groups of four to eight, participants write, on slips of paper, three review questions that address prior learning. They stuff each question into a balloon and inflate it. Then, they put the answers on three more slips of paper, which you collect and set aside to use later (keep them together in a bowl or bag). Collect all balloons and gather the entire group together. Participants should remain standing. Play some "balloon-batting" music (like *Celebration* by Kool & the Gang or *Who Let the Dogs Out* by Baha Men) while participants knock and bat the balloons around the room with their hands or head. When the music stops, everyone holding a balloon pops it to release the question inside. Participants who end up with their own question should exchange questions with someone else. Then, you draw one answer and read it aloud. People who think they have the question that matches the answer should raise their hands. The participant with the correct question wins the round. (There may be more than one question that matches each answer. In that case, the participant whose hand was up first—if correct—wins.)

VARIATIONS
★ Small group members tally up their correct answers; whichever group answers the most questions (or questions the most answers!) wins thirty seconds of public celebration.

★ Each small group writes one easy, one medium and one hard question and places them inside color-coded balloons (maybe red balloons for hard questions, yellow for medium and green for easy).

8 Bingo

Create bingo cards with nine spaces in a 3 x 3 array. Mark the center space "Free" and fill in the rest with answers to review questions. (For a more challenging game, sprinkle the bingo cards with one or two false answers.) Encourage participants to respond to each call with fun sounds, like a big groan if there's no match or a "Woo-hoo!" if there is. Players who get three in a row must rise to their feet and shout, "Bingo!"

VARIATION
★ Play kinesthetic bingo in teams of seven or eight people. For each team, create giant 3 x 3 bingo cards on the floor with the answers on pieces of paper that you have taped in place. Teams stand to the side of their cards. Display the questions one at a time on an overhead projector; teams send one member to stand on the matching answer. When a team has three players standing in a row, they jump up and down and call, "Bingo!"

⑨ Brainstorming

Brainstorming can confirm that learners are on the right track and help everyone gather many useful ideas, especially in an environment that allows creativity and doesn't judge any brainstorming suggestions as wrong or irrelevant. Put participants into groups or teams of four to five people; alternately, if the participants are already in teams, get their attention by asking them to point to the team leader. Now you are ready to introduce a topic for brainstorming. Follow these steps to make the directions very clear and to help the teams work efficiently:

❖ *Give the participants an incentive for doing it, perhaps by identifying a practical benefit.*

❖ *Tell teams how many items you expect them to come up with as they brainstorm.*

❖ *Have the teams designate a note taker before the activity begins.*

❖ *Provide an example of how to brainstorm to set them off on the right track.*

❖ *Get them going by saying something like, "Great. We're ready. Our goal is to list nine or more items in just three minutes! Now, turn to your team leader and say, 'Let's do it!'"*

VARIATIONS
★ When they complete their list, teams stand up and share their results with other teams.

★ Use Jigsaw teams for brainstorming (Jigsaw activities are explained in this chapter).

★ A person from one team (perhaps the team leader) stands and shares with the entire group the results of his or her team's brainstorm.

★ Teams send out one "spy" to collect two ideas from other groups and bring them back to the team.

⑩ Calling Cards

After exploring a particular topic, it's good to let the audience gather thoughts and ideas about it from each other. Give each person one index card and have him or her write on the front of it three important things they learned about the topic. To add to the atmosphere of busy importance, play Baroque music (in a major key). Instruct your audience to leave their cards face-up at their seats but to grab their notebooks. For five minutes have them wander around the room, reading other note cards and jotting down new ideas or concepts that they see.

VARIATIONS
★ In groups or teams, participants brainstorm everything they can about a topic. Keep notes on a big sheet of butcher paper. Group members circulate the room looking at the other brainstorming efforts and finally update their own brainstorms with information they learned from the others.

★ Groups or teams create graphic organizers of a review topic and circulate the room looking for new ideas to add to their own graphic organizer.

★ Save all the calling cards and post them on a bulletin board or save them for review activities later.

⑪ Group Quizzes

Not only do group quizzes put some healthy performance anxiety and stress on your audience, they also really demonstrate to participants how much they've been able to learn from each other. Break your audience into an even number of small groups. Each group creates a list of ten questions that can be answered in less than thirty seconds and with fewer than twenty-five words. Once they've made their lists, ask half the groups to remain seated and the other half to walk over to join one of the seated groups (and remain standing). The standing groups quiz the sitting ones with their questions. A scorekeeper awards three points for a perfect answer, two points for a "close" answer and one point for making a stab at it. The goal is to score thirty points. When the first quiz is complete, the groups switch places. The standing group sits down to be quizzed by the group that just answered their questions (and the sitting group stands to deliver the quiz). As a whole group, celebrate high scores at the end of the second round.

VARIATIONS

★ On index cards, participants write two questions (with answers) that can be answered in thirty seconds or less. They take turns quizzing partners, then return to their small groups or teams to share what they learned.

★ Small groups of participants design a brief presentation about content from the lesson and deliberately plant three mistakes in it. The groups pair up and take turns standing to give their presentations to each other. The listening group has to figure out what information was incorrect and how to fix it. When everyone has finished, the leader or a representative from each group reports to the rest of the class the mistakes they planted and how the other group fixed them.

⑫ Circle Add-Ons

A group or team of participants sits in a circle. The team leader says one true thing about a concept they all just learned. The person next to him or her repeats it and adds one fact, feature or distinction. The third person repeats the first two things, and adds another. Go around the circle until everyone has recited and added on to the list. Once everyone has added to the list, go around the circle one more time so everyone has a chance to recite the complete list. (That ought to keep everyone paying attention!)

VARIATIONS

★ Simplify it. Each person repeats any one of the statements (not the whole list) before adding one to the list.

★ Each person creates and performs a gesture that can be a memory aid for the item they add to the list. As team members take turns reciting the list, their teammates perform their gestures to help them remember.

★ The groups stand in a circle. When it is one person's turn to add to the list, he or she steps into the center of the circle to act out an item to add to the list. As they recite the list, the group members also have to act out the items in the center of the circle.

⑬ Compare and Contrast

Comparing and contrasting material works as both an introduction to new concepts and a review of old ones. The research on compare and contrast activities suggests that they are powerful learning tools (Marzano et al., 2001). In groups of three to six, have participants identify the features or issues that one assigned topic shares (or is at variance) with another. Next to each item, the group should explain the comparison or contrast to justify their choices.

VARIATIONS

★ Compare and contrast material to baseline standards instead of other topics.

★ Compare and contrast one group or pair's work to the work of other groups or pairs.

★ Compare and contrast material to printed research, Internet sources or similar compilations.

★ Before participant teams begin a compare and contrast activity, have them devise a rubric or checklist of what to look for and by what standards they intend to compare topics. Once they have this checklist, ask them to confer with other teams to refine their compare/contrast requirements. Finally, when the teams have finished comparing and contrasting the material, have them share their results with the entire group.

★ Individual participants decide how they are going to organize elements for a specific content. For example, they could organize a novel by plot, characters, conflicts, themes or setting. An historical event might be analyzed according to the countries involved, key people, political issues or extenuating circumstances (like geography or economy). Participants would then use graphic organizers to arrange the information in novel but meaningful ways.

★ At the conclusion of a compare and contrast activity, individual participants find partners outside of their original group. They then compare and contrast their notes with each other by identifying similarities and differences in their notes and making written updates to reflect new learning.

⑭ Divide and Conquer

Teams of four to eight participants split in half. One half stays together and the other half joins another team. The combined teams discuss the relevance of newly learned material for four minutes. (To enhance their productivity, give them questions or topics to focus on.) Finally, all participants return to their original teams and share what they learned.

VARIATION

★ Have everyone read a single document and then form groups or pairs to discuss how it fits in with the current topic or prior learning.

15 Fairy Tales

Announce to everyone that you are going to have some story time. In groups or teams, participants choose a fairy tale to rewrite (like *Little Red Riding Hood, The Three Little Pigs* or *Cinderella*.) Without divulging any of the other steps of the activity, ask them to spend seven minutes summarizing the fairy tale story in exactly seven sentences, the first of which must begin, "Once upon a time…" and the last of which might end, "…and they all lived happily ever after." Next, ask them to brainstorm ten to fifteen key terms or concepts from the topic or unit they have just learned. When this is complete, ask them to reduce the list of key terms to the seven most important ones. Finally, have them rewrite their fairy tale summary so that each sentence includes one of the seven key terms. They must use one term per sentence, without repeating any. The newly adapted story will make humorous points about what they have learned. The teams take turns reading their stories aloud to the rest of the group.

VARIATIONS

★ Have teams contribute tokens to a class pool (tokens can be personal items like a pencil or an earned privilege like an extra bathroom pass). After hearing all the teams' stories, participants vote on the funniest one (with the exception of their own). Use 3" x 5" cards for secret ballots. The team that wrote the winning story collects the pool.

★ Give each group seven overhead transparencies and a marker so they can illustrate each sentence of their stories. If you have enough, flip charts work well, too.

16 Feedback

Timely, specific feedback that directly addresses a learner's performance is an essential part of the learning process and can be added meaningfully to more than half of the activities in this book. One thing that clearly helps in the learning process is feedback (Marzano et al., 2001). At the end of content-heavy activities, ask team members or partners to pause, reflect on what they've done and give useful feedback to each other. Generic comments like, "You did great," are not feedback. Until participants are accustomed to giving specific feedback, provide structure for it. Say, "Talk to your partner about how many or how few vocabulary words he or she used in their story," or, "Did your partner present a clear and organized summary or just ramble on without direction?" Prompt feedback that helps learners correct or improve their performance is the most useful. To encourage participants to give each other lots of feedback, set a minimum time of forty-five seconds for each person to talk.

VARIATIONS

★ Provide participants with a rubric so everyone gets feedback on the same issues. For example, for feedback on an oral presentation, ask partners to evaluate things like eye contact with the audience, audible voice, lively manner and informative content.

★ Record a learner's performance on audio or video and let him or her watch it while a partner gives feedback on it.

★ Participants get anonymous feedback on index cards from everyone in their group.

17 Filling Potholes

This activity works best with an audience that takes lots of written notes. Each participant examines his or her notebook and identifies the "weakest" page (the page missing the most information) from the last unit or learning segment. On that page, he or she writes a list of questions about the topic to be answered. Everyone slides his or her notebooks (with that page exposed) to the person on the left. Give participants one minute to fill in as much of the requested information as they know; pass the notebooks once again to the left. When the notebooks are back in the hands of their owners, give everyone another minute to read what's been added to them. If participants need more information about what's been written in their notes, they can ask for it at this time.

VARIATIONS

★ Add a kinesthetic element to the activity by leaving the notebooks in place and moving the participants to the next place in the circle every minute.

★ Do this activity orally and in groups. After identifying the weakest page, have participants take turns reading their questions aloud for the rest of their group to answer; they can add the missing information to their notes.

18 Fishing for Gems

At the conclusion of a unit or topic, give everyone two index cards. On each card, participants write something from the lesson that they found very valuable or important. Then, have participants mix and mingle with each other, explaining why they chose what they did and exchanging interesting cards with each other. The goal of the activity is for everyone to swap cards with at least two other people before returning to their seats.

VARIATION

★ Participants write two questions on one index card. Then, they write the answers to the two questions on a second card. Mix up the cards in a big bowl or bin. Everyone draws out two cards (they'll get either questions or answers). Then, they find the participant with the corresponding questions or answers to the cards they drew.

19 Graphic Organizers

Graphic organizers use words and short phrases to arrange information about a topic in a visual, non-linear way. Chapter 3 describes how to use them to help your audience identify what they would like to know about an upcoming topic; they are also ideal tools for helping participants understand what they have learned at a lesson's conclusion. Tables, flow charts, idea webs, pictographs and Venn diagrams are all examples of graphic organizers that are quick and easy to make. Encourage participants to enhance their graphic organizers with color and non-linguistic symbols to make them even more memorable. For review of a topic, hand out incomplete graphic organizers for individual participants or teams to finish.

Group Mapping Activities Bring Out the Joy of Learning

VARIATIONS

★ Break a topic into sections and assign each section to a different team of students. Each team is responsible for creating a large, brightly colored graphic organizer of the material. Post the graphic organizers around the room for a gallery walk.

★ Distribute skeleton idea webs on butcher paper to student teams. Have each team fill them in most of the way, but leave some parts empty. When they are finished, have every team take a marker as they visit the other idea webs, trying to add one piece of information to each.

★ Two teams create information tables of the same chapter and later meet to merge the information.

★ Two individuals create personal graphic organizers and then merge their information into a single, larger graphic organizer.

★ Cover a wall with butcher paper (or sheets of flip-chart paper) to form a huge piece of paper. You will create a colossal idea-web skeleton and then assign each portion to participant teams to fill in. Once they've gotten most of the topic mapped, participants are free to add any details they think are missing from other teams' sections. At the end, individual participants copy down the salient points on personal idea webs.

★ Play Leap Frog with graphic organizers! At the end of a session, have participants create individual idea webs or flow charts of what they have learned. At the beginning of the next class, they try to recreate the exact same graphic organizer from memory (without peeking). Then, participants compare their two graphic organizers and update the second with key information from the first.

20 Group and Regroup

Grouping and regrouping is a way to help students remember particular bits of information by using them in a variety of ways. Post a list of key terms (fifteen to twenty total) on an overhead projector or have participants brainstorm their own list of topic items to display on butcher paper. In pairs or teams, they group the items in as many ways as they can think of; have them write their groupings down and title each one. Let them be creative but make them justify each grouping! The following grouping ideas should help them get started:

❖ *degree of difficulty*

❖ *chronologically, geographically, politically or economically*

❖ *practical usability (or when they are likely to use it in real life)*

❖ *"gee-whiz" versus "yawn"*

Groups can color-code or add other visuals to their groups. Eventually, they should share them with other students or with the entire class.

21 If-Thens

This strategy is a kinesthetic affirmation that helps students use their bodies to influence their minds. Make a suggestion about how you would like them to feel in the first part of your directions and follow it with a specific action for them to take—and model it. (*"If you feel ready to move on to our next topic, then take a slow, deep breath!"*). Most people will copy the action for the simple reason that everyone around them is doing it; because your words and the action are linked in their minds, the suggested feeling often follows the requested behavior.

The first time you use this strategy, it's best to ask your group to do something they would have done even without your direction. For example, if they've been standing for a while, say, "If you learned something new from your partner, then please take your seat." This helps form a bond of trust between you and your audience by signaling that you act in their best interest. Finally, avoid overusing If-Thens; they lose their novelty (as does anything) if they become just another part of the routine.

Here are some If-Then directions that work in any context:

❖ *"Take a slow, deep breath and hold it for a moment. Now, exhale. If you feel confident you can do well on this quiz, please begin."*

❖ *"If you are ready to have some fun, please stand up and find a partner from the opposite side of the room."*

❖ *"If your group is ready to create its graphic organizer, please send one representative to come get your materials."*

22 Jigsaw

Jigsaws are commonly known activities that have excellent application to our need to help learners identify their knowledge. Participants come together in teams like jigsaw pieces fit together in a puzzle. The jigsaw activity involves two groupings: expert groups and puzzle groups. Expert groups and puzzle groups should be between four and eight students in size.

Participants break into expert groups of equal size. Each group is assigned a topic to discuss or problem to solve together so they can become "experts" on the issue. When all the expert groups have had enough time to learn their material, participants leave to form their puzzle groups. Puzzle groups contain one member of each expert group. Once they are in their puzzle groups, each participant shares the information they learned in their expert groups. Finally, each person returns to their expert group to share what they learned from the other members of their puzzle group.

Note: To eliminate chaos and confusion about who goes where, give participants index cards that identify their expert group and puzzle group before you begin. For example, label the expert groups by color and puzzle groups by number. One student might get a card that says, "Blue 4." All the blues (or reds or yellows) meet for the expert group; all the fours (or fives or threes) find each other for the puzzle groups.

VARIATIONS

★ Students form expert groups to learn about a topic. They designate one person to be their delegate and send them out to visit another group. Once every expert group has a visitor, they share with the visiting delegate everything they know about their topic. Delegates return to their expert groups and share what they learned from other groups. To expose participants to more information, send a new delegate to visit the next group. Repeat this cycle until everyone has learned about all the topics.

★ Each group makes a large graphic organizer of what they learned, then move into jigsaw groups to get ideas from other graphic organizers and bring them back. The original groups update their graphic organizers with the new information and post them on the wall.

> **The fast-moving world inside your body and brain turns every idea, feeling, action, belief, sensation or decision into a state.**

23 Ketchup Catch-Up

Halfway through the day, put participants into pairs. One partner will take the role of "Mustard" and the other will be "Ketchup." Mustard will give Ketchup a summary of everything learned that day (as if Ketchup had arrived late and needed to catch up on what the class had been doing). After a few minutes, they switch roles.

VARIATIONS

★ Intensify the activity by putting a forty-five second time limit on each summary, so Mustard will have to quickly identify key points of the learning.

★ Rearrange the pairs to trios. Two people will play the role of Ketchup and one will play Mustard. Take turns so each person has the chance to summarize the learning to the other two.

24 Lyrical Learning

Provide the lyrics to ten songs everyone already knows (like *Happy Birthday* or *Row, Row, Row Your Boat*) or ask the audience to brainstorm a list to use. Put the audience in teams of three to six people and have them stand up and take a deep breath. While they are still standing, have each group choose the fifteen most important key words from the most recent learning segment or unit. Then, have them sit down and reduce the list to the top ten key words. Using those words, the teams rewrite the lyrics to one of the songs on the list. Finally, the teams create choreography for the songs and perform them for the rest of the group.

VARIATIONS

★ Teams create song sheets to pass out to other groups to sing along with. This will help everyone improve retention of content.

★ After each team presents a song, the other teams debrief, write down what they learned and give feedback to the performing team on index cards.

★ Spend five minutes each day for a week revising and rehearsing the songs to maintain content knowledge and to get top-notch performances.

Time Schedule for Complex Learning

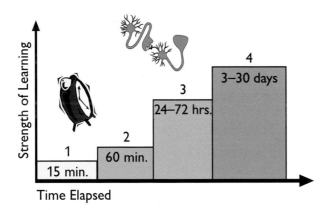

Strength of Learning (vertical axis)

1 — 15 min.
2 — 60 min.
3 — 24–72 hrs.
4 — 3–30 days

Time Elapsed (horizontal axis)

1. Initial connection is made. Synapses are formed or modified within the first 15 minutes.
2. Most explicit learning is held and evaluated by hippocampus. Synaptic adhesion strengthens.
3. At night, new learning is organized and coded. Hippocampus distributes it to the cortex by neural repetition for long-term storage.
4. Integration into related networks may occur if stimulation is provided for it.

25 Musical Messages

Each person writes three review concepts on a sheet of paper and leaves it at his or her desk. Then, everyone stands with a pen or pencil in hand and plays a version of Musical Chairs. Play some cheerful or silly music for twenty to thirty seconds while they walk around the room. When you stop the music, everyone quickly finds the nearest desk to sit at. The last person to take a seat has to read off the three ideas from the list on the desk. If those ideas have already been read aloud, the participant has to think of new ones on the spot. Play the game for five rotations. Then, everyone returns to their seats and adds on to their own lists what they heard from others during the game.

VARIATIONS

★ Enhance this activity for auditory learners by not leaving lists of review items at the desks. Participants will still scramble for a seat when the music stops, but instead of reading off a list, they verbalize a review idea to the people on either side of them. Allow participants to carry a pencil and paper so they can write down any ideas they like that they hear from others.

★ Participants carry their notes through a few rounds of traditional Musical Chairs. When someone is left standing, he or she has to read three review concepts aloud without repeating any that previous classmates have read.

26 Nonlinguistic Representation

Alone or with a partner or team, participants arrange recent learning into some kind of graphic organizer, like an idea web, matrix, pictograph or flow chart. When they are finished, they find a partner or another group to share their work with and to give and receive feedback.

VARIATIONS

★ Participants create three-dimensional representations with clay or decoupage.

★ Participants transform individual facts or items into Charades-like movements or actions.

27 Paper Airplane Follow-Up

On a regular piece of paper, each person writes his or her name and e-mail address plus two ideas he or she plans to implement within thirty days. Play songs like *Leaving on a Jet Plane* (by Peter, Paul and Mary) or any recording of *Fly Me to the Moon* (by Bart Howard) and have everyone fold their paper into an airplane (have a design handy for people who don't already know how to make one). When all the paper airplanes are ready, change the music to something wilder, like *Magic Carpet Ride* (by Steppenwolf). The whole class tosses planes around the room for about thirty seconds. When you stop the music, tell everyone to keep the planes they are holding (make sure everybody has someone else's). Ask participants to save the planes for thirty days and then email the planes' owners to support them in the goals that they had written down.

VARIATIONS

★ Use paper airplanes to choose secret gift exchange buddies or birthday partners.

★ Use paper airplanes to choose partners or groups for projects. Try handing out pieces of paper with topics on them for students to fold into airplanes. After they've tossed them around the room for a while, students unfold the planes and find the other people holding the same topic or group marker.

★ As a team review project, have participants create one plane per team. When they are finished, have an "air show" with all the planes. Award points for design, distance and accuracy. Also award points to teams that included important review items on their planes that the other teams forgot about, as well as the quality of their content.

28 Point to the Place

Point to the Place reinforces learning from an activity by sending participants back to the same location for context. This is both reassuring and confidence-building ("Hey, I remember this stuff!"). For something small you could say, "Point to the place in the room where you paired up with a neighbor ten minutes ago. Good memory!" For something more involved, try, "Go to the table where your group worked on its graphic organizer yesterday," or, "Sit in the same chair you were in during last week's brainstorming session."

29 Quick Draw

On a sheet of paper, have everyone draw a picture, flow chart or stick figure that best illustrates the concept they just learned. Then, have them turn to their neighbor for feedback on their picture and specific suggestions on how to enhance it. (Feedback should be content specific, not about artistic execution or ability.) Finally, everyone stands up, finds a new partner, shares their enhanced illustrations and explains the concepts behind them.

VARIATIONS

★ Encourage the audience to draw or doodle as you lecture, in order to make very visual notes of their questions or new content.

★ Stop the lecture and have learners exchange notes with a neighbor. Then, continue and ask them to take notes for each other. Make sure each person ends up with his or her original notes before you finish.

★ Before a new lesson, pass out copies of a skeleton graphic organizer for people to fill in as you talk.

★ Give colored pens to participants so they can make their notes more interesting. Introduce them to common graphic organizers like flow charts or idea webs so they can experiment with pictures and symbols.

30 Read and Share

This activity enables participants to move quickly through a body of text by reading it as a team of four to seven people. Select a chapter or other material that covers a relevant and interesting aspect of the content. (Don't use fluff or filler but rather something you'd like participants to master.) Make sure you choose something that all your participants are capable of reading. Sit the team members together and have them divide up the text into consecutive chunks of relatively equal size. Give them two minutes to read their chunks silently. (People who finish early can go on to read the last paragraph.) Then, give the teams ten minutes for each person to share what he or she learned from the reading and how it fits with the rest of the unit you are teaching.

VARIATIONS

★ Allow participants to read their segments at their own seats before joining their teams to discuss them.

★ Allow participants to lean up against a wall or lie on the floor to read their segments.

★ After everyone has finished reading but before they've discussed it with their team, give them two minutes to write summary statements about their segment.

★ After everyone on a team has shared their reading, give them time to create a summary paragraph of the whole selection.

★ Have team members visit other groups to share what they learned.

㉛ Repeat After Me

When used sparingly and carefully, Repeat After Me engages the learner and reinforces key ideas or hard-to-pronounce, unusual vocabulary terms. Introduce it with a simple, "Listen up. We have a new word today. It's Latin for 'seahorse' and it's the critical temporal lobe structure that affects learning and memory. The word is 'hippocampus.' Everyone repeat after me. Hip-po-cam-pus." Don't make them repeat it more than two or three times.

VARIATIONS

★ Let participants identify and learn a new word at the same time each day in a ritualized activity.

★ Teach a new word each day, as well as lead an oral review of the last five words and their definitions.

★ Orally review the five previous vocabulary words and then assign to participants a written activity about them.

㉜ Resident Expert

Post the titles of four to six topics in various locations in the room. For each, ask for a show of hands of people who could answer at least one question about that topic. These temporary "experts" go stand next to the topic title (there may be several experts per topic). Divide the rest of the participants into as many groups as

you have topics. Send a group to each topic location to ask the resident expert(s) five questions. After three minutes, the groups rotate to the next topic location until every group has asked five questions of every expert.

VARIATIONS

★ After answering the questions, the resident expert(s) switches places with a person from the visiting group. When the groups rotate, the former expert moves on to the next topic and the new expert stays behind to answer questions. (After all, they just heard the answers to five questions about that topic; they are experts themselves!) This gives the new expert a chance to demonstrate what he or she has learned and the former expert the opportunity to learn about another topic.

★ Before visiting the experts, the groups write five questions they'd like to ask about each topic.

★ Play for points: experts versus visitors! Every question the experts answer correctly earns them two points; every question the experts answer incorrectly awards the visiting group one point. After five minutes, total the points and let the winners celebrate.

㉝ Ring of Fire

Groups of five to nine participants arrange their chairs in a circle about ten feet in diameter and select someone to start. (Refer to the Chapter 3 activity, Identify the Person Who…, for ideas about how to creatively designate someone to begin the activity.) The person selected moves his or her chair to the "hot seat" at the center of the circle. The rest of the group fires review questions at the hot seat until that person answers three correctly (not necessarily in a row). The group applauds his or her success; the person in the hot seat chooses the next participant to take it. Rotate until everyone has had a chance to answer questions. It's an excellent way for participants to see how much they actually know.

VARIATIONS

★ If groups finish early, have them double up for "Super Ring of Fire."

★ A group that finishes early starts another round for bonus points.

★ Groups write out their questions in advance and share them with each other so everyone has time to prepare. In this case, have the person in the hot seat answer three questions correctly in a row.

34 Sentence Affirmations

Sentence Affirmations allow learners to verbally clarify a word or words that are important to a sentence or thought. Set up the activity by saying something like, "Today, we'll be exploring four things. They are A, B, C and D. Now, how many things are we exploring today?" The audience would respond with, "Four!" You could also announce, "When I say, 'Go!,' find two other partners and introduce yourselves," and then ask, "How many partners will you find quickly?" This keeps your audience "in the game" and verbally engaged in your presentation. Note how this activity differs from Unfinished Sentences in Chapter 3, which requires the audience to guess which

word would correctly complete a sentence. Sentence Affirmations are a clarification and short-term memory device rather than a test of prior learning.

35 Snow Ball

Participants divide a sheet of paper into four quadrants. Have them write something they learned in the first quadrant, then crumple up the paper and throw it to someone else. The person who catches it writes a comment in the first quadrant about what the first person said (like an extension of the information or a correction) and then writes something new in the second quadrant. Next, he or she crumples it up and throws it to a third person, who comments on the information in the first and second quadrants and adds more to the third. Repeat this one more time so a fourth person can fill in the last quadrant. Time the paper tosses so everyone throws them in unison, like a snow ball fight.

VARIATIONS

★ In the first quadrant, participants begin a sentence about the content that the next three people have to continue.

★ Participants write three true things and one false thing on their papers. Whoever catches the paper can work with a partner to determine which of the statements is incorrect.

> *Understanding **why** you should manage states is just as important as knowing **how** to manage them.*

36 Think-Pair-Share

The same activity that worked so well in Chapter 5 for making learners accountable to a peer is also valuable tool for refreshing and revising learning. It is ideal for content review. Its basic steps are:

❖ *stand up and mentally reflect on your topic for a moment;*

❖ *move around the room to find a partner;*

❖ *share with your partner your prior learning; and*

❖ *thank your partner and return to your seat.*

The secret is to create and explore fresh variations so the activity is relevant to your learners. If your technique isn't varied constantly, it will get real old, real fast.

VARIATIONS

★ Participants turn to the person sitting next to them and teach him or her something they just learned.

★ One partner role-plays an adult; the other role-plays a five-year-old child. Each partner explains the last topic to the other as they think their character would do, using speech patterns and hand gestures. Simplicity is key.

★ One partner plays the role of a world-renowned expert on a topic and the other partner plays the role of a reporter who asks questions for two minutes. Give each person a moment to get into character.

★ Teach a partner a key point from the last ten minutes of instruction by using only your hands and body. Then, review what you "said" with both gestures and words. Switch and have the other person do the same for a different topic. This strategy is great for embedding new learning into the right hemisphere of the brain.

★ Split your audience into two groups of equal size. Have one half stand in a tight, outward-facing circle and the other half around them in a larger, inward-facing circle. Each person should be directly in front of another. For thirty seconds, the inside person teaches the outside person something he or she has learned. Then, they switch roles. At the end of another thirty seconds, everyone in the outside circle says goodbye and moves to the right. The people in the inside circle stay put. The newly formed pairs go through another round of thirty-second lessons. Repeat this rotation five or six times.

Think-Pair-Share Is a Valuable Tool for Refreshing Learning

37 Summarize Learning

Summarization is a useful but rarely taught skill. Before asking learners to summarize new material, remind them of these key steps:

❖ *think about the meaning of the material;*

❖ *create a new topic sentence; and*

❖ *delete, substitute, generalize and categorize concepts.*

Give participants a defined body of content, like the last fifteen minutes of a lecture, a chapter in a book or a website. Then, give them ten minutes to summarize the material on paper. Allow them to work in pairs. When they finish, they can share their results with other pairs or hand in their work.

VARIATIONS

★ Teams agree on a step-by-step process for summarizing content, and divide up the work or do it together. Then, one team shares their work with another team.

★ One participant walks through the steps of the summary process and calls on his or her partner for help. Then, they both write out what was summarized. Switch roles when it is time to summarize a second process during this activity or a later one.

38 Timeline Review

Before the end of the day, have a deliberate "accident." Mix up your transparencies or notes and then let selected participants (or volunteers) unscramble them for the review session.

VARIATIONS

★ Have the group do a word association from the previous day's lesson. Set a goal of at least twenty-five words, ideas or activities. Write all these on sticky notes or small pieces of paper. Then, give small groups or teams seven minutes to put them in the exact same order in which they were presented the day before. Once they finish, have them share their timeline with another team to check for accuracy. Let them know it's OK if they recall something out of order. The process, not the outcome, is what will help them understand and recall knowledge better.

★ Allow volunteers or pre-selected participants to use your computer presentation, overhead transparencies or props to quickly re-teach what you just taught to the group. Ask them in advance to put two things out of order. The rest of the group needs to figure out what has been scrambled. After two or three minutes, lead the group in a standing ovation for the presenters.

39 Topic Tag Lines

At the end of an activity, put people in pairs to turn the main idea of the topic into a very simple but memorable tag line or rhyme (like you see on promotional posters for movies). For example, when I teach about the limitations of the hippocampus, I say we must not overwhelm our audience with too much content. A possible tag line for this concept could be, "Too much, too fast won't last." Other examples of topic tag lines are scattered throughout every chapter of this book. Tag lines do not have to rhyme—they just have to be catchy.

VARIATIONS

★ Give pairs or small groups five minutes to choreograph their rhyme or tag line. Then, have them share it with another group or with the entire audience. Call for nominations for the "Best Rhyme of All Time" or "Best Line of All Time." Offer a silly prize or privilege for winning.

★ Award bonus points to participants who remember and re-enact past tag lines from an earlier activity. Give more points if they can remember rhymes from several weeks before.

40 Wacky Words

Devise a list of unusually descriptive adjectives and phrases and display them on an overhead projector. Use words like "jaw-dropping," "five-legged," "dripping wet," "earth-sucking," "heartfelt" or "sweeter than sugar." Participants find partners for a think-pair-share activity and pick one of the phrases from the list. As they review prior learning, have them use the phrase as often as possible. This insertion will help them remember what they taught to each other. More advanced learners can play with two or three phrases from the list.

41 Write Now!

Help learners really remember new knowledge by asking them to write important information in a novel way. Build suspense by adding steps to the directions one at a time. For example, say, "Please get something to write with," and pause. Continue with, "Show your neighbor your writing tool. If theirs is as nice as yours, say, 'Wow!' Now, find something to write *on* (or, *turn to page...*) and write this down. The first word is...." Telling others to write something will get their attention, but avoid overuse. For best effect, use this tool *only* when you have something really important for students to capture.

Alert participants to important information with announcements like:

❖ *"Write this down even if you only write down one thing all day."*

❖ *"I'll talk for just three minutes. Then, you'll write down three things."*

❖ *"Write nothing down. You talk and your neighbor will write for you."*

❖ *"Prepare a generic graphic organizer. As I talk, add information to it. Every few minutes I'll remind you to add something new."*

❖ *"Write this down with your opposite [non-dominant] hand."*

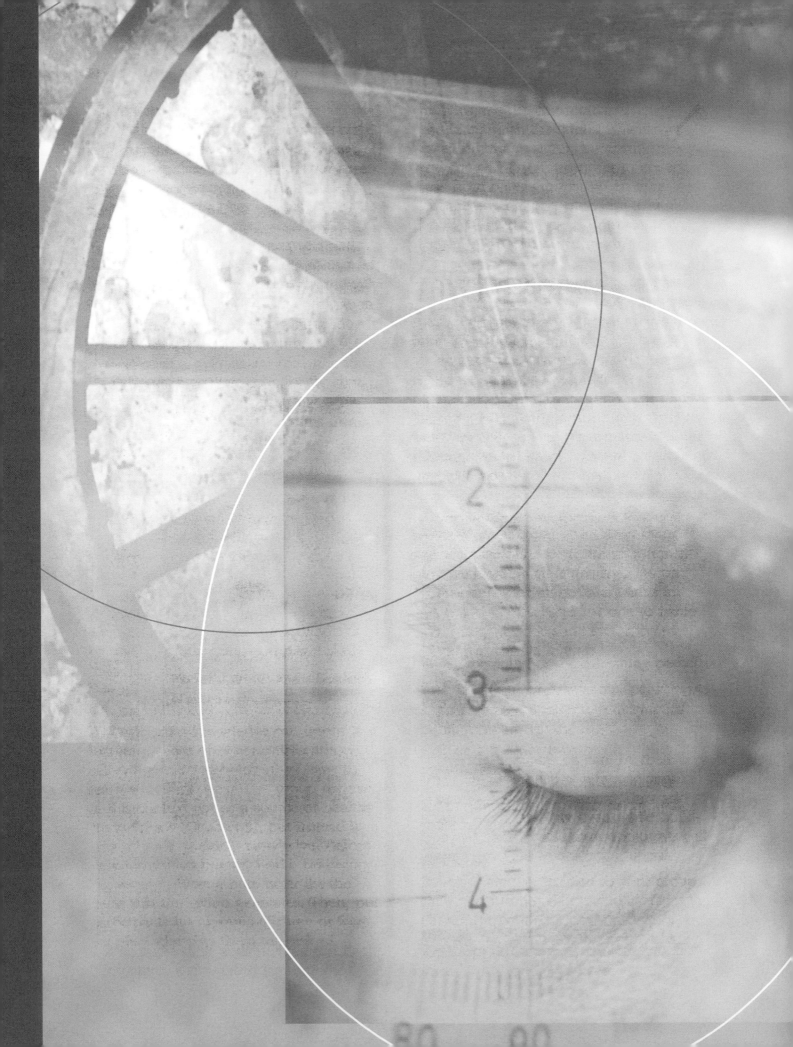

Chapter 9
"Peace & Quiet"
States of Reflection & Calm

What Is This State?

Like most states, reflection and calm have both cognitive and emotional aspects. The cognitive side is an awareness of being able to relax; the emotional side is feeling no threat or danger. You have to feel safe to enter this state. Broadly speaking, stress in this state is low, at least for the moment.

just a few minutes. Younger learners may become mischievous if you let them stay in this state for too long. Members of a mature audience will find it much easier to maintain; individuals who have trained in meditative techniques can even access it at will.

Why Is This State Important?

This state is fundamentally important to all presenters because certain learner behaviors can appear only during this state. For example, it is easier to be humble, honest or reflective in this state. Also, if students feel that they can be peaceful and calm in your presence, they are likely to want to return to that state (and enroll in your course) again and again.

How Long Does This State Last?

Peace and quiet typically do not last very long. Participants will often start to feel bored and some begin to feel stress after

What Brain Activity Is Involved?

Entering this state requires both the suppression of brain activity in some areas and the activation of the brain in others. The frontal lobes suppress areas of the brain, such as the occipital and parietal lobes, as well as activate positive memories from the temporal lobes. The brains of learners also suppress activity in areas like the amygdala, the brain's emotional center. Peaceful people usually exhibit low alpha waves or high theta waves. Levels of the stress hormone, cortisol, drop markedly; for several decades research has shown a high correlation between cortisol levels and stress (Rodin, 1980; Cacioppo, 1994).

Brain Waves of Learners in Peaceful States

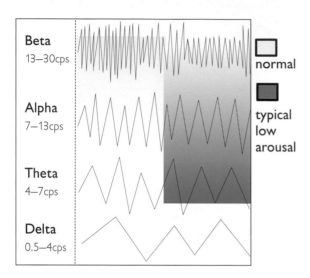

Beta
13–30cps

Alpha
7–13cps

Theta
4–7cps

Delta
0.5–4cps

normal

typical low arousal

Understanding Specific Brain Wave States

Beta High Activity: excitement, debate, exercise, complex projects, competition
Alpha Focused: in control, reading, writing, watching, drawing, problem-solving, talking
Theta Slow: spacy, unfocused, drowsy, dreamy, more receptive to suggestions
Delta Nonconscious: deepest sleep time, very slowed down, no reactions

Body Language of This State

Some learners lean back, letting their posture relax, their shoulders drop, their eyes glaze over, their breathing slow and their muscles relax. But this state is displayed just as frequently by sitting quietly in a chair, lying on the floor or putting your feet up. Cultural variations and varied circumstances might change what you see and hear.

Generalizations

Too few learners will trigger this state on their own. Never assume that your audience even knows how to access it! In a busy world, fewer and fewer people are able to reliably enter a state of calm; many people will be grateful to learn from you how to do so.

What Food Affects This State?

There are no guaranteed foods for relaxation. Avoid caffeine (coffee, tea, soft drinks or chocolate) and other stimulants. Foods that contain tryptophan and calcium often have calming effects. These foods include complex carbohydrates, like rice, pasta and potatoes, as well as turkey, milk, cottage cheese, tofu, avocados, almonds, walnuts and bananas.

What Music Affects This State?

Generally, calming music can both increase learner satisfaction and lower anxiety (Blood & Ferriss, 1993). Researchers found that customers moved almost thirty percent more slowly when stores played Muzak® than when they played contemporary, easy listening music or even no music at all (Dorfman, 1984). In other studies, soothing music lowered cortisol levels, heart rate and blood pressure (Geden et al., 1989; Lorch et al., 1994). Music can even support immune system functioning (McCraty et al., 1996).

To What Extent Does Testing Influence Student Stress Levels?

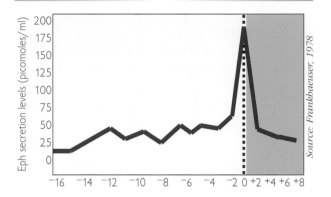

Source: Frankhaeuser, 1978

Levels of epinephrine shown over a 2-week period before, during and after a thesis exam for college students.

Key Basic Concepts

Peace and quiet should be elicited cautiously. Why? It's a delicate state and a good one to use but it takes time to get into and time to get out of. You must have enough time to transition properly. What encourages this state? A lack of stress or threat and a positive feeling of safety and calm. Students must be able to enter this state before they can look inward and become reflective. The better you become at managing your student states, the more effective you'll be as an instructor.

Learners will sweat if met with threat. Manage the stress or they'll achieve less.

Getting your audience into this state is easy. Use calming voice patterns, play soothing music, remove distractions and let them enjoy a feeling of control. Yoga postures can increase the sense of calm as well as focus a learner's attention and improve concentration, too. Additionally, yoga will usually decrease stress and muscle tension. But instead of announcing that you're going to introduce yoga postures and movements into an activity, simply say, "Let's try something different. Follow along with me." Always anticipate and diffuse resistance to avoid direct conflict that would raise stress levels. Set up any new activity by leading your audience into it gently and with certainty and empathy.

Strategies to Promote Reflection and Calm

Keep in mind that many things will calm learners down. This segment, however, focuses on ways to help participants consciously enter a very relaxed state without falling asleep. That means you must emphasize slow movements and gentle exertion in peaceful situations. Still, you want learners to experience control over their minds and bodies, not just to go along with things that you tell them to do. It's far more engaging and powerful for your audience members to be able to later replicate the feelings they experience during your presentation than for them to be led by you into this state for only the one moment.

Our Brain Adapts to Distress and Creates a New Allostatic State

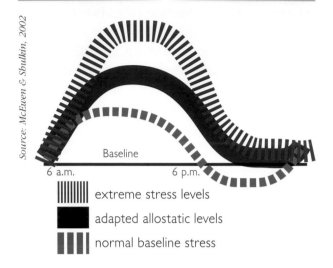

Source: McEwen & Shulkin, 2002

Baseline

6 a.m.   6 p.m.

||||| extreme stress levels

■ adapted allostatic levels

||| normal baseline stress

1. Baseline is healthy (green bar) stress.
2. Sudden exposure to extreme distress (red).
3. If all is well, subject returns to baseline (green).
4. Chronic exposure to extreme distress (red) forces changes in the brain. In comparison to distress, the adapted allostatic levels of stress (blue) feel almost good!
5. Over time, the subject's new baseline of stress in daily life becomes distress (blue).

① Acknowledgements

Acknowledgements work best right after the completion of an activity or project. Giving acknowledgements increases the likelihood that there will be more sincerely positive things to say about a classmate. When an activity is finished, have participants find partners. Direct everyone to take a few slow, deep breaths, close their eyes and reflect on the contributions that their partners have made to the course, class or project. After about thirty seconds, tell participants to open their eyes and make eye contact with their partners. After about ten seconds of silent eye contact, let them verbally acknowledge each other; the first partner speaks for thirty seconds and then the second one does.

VARIATIONS ★★☆

★ Have four to seven participants form a circle. Put a chair in the middle to represent the "seat of honor." One participant takes that seat and for fifteen seconds the others silently reflect on his or her contributions. Then, they take turns complimenting the person in the seat of honor. Have a timekeeper ensure that after one minute of compliments, the next participant takes a turn.

★ Two teams of the same size form a double circle, one team facing outward and the other team facing inward so they all see each other. Play soft, melodic music as teams arrange themselves. When you stop the music, have participants spend about ten seconds making eye contact and verbally acknowledging each other's accomplishments. When you start the music again, the participants in the inner circle stay put while the participants in the outer circle rotate one person to the right. When the music stops again, they spend another ten seconds acknowledging each other.

★ Give everyone an index card. Ask them to focus on one person in their group or team and write out what they appreciate about his or her contributions (not how much they like a hairstyle or clothing).

② Body Relaxers

Countless postures and slow movements will relax and calm the body. Postures that first tense the body before relaxing it will especially help participants access a state of peace and quiet. Additionally, comfortable postures that allow the body to unwind are beneficial to this state. T'ai Chi, an ancient set of postures and movements, is possibly the most relaxing series of exercises of all. Purchase a video or book about T'ai Chi to learn what it looks like and how to use it.

VARIATION

★ *Brain Gym*, the book by Dennison and Dennison, contains several relaxing poses. In the posture, "Cook's Hook-up," learners stand with one leg crossed over the other. They extend both arms to the front and cross and clasp their hands (palms together) so the left hand is on the right and the right hand is on the left. Once the hands are clasped, learners pull the clasped, crossed hands inward toward the chest so the elbows are down and the hands are up. This creates a tangled "hook-up" with a built-in cross lateral posture. Finally, the learners relax, inhaling slowly through the nose and exhaling through the mouth. Hold this posture and breathing cycle for one minute. Most learners find it very calming. Anyone who has difficulty doing it standing up can also do it while sitting instead.

③ Breathe through the Nose

Within normal parameters, higher temperatures generally trigger arousal and cooler ones tend to calm the brain. Breathing through the nose cools air as it enters the body and relaxes the mind. This is one way to calm learners, particularly when the room temperature is too warm. Relax your audience by first encouraging them to get into a comfortable position and then guiding their breathing. Suggest that they uncross their legs and let their hands drop to their sides. Direct them to inhale slowly through the nose and hold the breath for a moment, then exhale slowly through the mouth. Repeat this cycle several times until the audience is very relaxed. Be sure to use gentle words and a quiet tone throughout.

VARIATIONS

★ Add Body Relaxers postures to the breathing to enhance the relaxation.

★ Play slow-moving, peaceful music during the breathing exercises to lower participants' stress level.

④ Environment

It should come as no surprise that we feel very much at peace when we are in control or feel comfortable about what's in our environment. For this activity, have participants work in pairs or teams. Give everyone two minutes to discuss the immediate environment and some changes they'd like to see in it. Then, have participants narrow down the list to things that can be accomplished in five minutes or less. Finally, ask each participant pair or team to choose one item on their list and elect a spokesperson share it with the entire group. If the suggestion is possible, free and practical, give them the go-ahead to make the change. If it's not, put it "on hold." When all the participants or pairs have finished sharing their suggestions, play some background music and let them make the agreed-upon changes to the environment. You'll be surprised by some of the positive changes that surface in both the new environment and in the moods of your learners.

VARIATIONS

★ Have participant pairs brainstorm changes to make in the environment. Then, have them share their ideas with the entire group. Everyone will discuss and decide which changes are the best to make.

★ Participant teams decide which one change they would like to make. Then, all the team leaders meet separately to pick the top three changes from among all the teams and present them to the entire group.

★ The entire group brainstorms changes they would like to make to the environment; have a volunteer list the suggestions on chart paper, an overhead transparency or the white board. When the brainstorming session is finished, everybody votes on one change to implement.

5 Focusing Strategies

Being at peace involves either a release of stress or a good deal of suppression. Both of these things require the frontal lobes to work overtime at blocking out all the unwanted noise and chatter, dis-

tractions or music that might interrupt the state of quiet. The value of teaching focusing strategies is that you only need to demonstrate them once or twice before your audience will know and use them forever. These simple focusing strategies are not usually taught and you cannot assume that every learner intuitively knows what they are. Before teaching participants the following strategies, create a calming atmosphere by slowing the pace of your words and reassuring your audience that they are about to enjoy a positive experience.

❖ *Think about the "Why" of an activity. Why do you want to reach a particular goal? Answering this question sets up the next part of the process.*

❖ *Focus on what you're trying to accomplish. Make the goal or task vivid in your mind by drawing a mental a picture of the goal. Add in your imagination bold color and realistic sounds to accompany the goal so you can experience its positive attributes.*

❖ *If unrelated thoughts enter your mind, simply acknowledge them ("Yes, that's another thought.") and let them go. Give them the minimal amount of attention possible.*

❖ *Finally, constantly refresh and strengthen the goal. Surprisingly, in the end, it is just boredom or lack of guidance that causes us become lax about reaching our goals.*

6 Journaling

Writing about quiet, calm topics will generally create a quiet, calm state. Assume that your audience already knows the journaling process and that they are comfortable with it. You'll just need to provide them a theme or question to get them started. Be sure to give participants enough time to journal their way into a calm state. Generally, eight to ten minutes is sufficient.

Reflection and Journaling Are Tools for Peace and Quiet

VARIATIONS

★ Play some quiet, reflective music as participants write in their journals.

★ Model it! Describe a recent personal story or event from your own life that elicited feelings of calm or peace. Express your feelings about that event and share how you might have written about it in your own journal.

7 Music and Drawing

Music can induce just about any state from excitement to sleep. Triggering peace and quiet with music, however, means drawing a fine line between serenity and drowsiness. First, play music with an unhurried (but not too slow) tempo. The range of fifty-five to sixty-five beats per minute is just about right. Anything faster than that might be too arousing.

But listening to music is not enough! Make the experience more engaging with drawing. Give each participant a blank sheet of paper. Tell them to hold their pens in their non-dominant hands to remove any sense of pressure to be artistic and to activate the non-dominant hemisphere of the brain. Otherwise, drawing can be a very cognitive experience (Jensen, 2000). When everyone is ready, instruct participants to draw the emotions that the music stirs inside them. In other words, have them turn what they hear into something they can see. Many participants will change their minds several times about what they want to draw (just silently give them more paper when they need it) but insist that they keep using their non-dominant hand. This activity is not about how well they can draw; it's about how well they can put on paper the feelings that the music evokes. That's what will make this a personal exercise. After about three minutes, participants will be getting into the groove of moving and drawing to the music. After about five minutes, stop the music and have participants share their drawings (and their feelings) with a partner.

Try drawing to music like:

❖ *All the Seasons of George Winston: Piano Solos* from Windham Hill Records

❖ *Devotion: The Best of Yanni* from Private Music

❖ *Paint the Sky with Stars: The Best of Enya* from Warner Brothers

❖ *Peace and Quiet* and *Another World* by Harry Pickens, from The Brain Store® (Consumer note: Potential conflict of interest by the author duly noted.)

8 Mental Vacation

This relaxation activity can calm learners to very serene, focused and poised states for learning. Most relaxation sessions can be performed in two to four minutes. The process is simple. Ask participants to close their eyes. Invite them to inhale slowly through the nose and exhale slowly through the mouth as they relax their bodies. Invite them to raise their shoulders, tighten the shoulder muscles and then drop them. Go through the parts of the body one by one, raising and lowering the legs, neck, shoulders, back and fists, always reminding them to inhale through the nose and exhale through the mouth and keeping the rest of their body relaxed.

Next, ask them to mentally picture a very peaceful and relaxing getaway or vacation spot. Prompt them to imagine the sights, sounds and feelings that accompany their mental vacation and allow them time to enjoy it. Suggest that they carefully note the details that make the place colorful,

attractive or comfortable. Continually emphasize that they are really enjoying themselves. Encourage them to mentally live one completely relaxing day, a second one and then another one. In other words, send them on a virtual vacation. When you are finished, give them time to bring their minds back to the present before asking them to open their eyes. Direct their thoughts gently back to the room, to their classmates and then the topic at hand.

9 Reflection and Planning

Reflection can be an uncomfortable process for learners who are always on the go. You'll need to actually walk your audience through the steps for reflective thinking. They can be either sitting or standing calmly and peacefully, as long as their eyes are closed. Guide them through a review of their day, prompting them to think about their behaviors and how other people responded to those behaviors; ask them to reflect also on their thoughts and feelings. Encourage participants to dig deep into their minds to gather their thoughts and to review events in sequence. Depending on the age and experience of your audience, you may want to suggest a topic for reflection.

VARIATIONS

★ Music can enhance this state, as long as it is unrecognized by the participants. You don't want their brains to distract them by signalling, "I know that music!" Choose music with low BPMs (beats per minute) and with few or no compositional surprises. Much of Enya's music is appropriate (although often recognizable), as is music by Daniel Kobialka. The Brain Store® CD, *Peace and Quiet* (by Harry Pickens), also contains very reflective selections (potential conflict of interest by the author noted).

★ Planning is a possible follow-up to the reflection process. First, encourage learners to dream about their goals. Then, have them summarize the accomplishment of their goals—no matter how ambitious they are—in just five steps. Finally, have them simplify the five steps into one short sentence.

★ With pictures, participants illustrate a story board of themselves achieving personal or academic goals.

10 Settling Time

If you've dumped into your learners' heads a lot of content to process or review, it may be appropriate to take a short "brain break." I call this "Settling Time" because neural connections need time to let the new learning "settle" into place. Sometimes it's smart to just do nothing during this time. Now, it's not always easy to just do nothing, partly because parents and administrators always want learners to look busy. But it's also hard to do nothing because you never know when you're finished! To

define a clear beginning and end to doing nothing, bracket it with distinct activities. For example, begin "doing nothing" by having participants stand up and take a deep breath. Then, have them take at least eleven giant steps as slowly as possible. Once they've stopped moving, ask them to find a spot in the room where they feel (mostly) calm. From that point, end "doing nothing" by giving them instructions for their next activity.

VARIATIONS

★ Participants journal for a few minutes.

★ Release the audience to lunch or a snack break.

★ Let participants listen to some music, just for pleasure.

★ Have participants do some classroom chores that you consider mindless or routine.

11 Storytelling

Two things are critical to telling a story that evokes a state of peace and quiet. First, find a calming story that allows everyone to relax. Second, make listening to a story an active (but gentle) process for all learners. You didn't think I was going to let you just read a story aloud to your entire group, did you? You should know me better than that—I'm all about active learning!

Find a story you want to use and find a way to distribute it. You might print handouts of it, give everyone a copy of the book it is in or post it on an overhead projector. Once everyone has access to the story, put participants into teams to take turns reading it aloud to each other. You can help the groups decide who begins by saying something like, "Point to your team leader. Begin with the person to the left of the team leader and rotate clockwise. Each person takes a turn by reading one paragraph." (Refer to the Chapter 3 activity, Identify the Person Who..., for ideas about creatively choosing someone to start an activity.)

VARIATIONS

★ Partners take turns reading paragraphs of the story aloud.

★ Participants in teams stay alert and ready by reading just one sentence during their turn.

★ Play calming, peaceful music in the background.

12 Stretching

The simple act of sitting in chairs can create postural stress. So can sloppy body posture. Reduce that stress in your audience easily and safely with stretching. Introduce the activity by telling them that they are about to do something very important for their brains and spinal columns and have them take one deep breath. Then, have them stand up as an entire group or in their teams. Ask a volunteer or the team leaders to lead participants in forty-five seconds of stretching exercises that meet the following conditions:

❖ *the stretches move slowly;*

❖ *each stretch is accompanied by slow, deep inhalations and relaxed exhalations of breath; and*

❖ *participants stretch at least four different areas of the body, one at a time.*

VARIATIONS

★ Include some Brain Gym or yoga postures in the stretching.

★ Show a video of gentle stretching for participants to follow.

★ Play soothing music in the background.

★ Have participants first spend a minute planning which areas of the body they would like to target and what exercises would stretch those muscles.

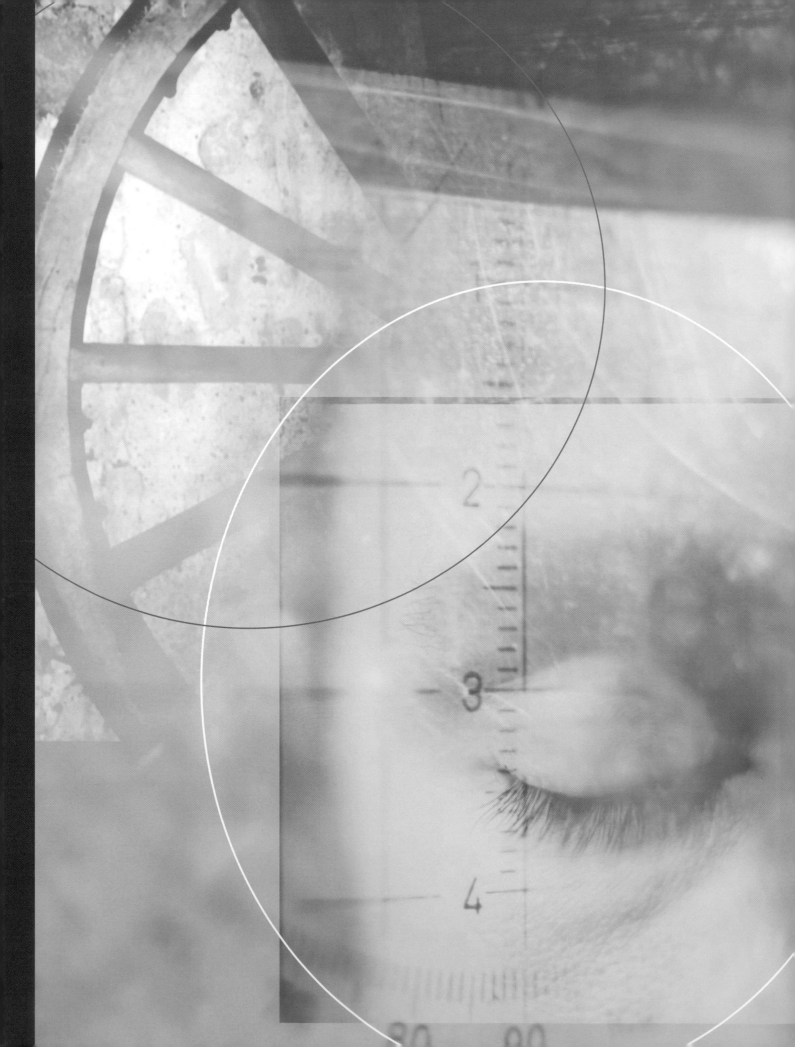

Chapter 10
"Yahoo!"
States of Celebration & Reward

What Is This State?

"Yahoo!" is the state of pleasure, joy and reward. It is stimulated in the brain with activities that either trigger a biological "pleasure point" or reactivate stored positive memories of past pleasure.

Why Is This State Important?

This state not only evokes positive feelings, but associates those positive feelings with a teacher, class or the school experience in general. This state is critical if you want your students to develop a love of learning, build strong, positive personal relationships in school and discover a genuine attraction to school that will keep them coming back. Overall, this is a state of increased dopamine (the "reward" neurotransmitter) in our brain. But what is this chemical? Why should you worry about your students feeling good?

An increased positive affect leads to improved flexibility in behavior and judgment (Ashby et al., 1999). Furthermore, high levels of dopamine are associated with greater flexibility in the brain's executive attentional system (Aspinwall & Richter, 1999). With students, too much

internal focus can promote feelings of negativity; however, dopamine promotes an external focus (Sedikides, 1992) that encourages greater feature recognition and a more global approach to processing a situation before making decisions. In short, when students feel better, they think better!

Having Fun Is a Social Reward

How Long Does This State Last?

We can only be in a state of bliss or pleasure for a short period of time. Why? First, we have a limited supply of dopamine to release into the brain. Second, things that trigger the release of dopamine rarely last. Third, some people feel undeserving or guilty about having too much pleasure, and think themselves right out of this state.

PET Scan of the Human Brain Shows Distribution of Dopamine Receptors for Pleasure

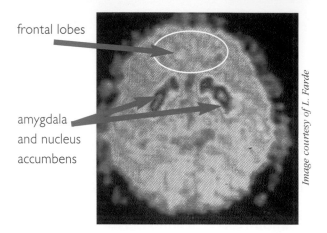

frontal lobes

amygdala and nucleus accumbens

Image courtesy of L. Farde

What Brain Activity Is Involved?

Catecholamines are a class of neurotransmitters that create arousal states in the central nervous system. (Think of them as "uppers" in your brain.) Dopamine is the dominant catecholamine in the central nervous system and actually represents more than fifty percent of all amines in the central nervous system (Cooper et al., 2001). The amino acid, tyrosine, is a necessary ingredient for dopamine production; the amino acid, phenylalanine, helps process tyrosine into mood-regulating products. Dopamine is produced and released in several brain areas, which include the septum, neostriatum, basal ganglia, nucleus accumbens and medial forebrain bundle. Dopamine beta-hydroxylase is an enzyme that converts dopamine into both epinephrine and norepinephrine, which give you energy to do something about the pleasure you feel. Dopamine is also a growth stimulant, and turbocharges

our neurons so they can grow for longer periods of time (Vaughan, 1997).

Body Language of This State

People in this state commonly demonstrate it by laughing, putting their hands up in the air, pumping a fist with pleasure, opening their mouth in a wide smile, jumping for joy or giving kind words to others. Perhaps the most consistent exhibition is inhaling deep into the chest and exhaling gently. Cultural variations and varied circumstances might change what you see and hear.

What Food Affects This State?

This state of pleasure is complex and can be triggered by many different types of food just by association. Stored memories often link certain dishes to pleasant events (celebrations or birthday parties), to a sense of reward (you deserved that hot fudge sundae for working so hard) or the temptation of forbidden foods that are temporarily available (like baked goods during the holidays). The foods of reward are not necessarily desserts; some may indulge in a corn dog at the county fair or share a drink with best friends.

Biologically, however, the raw ingredients of pleasure are foods high in phenylalanine, an essential amino acid. They include tuna, soybeans, blackstrap molasses, red meat, yogurt, chicken and cheese (most proteins, in fact). Remember: These foods do not spur dopamine production; they just supply the raw materials for it. Nutritional supplements of phenylalanine and vitamin B-6 contain the same raw materials. Phenylalanine is also found in chocolate.

What Music Affects This State?

Melvin Rigg conducted what was likely the first study on music that evokes a state of joy and celebration. He discovered that there is a statistically significant set of features in music that triggers this state, which includes accelerated tempos, major keys, simple harmony, ascending fourths in the melody, staccato notes, forte dynamics and iambic or anapestic rhythm (Rigg, 1937). These elements are all found, for example, in Beethoven's *Ode to Joy* and Handel's *Messiah*.

Key Basic Concepts

Successful problem-solving, strong social bonding, victory, accomplishment, high status, recognition, repetitive gross motor movement, celebration, falling in love and, unfortunately, drug abuse are all events that elicit the state of joy. A remarkable finding in neuroscience was that the pleasure neurons actually peak at the moment just *before* a predicted reward, not after it (Schultz et al., 2002). In other words, your ability to anticipate positives (favorite activities, privileges, points, etc.) is equally or more important to achieving pleasure than the actual experience of the positive event!

This anticipation can only occur when the brain has already had a taste of the "reward" behavior. For unusual or new positives, the reward itself triggers joy. Remember that rewards include anything that is highly anticipated and desired by someone. Rewards do not have to be as extravagant as winning the lottery! They can sometimes be as simple as giving a learner permission to silently read a favorite book for fifteen minutes.

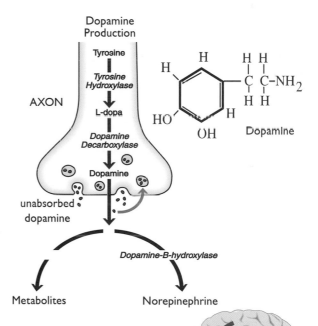

The Chemical Basis of Feeling Good and Being Happy

Dopamine has multiple pathways. One circuit originates near the hypothalamus (in green). Another pathway begins in the substantia nigra and travels to the caudate nucleus (blue). The third circuit begins near the top of the brain stem and pushes dopamine out to the frontal lobes (red).

One word of caution: This state cannot be achieved just by turning to your neighbor and saying, "You did great!" Not that there's anything wrong with talking to a neighbor—just that this comment is too weak of a stimulant to create a rush of dopamine. It takes more time and effort to artificially induce joy. Plan on needing thirty to sixty seconds of celebration to activate the necessary brain chemistry, depending on how intense the celebration will be. Realize as well that dopamine is released under many conditions. If an unanticipated reward event occurs (like a surprise party), dopamine is released. If an *anticipated* reward event occurs, even more dopamine is released. When an anticipated reward event *fails* to occur, some dopamine is released (in lesser amounts) prior to the expected pleasure event (but the benefits of dopamine don't last very long). Finally, all people need time to find attractor states of pleasure; for some of us that takes only seconds, for others, minutes.

> ## Dopamine Is Commonly Released During:
>
> - *successful problem-solving*
> - *strong affiliative bonding*
> (with friends, family or partner)
> - *winning/celebration*
> - *repetitive gross motor movement*
> (exercise like walking, tennis, etc.)
> - *anticipation*
> (of predicted rewards)

Strategies for Positive States

Keep in mind that many actions will put a smile on learners' faces (greeting them at the door is one such strategy for starting a class). This segment, however, focuses on things that learners can do themselves rather than activities you perform in front of them. Remember that the best learning occurs when students take an active instead of passive role. Our question, then, about bringing joy and celebration into our classroom is, "Do I just smile at my audience (a good idea) or do I get the audience to smile at each other (a better idea)?" Here are a few activities certain to raise dopamine levels in all your learners.

1 Celebrations

To effectively raise dopamine levels, celebrations have to occur when learners are in receptive states. They also have to be relevant and believable and must last long enough to signal the release of pleasure chemicals in the brain.

Receptive States: Keep in mind that there are open states and closed states. Open states are the most receptive to positive changes. Read the body language of your audience. Are their heads down or arms folded? Are they cold? If your audience exhibits the behavior of closed states, they are not likely to allow outside input (like a celebration) alter their mood or feelings. Open their states up with simple physical movements. Ask them to turn their bodies towards their neighbors to say hello. If they are seated, ask them to stand. Instruct them to point to a partner and compliment him or her. All of the actions physically open a brain state and make it easier to give and receive positive affirmations or celebrate. Still, they won't generate as much dopamine in the brain as a more complex, active orchestrated celebration will. Put your audience in motion to create the desired effect. Think in terms of multi-sensory immersion!

Relevant and Believable: Before participants give each other congratulations and affirmations, they must first accomplish tasks that deserve praise. Only tell learners they did a great job if they really did a great job. Otherwise, the affirmation is slightly disingenuous.

Duration: Celebrations are not transitions or quick activities that make learners feel good about being together and learning. They require time to fully activate the brain's pleasure chemicals so participants can enter the state of joy. The length of time needed by each individual varies, however, so keep a close eye on your audience to gauge their reactions. At the very minimum, celebration activities should last forty-five to ninety seconds.

End-of-Course Celebrations Bring Out the "Yahoo!" in Everyone

VARIATIONS

★ Play celebration music to enhance the experience. Many artists have recorded appropriate music. Try *The Best* (by Tina Turner), *Celebrate* (by Three Dog Night), *Celebration* (by Kool & the Gang), *We are the Champions* (by Queen) or the Hallelujah Chorus from Handel's *Messiah*.

★ Have teams stand in a circle around their own chairs or tables. Play some celebratory music and have participants walk around them with lots of motion and energy. Adjust the flow of traffic so that adjacent circles move counter-directionally. That way, participants see a steady stream of faces coming towards them as they walk. As participants encounter each other, each person congratulates every member of the other team. Tell them to be bold and make eye contact with each other, use names, give high fives, make positive affirmations and be enthusiastic.

★ Participants circle their tables for forty-five to ninety seconds. Then, ask them to move their team circles to visit other tables so they can congratulate other participants in the room. Keep that energy up! It will take two to three minutes of greeting people to rev up their brains' dopamine centers, depending on the intensity of their actions and how far participants have "bought into" the celebration. Any longer and your audience gets tired of the activity and loses interest.

★ In teams, participants write, on small slips of paper, affirmations or compliments that celebrate the completion of a project. Next, they roll up the papers and insert them into balloons, which they then inflate. Collect all the balloons and gather the entire group to the center of the room. Play celebratory, "balloon-batting" music and stand participants up to bat the balloons around the room. After about two minutes, give a signal for everyone to pick up a balloon and pop it to get the affirmation inside. Give participants time to read each affirmation to three other people and then have everyone cheer and celebrate a little bit longer.

★ For larger audiences of thirty to one hundred people, "car wash" celebrations can be lots of fun (this activity can be modified for smaller groups). Participants stand facing each other in two long lines about six to eight feet apart. Play some celebration music to set the mood. At your signal, the two participants at the same ends of each line start walking side by side down the center of the two lines like two cars driving through a car wash. As they pass, the participants standing in the lines call out their names (to add a personal touch) and "wash" and "bathe" them with cheers and applause. When these first two participants get about halfway down the length of the columns, the next two (from the ends of the double lines) start walking after them. This process continues as participants walk through the tunnel of cheers and are bathed in celebration. When a pair reaches the other end they take their places in line and join the cheering gallery. The celebration ends when everyone has had a chance to walk through the car wash to be bathed in good feelings and washed clean of negativity. For this activity to be effective, you must set it up quickly and keep it moving to maintain its momentum. Participants can only enjoy an activity of this intensity for a short while.

② Praise

Learners like praise and rarely get enough of it, although they are skeptical of praise that they think is shallow or unwarranted. Praise for something easy or routine is hollow. Make sure you only use praise when an audience would truly appreciate it. Wait until participants have just completed a task that they thought was challenging, time-consuming or complex. Then say, "Turn to your teammates and say, 'Great job!'"

VARIATIONS

★ Give participants an opportunity to praise others so that the flow of praise is not always from teacher to learner. Participants write, on index cards, something they have recently done that they would like praise for. They hold these cards at chest level, facing out, so everyone can read them. Play some celebratory music and have participants walk around for one minute, displaying their cards and giving specific praise to at least five other people. When giving the praise, they use each person's name and include a positive comment about his or her accomplishment.

★ Put participants into teams and have each person take out a sheet of paper. At the top of their papers, participants write their names and a brief description of something they did for which they would like praise. Then, each participant passes his or her paper to the teammate on the left and accepts the paper from the teammate on the right. Give everyone fifteen seconds to write a specific praise statement on the page and prompt them to pass it to the next person. The last person to write on the page should fold it in half so the owner can't read it. When the folded pages are back in the hands of their owners (remind them not to peek!), have everyone stand up and find a partner from another team. Then, partners exchange "praise papers" and read to each other what their respective teammates wrote.

Rewards Come in Many Forms; For Some, It's a Quick Snack

③ Problem-Solving Success

Our frontal lobes release dopamine when we complete challenging problems—nature's way of rewarding us for doing well. Dopamine release comes from success, not struggle; give learners plenty of opportunities to succeed before challenging them. Stair-step the problem-solving process to encourage your learners. Consider the structure of the television game show, *Jeopardy*; most contestants start by answering questions at the "$100" level and work their way up to questions at the "$500" level. Similarly, give your audience problems that are a little easier than average to help them gain speed and build psychological momentum. Once they are successful with the easy problems, they'll be revved up for the harder ones. Their brains will already be primed for success and they'll be motivated to tackle the challenge. Once they solve their problems successfully, have them congratulate their neighbors, partners or teammates and enjoy the feeling of making progress.

VARIATIONS

★ Invent a game show with questions of escalating difficulty. Throw into the mix several fun trivia questions that any participant could answer.

★ Have participants create game show questions and classify them as "Easy," "Medium" or "Hard." Separate the questions by level of difficulty into three bins or baskets. Participants take turns answering questions at the front of the room. Start with an easy question; if they answer it correctly let them advance to a medium one, and then to a hard one. Have the rest of the group cheer for every correct response.

4 Repetitive Gross Motor Movement

In general, three to ten minutes of repetitive gross motor movement—swimming, walking, cycling or marching—can get the dopamine flowing in your brain (Sutoo & Akiyama, 2003). (You may have noticed that you almost never return from a brisk walk in a bad mood.) If students need a little "pick-me-up" activity, send them outside for a ten-minute walk with a structured, positive conversation assignment, like discussing with a partner some of the things in life for which they are grateful. A few laps power-walking around a track (if one is available) will keep the group more or less together so they can benefit from each other's positive energy. They'll return to the room in better state of mind.

VARIATIONS

★ Combine marching with other physical movements such as raising the legs high, swinging the arms or beating an imaginary drum.

★ Accompany marching with music like *Anchors Aweigh*, Verdi's *Triumphal March*, the *Radetzky March* (Op. 228) by Johann Strauss, Sr., the *Persian March* (Op. 289) and *Egyptian March* (Op. 335) by Johann Strauss, Jr., or Liszt's *Rackoczy March* from *Hungarian Rhapsody No. 15*.

5 Social Bonding

The powerful bonding that comes from the love of family and friends can stimulate dopamine. Have you ever noticed joyful reunions at airports? Lots of dopamine there! Have you ever fallen in love? Lots of dopamine there, too! Bonding activities increase a participant's investment in his or her learning, as well as promote empathy for the learning of classmates. Over time, encourage learners to get to know each other better.

VARIATIONS

★ Establish rituals like "Student of the Day," in which one person gets a chance to share with the rest of the group some of his or her personal history or favorite hobbies.

★ Create learning teams with members who care about each other, stick up for each other and support each other through their wins and losses. Team keep track of their daily "highs" and share them with the group.

★ Share something from your own life with your audience every single day to increase your personal connection with them. Never go too long, however; keep your stories to three minutes or less.

6 Winning or Achieving Success

Nothing breeds success like more success. It also can trigger a surge of dopamine, too! When a team wins a competition, dopamine surges. When a team completes a difficult project—anything from meeting a yearbook deadline to building a complex model that works—dopamine surges. Usually, the greater the challenge, the longer it takes to achieve and the higher the stakes, the bigger the dopamine surge. So what's the secret to making success a valuable tool for engagement? Even while learners are hard at work on a task, give them time to plan their concluding celebration. This will keep them focused on their goal and (remember the effects of anticipation?) will intensify their positive feelings when it does come time to celebrate.

VARIATIONS

★ Have teams report often on their progress towards their goals; encourage them to celebrate milestones towards achieving success. To maintain a climate of celebration, encourage participants to cheer or applaud other teams as they give their progress reports.

★ Have each team designate a member to be in charge of team spirit. That person will use rituals, favors or noisemakers to celebrate small successes as well as big ones.

7 Prediction of Reward

The pleasure neurotransmitter, dopamine, is well known to help us feel good. Surprisingly, research suggests that activating memories of past pleasure sometimes triggers the same effect that experiencing new pleasure does (Koob, 2000). By reactivating a past pleasure in the classroom, you can affect your learners in the same way that working hard to bring them new pleasure does. If a positive event, shared by all the members of your audience, has recently occurred, use the memory of it to evoke strong positive states when you need them. Say something like, "Remember the field trip we had last week? How many of you had a good time?"

Additionally, evidence suggests that hinting at upcoming pleasure will trigger pleasure in learners' brains as much as if it has already happened (Schultz et al., 2002)! Parents frequently do this with children by telling them things like, "Now, be good. Next week we're going to Disney World. Are you excited about that?" When you're going to do an activity that students genuinely enjoy, introduce it with a teaser along the lines of, "Before we get to the main event, let's find out who is ready for it. If your team is prepared to move ahead, raise your hands and say, 'Yes!'" In short, draw out the anticipation of the event by referring to the event itself. This extends the pleasure an audience will derive from it.

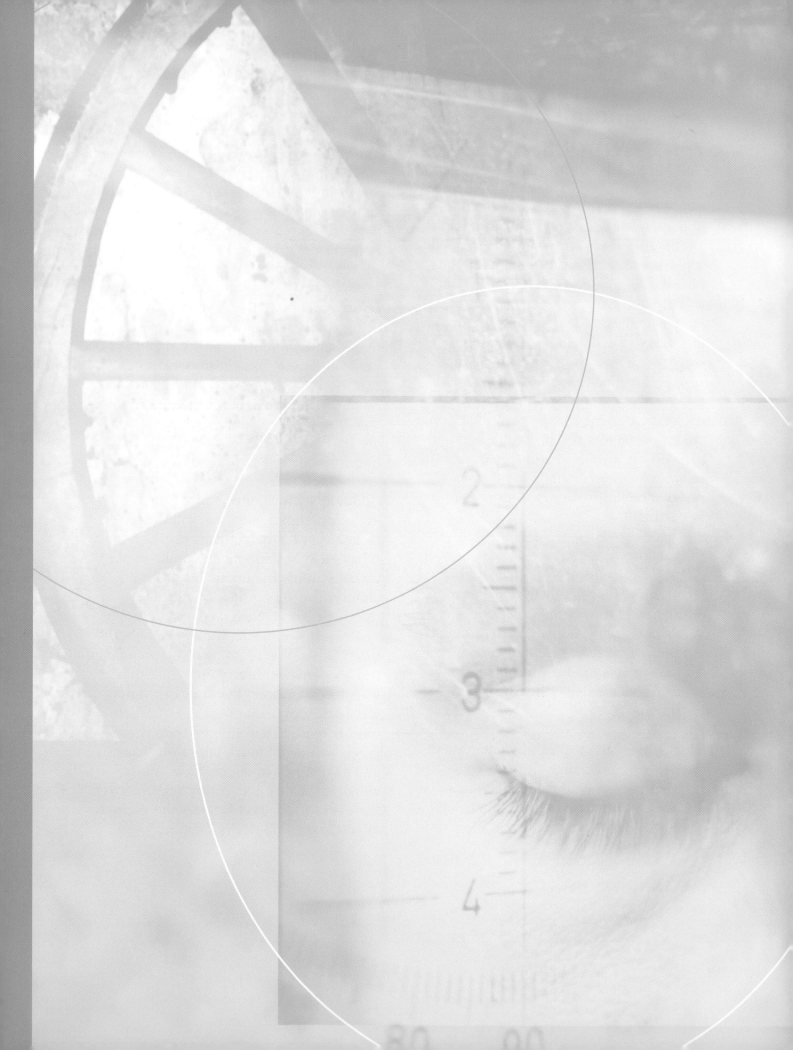

Chapter 11

"How Do I Do It?"

Methods to Mastering State Management

The powerful tool of state management is simple to understand but far from easy to use. Sometimes its nuances drive me crazy! I've tried to share as much of my knowledge as I can in this book. As you may guess, there is much more to learn besides the names of activities—there's all that practice and experience to be gained from simple trial and error, too. I have been learning and using state management since I was first introduced to the concept in 1985, but even though I've had a head start, I'm still learning.

I'm not a comedian, I don't have natural stage presence and I am generally a private person. Still, if I can facilitate my audience's learning, then I can make a real difference in the world with only average presentation skills. This final chapter contains not only the basic steps of how to manage states, but also many delivery techniques I've discovered over the years. I think you'll find it one of the most valuable chapters of this book. It is arranged as a forum to answer many questions that you are likely to ask. Let's walk through them.

Where Do I Start?

Start with a sequence or model to learn from. Sometimes a framework makes it easier to move forward and act confidently. One sequence you could try is:

1. Choose your target state.

2. Read present states.

3. Plan your strategy.

4. Create a back-up plan.

5. Frame the state change.

6. Begin to change the state.

7. Monitor and adjust the activity as needed.

A model like this one is good to have because it simultaneously gives you the big picture as well as the individual steps you need to take to get there. The next section should answer your questions about how to do this.

isn't this what we do every day?

Seven Easy Steps to Changing States

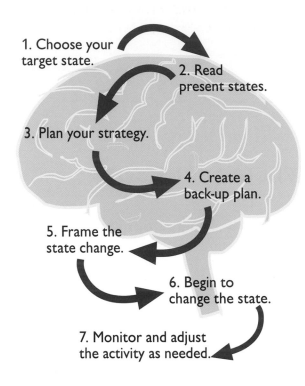

1. Choose your target state.
2. Read present states.
3. Plan your strategy.
4. Create a back-up plan.
5. Frame the state change.
6. Begin to change the state.
7. Monitor and adjust the activity as needed.

How Do I Learn to Read States Better?

The model suggests that you first learn to read states. Until you know what states you have in your audience, it's hard to decide what you're getting and what you need. Begin to pay more attention to the expressions, mannerisms, gestures, postures and comments of people you meet or work with. Soon you'll not only be able to understand but also to predict states well. Here are some active strategies to help you learn to read states better:

❖ *People-watch* at malls, stores or restaurants. Then, check your perceptions against what you see them do.

❖ *Watch television with the sound off* and try to figure out what the characters are doing and saying. Turn the sound back on and check your accuracy.

❖ *Sit in on another teacher's presentation.* Choose a seat in the middle of class but off to one side, so you can observe learners in the front and the back of the room. Predict their behaviors based on your perception of their states; then, verify your predictions.

❖ *Start close to home.* If you have siblings, family members, a roommate or a spouse, you have plenty of opportunity to practice reading states. Make a prediction and then verify it by waiting to see what they do next. You could also simply ask the questions, "What were you thinking just now?" or, "Did something just upset you? I'm curious."

❖ *Begin with just one state.* Learn the symptoms of that particular state until you're familiar with it. Then, try out some of these strategies to get your feet wet with state management while gathering valuable feedback.

When you're ready, practice further by reading the states of the people in the front row of your next audience. Start with a few learners, probably those sitting closest to you. Over time, work your way back until you have a pretty good idea of the state of the entire audience. Many presenters have never really tried to read states and are not used to it; it can be intimidating at first. Use the information from the beginning of each chapter for clues that will help you read your audience.

Some states appear reliably; those are probably the built-in, emotional states like the startle effect, sadness or disgust. In a classroom, you'll commonly see states of anticipation and curiosity. (Hopefully, you'll rarely see states of frustration, apathy and anger.) You'll also find high-energy states and calming states as well as states of affirmation and self-confidence. Remember: Because we work with a wide range of populations, you may have some audience members in states of hunger, stress or even under threat. But look for the most common states that influence learning. They are:

❖ anticipation and curiosity
   ("I'm hungry to learn")
   (leaning forward, eyes wide open, not blinking)

❖ frustration, distress and tension
   ("I'm not getting what I need")
   (tightened jaws or neck, expressive foot or hand tapping, closed posture)

❖ confusion and feeling lost
   ("I don't get it")
   (head turned, wrinkled or furrowed brow, hand touching face)

❖ ah-ha!, self-confidence or celebration
   ("I got it!")
   (deep breaths, smiles, hands in the air, relaxed posture, sharing verbally with others)

❖ boredom and apathy
   ("I don't care")
   (slumped posture, hunched shoulders, eyes glazed over, no focused expression)

❖ fear and duress
   ("I'm very uneasy")
   (closed postures, eyes looking away from front of room, short breaths)

There are probably thousands of possible states available to us. The ones listed above represent only a few of the common states you'll see in your classroom.

How Do I Know What My Target States Are?

Target states are the states you want your students to enter as you move ahead through your presentation. All teachers, trainers or speakers should know their preferred audience target states; whether it's a reflective state or high-energy state, figure out which one is needed to move an audience's learning forward.

Which State Change Should You Use?

"Yikes!"
use to energize or create emotions

"Yahoo!"
use for celebrations, to reward behaviors or have fun

"I Got It!"
use to deepen learning, build confidence or strengthen understanding and recall

"Uh-Oh!"
trigger healthy concern, create a vested interest in upcoming learning

"Huh?"
use for getting attention, building curiosity or generating confusion

"Ah-hh"
use to improve focus, enhance comfort and lessen sense of stress or threat

"Peace & Quiet"
use to calm, turn thoughts inward, focus minds, promote relaxation and reflection

High Energy

Low Energy

For example, if your audience is falling asleep because the room's too hot or you notice that no one has moved for a while, *your target state is going to be an arousal state.* You can choose which arousal state you'd like to use, but you have to choose *something* if you want to wake up your group. I've listed the arousal states in this book and added comments to guide you as you make your hypothetical selection:

Arousal States

"I Got It!"
(But are you sure they know it?)
"Huh?"
(possibility)
"Yikes!"
(possibility)
"Movin' On"
(But have you completed the topic?)
"Uh-Oh!"
(possibility)
"Yahoo!"
(Do they have anything to celebrate yet?)

Calming States

"Peace and Quiet"
(not what you want)
"Ah-hh"
(too relaxed)

Now that they are arranged in this way, you can see that you really have only three options from this long list of states: "Huh?," "Yikes!" or "Uh-Oh!" The other states drop out of contention. To wake my audience up, I'd probably choose "Yikes!," but you could do just well with "Uh-Oh!" or "Huh?" (I tend to go to extremes because it's easier for me to back down in intensity than ramp it up.)

What Are My Options for Reaching the Target State?

First, think about a particular teaching problem you want to solve. Then, find the chapter in the book that matches the target state that would help you solve this problem. Let's say your audience is apathetic and lacks focus or motivation and you want them hungry to learn something new. Open up Chapter 3, "Huh?," and browse through the list of activities you can use to trigger an arousal state. Pick one that meets your needs. It should:

❖ *fit your target state;*

❖ *be appropriate for the age of your group;*

❖ *have the qualities that move your group forward; and*

❖ *be an activity that you understand and can do well.*

> ### Example of Step-by-Step State Changes
>
> 1. *"Take a slow, deep breath... and exhale."*
> 2. *Please stand up and push your chair in."*
> 3. *"In 10 seconds, when I say 'Go,' take 10 giant steps. Ready, set, go!"*
> 4. *"Please find a partner."*

How or Where Do I Begin to Use These New Strategies?

Remember that the strategies you use have to be appropriate for both you and your audience. Read an activity carefully and rehearse it in your mind. Plan out the two extremes: the best-case scenario (how will you use your tools to achieve this?) and the worst-case scenario (what will you do if the activity bombs?). Because you'll have your responses already prepared, there will be no surprises. By preparing for both extremes, you'll be able to handle anything.

Everyone has his or her own system of adding new elements to their work. Some of us need a visual prompt. If you are one of those trainers, consider using a stack of index cards as an activity pack that you can easily flip through. Post the details of three activities on posters at the back of the room to refer to while you teach. You could also jot down the steps of your lesson on a 3" x 5" card (or prepare an overhead transparency with words and phrases to prompt you) and keep it right in front of you. Use your "cheat sheet" during your next presentation. If you have a kinesthetic style of learning or remembering, do a dress rehearsal of the strategy in an empty room to make a muscle memory of the process. If you're an auditory learner, sit down in a quiet room and talk yourself through the activity twice so you feel comfortable about what to say. When you are confident that you know the activity, you're ready to try it out.

But what if you hear a little voice in your head before you use the activity asking you, *"Aren't these strategies a little silly? Won't I do better with 100% lecture?"*

Most of us who are workshop leaders, teachers, staff developers or trainers started out by using lecture as our primary teaching strategy. Only *over time* did we switch to an interactive style. Why? Evidence suggests that participants who actively participate also learn better. If you do all the talking, you're doing too much. For your audience to learn, they have to think, talk and write. Keep in mind the following:

❖ *Most learners these days are accustomed to active learning and are critical of presenters who don't offer it.*

❖ *Learners would rather experience a crude attempt at active learning than sit through a lecture for an entire presentation. Your active learning lessons don't have to be perfect and you have little to lose by trying them out.*

❖ *You'll only be new to active learning once. After that, you'll have some experience and will be more confident. We've all been wet behind the ears but there is no way to overcome that lack of experience except to prepare and go for it!*

❖ *Get honest feedback from your audience and gauge their interests so you know how to proceed. Use feedback forms or ask questions that are easy to answer. For example, you could begin a class by asking something like, "Today, would you prefer that I teach with only lecture, a mixture of lecture and hands-on learning or mostly active learning?" To get feedback about how to improve your presentation the next time you give it, you might conclude by asking, "In general, do you think this class had too much active learning, too much lecture or just the right balance?" The feedback will be priceless.*

But what if you're rehearsing your upcoming strategy (as you should) and a second voice pops up in your head? Maybe it's a fearful one that says, *"I can't use these strategies. My class moves too fast—I just don't have the time!"*

Remember the first time you learned to drive? The very act of getting your driver's license was stressful! Then there was all that information you had to absorb, decisions to make at every intersection, traffic safety rules to keep in mind, remembering the directions to your destination and developing the motor skills to move the car. It was pretty overwhelming at first but you eventually mastered driving, one sub-skill at a time. It's the same when you visit a foreign country and don't know the language very well—the native speakers all speak so quickly! But the more time you spend there, the more you are able to understand them. With practice, using these active learning strategies in class will come naturally if you just relax and tackle one skill at a time.

If your perception is that your classes zip by out of your control, slow down. That's a signal to engage your audience more, to actively involve participants and to stop talking so much. Keep the mantra, "More of them and less of me," at the front of your mind and you'll have plenty of time each session to think, plan and prepare. Let the learners do the reading, thinking, deciding and doing. You are not a one-person band playing all the instruments; you are an orchestra conductor directing the activity of your entire group. The participants are the show, not you.

Once you've selected your activity (and summoned the confidence to try it), you'll need some help with those state changes. This help comes in the form of a "frame."

What Are Frames and Why Use Them Before the State Change?

Do you have any pictures or paintings in your house? Are they in frames? Why do I ask? Because most people will tell you that the frame is an important part of the aesthetic and functional experience of the picture. A few years back I bought a frame that cost more than the painting I put in it. But without the frame, the painting was almost useless to me. In the same way that pictures require frames, most activities require frames before you begin them. A frame is an *intentional bias* that you place on any upcoming event (lecture, change in routine, video, state change, exercise, stretching, etc.) or person to skew the odds of success (in your favor).

Framing is a tool used to create an intentional bias.

It helps avoid:
- apathy
- confusion
- demotivation

Framing changes the brain's response to something because you have influenced it to do so. Be proactive and seek the reaction you want. Framing can lower or raise stress levels. You can use it before, during or after an activity, lecture, event or decision.

HOW TO FRAME?

- Research
- Reasons
- Compelling Questions
- Inspirational Stories

Before you ask students to do anything, frame it first! One example of framing an activity before asking students to stand up for it is: "We've been sitting too long and it's good to move around now and then. Everyone take a slow, deep breath...good...exhale. Now, please stand up!" You gave participants a valid reason to stand up—you "framed" the activity for them.

A very common frame from everyday life is, "I have good news and bad news. Which do you want to hear first?" This frame prepares and cushions the listener for upcoming information. Frames change or manage the state of the audience until the activity can carry the state by itself. Frames are typically created with:

- ❖ *a personal anecdote to set up an activity;*

- ❖ *research to justify why someone should do it;*

- ❖ *a comment to provide a simple rationale;*

- ❖ *some sort of contrast to create a bias for success; and*

- ❖ *a compelling question that helps the audience justify why they would want to do the following activity by answering it.*

I'm sure you're pretty savvy now that you've reached this part of book, so I'll forge ahead with some specific examples for adding frames to activities you have learned about:

No Frame: "Everyone get up. Find a partner. Share what you've learned with them."
Useful Frame: "Answer me by raising your hands. How many of you have found that when you teach something to others, you also learn it better? I thought so. Let's try that concept out. Please stand up and find a partner. You each have one minute to share what you've learned."

The frame of this sharing activity was *evoking each participant's past experience to validate the purpose of upcoming activity.*

Anticipatory Set.

No Frame: "Everyone up. Please push your chair in. I'm going to play some music in a moment. When the music begins, please walk around to wake up."

Useful Frame: "I just read a study in *Clinical Autonomic Research* suggesting that brisk walks affect both the heart rate and brain chemistry. The heart rate stuff I could have guessed, but I'm curious about the brain chemistry stuff. Let's try an experiment. Please stand up and push in your chairs. Now, take a deep breath. In ten seconds, when I say 'Go,' walk clockwise around the room until the music stops. Ready? Get set. Go!"

The frame around this activity was *citing relevant or interesting research.*

No Frame: "In a moment, we're all going to play a game you might have played as children. It's called 'Ball Toss.' Please stand up and form circles of six people."

Useful Frame: "We're going to try something different, so everyone take a deep breath. Now, please stand up and push your chair in. How many of you would like to combine learning and fun in a quick review? Great! Let's do it. First, you'll need some partners. In a moment, when I turn on the music, start walking. When the music stops, form a group with the five people nearest to you and wait for further directions."

Here, the frame was the *pleasurable combination of fun and learning* in the form of a compelling question.

No Frame: "Please stand up. Let's all stretch for a minute before we continue."

Useful Frame: "I noticed that some of you came in long before we even started today. Before we continue, I think getting out of our chairs for a minute would be

good for our backs and ease some stress. First, take a slow, deep breath and exhale. Good. Now, please stand up and slide your chair in. Perfect. Have you ever noticed that some people are extroverted and love to find an adventure? Identify the person at your table who looks like they have the most fun in life. That person will be your temporary leader. When I give the signal, they'll lead you in forty-five seconds of stretching and deep breathing to wake up your brains. Ready? Get set. Go!"

The activity was framed by *promoting good health and relieving stress.*

If you don't frame it, they probably can't picture it!

Frames are not a secret. The best persuaders, salespeople, comedians, politicians and teachers use them *all* the time. Once I had someone sit in on one of my presentations and count how many times I used frames. Thirty-five frames in a day and a half! Because they are necessary, you really can't overdo them. In general, they are most effective before an activity, but you could also use them to conclude one. There is actually no bad time to use them, unless they interrupt the flow of a lesson. If any activity in this book does not work for you, the most likely way to improve it for next time is to work on your framing. It is the number one reason activities succeed or fail. Again, "If you don't frame it, they probably can't picture it!"

How to Stair-Step Your Audience to Your Target State

Remember this concept to save yourself a lot of grief: Humans are not very good at going from zero to sixty or from sixty to zero miles per hour. In general, we need prior warning and some time to ease ourselves into a big change. In practical application, this means you'll have to keep in mind where your learners' mental focus is at the moment and which state you want them to enter during the activity you propose. Then, you'll need to bring them through some interval or intermediary states. If students enter the room all pumped up from recess, they'll need some time to unwind before you can successfully ask them to focus. If they're all slouched over and half-asleep from lunch, don't expect them to jump up and dance at the crack of a whip.

Instead, use states of transition or gradually change states. Have learners take a deep breath, ask a question that invites them to raise their hands, and get them to stand up for an activity before finally asking them to move around the room. Imagine that you are leading your audience up a flight of stairs, one step (state) at a time. Unless we are faced with an emergency, our only viable option to move a group from one state to another is take things in small increments. The best bit of advice I can give is also among the simplest:

One at a Time!

You can only "stair-step" your audience into new states if you do things one at a time. You reduce confusion if you do things one at a time. You eliminate questions and increase clarity if you do things one at a time. I have broken an activity into an outline of its basic steps to demonstrate this concept. You tackle each step one at a time; after completing each step, pause until your audience catches up.

1. "Let's do something different." (frame)

2. "But first, take a deep breath." (mild change to state of anticipation)

3. "Please stand up." (Pause and wait until the audience stands.)

4. "Good. Now, push your chair in." (You could combine steps 3 and 4 if seems more efficient.)

5. "By raising your hands, show me how many of you would like to combine learning and fun for a quick review?" (more frame)

6. "Great! Let's do it. First, you'll need some partners. In a moment, when I turn on the music, start walking. When the music stops, form a group with the five people nearest to you and wait for further directions." (Pause and wait to ensure that participants walk, stop and listen while you give your directions.)

7. "Now, count how many people are in your group." (activate the state of anticipation)

8. "If you have either fewer than five or more than seven people in your group, please raise your hands." (You are gathering information.)

love this step by step example

9. "Wow! It looks like we are all in groups of just the right size. Everyone turn to a partner and say, 'We're just right!'" (state of affirmation and self-congratulations for following the directions correctly)

10. "Now we are ready to begin with our activity." (state of curiosity)

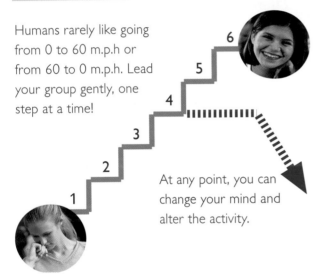

Changing States in Others? Respect the Gradient!

Humans rarely like going from 0 to 60 m.p.h or from 60 to 0 m.p.h. Lead your group gently, one step at a time!

At any point, you can change your mind and alter the activity.

Words of Caution

One thing you may have noticed is that I didn't tell my audience that I was going to change their state. Every year I watch fifteen to twenty-five presentations by other staff developers, many who are still learning how to manage states. They say to their audience, "Next, I'm going to change your state." That's a *huge* mistake! Why? Because it puts the audience on guard and creates resistance. It's like a magician saying to the audience, "I'm going to distract you with my left hand,

so don't look at my right hand." You ought to be able to teach or train for months without ever even using the word "state." Never tell your audience that you're managing their states—just do it.

Another thing you may have noticed is that when you break an activity into its smaller parts, it seems very detailed and tedious. Nothing could be further than the truth! I've only outlined it to clarify how serious I am about taking things one at a time. In reality, a sequence goes by so fast that the audience experiences it as fast and fun and their anticipation builds. Avoid overwhelming your audience with information and focus instead on managing their states for the brief time you are with them. Yes, it will take practice to pull it off, but when you do it well, it's a thing of functional beauty!

Why Have a Back-up Plan?

Although I don't always have a deliberate back-up plan, I have enough experience managing states to pull something out of my hat if things don't go right. But you just read an entire book about changing states. How could something go wrong? Easily.

Even if you get the majority of your audience to respond a certain way (which, considering how different we all are, is quite an accomplishment) you might wonder what went wrong with the non-responsive participants. The answer is, possibly nothing. Managing states is an ongoing process that requires some prep work. First, make it a point to create a backdrop of positive emotions for all of the activities listed in this book. Have upbeat music playing when the first person arrives. Turn the room into an inviting, clean, positive environment. Share a smile, a cheerful attitude, your sense of humor and trust with your audience. Make them feel good. But that's just the start! Here's why you'll need a back-up plan.

These state-changing tools are intended for ordinary circumstances with normal healthy brains. If you are teaching a group of learners who have oppositional or attentional disorders, you'll need to modify your approach. If your participants have learning delays, spectrum disorders or phonological processing deficits, you'll need very extreme adaptations or very different tools. If you cannot use these tools because you work in a high-security environment where people are not allowed to leave their seats, again, you'll have to make significant adaptations and modify these tools. By now, you should have gotten the message: Know your audience and adapt to them.

Take a peek—we're all unique!

In general, you will see gender, stress and behavioral differences in how your groups respond. If you know this in advance, you will not be surprised when it happens. Even how you put participants into groups can affect their stress levels. How many, how close, how familiar are they with each other and what is the activity? That said, consider the results from the following studies, which suggest these generalizations about using states. Keep in mind that there are always exceptions, but if you read about this research in context, you will find it helpful.

❖ Unlike shy children, socially competent children approach novelty and form new social groups without stress responses (Schmidt et al., 1997). Expect some children to be awkward during sharing activities and be patient with them. *This may apply to adults, so be ready for it.*

❖ Women and girls are more likely to seek help from others and give help to others than men and boys do. This is consistent across cultures (Edwards, 1993). *Expect most males to share fewer ideas and ask for fewer ideas than females. Do not take it personally.*

❖ Spatial crowding will often stress males but calm females (Brown & Grunberg, 1995). *Men will often hover at the outer edges of social groups; women will often cluster in the center groups. Be aware of this pattern.*

❖ The higher the stress level, the more likely women are to be nurturing (Repetti,1997); men's stress responses are tied to sympathetic system arousal and tend to be less familial (Repetti et al., 2000). *Stress is higher for most educators later in the day, later in the month, around testing time, during parent-teacher conferences and later in the school year. Under stress, women often become more supportive of each other than men do.*

❖ Learners experiencing frequent and uncontrollable stress (abuse, marital separation, financial hardship, child care issues, prolonged sickness, etc.) may have maladapted to the distress by creating an allostatic load. This can create extremes in responses to healthy stressors (McEwen, 2002) such as decreased motivation prior to an activity or prolonged anxiety following an activity. *Some members of your audience will complain that social or physical activities are either stupid or stressful. Be sympathetic, but don't change your plans for the sake of five percent of your audience. You can never please all of the people all of the time; if you threw out everything that was uncomfortable to somebody in your audience, you would end up doing absolutely nothing.*

❖ Although males will form social groupings, they are more likely to base them on hierarchies of status or power rather than newly generated intimacy (Baumeister & Sommer, 1997). *Females are more likely to enjoy groupings based on variety, social intimacy or tastes and interests. Males are more likely to prefer groupings by job title, work experience or skill level. Remember, though, these are only generalizations.*

❖ During games, woman and girls are more social and less aggressive than males (Girdler et al., 1997). *Often, men and boys will become a little competitive during play.*

Don't make judgments about participant personalities or speculate on their deep-seated motivations; just work to keep them out of negative states. What's your bottom line? Avoid thinking that everyone will respond the same way to state management. If you can change the state of most of your group, most of the time, with minimal resistance, you are doing a great job. People are unique and it takes a great deal of flexibility to meet the needs of everyone. Forgive yourself when necessary and, though it is worthwhile to pursue mastery, adjust to the realities of human uniqueness.

Audience Resistance Can Build When States Change Too Slowly

What If My Audience Is Resistant?

You may also find certain people in your audience who mount resistance to your some of your state managing. Why? Because of three likely reasons:

1. *You forgot to use a compelling frame.* The use of frames will reduce resistance dramatically. In other words, use a frame to put your audience at ease (create a rational context for action); then, take action and move quickly, without hesitation. Still, you may find that some learners seem to fight tooth and nail over any change of states.

2. *Some audience members are withdrawn.* The participants most likely to resist state changes are the less social or less active. Many people are often lonely or anxious. These individuals have a greater likelihood of lower heart rates and frequently demonstrate emotional withdrawal in novel social settings. Additionally, they have a tendency to withdraw from complex social environments because they feel overwhelmed by the stimuli and have less conscious control over their focus (Cacioppo et al., 2002). Do not take their non-responsiveness personally. Many slow or resistant responders share some tendencies seen in people with high-functioning autistic spectrum disorders, oppositional personality disorders, attachment or stress disorders or even damage to the regulatory mechanisms of social contact (Raine et al., 2002).

3. *Speed is essential.* Move too slowly and you'll get caught off guard! If participants mount resistance, remember that it is *just an adaptive response* and should *never be taken personally.* Evolutionarily, predators (or instructors suggesting a change) attack quickly and thoroughly. Any moments wasted on deliberation allow the prey (or an audience comfortable with the status quo) to counter-attack or increase its chances of escape. Be particularly careful not to evoke defensive reactions in your audience since their instinctive, reflexive escape actions will be instantaneous (Ohman et al., 2000). Otherwise, your audience could mentally flee the learning environment you are trying to establish. When presenters struggle with the realities of managing states, it's usually because they didn't frame it properly, move quickly enough or couldn't adjust on the fly.

This is a crucial fact about states: They are fast-moving targets. Although initially you'll be cautious, in time you'll want to move quickly. Why? Because people are only in particular states for a short time. Any activity you use to change a state will lose its effectiveness *because participants will have moved on to another state.* As a presenter, many times I have planned on doing one thing, missed my moment (or it never came) and had to elicit a brand new state for my audience. This "thinking on your feet" is characteristic of good trainers who have an intuitive understanding of what appropriate states are.

Remember to Adjust Your Activities as Needed

There are two good reasons you'll need to adjust your state changes constantly. First, students can tire of a particular activity, even a sound one based on good research, so you'll want to vary them. Every activity can be altered, tweaked or rearranged to ensure novelty. I rarely use the same activity twice in a row. There are far too many ways to vary them to need it. If you're starting to get the "Ho-hum, been there, done that" response, don't take it personally. Just adapt and move on.

Second, you'll need to adjust to specific individuals who may strain your values or creativity. Have the attitude that you can bend but won't break. Sometimes I'll go up to an individual during a rest period and say, "I noticed you seemed pretty quiet today. Is everything okay?" This simple act of caring and interest usually opens the door. Sometimes the person will say, "I'm okay—I just think some of the stuff we're doing is a little hokey."

You might respond to that with, "Thanks, I appreciate the feedback. I know some things I do don't appeal to everyone. But if you hang in there, I think you'll find other things quite valuable. By the way, what's your subject area?" Notice that I listened, expressed interested in what was said and never got defensive. Sometimes that's all you need to convert someone into a more willing (and less resistant) participant.

Every now and then, you even can give someone some private space and leave him or her alone for a few hours or a day, especially if you have relevant insight to their personal background. Don't make it a habit with any one student, though. The longer a learner stays in a counterproductive state, the chances increase that non-productivity will become an attractor state, one he or she will enter easily and often. Time reinforces the states we are in, good and bad states alike. On the bright side, they are self-reinforcing, so the more you engage your audience by using the tools of this book the more likely it is they will become thinking, learning and growing human beings.

What If These State-Management Tools Don't Work for Me?

If you are still unsuccessful at managing states, it may be that you are not quite skilled enough to use them and just need more practice. Reread sections of this book that you may have glossed over the first time. When we are disorganized, miss cues, have sloppy materials, say the wrong things, lack clarity, talk too much, leave out key terms or have no rapport with our audience, it's likely we'll present a substandard activity. If this happens to you, stay confident and don't let a setback affect you. We've all messed up these tools at some point! Getting specific feedback and lots of practice will solve this problem quickly. That said, remember that these tools cannot replace intelligent lesson planning, relevant, meaningful curriculum or establishing positive, personal relationships. If those elements are missing, success will forever elude you.

What If I Goof Up While Managing States?

Making mistakes only happens to those who refuse to take risks. Goofing up, however, isn't a crisis. First, over-practice so you feel confident that you know what to do before you start. Second, prepare in advance a phrase to use if things get wobbly and you're struggling to coordinate the activity. You might say, "Please have patience. I'm learning this, too!" or, "While I catch my breath, take thirty seconds to review one of our vocabulary words with your partner." You could even try the lighthearted, "Oops! Even the big cheese gets holes in her brain occasionally. Please bear with me until we get it right."

Finally, remember that most audiences will be very patient with you. If you're giving the strategy an honest try with lots of rehearsal behind time you, the fact that you are doing something rather than nothing is likely to produce a positive, measurable result (Shapiro & Shapiro, 1997). Everything really depends on the relationship you have with your audience and the expectations you share. As long as your rapport is good, they'll be quite forgiving.

I've been sloppy over the years and messed up more of these tools than I'd like to admit. But every year I get better and make fewer big mistakes. (My small mistakes are often errors of omission or experimentation. If I don't innovate, I'll get stale.) Mistakes are excusable; tired routine is not. To stay fresh and exciting you have to be willing to go out on a limb.

But always give yourself credit for trying! Choosing the right tool for the right time and implementing it correctly can be very challenging. Remember that nobody (and I mean *nobody*) ever learned all these things in a day, week, month or even a *year*. Add to your mantra the following: "One at a time. Forgive mistakes. Acknowledge the effort. Learn from it."

Remember to Manage the Most Important State of All: Yours!

Your audience members are far more tuned into your states than you would imagine. Though this happens more often with younger students than an adult audience, it can occur with any strong relationship. The state you're in is highly contagious. If you're peppy, they'll be peppy. If you're down, they'll be down. You have to manage your own states as if

your life depends on it—and your professional life does! Here are some of things I do to prepare for an audience.

The night before my presentation:

❖ *review audience background*

❖ *check for any special interests or needs*

❖ *review my notes and walk through them all*

❖ *lay out my wardrobe*

❖ *plan my morning to the smallest detail*

❖ *come home early and get plenty of sleep*

The day of my presentation:

❖ *eat high protein foods and take nutritional supplements*

❖ *arrive earlier than I need to, so I can relax while I get ready*

❖ *make sure I have water to drink and upbeat music on hand*

❖ *set everything up before (not as) the audience arrives*

❖ *take a short walk to mentally plan and relax*

❖ *focus on what it is that I'm grateful for in life*

❖ *be fully present so I can meet and greet my audience when they arrive*

I consider my health first and foremost. No matter who makes up my audience, they deserve my best effort. I manage my states as best I can. I keep my stress low so I can answer questions and be helpful, not snappy. Sometimes I'll skip my breaks because people bring me books to autograph, so I have to be mentally (and physically) ready for that possibility. (I am always grateful for the opportunity to autograph anything, since it is not only a way to make a difference in the world, but because those folks are paying my bills.) As a publicly visible person, I've discovered that none of the states that I enter when I work are private. That's a large pill to swallow, but it's the part of the job, too. I have to be guarded and aware at all times of my states, since they are constantly conveying messages to others.

Rituals or Group Traditions Can Solve Many Problems

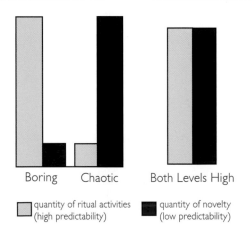

| Boring | Chaotic | Both Levels High |

◻ quantity of ritual activities (high predictability)   ◼ quantity of novelty (low predictability)

Effective rituals regulate brain chemistry. You should have 15 to 25 rituals to share with your audience, which must meet *all* of the following criteria:

- solve a problem
- are highly predictable
- put learners in a productive state
- create a sense of community
- are easy for everyone to do

Final Notes

Every brain state described in this book has been well-researched. Still, keep in mind that we are in a groundbreaking era of educational theory and practice. For the first time ever, we can apply what we know about the brain directly to educational practices. I know some researchers are uncomfortable with this concept and that's a shame. If it turns out that this book contains some errors of enthusiasm because it applies some aspects of the science *before* its time, I *don't* apologize. Active experimentation comes with the territory. None of the strategies listed here will harm a learner. And, as usual, you can trust in your relationships and good judgement to be your safety net during any learning experience.

Therefore, you have much to gain every time you engage your audience with an activity from this book. I wish you the best of states. May all your presentations be as lively as a flea-infested monkey brushing off fire ants while running from a herd of blind elephants through the middle of the annual Banana Throwing Festival! (Did that silly description just change your state? I hope so!)

Bonus Guide
10 Guidelines
to Ensure Success with Tools for Engagement

1 Room Set-Up Matters

The more your room furnishings are fixed in place, the less flexibility you will have to choose your activities. If you have the option, select chairs, tables and dividers that can be moved from place to place. If your room is small, ask learners to push their chairs under their desks or tables each time they stand up to increase room space by about five percent. Ask volunteers to help you move large pieces of furniture; mark the floor with tape so you can return pieces to their original spots or work out (in advance) an arrangement with the custodian to restore the room to its usual condition.

If you are in a room with permanent seating, like an auditorium, give specific directions so your audience knows how to mix themselves up. For example, say, "Please stand up. Turn and head towards the aisles. You have ten seconds to gather at the sides of the room." When everyone has made their way there, continue with, "Great! Now, shout out the month of your birthday and find a partner with the same birthday month."

My favorite seating arrangement for college or adult learners is at rectangular or circular tables with six to eight people seated at each one. Smaller tables with fewer people are better for elementary school learners. At middle and high schools, four or five students at a table are best.

2 Actions Speak Louder than Words

What you do will always communicate more than what you say. If you believe in a strategy, use it. Teachers tell tales of attending continuing education or graduate school classes in which their instructors constantly told them about certain strategies but never actually modeled them. I have a simple motto:

If you don't live it, you don't believe it.

When it is time to use an activity, avoid over-explaining your directions. It not only makes you look unsure but also wastes your audience's time. Put a simplified version up on an overhead. Use gestures and other nonverbal messages to help make your point. If you can't explain an activity easily and clearly, you're trying to do too much at once. It's better to explain the next thirty seconds with just two sentences than ramble on for three minutes. Say only enough to get the effect you want, pause and then repeat your directions. If learners don't understand what you're trying to do with them, get their attention before you talk next time. Then, use a metaphor or analogy to illustrate your directions. Finally, have them pair up and repeat the directions to each other before beginning an activity.

3 Remember: Students Already Change Their Own States!

You may be concerned that state management seems like manipulation. Yet almost all learners (with or without healthy brains) self-regulate (manipulate) their own states every day! They want to enjoy positive states and appreciate it when others help them do so. In fact, trying to stay in positive states occupies them from dawn to dusk. Younger learners (from ages 3 to 8) are always interested in changing their states. They often self-regulate via:

❖ *laughing or crying*
❖ *running or horsing around*
❖ *drinking juice, soft drinks or water*
❖ *smiling, laughing or listening to jokes*
❖ *resting or closing their eyes*

Learners from ages eight to twenty-five influence their states differently than younger students. Their choices may include:

❖ *reading a hobby book or teen magazine*
❖ *watching a movie*
❖ *going out to eat*

❖ *spending time with friends*
❖ *driving somewhere new (to a lookout point or another part of town)*
❖ *shopping*
❖ *cruising around or hanging out*
❖ *going to sporting events*
❖ *expressing affection or engaging in romantic activity*

Learners older than the age of twenty-five change their states in still other ways:

❖ *traveling or watching travel shows*
❖ *spending time with children or grandchildren*
❖ *spending time with pets*
❖ *meeting with friends*
❖ *practicing hobbies, like gardening or needlepoint*
❖ *entertaining friends or eating out*
❖ *reading or watching movies*

Changing our states is a large part of what we do all day. So, when I encourage you to use purposeful state management in a learning situation, realize that people are used to the concept. They just haven't given it a label.

4 Err on the Side of Enthusiasm

Use these tools with a positive attitude and a smile. When you make mistakes with these tools (and trust me, we all do), remember that your audience will forgive you for them. They'll forgive you because they appreciate an honest effort by a well-meaning presenter who can laugh at him- or herself. They will not, however, want a long-winded explanation from you about why you messed up an activity (or any excuses at all). Just say pleasantly, "Oops, back to the drawing board. Sorry, everyone! Let's all find our seats and shift gears for a moment." Do not try to talk your way out of it. Apologize quickly, make light of it and get on with the presentation. Nothing, and I mean nothing, is a disaster until you treat it like one.

5 Never Waste Your Learners' Time

Every activity you use during a presentation should have purpose and reason behind it. If all you want to do is to raise heart rates or wake up your audience, say so. ("It's a good time for a recharge! Everyone please stand up! Find the nearest person with whom you haven't yet partnered today.") Explain why you are asking them to do something, but do it so quickly and matter-of-factly that your audience accepts it without debate and moves on. Never introduce an activity apologetically. If it's a bad one, don't do it. If it's worth doing, do it with enthusiasm.

If learners want to know *why* you are using so many active learning techniques, tell them. (I prefer to tell them after, not before, the activity.) Let them know that you are orchestrating their learning experiences with activities that influence brain states so they can learn better (Chapters 3 through 8 and 10) or enhance the actual learning itself (Chapter 9).

6 Practice Orchestrating Positive States in Others

States rule our lives. Get good at putting other people into positive states and you'll never lack for friends or employment. You'll probably even live a healthier life! Nothing is more important to you or your

participants than favorite states of mind. What they'll remember best about your presentation is *what states they entered while they were there.* If a state was boredom, they'll associate boredom with you and your classroom. If something is not working in your presentation, change the audience's state to a better one and continue. If you think that's not your job, that you weren't hired to be an entertainer, comedian or master of ceremonies, think about it this way:

You were hired to facilitate learning. The environment you create, the content you teach, the expressions on your face, the organization of your material and even the timing of your delivery affect audience states. You have much more influence on their learning experience than you give yourself credit for. If you don't value learning, find another job. If you do value it, realize that states and learning are intertwined and there are absolutely no exceptions to that rule. Negative states in an audience make your presentation a bad experience for everyone.

7 Organize State Management Tools

Organize the tools in this book so that they are more accessible to you. When you actually want to use a tool during a presentation, you'll have very little time to look it up in a book. I have listed ways that I organize my own tools. In general, I put them in groups, but no system is better than your own. If my system isn't helpful to you, don't worry— you will probably come up with one you like better.

Target States (8):
List your five favorite strategies for achieving each state:

"Huh?":   "Ah-hh":

"Yikes!":   "I Got It!":

"Uh-Oh!":   "Peace & Quiet":

"Movin' On":   "Yahoo":

Social Grouping Systems (5):
List your five favorite strategies for creating social grouping structures:

Existing team members:

Finding new partners (2 or 3 people):

Casual, instant groups:

Individual work:

Entire audience:

Activities
List your five favorite strategies for each activity type:

Content-based:

Content-free, process-based:

Designating a teammate:

Transitions between content:

Short activities (two minutes or less):

Longer activities (two to fifteen minutes)

Finding new partners

8 Stretch Your Skill Level Every Day

If your audience is in an "unteachable" state (probably very high energy or very low energy), consider it an opportunity. Use your tools to bring them into a learning state, gradually if necessary. You will only improve by testing your skills and challenging yourself. I have accepted work that was not easy, convenient or close to home, not because I needed the money but because it seemed like an experience I could learn and grow from. Accept hard assignments that give you the chance to learn! Every excellent professional I know has

1. accepted continually more challenging assignments;

2. requested feedback and learned from it;

3. taken risks and tried out new material;

4. made a total commitment to improve with every presentation; and

5. really loves the work.

If you say that you are doing what you love, that's a good start. But I know presenters who love what they do but are not very good at it. Why not? They are not truly committed to achieving excellence. They ignore the first four items on the above list, even though they are just as necessary as the fifth item for a successful career as a presenter—if not more so.

9 Use Strategies to Improve Students' Test Scores

Improving test scores is not part of my mission statement as an instructor, but state management tools do help raise them. I don't like thinking about teaching strategies or theories of learning solely as vehicles for boosting test scores, but when we manage learner states better, learning increases. And when learning increases, higher test scores usually follow. It's an almost inevitable outcome.

Learning
The very first step towards boosting test scores is improving learning. Each of the chapters in this book will help with that, especially "Huh?" (Chapter 3) and "I Got It!" (Chapter 8). In fact, any of these states will work at any level of education, from K–12 through adult.

Environment
The environment plays any important part in affecting test scores, too. Learners score better on tests they take in the same rooms in which they learned the original material. If you cannot control this circumstance, give your test in a room in which a major review of the material was performed.

State Management
Taking a brisk walk before a test will increase the arousal chemicals of norepinephrine and epinephrine. During the test, allow learners get up and stretch every fifteen to twenty minutes. Although walking is better for the body (but not necessarily for the testing environment), the mere act of standing can also increase blood flow to the brain by five to ten percent.

Finally, results from several sources have shown that eating a snack within thirty minutes of a test *does help* improve test scores. For short tests (thirty minutes or less), any sugar snack, from a candy bar to a piece of fruit, is fine. The brain will overreact, however, if a learner puts too much sugar in the system (Simontacchi, 2000). For longer tests (thirty minutes to two hours), encourage learners to eat proteins (yogurt, eggs, lean meat, tofu) or complex carbohydrates (whole grain breads, nuts, pasta, potatoes). Finally, for some learners, sucking on a peppermint or chewing a piece of gum is a slow, steady source for energy and brain state regulation (Levine et al., 1999). Anything eaten more than two hours before a test will have little or no effect on the student.

10 Model These Tools for Engagement

People use these tools all the time, every-where. Some just use them more purpose-fully than others. The next time you watch television, pay close attention to how announcers frame a news story ("You're not going to believe our next story!" or, "If you own a pet, stay tuned for our next segment—it's a shocker."). A better way to learn, though, is to see first-hand how skilled educators and presenters use these strategies.

You'd be surprised by how many of the world's top presenters already use these tools, although they don't label or explain them in the same way. Many of them present at the major conferences. The *Learning Brain Expo*® is one such confer-ence for educators and trainers where you can see many quality presenters implement the ideas and strategies in this book. This website, *www.brainexpo.com*, has more information about this event.

Bonus Guide
10 Insider Secrets
for Highly Effective Presentations

What If I Can't Even 1 Get My Group's Attention?

Remember that the more time your audience spends participating and the less time you spend talking, the better. But environments can get noisy. The tools listed in Chapter 3, "Huh?," can help you solve this problem because they involve more participation. Artificial noisemakers can quiet people in a group, but enlisting their participation and cooperation is a more reliable solution, though perhaps trickier. There are, however, times when one becomes desperate.

If you are a little frustrated and want to add some novelty to your request for quiet, say to your group, "Please! You shhhhhhould be listening carefully!" That "sh" extension in the middle of a word usually does the job. If not, you can then resort to the use of a noisemaker. It's a good idea to have several whistles on hand for different purposes. Try a shrill coach's whistle or small, plastic, toy whistle when you have to make yourself heard above a lot of noise. A set of chimes, a bicycle horn or even one of those noisy party ratchets that spins around a post would also be effective.

A more moderate option is to use a (less obnoxious) wooden train whistle (sold at a model train store or in a trainer's catalog) to quiet a group down when it's time to stop conversation or a discussion activity. When you blow the whistle, also raise your hand; ask that learners respond to the sound by quieting down and respond to your prompt by raising their own hands. Engage participants in this ritual by having a volunteer take over after you have modeled and practiced for a week. Then, devise a signal system so the volunteer knows when you want him or her to blow the whistle and get the group's attention. Change volunteers regularly and let each one pick the person to lead the ritual during the following week.

INSIDER SECRET
The very first two or three times you use the whistle, follow it up immediately with a short "shhh-hh." This connects the sound of the whistle to the message to quiet down. After a few repetitions, you'll never again have to shush the group verbally because the sound of the whistle will trigger their unconscious memory of your shush request.

How Do I Consistently 2 Put My Group in the Same Positive State?

Although there are no guaranteed state management tools, some are very reliable. Yelling, "Incoming!" or setting your hair on fire generates a consistent response. Inducing trauma, however, is a poor way to manage states. In the short term, the tools of this book have the advantage of novelty. People respond to new things with curiosity and even excitement. But over the long haul, you'll encounter the problem of habituation. Typically, people become accustomed to their states changing. Although habit and predictability have their uses (a mere prompt or reminder will trigger a state), they also have their downsides (boredom). So how can you be sure of your ability to consistently trigger your target states? You'll have to do some planning.

The best plan I know is to establish rituals. A ritual is an event performed by a community for a mutual gain. We enact countless rituals in our society, including funerals, birthday and anniversary celebrations, holiday meals, gift exchanges, Tax Day in April and the planting rites of spring. Some communities observe the annual ritual of Mardi Gras; others host a hula festival or Derby Week. The more often rituals are performed and the longer they endure as the years go by, the more likely they are to be meaningful. In a learning environment, it's up to the instructor to create and maintain rituals that work.

Enduring rituals share several key ingredients, without which they would fall apart. Each ritual must:

❖ *solve a problem (create unity among chaos, redirect attention, etc.)*
❖ *invlove everyone (to create community, it must include your audience, not just you)*
❖ *put everyone into positive states (or they'll feel worse than before they started)*
❖ *be easy to do (no special skill required or it becomes exclusive)*
❖ *be consistent—when A occurs, B always follows (participants must be able to predict it every time)*

There you have it—the five requirements of any ritual. I am listing a few examples of classroom rituals. In parentheses after each one, I address the ritual criteria detailed above to show how they qualify.

Stretching
(Problem: the group is stiff. Everyone participates; when they are done, learners feel less tense; anyone can stretch; stretches are scheduled each day after announcements.)

Grateful Reflection
(Problem: people want to connect with others and move around. Everyone participates; learners are inspired by voicing aloud what they are grateful for, what they have learned and what the day promises; no special skills are required for walking; walks are scheduled every day after the math lesson.)

Call-Response Wrap-Ups
(Problem: group needs a sense of closure. Everyone participates; call-responses are fun and raise spirits; anyone can clap their hands and answer as part of a group; call-responses happen right before learners leave the room.)

Return Responses

(Problem: need to settle and align group. Presenter directs the audience by saying, "If you made it back on time, raise your hand and say 'Yes!'" Everyone participates; it's a positive and affirming gesture; anyone can raise a hand and answer as part of a group; the ritual is performed every time the audience returns to the room.)

Now that you are starting to get a feel for what rituals are, you may wonder if they make sense for your presentation style. Guess what? You already use them! You just might not use rituals that meet all the criteria. Many of my teachers in elementary and high school started class each day with a roll call. They way they performed the ritual, however, was terrible. Although it was predictable and solved a problem, it involved too few students and flat-out bored them. But you could easily change how roll call is done and turn it into a positive ritual.

What if you assigned participants to teams? What if you gave each team a number? What if each morning the team leaders stood and announced whether or not all of their teammates were present that day? If they were, the team could stand and cheer. If not, they would stay seated and just clap for the people who were present. Finally, each team leader would post the absent teammate's name on your daily roster. With an audience of forty, the entire process would take about forty seconds for eight teams of five each. Every participant has a role to play in the ritual and you still get roll taken. Simple, fun, energizing—what more could you ask for?

It will require energy to establish rituals in the first place. When I first begin a "start up the class" ritual, I walk around the room, rounding up the students and reminding them how to participate. If I point out, for example, that the call-back song is playing, they will start linking the music to the act of returning to class on time. After a few repetitions, they don't need much help; the group will take care of itself. The only drawback to rituals is that they become tiresome over time. Most rituals are effective for only two to four weeks. Solve that problem with a suggestion box for ideas on how to vary them. Fun rituals that occur less frequently and require less physical or mental energy may last as long as two to four months. You'll know when a ritual is on its way out because the participation level drops over time.

INSIDER SECRET

You can use rituals in a one-day or half-day presentation, but you will have to establish a conditioned response with the audience first. Perhaps every time you say something twice, your audience repeats it. Or, at the end of each lesson topic, have participants turn to their neighbors and say, "That makes sense!" Set rituals in place within the first few minutes of a session and use them to manage group responses for the duration.

3 What Are Some Less Active State Management Tools?

Many common state changers are *not* discussed in this book, primarily because they are done *to* participants rather than *with* them. For example, I didn't talk about any of the following:

❖ *giving food to students (though that would clearly change a state of hunger)*

❖ *blowing an air horn (That definitely gets attention, but I'd rather involve students in the process and avoid the more gimmicky things that teachers and trainers already know.)*

❖ *performing vocal, visual or magic tricks (These shows might be entertaining, but they simply do not engage the learners in the same way as having them do the magic or having them sing the song.)*

If the learners do not actually do an activity themselves (but only watch the presenter do them), it's probably not mentioned in the earlier chapters. This limits, of course, the number of state changers that I can describe, but I believe it makes the ones I do choose a better selection.

There are actually many subtle state management tools that you can use, but most of them are best suited for capturing interest and shifting attention than anything else. They will not involve or engage the audience as much as the ones listed in previous chapters but they are all still good to know! However, do not use them *instead of* the active tools in this book—use them *in addition to* them, when appropriate. Some of these more passive, less active state changers can be performed by you; others can be performed by one or more participants:

- change where you stand in the room
- read a dramatic story
- post written affirmations and have learners read them
- laugh or tell a joke
- wear a special hat or clothes

- sing or play an instrument
- blow an unusual whistle
- display unexpected facial expressions
- change the tone of your voice
- passionately read an inspirational quotation
- make special gestures
- make oral affirmations
- switch to a video or overhead transparency
- mime a key point and ask your audience to guess it
- bang on a desk
- stand on a chair or table
- use music (or change the type of music you use)
- have participants wear funny hats or costumes, or use props
- point to something and ask for information about it
- have a team stand up to speak as the rest of the audience sits and listens
- turn your back on group for a moment
- scream, pause and stand in silence
- show an unusual object
- use noisemakers or other gimmicks
- change lighting from one extreme to the other
- knock on the door and wait
- perform a magic trick
- leave the room for a few seconds
- hand out food (popcorn, snacks, etc.)
- bring in flowers
- switch participants' seats
- lead the audience outside for a few minutes
- move to a new classroom for a few minutes
- have participants find and touch subject-related objects
- introduce an animal to the group
- rearrange the chairs

4   Use Positive Peer Pressure

If you wonder how you are going to convince an audience to participate in all the activities that are listed in this book, practice peer pressure. If everyone else is doing something, then an individual learner will find it easier to join in. By creating a climate of participation, it is likely that you'll invite more involvement. Creative, positive peer pressure attracts learners in fun, adventurous ways.

❖ *Establish semi-permanent teams that last from three to six weeks and assign roles to each team member. Depending on the purpose of the team, establish roles like leader, secretary, timekeeper, scorekeeper, materials gatherer or cheerleader.*

❖ *Create instant groupings with ideas from the "Mixer Walk" activity in Chapter 4.*

❖ *Have everyone take ten giant steps in any direction and then form groups of four. Or, immediately pair participants by asking them to work with the person in the seat next to them.*

5   Follow Through on Every Activity

Most of the activities in this book seem complete, but they aren't. Each one of them would benefit from enhancements. Deepen participant learning by allowing time for debriefing, sharing or reflecting on it.

❖ *At the conclusion of an activity, ask your audience how they fared.*

❖ *Have participants give you written feedback on index cards.*

❖ *Have partners share with each other their opinions about how an activity went.*

❖ *Have participants give to partners or group members specific feedback about their performance on an assignment.*

❖ *Ask partners or group members to thank each other for their help before returning to their original seats.*

❖ *While an activity is still fresh in your mind, make personal notes about how it went and what you can do to improve it next time.*

INSIDER SECRET

Do not employ all of these suggestions at one time—that would be overkill! But do keep in mind that learning never ends. Find ways to expand and upgrade the tools listed in this book so they fit your personal presentation style. Modifications could be as simple as adding a discussion or as complex as assigning a multiple week project. With a touch of boldness and a lot of reflection on your part, you'll become a real pro at using these tools for engagement.

6 Always Have a Back-Up Plan

The best-laid plans can fail. Easy-to-work-with groups can turn on you. Simple activities can go wrong. Expect that it will happen to you someday! An explanation about what went wrong may be informative, but it will not satisfy your audience if you have nothing else to offer. Be ready with a back-up plan.

INSIDER SECRET

Keep a list in the back of your mind of ways to make a quick, definite exit from a chaotic moment. You could tell a personal story, lead a slow stretch, make a good-natured joke or give learners an assignment. Sometimes the best back-up plan is a diversion. "Oops! I just realized it's time for a break. Let's sort this activity out and finish it up later. I'll see you all back in fifteen minutes!"

7 Start with a Few Simple Tools First

Stair-step yourself into confidence. This book has more than 150 primary activities and 350 additional variations on them, but you only need to learn one of them before your next class, course or training. Just one! Learn it, practice it and master it. Once you're good at it, your confidence will soar and you'll be ready for the next one. Learning these activities one by one is better than attempting to use several of them in your next class and failing at most of them. Focus on just what you need to get started. Go easy on yourself and only use and practice one new activity at a time.

It is better to learn ten tools and five ways to vary each of them than to try to learn fifty tools!

INSIDER SECRET

Focus on learning fewer things better. Although I endorse every item in this book, I do not use every single one in a presentation. I don't have time. But I sure know how to tweak each of my favorites in order to vary them and keep them fresh. Simplicity is the key: Learn fewer tools, but learn them better.

8 Get Help

Think of music as a teaching partner that will help you manage states. If you aren't already using music, start. So many other teachers and trainers use music during their presentations that the ones who don't seem out of date.

The idea of using music to enhance a presentation is traditional and hip, and fast becoming universal. If you teach in a classroom, buy an inexpensive CD player and lock it up when you aren't using it. If you are a staff developer, purchase a CD player with the best sound you can afford so that everyone in a large auditorium or meeting room can hear the music you play. (The quality of sound can affect a learner's state positively or negatively.) When you're ready for a CD player with even better sound and features, invest in one. I began with a tape player and one cassette. Now, I typically bring to my presentations twenty-four CDs and a sound system that can fill an auditorium.

INSIDER SECRET
I travel with a Bose Acoustic Wave® Radio/CD player (two models are available with an educator's discount). This system requires no additional speakers and has held up well.

9 Find Reliable Sources of Music

Choose one or two CDs at first and familiarize yourself with their songs and how to use them in your lessons. Buy used CDs to keep your costs down and buy compilations for a wide variety of selections. There are dozens of them with names like, "Juke Box Hits from the 1960s," "Dance Dance 2001" or "R & B Classics." I also recommend getting a CD burner to compile your own CDs. Also, try CDs from training and education catalogs that are designed specifically to evoke particular learner states.

I am a strong believer in positive karma. Always pay for *any music* downloaded from the Internet or copied from a friend.

Artists are entitled to compensation for their music. If you are giving a paid presentation, get a site license. After all, you are using an artist's work and benefiting from it monetarily. (Music played only within a school does not require a site license.)

INSIDER SECRET
Contact the American Society of Composers, Authors and Publishers (ASCAP) about getting an annual blanket license. Visit their website, www.ascap.com/licensing, *for answers to questions about licensing terms and requirements. Broadcast Music, Inc. (BMI) also offers a general license for songs in their catalog. Visit their website,* www.bmi.com, *for information about these requirements and a song list.*

10 Choose Your Music Carefully

Choosing the right music to play at the right time is both a science and an art. The best way to get started is to decide which situations will require music, then collect music to fit those situations.

Make compilations with a variety of selections for various circumstances. Once you feel comfortable with your first one, start adding more CDs to your collection. Although you could use an endless list of criteria for choosing suitable music, these three considerations are a good start:

1. Target State

What state are you trying to elicit? Pay attention to what happens to your body and mind as you listen to a song. Note its tempo and the number of beats per minute (BPM). Songs in the range of thirty-five to fifty BPMs will be calming; those in the middle range of fifty to seventy BPMs will be move faster (this is a good pace for seat work); 100 to 160 BPMs will really get things moving.

2. Age of the Listener

Ask yourself what generation you'll be working with. If your audience is primarily senior citizens, forget hip-hop! Use an energetic, up-tempo Big Band selection instead. If you'll be working with baby boomers, play music from the 1960s and 1970s. Learners from the ages of six to twelve enjoy the trendiest music available. Basically, consider the generation of your audience and play whatever they listened to in high school or college.

3. Type of Music

Should you play music with lyrics or instrumental music? In general, use music with lyrics only for transitions, games that require them and special occasions. Instrumental music is better for most situations. Your audience should never be talking, sharing or brainstorming and have to compete with words. Classical, jazz, country, rave, folk tunes, polka, Eastern music, chanting, Polynesian music, rock n' roll, smooth jazz, hard rock, Chinese music, easy listening, flamenco, Greek and countless other genres all have instrumental selections. Besides, if you limit yourself to one kind of music you'll miss some great alternatives.

I've listed particular pieces of music that are suitable for each of the learning states in this book. You can slowly add them to your collection as you become more comfortable with their sounds and tempo. I am very partial to The Brain Store's® collection of CDs because they are produced with specific states in mind; all of these suggested titles are commercially available.

♪♪ "Huh?" Arousal States for Learning

- *Flight of the Bumblebee* (Nicolai Rimsky-Korsakov)
- *Morning Mood* (Edvard Grieg; Peer Gynt Suite, No. 1)
- *Toy Symphony* (Leopold Mozart)
- *March of the Toy Soldiers* (Tchaikovsky, *Nutcracker Ballet*)
- *Energizers To Go* CD* (2003, The Brain Store®)
- *Let's Get Ready To Rumble!* (Michael Buffer, from *Jock Jams*, 1995, Tommy Boy Music)
- *Peter and the Wolf* (Sergei Prokofiev)
- *Getting to Know You* (Rodgers and Hammerstein, *The King and I*)
- Theme from *Rocky (Gonna Fly Now)* (Bill Conti)
- 1984 *Olympic Fanfare and Theme* (John Williams)
- Main Theme from *Star Wars* (John Williams).
- *Fanfare for the Common Man* (Aaron Copland)
- *Triumphal March* from *Aida* (Giuseppe Verdi)
- *Grand March* from *Aida* (Giuseppe Verdi)
- *Persian March* (Johann Strauss, Jr.)
- *Egyptian March* (Johann Strauss, Jr.)

- *Radetzky March* (Johann Strauss, Sr.)
- *Wedding March* from *A Midsummer Night's Dream* (Felix Mendelssohn)
- *Rackoczy March* from *Hungarian Rhapsody No. 15* (Franz Liszt)
- Theme from *Peter Gunn* (Henry Mancini)
- *Tequila* (The Champs)
- *Walk Right In* (The Rooftop Singers)

"Yikes!"
High Energy States

- *Energizers To Go* CD* (2003, The Brain Store®)
- *Whip It* (Devo)
- *I'm Walking* (Fats Domino)
- *I'm So Excited* (Pointer Sisters)
- *Shake It Up* (The Cars)
- *I Like to Move It* (Reel 2 Reel)
- Theme from *Hawaii Five-O* (Morton Stevens)
- *We Didn't Start the Fire* (Billy Joel)
- *Eye of the Tiger* (Survivor)
- *William Tell Overture* (Gioachino Rossini)
- *The Locomotion* (Little Eva)
- *New Attitude* (Patti LaBelle)
- *Takin' Care of Business* (BTO)
- *Hooked on Classics* CD (2002, K-Tel Entertainment)
- *1812 Overture* (Pytor Ilyich Tchaikovsky)
- *Ride of the Valkyries* (Richard Wagner)
- *YMCA* (Village People)
- *La Bamba* (Richie Valens)
- *Shout* (Isley Brothers)
- *Jellyhead* (Crush)
- *C'Mon N Ride It (The Train)* (Quad City DJs)
- *Endless Summer: Donna Summer's Greatest Hits* (1994, Polygram Records)
- *Dance, Dance, Dance: The Best of Chic* CD (1991, Atlantic)

"Uh-Oh!"
The State of Healthy Concern

- *Help!* (Beatles)
- Theme from *Mission Impossible* (Lalo Schifrin)
- Theme from *Twilight Zone* (Bernard Herrmann)
- Theme from *Pink Panther* (Henry Mancini)
- Theme from *Dragnet* (Walter Schumann)
- *Bad Moon Rising* (Credence Clearwater Revival)

"Movin' On"
Transitions

- *Energizers To Go* CD* (2003, The Brain Store®)
- *Flight of the Bumblebee* (Nicolai Rimsky-Korsakov)
- *Tequila* (The Champs)
- Theme from *Batman* (Neal Hefti)
- *Whip It* (Devo)
- *I'm So Excited* (Pointer Sisters)
- *Shake It Up* (Cars)
- *I Like to Move It* (Reel 2 Reel)
- Theme from *Hawaii Five-O* (Morton Stevens)
- *William Tell Overture* (Gioachino Rossini)
- *The Locomotion* (Little Eva)
- *New Attitude* (Patti LaBelle)
- *Hooked on Classics* CD (2002, K-Tel Entertainment)
- *1812 Overture* (Pytor Ilyich Tchaikovsky)
- *Ride of the Valkyries* (Richard Wagner)
- *La Bamba* (Richie Valens)

"Ah-hh"
The State of Well-Being

- *Urban Gypsy* CD
  (Marc Antoine, 1995, GRP Records)
- *Don't Worry, Be Happy* (Bobby McFerrin)
- *Whistle While You Work* CD*
  (2002, The Brain Store®)
- *Reach Out (I'll Be There)* (Four Tops)
- *You've Got a Friend* (James Taylor)
- *We Are Family* (Sister Sledge)
- *I'll Take You There* (Staple Singers)
- *You Can Make It If You Try*
  (Sly and the Family Stone)
- *Take it Easy* (Eagles)
- *Circle of Life* (Elton John)
- *When You're Smiling* (Louis Armstrong)
- *What a Wonderful World* (Louis Armstrong)
- *Wind Beneath My Wings* (Bette Midler)
- *Fly Me to the Moon* (Bobby Darin)
- *Heigh-Ho* (from Disney's *Snow White*)
- *Zip-A-Dee-Doo-Dah*
  (from Disney's *Song of the South*)
- *Day-O (Banana Boat Song)*
  (Harry Belafonte)
- *Matilda* (Harry Belafonte)
- *Jump Down, Spin Around* (Harry Belafonte)
- Recordings by Red Grammer
- Recordings by Hap Palmer
- CDs from The Learning Station

"I Got It!"
In-Depth Learning with Confidence

- *Energizers To Go* CD*
  (2003, The Brain Store®)
- *That's the Way I Like It*
  (KC and the Sunshine Band)
- *I Feel Good* (James Brown)
- *I Can See Clearly Now* (Johnny Nash)
- Theme from *Rocky* (Bill Conti)

- Theme from *Raiders of Lost Ark*
  (John Williams)
- *The Best* (Tina Turner)
- *We Are the Champions* (Queen)
- *Celebration* (Kool and the Gang)
- *Hallelujah Chorus* from Handel's *Messiah*

"Peace and Quiet"
States of Reflection & Calm

- *Peace and Quiet* CD*
  (2002, The Brain Store®)
- Compositions and recordings by
  George Winston
- Compositions and recordings by
  Michael Jones
- Recordings of Eric Satie compositions
- *The Goldberg Variations*
  (Johann Sebastian Bach)
- *Music for Airports* CD
  (Brian Eno, 1998, Polygram Records)
- *Inner Rhythms* CD
  (Randy Crafton, 1996, Relaxation)
- Recordings by Daniel Kobialka

"Yahoo!"
States of Celebration & Reward

- *Holiday* (Madonna)
- *Hallelujah Chorus* from Handel's *Messiah*
- *Everybody Is a Star*
  (Sly and the Family Stone)
- *Ninth (Choral) Symphony*
  (Ludwig von Beethoven)
- *Celebration* (Kool and the Gang)
- *1812 Overture* (Pytor Ilyich Tchaikovsky)
- *Dancing in the Street*
  (Martha and the Vandellas)
- *Joy to the World* (Three Dog Night)

* Available from The Brain Store® at www.thebrainstore.com

INSIDER SECRET

If you don't have enough time to play music while teaching, you're talking too much. If you don't have enough time to select and use CDs during your presentation, you're talking too much. When my audience is busy doing an active learning assignment, I use that time to get my next music selection ready. That way, I'm always one step ahead. Participants often think I have the whole day cued up in advance—I don't. I only have one song cued in advance, but I rely on this motto for presenting: "More of them and less of me." *Using music will become second nature if you start simple, by choosing music according to the three qualifiers detailed above and preparing it while learners are busy. Trust me—with practice, you'll become very comfortable with music in your lessons and enjoy the process.*

Bibliography

Ahern, G. L. & Schwartz, G. E. (1979). Differential lateralization for positive versus negative emotion. *Neuropsychologia*, 17(6), 693–8.

Alexander, P., Kulickowich, J., & Schulze, S. (1994). How subject-matter knowledge affects recall and interest. *American Educational Research Journal*, 31(2), 313–37.

Allen, Richard (2002). *Impact Teaching: Ideas and Strategies for Teachers to Maximize Student Learning* (pp. 112–37). Boston, MA: Allyn and Bacon.

Alloy, L. B. & Abramson L. Y. (1979). Judgment of contingency in depressed and non-depressed students: Sadder but wiser? *Journal of Experimental Psychology: General*, 108(4), 441–85.

Ashby, F. G., Isen, A. M., & Turken, A. U. (1999, July). A neuropsychological theory of positive affect and its influence on cognition. *Psychological Review*, 106, 529–50.

Aspinwall, L. G. & Richter, L. (1999). Optimism and self-mastery predict more rapid disengagement from unsolvable tasks in the presence of alternatives. *Motivation and Emotion*, 23, 221–45.

Baars, B. & McGovern, K. (1996). Cognitive views of consciousness: What are the facts? How can we explain them? In Max Velmans (Ed.), *The Science of Consciousness: Psychological, Neuropsychological and Clinical Views* (pp. 63–95). New York, NY: Routledge.

Barker, L. W. (1991). The use of music and relaxation techniques to reduce pain of burn patients during daily debridement. In C. D. Maranto (Ed.), *Applications of Music in Medicine* (pp. 124–40). Washington, DC: National Association for Music Therapy.

Bartlett, Dale (1996). Physiological responses to music and sound stimuli. In D. Hodges (Ed.), *Handbook of Music Psychology* (pp. 343–85). San Antonio, TX: IMR Press.

Baumeister, R. F. & Sommer, K. L. (1997, July). What do men want? Gender differences and two spheres of belongingness: Comment on Cross and Madson. *Psychological Bulletin*, 122(1), 38–44.

Bennett, Alan Weinberg & Bealer, Bonnie (2002). *The Caffeine Advantage: How to Sharpen Your Mind, Improve Your Physical Performance, and Achieve Your Goals—The Healthy Way*. New York, NY: Free Press.

Bernstein, G. A., Carroll, M. E., Dean, N. W., Crosby, R. D., Perwien, A. R., & Benowitz, N. L. (1998, August). Caffeine withdrawal in normal school-age children. *Journal of the American Academy of Child and Adolescent Psychiatry*, 37(8), 858–65.

Berridge, K. C. (1999). Pleasure, pain, desire, and dread: Hidden core processes of emotion. In D. Kahneman, E. Diener, & N. Schwarz (Eds.), *Well-Being: Foundations of Hedonic Psychology* (pp. 527–559). New York, NY: Russell Sage Foundation.

Blood, D. J. & Ferriss, S. J. (1993, February). Effects of background music on anxiety, satisfaction with communication, and productivity. *Psychological Reports*, 72(1), 171–7.

Bonny, H. L. (1983). Music listening for intensive coronary care units: A pilot project. *Music Therapy: Journal of the American Association for Music Therapy*, 3(1), 4–16.

Bradley, M. & Lang, P. (2000). Measuring emotion: Behavior, feeling and physiology. In Richard Lane, Lynn Nadel, G. L. Ahern, J. J. B. Allen, A. W. Kaszniak, S. Z. Rapcsak, & G. E. Schwartz (Eds.), *Cognitive Neuroscience of Emotion* (pp. 242–276). New York, NY: Oxford University Press.

Brown, K. J. & Grunberg, N. E. (1995, December). Effects of housing on male and female rats: Crowding stresses males but calms females. *Physiology and Behavior*, 58(6), 1085–9.

Brownley, K. A., McMurray, R. G., & Hackney, A.C. (1995, April). Effects of music on physiological and affective responses to graded treadmill exercise in trained and untrained runners. *International Journal of Psychophysiology*, 19(3), 193–201.

Buzan, Tony & Buzan, Barry (1996). *The Mind Map Book: How to Use Radiant Thinking to Maximize Your Brain's Untapped Potential*. New York, NY: Penguin.

Cacioppo, J. T. (1994, March). Social neuroscience: Autonomic, neuroendrocine, and immune responses to stress. *Psychophysiology*, 31(2), 113–28.

Cacioppo, J. T. & Berntson, G. G. (1992, August). Social psychological contributions to the decade of the brain: Doctrine of multilevel analysis. *American Psychologist*, 47(8), 1019–28.

Cacioppo, J. T., Berntson, G. G., Sheridan, J., & McClintock, M. (2002). Multilevel integrative analysis of human behavior: Social neuroscience and the complementing nature of social and biological approaches. In John T. Cacioppo, Gary G. Berntson, Ralph Adolphs, C. Sue Carter, Richard J. Davidson, Martha K. McClintock, Bruce S. McEwen, Michael J. Meaney, Daniel L. Schacter, Esther M. Sternberg, Steve S. Suomi, & Shelley E. Taylor (Eds.), *Foundations of Social Neuroscience* (pp. 21–46). Cambridge, MA: MIT Press.

Cacioppo, J. T., Ernst, J., Burleson, M., McClintock, M., Malarkey, B., Hawkley, L., Kawalewski, R., Paulsen, A., Hobson, J., Hugdahl, K., Speigel, D., & G. Berntson (2002). Lonely traits and concomitant physiological processes: The MacArthur Social Neuroscience Studies. In John T. Cacioppo, Gary G. Berntson, Ralph Adolphs, C. Sue Carter, Richard J. Davidson, Martha K. McClintock, Bruce S. McEwen, Michael J. Meaney, Daniel L. Schacter, Esther M. Sternberg, Steve S. Suomi, & Shelley E. Taylor (Eds.), *Foundations of Social Neuroscience* (pp. 839–52). Cambridge, MA: MIT Press.

Cacioppo, J. T., Gardner, W. L., & Berntson, G. G. (1999) The affect system has parallel and integrative processing components: Form follows function. *Journal of Personality and Social Psychology*, 76, 839–55.

Cacioppo, J. T., Gardner, W. L., & Berntson, G. G. (1997). Beyond bipolar conceptualizations and measures: The case of attitudes and evaluative space. *Personality and Social Psychology Review*, 1, 3–25.

Cahill, L., Prins, B., Weber, M., & McGaugh, J. (1994, October 20). Beta-adrenergic activation and memory for emotional events. *Nature*, 371(6499), 702–4.

Carlson, M. & Earls, F. (1999) Psychological and neuroendocrinological sequelae of early social deprivation in institutionalized children in Romania. In Carol Sue Carter, I. Izja Lederhendler, & Brian Kirkpatrick (Eds.), *The Integrative Neurobiology of Affiliation* (pp. 419-428). Cambridge, MA: MIT Press.

Carper, Jean (2000). *Your Miracle Brain*. New York, NY: HarperCollins.

Carver, C. & Scheier, M. (2001). Optimism, pessimism, and self-regulation. In Edward Chang (Ed.), *Optimism and Pessimism: Implications for Theory, Research and Practice* (pp. 31–51). Washington, DC: American Psychological Association.

Casey, B. J., Trainor, R., Giedd, J., Vauss, Y., Vaituzis, C. K., Hamburger, S., Kozusch, P., & Rapoport, J. L. (1997, January). The role of the anterior cingulate in automatic and controlled processes: A developmental neuroanatomical study. *Developmental Psychobiology*, 30(1), 61–9.

Charnetski, Carl; Brennan, Francis, Jr.; & Harrison, J. F. (1998, December). Effect of music and auditory stimuli on secretory immunoglobulin A (IgA). *Perceptual and Motor Skills*, 87, 1163–70.

Clore, G. & Ortony, A. (2000). Cognition in emotion: Always, sometimes or never? In Richard Lane, Lynn Nadel, G. L. Ahern, J. J. B. Allen, A. W. Kaszniak, S. Z. Rapcsak, & G. E. Schwartz (Eds.), *Cognitive Neuroscience of Emotion* (pp. 54–6). New York, NY: Oxford University Press.

Cockerton, T., Moore, S., and Norman, D. (1997, December). Cognitive test performance and background music. *Perceptual and Motor Skills*, 85, 1435–8.

Cooper, J., Bloom, F., & Roth, R. (2001). *The Biochemical Basis of Neuropharmacology* (pp. 111–32). New York, NY: Oxford University Press.

Crabbe, J. C., Wahlsten, D., and Dudek, B. C. (1999, June 4). Genetics of mouse behavior: Interactions with laboratory environment. *Science*, 284(5420), 1670–2.

Damasio, Antonio (1994). *Descartes' Error: Emotion, Reason, and the Human Brain*. New York, NY: Avon.

Damasio, Antonio (1999). *The Feeling of What Happens: Body and Emotion in the Making of Consciousness*. New York, NY: Harcourt, Brace and Co.

Damasio, Antonio (2000). A second chance for emotion. In Richard Lane, Lynn Nadel, G. L. Ahern, J. J. B. Allen, A. W. Kaszniak, S. Z. Rapcsak, & G. E. Schwartz (Eds.), *Cognitive Neuroscience of Emotion* (pp. 12–23). New York, NY: Oxford University Press.

Darner, C. L. (1966, February). Sound pulses and the heart. *Journal of the Acoustical Society of America*, 39, 414–6.

Dorfman, Andrea (1984). How Muzak manipulates you. *Science Digest*, 92, 26.

Dossey, Larry (1993). *Healing Words: The Power of Prayer and the Practice of Medicine*. San Francisco, CA: HarperCollins.

Dunbar, R. (2002). The social brain hypothesis. In John T. Cacioppo, Gary G. Berntson, Ralph Adolphs, C. Sue Carter, Richard J. Davidson, Martha K. McClintock, Bruce S. McEwen, Michael J. Meaney, Daniel L. Schacter, Esther M. Sternberg, Steve S. Suomi, & Shelley E. Taylor (Eds.), *Foundations of Social Neuroscience* (pp. 69-87). Cambridge, MA: MIT Press.

Dwyer, T., Blizzard, L., & Dean, Kimberlie (1996, April). Physical activity and performance in children. *Nutrition Reviews*, 54(4), 27–31.

Edwards, C. (1993). Behavioral sex differences in children of diverse cultures: The case of nurturance to infants. In M. E. Pereira & L. A. Fairbanks (Eds.), *Juvenile Primates: Life History, Development, and Behavior* (pp. 327–38). New York: Oxford University Press.

Ekkekakis, P., Hall, E. E., VanLanduyt, L. M., & Petruzello, S. (2000). Walking in (affective) circles: Can short walks enhance affect? *Journal of Behavioral Medicine*, 23(3), 245–75.

Ekman, P. & Davidson, R. J. (1993). Voluntary smiling changes regional brain activity. *Psychological Science*, 4, 342–5.

Frijda, Nico H. (1986). *The Emotions*. Cambridge, MA: Cambridge University Press.

Furnham, A. & Bradley, A. (1997). Music while you work: The differential distraction of background music on the cognitive test performance of introverts and extroverts. *Applied Cognitive Psychology*, 11, 445–55.

Geden, E. A., Lower, M., Beattie, S., & Beck, N. (1989). Effects of music and imagery on physiologic and self-report of analogued labor pain. *Nursing Research*, 38(1), 37–41.

Gershon, Michael (1998). *The Second Brain: The Scientific Basis of Gut Instinct and a Groundbreaking New Understanding of Nervous Disorders of the Stomach and Intestine*. New York, NY: HarperCollins.

Girdler, S. S., Jamner, L. D., & Shapiro, D. (1997). Hostility, testosterone and vascular reactivity to stress: Effects of gender. *International Journal of Behavioral Medicine*, 4, 242–63.

Goldman, Mark (1999). Expectancy operation: Cognitive-neural models and architectures. In Irving Kirsch (Ed.), *How Expectancies Shape Experiences* (pp. 41–63). Washington, DC: American Psychological Association.

Greenwood, B. N., Foley, T. E., Day, H. E., Campisi, J., Hammack, S. H., Campeau, S., Maier, S. F., & Fleshner, M. (2003, April 1). Freewheel running prevents learned helplessness/behavioral depression: Role of dorsal raphe serotonergic neurons. *Journal of Neuroscience*, 23(7), 2889–98.

Grieco, A. (1986). Sitting posture: An old problem and a new one. *Ergonomics*, 29, 345–62.

Grigsby, Jim & Stevens, David (2000). *Neurodynamics of Personality* (pp. 164–88). New York, NY: Guilford Publications.

Haber, S. & Barchas, P. (1984). The regulatory effect of social rank on behavior after amphetamine administration. In P.R. Barchas & S. P. Mendoza (Eds.), *Social Cohesion: Essays Toward a Sociophysioplogical Perspective* (pp. 119–32). Westport, CT: Greenwood Press.

Harlow, H. & Harlow, M. (1973). Social deprivation in monkeys. In William T. Greenough (Ed.), *The Nature and Nurture of Behavior: Readings from Scientific American* (pgs.108–16). San Francisco, CA: W. H. Freeman.

Heybach, J. & Vernikos-Danellis, J. (1979). Inhibition of adreno-corticotrophin secretion during deprivation-induced eating and drinking in rats. *Neuroendrocrinology*, 28, 329–38.

Hobson, J. Allan (1994). *The Chemistry of Conscious States: How the Brain Changes Its Mind*. Boston, MA: Little, Brown and Co.

House, J. S., Landis, K. R., & Umberson, D. (1988, July 29). Social relationships and health. *Science*, 241(4865), 540–5.

Hume, K. M. & Crossman, J. (1992). Musical reinforcement of practice behaviors among competitive swimmers. *Journal of Applied Behavior Analysis*, 25, 665–70.

Ito, T., Larsen, J., Smith, N., & Cacioppo, J. (2002). Negative information weighs more heavily on the brain: The negativity bias in evaluative categorizations. In John T. Cacioppo, Gary G. Berntson, Ralph Adolphs, C. Sue Carter, Richard J. Davidson, Martha K. McClintock, Bruce S. McEwen, Michael J. Meaney, Daniel L. Schacter, Esther M. Sternberg, Steve S. Suomi, & Shelley E. Taylor (Eds.), *Foundations of Social Neuroscience* (pp. 575–97). Cambridge, MA: MIT Press.

Jeannerod, M. (1999, February). The 25th Bartlett Lecture. To act or not to act: Perspectives on the representations of actions. *The Quarterly Journal of Experimental Psychology*, 52, 1–29.

Jensen, Eric (2000). *Learning with the Body in Mind*. San Diego, CA: The Brain Store®.

Jensen, Eric (2001). *Arts with the Brain in Mind*. Alexandria, VA: Association for Supervision and Curriculum Development.

Johnston, Victor (1999). *Why We Feel: The Science of Human Emotions*. Reading, MA: Perseus Books.

Kelso, J. A. Scott (1997). *Dynamic Patterns: The Self-Organization of Brain and Behavior*. Cambridge, MA: A Bradford Book/The MIT Press.

Kirsch, Irving (1999). The response expectancy: An introduction. In Irving Kirsch (Ed.), *How Expectancies Shape Experiences* (pp. 7). Washington, DC: American Psychological Association.

Koob, G. F. (2000). Neurobiology of addiction. Toward the development of new therapies. *Annals of the New York Academy of Sciences*, 909, 170–85.

Krock, L. P. & Hartung, G. H. (1992, April). Influence of post-exercise activity on plasma catecholamines, blood pressure and heart rate in normal subjects. *Clinical Autonomic Research*, 2(2), 89–97.

LaBerge, David (1995). *Attentional Processing: The Brain's Art of Mindfulness*. Cambridge, MA: Harvard University Press.

Lane, R., Nadel, L., & Kasziak, A. (2000). The study of emotion from the perspective of cognitive neuroscience. In Richard Lane & Lynn Nadel (Eds.), *Cognitive Neuroscience of Emotion* (pp. 3–11). New York, NY: Oxford University Press.

Lavoie, Derrick R. (1999). Effects of emphasizing hypothetico-predictive reasoning within the science learning cycle on high school student's process skills and conceptual understanding in biology. *Journal of Research in Science Teaching*, 36(10), 1127–47.

LeDoux, Joseph (1996). *The Emotional Brain*. New York, NY: Simon and Schuster.

LeDoux, Joseph (1999). The power of emotions. In Roberta Conlan (Ed.), *States of Mind: New Discoveries About How Our Brains Make Us Who We Are* (pp. 123–50). New York, NY: John Wiley & Sons.

Lesser, Michael (2002). *The Brain Chemistry Diet: The Personalized Prescription for Balancing Mood, Relieving Stress, and Conquering Depression, Based on Your Personality Profile*. New York, NY: Putnam.

Levine, J., Baukol, P., & Pavlidis, I. (1999). The energy expended in chewing gum. *New England Journal of Medicine*, 341, 2100.

Levine, S. & Coe, S. (1989). Endocrine regulation. In Stanley Cheren (Ed.), *Psychosomatic Medicine: Theory, Physiology and Practice, Vol. 1* (pp. 331–83). Madison, CT: International Universities Press, Inc.

Levine, S., Lyons, D., & Schatzberg, A. (1999). Psycho-biological consequences of social relationships. In Carol Sue Carter, I. Izja Lederhendler, & Brian Kirkpatrick (Eds.), *The Integrative Neurobiology of Affiliation* (pp. 83–92). Cambridge, MA: MIT Press.

Lorch, C. A., Lorch, V., Diefendorf, A. O., & Earl, P. W. (1994). Effect of stimulative and sedative music on systolic blood pressure, heart rate, and respiratory rate in premature infants. *Journal of Music Therapy*, 31(2), 105–18.

Malyarenko, T. N., Kuraev, G. A., Malyarenko, E., Khvatova, M. V., Romanova, N. G., & Gurina, V. I. (1996). The development of brain electric activity in 4-year-old children by long-term sensory stimulation with music. *Human Physiology*, 22(1), 76–81.

Marzano, Robert J., Pickering, Debra, & Pollock, Jane E. (2001). *Classroom Instruction That Works: Research-Based Strategies for Increasing Student Achievement*. Alexandria, VA: Association for Supervision and Curriculum Development.

McCraty, R., Atkinson, M., Rein, G., & Watkins, A. D. (1996). Music enhances the effect of positive emotional state on salivary IgA. *Stress Medicine*, 12, 167–75.

McEwen, B. (2002). Protective and damaging effects of stress mediators. In John T. Cacioppo, Gary G. Berntson, Ralph Adolphs, C. Sue Carter, Richard J. Davidson, Martha K. McClintock, Bruce S. McEwen, Michael J. Meaney, Daniel L. Schacter, Esther M. Sternberg, Steve S. Suomi, & Shelley E. Taylor (Eds.), *Foundations of Social Neuroscience* (pp. 1127–40). Cambridge, MA: MIT Press.

Meaney, M. J., Sapolsky, R. M., & McEwen, B. S. (1985, February). The development of the glucocorticoid receptor system in the rat limbic brain. II. An autoradiographic study. *Developmental Brain Research*, 350(1–2), 165–8.

Millbower, Lenn (2000). *Training with a Beat: The Teaching Power of Music*. Sterling, VA: Stylus Publishing.

Miluk-Kolasa, B., Obminski, Z., Stupnicki, R., & Golec, L. (1994). Effects of music treatment on salivary cortisol in patients exposed to pre-surgical stress. *Experimental and Clinical Endocrinology*, 102(2), 118–20.

Ohman, A., Flykt, A., & Lundqvist, D. (2000). Unconscious emotion: Evolutionary perspectives, psychophysiological data and neuropsychological mechanisms. In Richard Lane, Lynn Nadel, G. L. Ahern, J. J. B. Allen, A. W. Kaszniak, S. Z. Rapcsak, & G. E. Schwartz (Eds.), *Cognitive Neuroscience of Emotion* (pp. 296–327). New York, NY: Oxford University Press.

Padgett, D. A., Sheridan, J. F., Dorne, J., Berntson, G. G., Candelora, J., & Glaser, R. (1998, June 9). Social stress and the reactivation of latent herpes simplex virus type 1. *Proceedings of the National Academy of Sciences of the United States of America*, 95(12), 7231–5.

Panksepp, J., Nelson, E., & Bekkedal, M. (1999). Brain systems for the mediation of social separation-distress and social-reward: Evolutionary antecedents and neuropeptide intermediaries. In Carol Sue Carter, I. Izja Lederhendler, & Brian Kirkpatrick (Eds.), *The Integrative Neurobiology of Affiliation: Proceedings of a New York Academy of Sciences Conference, March 14–17, 1996* (pp. 221–43). Cambridge, MA: MIT Press.

Pert, Candace (1997). *Molecules of Emotion: Why You Feel the Way You Feel*. New York, NY: Scribner and Sons.

Raine, A., Lencz, T., Bihrle, S., LaCasse, L., & Colletti, P. (2002). Reduced prefrontal gray matter volume and reduced autonomic activity in antisocial personality disorder. In John T. Cacioppo, Gary G. Berntson, Ralph Adolphs, C. Sue Carter, Richard J. Davidson, Martha K. McClintock, Bruce S. McEwen, Michael J. Meaney, Daniel L. Schacter, Esther M. Sternberg, Steve S. Suomi, & Shelley E. Taylor (Eds.), *Foundations of Social Neuroscience* (pp. 1023–35). Cambridge, MA: MIT Press.

Rapoport, J. L., Jensvold, M., Elkins, R., Buchsbaum, M. S., Weingarter, H., Ludlow, C., Zahn, T. P., Berg, C. J., & Neims, A. H. (1981, November). Behavioral and cognitive effects of caffeine in boys and adult males. *Journal of Nervous and Mental Disease*, 169(11), 726–32.

Repetti, R. (1997). The effects of daily job stress on parent behavior with preadolescents. Paper presented at the biennial meeting of the Society for Research in Child Development. (ERIC: ED 413 074)

Repetti, R. L., Taylor, S. E., & Seeman, T. E. (2000). Risky families: Family social environments and the mental and physical health of offspring. *Psychological Bulletin*, 128(2), 330–66.

Rickard, H. C., Rogers, R. W., Ellis, N. R., & Beidleman, W. (1988). Some retention, but not enough. *Teaching of Psychology*, 15, 151–2.

Rigg, Melvin (1937). Musical expression: An investigation of the theories of Erich Sorantin. *Journal of Experimental Psychology*, 21, 442–5.

Rodin, J. (1980). Managing the stress of aging: The role of control and coping. In H. Ursin & S. Levine (Eds.), *Coping and Health* (pp. 171–202). New York, NY: Plenum.

Ruhl, K., Hughes, C., & Schloss, P. (1987). Using the pause procedure to enhance lecture recall. *Teacher Education and Special Education*, 10(1), 14–8.

Saklofske, D. & Kelly, I. (1992). The effects of exercise and relaxation on energetic and tense arousal. *Personality and Individual Differences*, 13, 623–5.

Saper, C. B. (1996). Role of the cerebral cortex and striatum in emotional motor response. *Progress in Brain Research*, 107, 537–50.

Sapolsky, Robert (1986). Social Neuroscience: Autonomic, neuroendocrine and immune responses to stress. *Psychophysiology*, 31, 113–28.

Sapolsky, Robert (1992). *Stress, the Aging Brain, and the Mechanisms of Neuron Death*. Cambridge, MA: MIT Press.

Sapolsky, Robert (1998). *Why Zebras Don't Get Ulcers: An Updated Guide to Stress, Stress-Related Diseases, and Coping*. New York, NY: W. H. Freeman.

Schmidt, L. A., Fox, N. A., Rubin, K. H., Sternberg, E. M., Gold, P. W., Smith, C. C., & Schulkin, J. (1997, March). Behavioral and neuroendocrine responses in shy children. *Developmental Psychobiology*, 30(2), 127–40.

Schulkin, Jay (2000). *Roots of Social Sensibility and Neural Function*. Cambridge, MA: MIT Press.

Schultz, W., Dayan, P., & Montague, P. R. (2002). A neural substrate of prediction and reward. In John T. Cacioppo, Gary G. Berntson, Ralph Adolphs, C. Sue Carter, Richard J. Davidson, Martha K. McClintock, Bruce S. McEwen, Michael J. Meaney, Daniel L. Schacter, Esther M. Sternberg, Steve S. Suomi, & Shelley E. Taylor (Eds.), *Foundations in Social Neuroscience* (pp. 541–54). Cambridge, MA: MIT Press.

Sedikides, C. (1992). Mood as a determinant of attentional focus. *Cognition and Emotion*, 6, 129–48.

Shapiro, Arthur K. & Shapiro, Elaine (1997). *The Powerful Placebo: From Ancient Priest to Modern Physician*. Baltimore, MD: Johns Hopkins University Press.

Siever, Larry & Frucht, William (1997). *The New View of Self: How Genes and Neurotransmitters Shape Your Mind, Personality and Your Mental Health*. New York, NY: Macmillan.

Silberman, Mel (1996). *Active Learning: 101 Strategies to Teach Any Subject*. Boston, MA: Allyn and Bacon.

Simontacchi, Carol (2000). *The Crazy Makers: How the Food Industry is Destroying Our Brains and Harming Our Children* (pp. 173–202). New York, NY: Tarcher.

Standley, J. M. (1991). The effect of vibrotactile and auditory stimuli on perception of comfort, heart rate and peripheral finger temperature. *Journal of Music Therapy*, 28(3), 120–34.

Sutoo, Den'etsu & Akiyama, Kayo (2003, June). Regulation of brain function by exercise. *Neurobiology of Disease*, 13(1), 1–14.

Tamblyn, Doni. (2003). *Laugh and Learn: 95 Ways to Use Humor for More Effective Teaching and Training*. New York, NY: AMACOM.

Taylor, S. E. (1991). The asymmetrical impact of positive and negative events: The mobilization-minimization hypothesis. *Psychological Bulletin*, 110, 67–85.

Thayer, R. (2001). *Calm Energy: How People Regulate Mood with Food and Exercise*. New York, NY: Oxford University Press.

Thayer, R. (1987, January). Energy, tiredness and tension effects of a sugar snack versus moderate exercise. *Journal of Personality and Social Psychology*, 52(1), 119–25.

Uchino, B., Cacioppo, J., & Kiecolt-Glaser, J. (1996, May). The relationship between social support and physiological processes: A review with emphasis on underlying mechanisms and implications for health. *Psychological Bulletin*, 119(3), 488–531.

Vaughan, Susan (1997). *The Talking Cure: The Science Behind Psychotherapy*. New York, NY: Putnam.

Warburton, D. M. (1995, May). Effects of caffeine on cognition and mood without caffeine abstinence. *Psychopharmacology (Berl)*, 119(1), 66–70.

Weingarten, H. P. & Elston, D. (1991, December). Food cravings in a college population. *Appetite*, 17, 167–75.

Whiten, Andrew (1991). *Natural Theories of Mind: Evolution, Development, and Simulation of Everyday Mindreading*. Oxford, UK: Basil Blackwell.

Yeh, S. R., Fricke, R. A., & Edwards, D. H. (1996, January 19). The effect of social experience on serotonergic modulation of the escape circuit of crayfish. *Science*, 271(5247), 366–9.

Zillmann, Dolf (1984). *Connections Between Sex and Aggression*. Hillsdale, N.J: Lawrence Erlbaum.

About the Author

Eric Jensen has taught at the elementary, middle school and senior high school level, as well as at three California universities. In 1981, he co-founded SuperCamp, the country's most successful brain-compatible learning program for students. He helped introduce brain-based learning to Australia, Denmark, New Zealand, Sweden and South Africa. Jensen has authored twenty-two books, including the best-selling *Teaching with the Brain in Mind*, *SuperTeaching*, *Student Success Secrets*, *The Learning Brain* and *Brain-Based Learning*. He speaks at many major conferences; his work has been featured in *USA Today*, the *Wall Street Journal* and on CNN. He is currently a staff developer and member of the Society for Neuroscience. To contact the author, call (858) 642-0400. Email Diane Jensen at *diane@jlcbrain.com* to schedule staff development.

Brain-Based Training

For in-depth training on brain-compatible learning, attend the six-day workshop, *Teaching with the Brain in Mind*, to learn practical, motivational, research-based strategies that boost learning. Facilitators may wish to attend the five-day program, *Presenting with the Brain in Mind*, for tools to engage, inspire, motivate and change audience behaviors. The three-day *Fragile Brain* program addresses the needs of hard-to-reach learners, and teaches participants how to identify learners with behavioral or academic problems. These training sessions are hosted in several cities across the nation. Call (858) 642-0400 for a brochure, or visit www.jensenlearning.com for training dates and locations.

From The Brain Store®

For a FREE catalog of brain-compatible learning resources, call The Brain Store® at (800) 325-4769 or (858) 546-7555. Or, visit **www.thebrainstore.com** and browse the online catalog.

Learning Brain Expo®: An Amazing, Three-Day Brain/Mind Conference: Contact The Brain Store® or log on to **www.brainexpo.com** for registration and session information.

Read a FREE issue of the online The Learning Brain newsletter! Each issue of The Learning Brain newsletter represents more than 100 hours of research on the most recent neuroscientific discoveries. The articles are fully cited and conveniently available right at your fingertips—one mouse-click away! Receive hundreds of practical, brain-compatible teaching and training tips. Visit **www.learningbrain.com** and discover the future of learning.

Index